CONFRONTING
THE DECEPTION

Inflamed by 9/11, fired up by eight bad years

Tabitha Korol   8/4/19

To Audrey —
Happy Birthday! May this
book answer your questions about
today's world — and hope for a
better future.
                    Tabitha Korol

CONFRONTING
THE DECEPTION
Inflamed by 9/11, fired up by eight bad years

Tabitha Korol

©2018 by Tabitha Korol
All Rights Reserved

ISBN #978-1-986925-50-1

❧

To my wonderful grandchildren,
Madeline Olivia, Graeme Maxwell, and Ilana Yael.

I was driven to defend our America and Israel, our values and ethics,
during America's grim Obama years, which also brought with them
the rise of the Left, Progressivism, and the most dangerous Islamic ideology.

May my efforts and that of many who work to improve our future
be reflected in a better life for you and your families.
May you continue to love and respect our history, remain dedicated to America
and Israel, and be courageous when you're needed.

President Ronald Reagan said:
Freedom is never more than one generation away from extinction.
We didn't pass it to our children in the bloodstream.
It must be fought for, protected, and passed forward
so they may do the same.

ACKNOWLEDGMENTS

To my devoted husband, Sheldon, who is always there to encourage and support my every endeavor.

To Kevin O'Neil, my personal editor in the UK, for his incomparable wisdom and inspiring friendship.

To CAMERA (Committee for Accuracy in Middle East Reporting in America) and its dedicated team for providing the incentive to make political activism my late-in-life's work. Their forum furnishes in-depth research, historical background and comprehensive media monitoring; their people support with personal notes of encouragement and wishes for Yasher Koach (be strong!), the motivation one needs to make a difference.

To Rhoda Haimson, political blogger extraordinaire, and Joan Swirsky, author and journalist, for always posting my essays and offering their uplifting cheers and warm friendship. I sincerely regret that I've never met these feisty New Yorkers, but hope such a meeting lies in my future.

To Steve Stone, proprietor and editor of RenewAmerica.com, and Debbie Hamilton, Right Truth editor (ret'd), the first to accept my work for publication.

To those who administer the Jewish Virtual Library and The Religion of Peace websites, for their research and well-organized resources.

And to the wonderful people who use their own resources and work tirelessly to disseminate their writers' messages to reach the widest possible distribution. Thank you to Arutz Sheva, Centinel2012, Conservative News & Views, Constitution, Dr. Rich Swier, Grumpy Opinions, iPatriot, Israel News Talk Radio, Israel's Voice, Jewish Press, Jewish Voice of NY, Liberty News & Views, New Media Journal, News Nation Brewing, Right Side News, Snakehunter, Ted Belman, Town Hall Mail, Web Commentary, Western Free Press, and others, for all you do to keep our country ours.

TABLE OF CONTENTS

FOREWORD 8

ESSAYS
PART ONE: ISLAM

1. The Many Faces of Grand Jihad .... October 23, 2011 11
2. 1400 Years of Suspicion .... November 6, 2011 12
3. Baseless Bedouin Brouhaha .... December 20, 2011 15
4. Lawfare – Legal Warfare .... February 15, 2012 16
5. Myth-illogical Apartheid .... April 23, 2012 19
6. Beware of CAIR .... June 22, 2012 22
7. Goodbye, Columbus .... January 29, 2013 24
8. Violence of the Lambs .... March 22, 2013 26
9. Hunter is the Prey .... April 13, 2013 29
10. Sins Cast Long Shadows .... April 20, 2013 31
11. Not the Same God .... July 14, 2013 34
12. !Smitciv .... October 8, 2013 36
13. Wooing Wyoming .... January 20, 2014 39
14. A Quest for Commonality .... March 14, 2014 41
15. From Hijab to Jihad .... April 14, 2014 44
16. CAIR Visits Franciscan Sisters .... May 27, 2014 46
17. Jews Don't Behave Like Muslims .... July 27, 2014 48
18. Training for Treachery .... October 28, 2014 50
19. Pack of Wolves .... December 22, 2014 53
20. Destroy the History, Dread the Future .... March 16, 2015 56
21. Jihadis of Tomorrow .... June 8, 2015 58
22. A la Fiorina .... June 24, 2015 60
23. Mosquitoes in the Mosque .... July 30, 2015 64
24. Iceland's Meltdown .... September 21, 2015 65
25. Takk Fyrir .... October 4, 2015 68
26. A Very Syrious Matter .... October 15, 2015 70
27. Chelm .... December 8, 2015 73
28. Musings of a Muslim Father .... August 30, 2016 75
29. Engraved in Stone .... September 13, 2016 78
30. The Female Jihadi .... September 21, 2017 81

PART TWO: ACADEMIA

31. Jihad at Kent State .... October 29, 2011 84
32. Harvard, the Higher Madrassa .... January 18, 2012 85
33. UP on the Decline .... January 30, 2012 87
34. BDS — Bigoted, Deceptive, Shameless .... February 26, 2012 89
35. BDS — Agents of Destruction .... March 7, 2012 91
36. BDS — A case of Myth-taken Identity .... May 1, 2012 94
37. Textbook Taqiyyah .... August 3, 2012 97
38. Broken College, Office of Submissions .... February 4, 2013 102
39. Oberlin's Onus .... May 29, 2013 104
40. Cary's Canards .... August 20, 2013 106
41. ASA: Academics Surrender to Allah .... December 25, 2013 108
42. Communizing Common Core .... May 23, 2014 111
43. ASA, Anti-Semitic Association .... November 22, 2014 113
44. Purging Israel for Profit .... January 8, 2015 115
45. Veiled Pursuit .... February 3, 2015 118
46. The Moderate Vanguard .... February 14, 2015 120
47. Dawa at Chautauqua .... August 6, 2015 122
48. Precarity .... December 23, 2015 124
49. The Art of War .... December 30, 2015 127
50. Morality at Missouri U .... January 9, 2016 131
51. Changing Minds .... February 26, 2016 132
52. Mobocracy in Academia .... March 15, 2016 135
53. Joy of Witlessness .... March 23, 2016 138
54. Of Villainy in Vassar .... April 11, 2016 141
55. Offense by Design .... June 20, 2016 145
56. Offense by Design, pt. 2 .... August 1, 2016 148
57. An Education in Corruption .... October 30, 2016 153
58. A Choice of One .... August 21, 2017 158
59. Good Morning, Little Comrades .... October 19, 2017 160

PART THREE: MEDIA

60. The Value of One .... October 25, 2011 164
61. Foul Play .... November 16, 2011 165
62. NPR, Notorious for Palestinian Revisionism ... November 26, 2011 168
63. Restricted Vision .... March 8, 2012 170
64. A Twist of Hate .... April 7, 2012 172
65. Hardtalk, Hard to Swallow .... June 29, 2012 174

66. Lourdes of the Lies .... August 21, 2012 177
67. 60 Minutes of Mendacity .... September 29, 2012 179
68. The Palestine Khouri Doesn't Know .... October 11, 2012 181
69. Oren on Honesty .... January 3, 2013 184
70. Times Un-Square .... April 5, 2013 186
71. Two-Time Oscar Winner Two-Times .... April 24, 2013 188
72. Polluted Waters .... May 7, 2013 191
73. Honor for Dishonor .... May 15, 2013 194
74. L'Americaine .... October 30, 2013 196
75. Probing the Propaganda .... November 8, 2013 198
76. Nuremberg Revisited .... December 7, 2013 200
77. We Have MET the Enemy .... June 13, 2014 205
78. The Metropalistan Opera .... June 21, 2014 207
79. The Board Gets Nailed .... June 30, 2014 209
80. Guardian with Guile .... August 11, 2014 212
81. Men of Ideals .... September 10, 2014 215
82. No, No, Norah .... December 13, 2014 218
83. En Garde! .... January 16, 2015 219
84. Bias at the BBC .... January 19, 2015 221
85. BBC, A Mission Astray .... January 26, 2015 223
86. Dissociated Press .... March 4, 2015 226
87. Muslims Are Not Jews .... October 5, 2016 229
88. The Times That Try Men's Souls .... November 21, 2016 232
89. Israel in Dispute .... January 28, 2017 235
90. Asylum! .... February 8, 2017 238

CONCLUSION

Islam's Glaring Reality 242

INDEX

INDEX 245

ENDNOTES

ENDNOTES 247

Foreword

The destruction of The World Trade Center on September 11, 2001, affected Americans deeply. Although I knew no one in the buildings that day, these were nevertheless my people, New Yorkers and Americans. I had already moved to a midwestern suburb when I heard my co-worker in the next cubicle responding with unusual sounds to what she was hearing on her radio and then to her sister who was then in the second of the two Towers, negotiating her descent in the stairwell because the elevators were filled to capacity. She survived the ordeal; the elevator passengers did not. We later learned that 19 Muslims intentionally commandeered two planes and flew them into the Twin Towers, a third plane crashed into the western side of the Pentagon, and a fourth crashed in rural Pennsylvania. About 3,000 Americans were killed, including first responders.

I became a traumatized American, tears at the ready, more vigilant, more aware of our government and our world. I spent more time on the computer, dealing with, but not completely comprehending, the propaganda and misinformation we were receiving. I discovered CAMERA (Committee for Accuracy in Middle East Reporting in America) and began writing letters to the editors in response to their alerts to counter the deceptive propaganda. Friends and Internet readers were beginning to send me articles that were incorrect, intentionally biased, asking that I respond.

Imam Feisal Abdul Rauf's demands to construct a mosque, the Córdoba Center, on Ground Zero infuriated me. I recognized this as a mosque of conquest by its proposed architecture and choice of site; Ground Zero was sacred ground, still offering up plane and body parts. I also knew enough of Spain's history to be wary of the Córdoba appellation; Córdoba had become the seat of the Islamic Caliphate when the Moors conquered Spain in 711 — until the Catholics retook their country in 1492. Muslims called these years the Golden Era, when Jews and Christians were at the very bottom of the hierarchical structure of their society. Because control and rule varied with each caliphate, the degrees of subjugation, discrimination, restrictions, severe rules, a Jizya tax levied against each dhimmi (non-Muslim), intolerance, and pogroms also varied, but there was never freedom.

It will become evident as you continue to read the deceptive information that comes at us from every direction, Islam's purpose is to establish Islamic law, Sharia, throughout the world. The believers follow Allah's laws, sharia, which conflict with all Western laws; therefore, their will is to establish their laws over ours, whether by stealth or by force, as is decreed in their Koran.

I can't pinpoint a date, but it was soon after 9/11 that I discovered two baffling essays written by local high school students of journalism, published in a local weekly newspaper. Although presented as being pro-Israel, they were seriously skewed, allowing for the possibility that Muslims might not have been responsible for "the day that changed the world."

Islam is, foremost, a strict political ideology of world conquest couched as a religion, a civilization with a strict method of governance. It provides a set plan of action for vanquishing a region, such as the Middle East, destroying and forcing the populaces to convert to Islam, expecting to eventually include Israel. The greater part of the Koran commands to conquer, convert, or kill the dhimmis and its influence is seen worldwide as Muslims are changing the face of every country in Europe, turning against Jewish citizens with a unique approach, but already creating havoc for the host country's indigenous people.

Whereas the young journalist students should have been learning about the drastic changes occurring in England, France, Germany, the Netherlands, Norway and Sweden; the Islamic marchers' holding signs that spew hatred of democracy; their specific demands for accommodations; their violent riots and gang rapes; the grotesqueries of their bloodlust; and the murders committed in the name of their god against those who speak out against Islam, these students expressed a sympathy for the Islamic aggressors. They repeated the victimization mantra, never once considering the victims of that horrifying day and the families who were left to mourn for the rest of their lives.

There was obviously a serious blind spot in their training that prevented the young writers and their instructors from recognizing the menace that had come to our land, that had the effect of recruiting them into a pro-Islamic mentality. I have since come to realize that their parents had also to grant permission for the students' narrations to be published. And how many readers questioned the historic revisionism or Leftist views that the terrorists may not have been Muslim who flew those planes? We are speaking of the Religion of Peace, after all. Despite the photos and identities in the media, the children were taught to consider that the nineteen could have been Americans of other faiths.

Deception is the essence of the Left, and it has worsened since the above event. They are being taught to disrespect and dislike America, to devalue the freedoms we have, and they appear willing to destroy the advancements we've made since our founding. The eight years of Obama have brought us divisiveness, intolerance, street violence, and false narratives to influence the thinking of the gullible, particularly the students who will be the compliant, brainwashed next generation.

This book is an attempt to redress our endangered world by confronting the deception.

Cleveland, Ohio
April 2018

ESSAYS
PART ONE: ON ISLAM

THE MANY FACES OF JIHAD
Islamic conquest by the sword and by stealth.

Fourteen centuries after Mohammad, Muslims still despise the West, and remain willing to offer up their own lives to kill those who think and believe differently. Muslims believe that only jihad (holy war) can reestablish a true Muslim state to abolish injustice and bring people into their god's service — by eradicating other political systems by the sword — to preach, restore the Caliphate and destroy their enemies, infidels and Jews. Raised by devout, doting families, many are taught 7th century masculine values, trained to feel isolated from their host society, develop a group mentality, and while they may not be predisposed to doing harm individually, they can perform monstrous acts[1] collectively.

Jihad's purpose is establishing Allah's kingdom on earth, and expropriating booty and land. Defeat and death bring everlasting Paradise and spiritual benefit. The complete imperialism, Islam seeks to erase the past so the vanquished are culturally[2] disemboweled, with nothing left of religion or relics of historical importance,[3] their support system destabilized. The world is Islam's perpetual war zone.

Jihad uses deceptive sabotage to discredit Israel's struggle for peace and her very existence, insisting that Israel is an occupying entity on Arab territory, despite indisputable facts, through Bible and archaeological discoveries,[4] of a continuous Jewish presence for more than 3,000 years, Christians, 2000; Muslims, 1400; and no history exists of an independent Arab state.

Jihad is the myth that Mohammad ascended to heaven from the Dome of the Rock. Born in Saudi Arabia, he never set foot in Jerusalem. The mosque, originally a small prayer house, was erected by Umar, second Rashidun caliph, to establish supremacy over Judaism and Christianity.

Jihad revisionism states that Israel (not Iran) is the threat to peace and stability, Israel (not Hamas) causes Gaza's humanitarian problems, Israel (not Islamic countries) is apartheid; and Israel (not Palestinians) is the stumbling block to the two-state solution.

Spanning fourteen centuries, Islamic jihad caused the death of 890 million people (Jews, Christians, Zoroastrians, Hindus, Buddhists); the enslavement[5] of 28 million in Mauritania, Saudi Arabia, and Sudan and the death[6] of 85 million during transport; the massacre of thousands of Christians in Syria, 634 AD; monasteries ransacked, villagers slain in Mesopotamia, 635-642; inhabitants of entire towns killed in Egypt and Armenia; a great massacre before establishing rule in Cyprus; Tripoli's Jewish and Christian women and children sent as slaves to the Arab army; Carthage razed; and 32,454 jihad attacks to date[7] — death and destruction worldwide since 9/11.

Jihad demands accommodation by the host country: Sharia law accepted by the Archbishop of Canterbury, England;[8] violence evacuating the once-Jewish city of Malmo, Sweden;[9] the murder of Theo Van Gogh in the Netherlands;[10] physical attacks on citizens, riots, and no-go zones in France;[11] and demanding a triumphal rabat-style mosque[12] on Ground Zero.

Jihad is lawfare, an assault on freedom of speech[13] — instructing our media on addressing Islamic issues, and vetting our school books[14] to promote Islam.

Jihad is September 11; universities that permit Muslim Student Unions[15] to rage against Israel and Jews and establish Israel apartheid week; Oklahoma's anti-sharia laws challenged by CAIR;[16] and devout Muslims[17] in our Department of Homeland Security.

The asymmetrical war fought against Israel, that turns the aggressor into victim; rocket fire against Israel while claiming undue retaliatory force,[18] deadly flotillas[19] under the guise of humanitarian aid, using their youth as suicide bombers and inspiring martyrdom are all jihad tactics.

Jihad is having our own President Obama force Israel to comply with Mahmoud Abbas's demands and Secretary of State Hillary Clinton's warning against recognizing Jerusalem[20] as Israel's capital.

I urge the media to feel some moral obligation to report honestly to their readers, or these jihad tactics will continue until Islam conquers every country on the globe.

1400 YEARS OF SUSPICION
The four stages of Islamic conquest over 1400 years of brutality without mercy.

The first thing to catch my eye in the September 30, 2011 issue of *The Forward* was an article by journalist Nathan Guttmann, "American Jews and Muslims work together...," and a photograph with the caption, "Standing Together: American Jewish and Muslim religious leaders routinely work together. That's a substantial change from the past, when they often viewed one another with suspicion."

Was that all he could say about 1400 years of "brutality without mercy, invasions, wreaking ruin, slavery, violent destruction, calamity, razed to the ground, pillaged for booty" — descriptions taken from books on Islamic history. Suspicion? And should we refer to the annihilated *890 million people*[21] and their cultures as "Casualties?" And what should we call those who created the corpses, severed the heads, and took women and children into forced slavery? "Suspects?"

There are no moderates in Islam, neither can there be; the Koran is not a bible and there is no Golden Rule. *Sixty-one percent*[22] of the Koran is devoted to killing the infidel — any non-Muslim. Islam is filled with instructions[23] for its own proliferation, its preservation, protection, and replicated fidelity. It commands its followers to create a government that supports it and provides permission and methods to spread religion by war. Lands must be conquered; people converted or slaughtered, and women subordinated to avoid domestic rebellion. The religion provides inspiration, motivation, and unity. With one exception — Spain and the Spaniards' *Reconquista* of their own land in 1492 — there has never been another Islam-invaded country that was able to return to its previous culture.

These are the steps of Islamization:

Stage I of Islamic Conquests begins with Infiltration.

Migration: Muslims have migrated to America en masse, as they have in Europe. There are already pockets of neighborhoods in which they live apart from others, intentionally establishing their isolation with exclusively Islamic schools. Previous waves of immigrants brought people who eagerly assimilated to become proud Americans.

Appeal for humanitarian tolerance: From severely intolerant lands, they begin their appeal for tolerance. America had already learned to accept the "tired, the poor, the huddled masses yearning to breathe free." The "melting pot" welcomed new immigrants who lived adjacent to and among each other, and the children became Americans together. But the Muslim strategy is to demand special privileges, such as inviting the Muslim Brotherhood-affiliate, Muslim Student Union, into a Catholic-University,[24] rather than assimilate or attend secular schools, to break down the existing system.

Revise history: Muslims attempt to portray Islam as a religion of peace, and the Muslims as victims of misunderstanding or racism (bigotry) they're not a race). History books[25] are revised in America so as to secrete Islam's true jihadist history, just as Muslims have built mosques over razed churches, synagogues and temples to eliminate them from memory.

A high Muslim birthrate is encouraged in host countries to increase the Muslim population. The US Muslim population increased greatly in the 20th century, due to rising immigration and conversion, and a comparatively high birth rate. In 2005, nearly 96,000 people from Islamic countries became legal, permanent United States residents[26] than in any previous year.

Mosques are used to spread hate of the host country and culture. There are more than 2,000 mosques in America, and Muslims, led by Imam Rauf, are working hard to use our laws to establish a caliphate by constructing a rabat-style mosque of conquest on Ground Zero, designed to house a war room, resting places for jihadis, and not one with the typically round configuration for prayer. Rauf issued a threat if he could not build his mosque there, "Otherwise, the Islamists might get violent.[27]"

Islamophobia: Threats of Islamophobia, already prevalent, are used as a means of controlling our speech. Citizens are discouraged/forbidden from mentioning certain words for fear of "offending" — not identifying terrorists, preventing media attention to jihad attacks worldwide or local. Our media had failed to alert us to the 17,000+ jihadist attacks worldwide since 9/11, including the numerous Christian[28] villages burned to the ground, the Muslims who attacked and carved a Star of David[29] into the back of a pro-Israel Iraqi poet in St. Louis, or the US universities that do little to discourage hate crimes on campus. Now CAIR (Council on American-Islamic Relations) and the Muslim Brotherhood are in control of what our media may announce/write, and the Obama[30] administration is pulling back all training manuals used for law enforcement material and national security that refer to Islam, deemed offensive to Muslims, thereby eliminating the ability to reference those who endanger our national security.

Lawfare:[31] Threats of legal action for perceived discrimination, to criminalize honest discussion on and teachings of violence — using libel and defamation laws as weapons to intimidate democracy into silence. And the publisher who bowed to threats did not produce his book that contained cartoons of Mohammad.

Offers of interfaith dialogue to indoctrinate non-Muslims: These are perceived by many to be a form of outreach, such as reported by Nathan Gutman of *The Forward*. However, one of the rabbis in attendance was Rabbi Eric Yoffie, past-president of the Union for Reform Judaism, a branch that has been known to affiliate with leftist J Street,[32] whose solutions for peace are considered suicidal by most Israelis. They purport to speak for most American Jews, and claim to be pro-Israel, yet they receive their financial support from the pro-Palestinian, pro-Iranian George Soros, and have never taken a pro-Israel position on anything.

The next stages of the Islamization of America would be:

Stage 2: Consolidation of Power

Stage 3: Open war with Leadership and Culture

Stage 4: Totalitarianism, Islamic 'theocracy" and
    the full implementation of sharia.

So, what is it about this kind of conquest that Gutman and other journalists fail to understand? What will it take for the media and many of our population to acknowledge that Stage 2 is at hand?

BASELESS BEDOUIN BROUHAHA

Nomadic Arab tribes become squatters in Israel – another form of jihad.

The Economist self-describes its character as belonging to the radicals, yet it backed conservative Ronald Reagan, who would never have approved of that article. My conclusion after reading, "We Want Recognition too," was that *The Economist* economizes on truth, because it clearly misrepresents the facts with the intent to demonize Israel in every conceivable way.

The author, Wadi Naam, accused Israeli soldiers of knocking down Bedouin shacks "with abandon," without acknowledging that Israel is among the smallest countries in the world with high population densities that require proper urban planning to accommodate all its citizens. Bedouins have exceedingly high reproduction rates that require special attention.

Further, these nomads often choose to live in accordance with their historic lifestyle, in mean housing,[33] without paved roads, public transportation, electricity or water. These amenities are available to them in the established communities but cannot be routed in desert areas despite their expectation of entitlements — and Naam admits that the Bedouins refuse to budge! Soldiers do not destroy with abandon and construction is done with legal authorization under Israel's democratic law, the same privileges and restrictions that apply to all Israeli citizens.

His mention of a torched mosque is made completely out of context, without providing the impetus for the action, which was in retaliation to all the damage done by Arabs to Jewish antiquities, from undermining the Temple Mount, to destroying the graves of the 3,000-year-old Mount of Olives cemetery, to the defilement of the Church of the Nativity, to the bombing and burning of a church in Gaza and Jewish synagogues in Jericho, Nablus, Gush Katif; to the destruction of Rachel's tomb in Bethlehem and Joseph's tomb in Nablus, while also killing six soldiers; to removing soil containing precious relics and disposing it in a garbage dump. Need I say more? The mosque was torched by individual, angry, avenging citizens; they were not the government's representatives.

Additional unethical and immoral statements were made, referencing 1948 as an issue of ethnic cleansing, when these accusations have already been proven wrong. The establishment of the Jewish State brought her 850,000 Jews who fled increased Arab persecution as well as sudden attacks from seven Arab countries (Egypt, Syria, Jordan, Lebanon, Iraq, Saudi Arabia and Yemen). The Jewish refugees were given safe haven and welcomed as citizens to Israel, France, and the US. The 160,000 Arabs who accepted Israel's invitation to stay and become citizens now number more than a million and are gainfully employed and thriving.

Palestinian leadership and elite had evacuated their homes earlier to avoid the conflict and many followed by example. NOTE: Historian Shabtai Teveth reported that they were given oral instructions to leave. British High Commissioner for Palestine General Sir Alan Cunningham reported that Arab morale had collapsed. The Major of Jaffa, among the many who fled, was also a factor in the flight of Haifa's community. A British official, Palestine's Chief Secretary Sir Henry Gurney, recorded that the Arabs were deserted by their leaders — and the inhabitants of nearby towns followed suit. The Grand Mufti of Jerusalem Haj Amin al Husseini gave instructions for complete evacuation (for holy war/jihad) even while British, Jewish and Arab leadership were negotiating a truce. Those who fled were not offered sanctuary by their countries of origin but were forced to remain homeless pawns to be used strategically later. This was a heartless Muslim-upon-Muslim crime.

Finally, if there is no room for camels and Bedouins are forced to abandon their herds, this is what happens with increased population without room for expansion. Israel tries to accommodate all her citizens in the little land she has, which is one one-thousandth of the Arab land mass. Those who chose to leave their traditional enclaves with their "wide open spaces" enjoy life in the cities, and a full range of modern homes and services, such as in the modern city of Rahat. Those who choose to live in underdeveloped areas will, obviously, not have access to infrastructure; it is their choice. There are many Bedouins working to assist their own people in assimilation, but the truth does not suit the author's agenda.

The Negev Bedouins (desert dwellers) continue their centuries-old ways, living as squatters and tribal nomads, engaging in sectarian violence, except that now they have apparently concluded that they can get more, as the Palestinians do. They have seen that the Palestinian-Arabs[34] get far more "humanitarian" aid per capita than any other group on earth, and likely believe they can as well — or threaten with a Palestinian-style Intifada.

The Western world insists that Islamic assimilation is possible, and it is incumbent upon Israel to be the first to give up everything for the sake of the Arab world. The conflict is fundamental. The Koran prohibits assimilation and for Muslims this is truth.

LAWFARE – LEGAL WARFARE

Islam makes war against our Constitution by way of our legal system when violence is not practical. These are the Islamic WMDs (weapons of mass destruction) that we failed to recognize.

Islam and its destruction of the many cultures that once existed in the Middle East began in earnest, with uncompromising hostility and justification for violence, when

Mohammad's religious righteousness was repudiated by the Jews and Christians of Mecca and Medina in the 7th century. Islam's jihad activities continue their brutality to this day, with terrorist activities worldwide. They are commanded to conquer non-Muslims, usurp land, destroy antiquities, remove all remnants of the indigenous history, and slaughter rampantly — and reign supreme.

Where their violence would not succeed, Muslims have invaded by emigration as though to live harmoniously with their hosts, conquering by shunning assimilation and demanding special modifications. Their sophisticated propaganda machine accuses their innocent hosts of a variety of offenses, using "Islamophobia," a politically manipulative accusation designed to intimidate critics into silence, curbing the very terminology needed to report their activities.

Islam has grown due to its appeal to the socialists and communists who take on their cause and perpetrate anti-democratic and anti-Semitic ideologies in schools and universities, and the work of chaplains who infiltrate the armed forces and prisons to convert the vulnerable minds. Muslims have instituted BDS (boycott, divestment, sanctions) worldwide to inspire hate and financial and business disengagement from the target culture. Most dire are the Islamists found in our administration, severely affecting the way our government attends to America's business of foreign and domestic policies.

A more recent phenomenon, Lawfare, is a "soft jihad," a negative force that operates within our administration and court system. It is defined as the manipulation of the rule of law, and the humanitarianism thus represented, to achieve a military advantage, such as 1) the use of mosques as armories, command and control centers, and launching pads, and then using protections accorded religious sites under the laws of armed conflict, and 2) when militants hide among noncombatants in order to shield themselves from attack, or if attacked, use the civilian losses as accusations against the opponent's military defense, also known as "disproportionate warfare."

Lawfare's purpose is to silence free speech important to our national security and public concern; to delegitimize the sovereignty of democratic states (Israel); to hinder democracies from fighting and defeating terrorism; to confuse laws of armed conflict with those of human rights; and to prevent the application of human rights laws where they are most needed. Lawfare is "a revolution in military legal affairs." The lawsuits, implemented with bias and inconsistency within our democracy, are a means of intimidating, demoralizing, and bankrupting defendants. They are weapons of war to muzzle all criticism of Islam or exposure of its true nature and violence.

The first conference of The Lawfare Project, led by director Brooke Goldstein, met in New York just months ago, to address the abuse of Western laws and judicial systems to achieve strategic military or political ends, where violence won't work. It drew experts from around the world to focus on the increasing threat from Islamists' exploitation of our mutual legal systems.

The constituents agreed that Lawfare must be opposed in accordance with the tenets of democracy, and discussed the legal limits placed on fighting terrorism and the rights granted to terrorists. Particular attention was paid to the lawsuits that thwart our freedom of speech on issues of national security and public concern that attempt to delegitimize the sovereignty of democratic states (Israel), and their efforts to inhibit the right and ability of democracies to defend themselves against terrorism. The members concurred that they must question the intention behind the legal action, to see if it was created to pursue justice or to undermine and manipulate our very system of laws. Citing tedious and expensive defenses, the attendees agreed to a proactive approach — to file suits against the supporters of terrorism so that they, too, might be bankrupted.

Among the issues under consideration are:

Power of the state and an international court,
Incitement to violence and legitimate criticism of religion,
Legalities of hate speech,
Bias in international tribunals,
Limits of universal jurisdiction of our national security interests,
UN Power (non-democratic members) to dictate international human rights norms,
Flawed documents masquerading as legitimate analyses,
Classified material obtained from terrorists,
Laws and "Miranda rights" governing terrorists and unlawful combatants.

President Obama addressed the nation about the Ground Zero mosque, saying, "This is America and our commitment to religious freedom must be unshakable." But Islam promotes religious tyranny, which is not an inalienable right; freedom from religious tyranny is. Religious tolerance is why we have religious freedom; we must never tolerate religious tyranny. The Lawfare Project agreed that our resolutions must uphold respect for universal human rights, promote interfaith harmony, combat discrimination against individuals based on religion or belief, and promote respect for universal religious diversity, but we must never permit religion to rule.

Under our Constitution, any religious law that supports violence or the overthrow of our government for blasphemy is a criminal act, ranging from a felony to an act of treason. Our US Constitution must be used as our guideline to define the enemy and its (mis)use of our laws. The Lawfare Project must ensure that our Constitution is diligently upheld and protected from Islamic assault.

MYTH-ILLOGICAL APARTHEID
Islamic war tactics include unsubstantiated accusations, slander, against Israel.

The Jews created one of the most progressive democracies in the world, most accepting of minorities, yet they're branded racist by Islamists, themselves severely discriminatory. Jews resettled peacefully in their homeland of 3,000+ years but are called colonialists by those who seize land by force. Muslims waged pogroms against Arab Jews and today clear their land of Christians in astounding numbers, but Israel is accused of ethnic cleansing. Seven million Jews on 1/1,000th of the Middle Eastern land mass are called imperialist by 1.5 billion Arabs on their previously conquered continent. Iran threatens to obliterate Israel, but the US tells Israel to use restraint and make concessions. Arabs hold Judea and Samaria steadfastly; Russia holds Japanese islands; Communist China rules Tibet, Turkey holds parts of Cyprus, and Germans live and rule in East Prussia, but Israel is the "occupier." Human Rights violations are cited against Israel 75 percent of the time at the UN, while Arabic genocide continues unabated in Sudan, Congo, and Rwanda, and Arab women are under constant oppression.

One of the leading accusations used by the anti-Semitic BDS (Boycott-Divestment-Sanctions) movement to delegitimize Israel is an illogical one — the false, multi-faceted condemnations of APARTHEID — fashioned after the policies of South Africa and Nazi Germany. And the BDS minions espouse Islam's deadly dogmatic propaganda against world Jewry. The fabricated indictments against the Jewish State are flagrant inversions of reality (aka revisionism), a serious threat to Israel and the Jewish students — and that these myths are supported by a remorseless academia attests to the universities' ignominious collaboration with Islamic jihad against the Jewish people.

Myth: The Apartheid Wall/Barrier
Mainstream media took up the cause of "victimized" Palestinians who were denied entry into Israel with the construction of a barrier fence between the two cultures, but rarely mentioned is its true purpose and value — that of protecting Israelis from Palestinian terrorists, their suicide murderers, rockets and missiles. Neither does the media reference the innumerable defensive walls erected worldwide:[35] the Great Wall of Morocco (security belt) against Soviet Polisario rebels; South Korea's barrier against North Korea; India's wall against Pakistan; Botswana's electric fence against Zimbabwe's ethnic cleansing; Saudi Arabia's fences against Iraq and Yemen; Turkey's partitioned claim of Cyprus; Thailand's against Malaysia's Muslims; Pakistan's against Afghanistan; Uzbekistan's against Tajikistan; the UAR's against Oman; Kuwait's against Iraq; the US's wall against Mexico, and the many other signs of nations living in fear of their aggressive neighbors.

Myth: Palestinians should have the Right of Return

War creates refugees. Had Arab leaders accepted the UN partition instead of launching a war to seize the whole British Mandate, there would be two adjacent states today, with no Palestinian or Jewish refugees. Most of the 850,000 Jews who escaped Arab persecution settled and became citizens in Israel; 160,000 Arabs stayed and became citizens in Israel; but between 472,000 and 750,000 Palestinians fled in response to Arab armies' orders and were then shunned by their brethren to become a propaganda weapon against Israel. The lands to which they should be returning are their original Islamic lands of Jordan, Lebanon, Yemen, Syria, etc.

Israel's Law of Return is consistent with her just purpose and noble cause: a haven for the Jewish people, regardless of race and national origin — that a state may employ a preference in granting citizenship to undo the effects of prior discrimination, as with the British decision of 1939, which barred Jewish immigration to Mandatory Palestine and returned millions of Jews to their death in Europe. Similar laws of return exist in other democracies, Germany, Ireland, Finland, Greece, Poland, Hungary, Bulgaria, Slovakia, the Czech Republic, Slovenia, Croatia, yet BDS groups do not denounce these nations.

Myth: Ethnic-Cleansing Charge

This charge against Israel began with the settling of European Jews after WW II, and a quotation erroneously attributed to David Ben-Gurion, in 1937, "We do not wish and do not need to expel Arabs and take their places. All our aspiration is built on the assumption — proven throughout all our activity in the Land [of Israel] — that there is enough room in the country for ourselves and the Arabs," and reiterated ten years later to build good relations with their Arab neighbors. But Arabs announced the opposite to their brethren, instilling hate, resentment, and fomenting a determination to annihilate Israel.

Myth: Israel steals Palestinian Water

The water charge against Israel began in the 1920s, with Palestinians' charging that the Israeli military authority controls most of the West Bank's water. One accusation says 73 percent is piped back to Israel with another 10 percent used by illegal Jewish settlers; another says 83 percent. But B'Tselem's report, used to support the allegations, proves nothing of the sort.

Israel obtains about 50 percent of its water from the Sea of Galilee and the Coastal Aquifer, both entirely within Israel's pre-1967 lines; 30 percent comes from the Western and Northeastern Aquifers of the Mountain Aquifer system, which straddles the Green Line, but most is under pre-1967 Israel. Israel's Mediterranean coastline is at a lower elevation than the West Bank, and the water follows the flow of gravity. Compared to when Jordan occupied the West Bank (1950s), the Palestinians' share of aquifers increased by a considerable amount under Israel's administration. The truth: Palestinians use Israeli water! And compassionately, despite Israel's limited water supply, Israel provides water to ten dry villages in South Lebanon.

Myth: Israel discriminates against its citizens

Of 6.7 million citizens, 20 percent are non-Jews (about 1.1 Muslims, 130,000 Christian, 100,000 Druze). Israel is the only country in the Middle East that offers Arabs and Arab women equal right to vote. Arabs hold various government posts, including eight seats in Knesset (Parliament) and a Supreme Court Justice. There are hundreds of Arab schools attended by 300,000 Arab students. BDSers communicate that Arabs are not welcomed into military service — also untrue. Arab volunteers are accepted — but Israel will not force Arabs to fight their brethren. Citizens may live anywhere; housing is not government-controlled based on religion or ethnicity. After almost 230 years of US independence, America has still not integrated all her diverse communities; 60 years after civil rights legislation, discrimination has not been eradicated. Neither country has solved all its social problems.

Myth: Israel restricts Palestinian travel

Palestinians complained about roads forbidden to them, making it difficult to for them to get to work and for pregnant women to travel for healthcare. The Associated Press reported about restricted roads for Palestinians and B'Tselem mimicked the accusations, adding that Palestinians were prohibited from crossing some of those roads with vehicles. The full truth was omitted — that the roads were open to all Israeli citizens (Jew and Arab), foreigners, and tourists. Nationality-based restrictions (not religion — or ethnicity-based) were made on Palestinian vehicles in 1993, after the rise in Palestinian political violence, when drive-by shootings resulted in drivers' deaths. Security far outweighs Palestinian rights.

The consequence of the Oslo Accords was three separate administrative divisions, but the violence of the Second Intifada necessitated complete prohibitions on Palestinian movement into Israel and between the West Bank and Gaza Strip — to protect all people in Israel and Israeli settlements.

Also omitted from biased reporting is that Israelis were also restricted from driving through regions controlled by the Palestinian Authority.

BDSers never speak of Saudi Arabia's Muslim-only roads, and privileged Muslim-only cities of Mecca and Medina and its environs, while Jerusalem, Israel's holiest city for Jews, is open to tourists of every faith. Note that Mahmoud Abbas announced that a Palestinian state would be closed to Jews and homosexuals.

These myths are inventive, designed to create a militarily weak Israel that would be replaced by a new Islamic state whose defenseless Jewish citizens could be massacred. The variety and number of myths are endless, too numerous for one essay, but they are myths nevertheless and easily refuted. Israel is the only open liberal democracy in the entire Middle East where all her citizens live infinitely better than do the people of Arab nations.

It is time to stop pretending that the Muslim students' hate and sedition is "free speech" and acknowledge that they adamantly fight for their own free speech while suppressing the speech of others. The hostile campus climate they create serves to intimidate visiting pro-Israel speakers and remove opposition from the room, thereby insulating themselves from criticism for their radical ideologies.

It is both immoral and against our democratic values to fund anything related to BDS and the "Israel Apartheid" movement. It is time to stand for honest free speech and academic integrity and to stop the hate and sedition that is cloaked in "free speech." Whether this scourge has been permitted out of weakness, complacency, ignorance, or fear of retribution, be aware that the smaller your contribution to restoring democracy to your school and to our nation, the direr will be the consequences in the future. Tolerance of Islamic intolerance is not tolerance, but the ultimate destruction of our civilization.

BEWARE OF CAIR

The purpose of CAIR, an extension of the Muslim Brotherhood, is to influence and destroy from within.

One of the most pervasive strategies of the global Muslim Brotherhood (MB) is their many organizations and initiatives, all usually led by the same individuals, of which CAIR[36] (Council on American-Islamic Relations) is one. Their nature, plans and purpose are known: to destroy Western civilization from within through sharia adherence, to advance a jihad against the Jews and Christians using violence as needed, but also with stealth in America, dangerous to non-Muslims in free and open societies.

Headquartered in Washington, DC, blocks from the White House, CAIR has known ties to international terrorist groups. It was named co-conspirator in The Holy Land Foundation[37] trial of radical Islamic terrorists, which exposed their scheme to disguise payments to Hamas suicide bombers and their families as charity[38] and ruled a criminal organization by the Department of Justice. They boast a "great deal of success" at having infiltrated our government.

In 2008, CAIR instructed our government and schools in Columbus, Cincinnati and Cleveland, Ohio, on Islamic sensitivities and requirements, and met with with officials at Kent State, Cleveland State, John Carroll, Case Western Reserve, and Baldwin-Wallace,[39] Oberlin College and Hathaway Brown. Jihadis are subverting our educational system, demanding preferential treatment, and using petro dollars for new university political-science departments and department chairs in Middle Eastern studies, and anti-American and anti-Israel preaching.

Thanks to Brigitte Gabriel, founder of Act! For America, we know of $20 million given to the University of Arkansas; $5M to the University of California, Berkeley; $22.5 million to Harvard; $28 million to Georgetown; $11 million to Cornell; $5 million each to MIT and Princeton; $1.5 million to Texas A&M; $5 million to Columbia; and unnamed amounts to such as UC Santa Barbara, American University, Rice, Duke, and others, with the certainty that more will be forthcoming to our area schools. We learn of new accommodations weekly where companies and schools are forced to apologize[40] and subordinate their own rights for offending a Muslim.

Muslims already have equal rights to life, liberty and the pursuit of happiness in the United States. Their women, confined in cloth prisons, are deprived of rights under their own sharia laws. No other group of immigrants has ever had to organize to be so understood, but then they are like no other group. They are here to conquer, not to be understood.

CAIR has come to impose its dogma and sharia law on those who value freedom. When any foreign element comes to a new nation and demands the latter adhere to their laws, they come not to assimilate, but to conquer — if not through violence, then through stealth or civilizational jihad. They have demanded and influenced our schools, businesses, media, film industry, and our government, and they have been accommodated by the unwitting, uninformed, ill-informed, apologists, and the enablers who perceive that they will benefit from this menace. Whether by stealth or violence, their goal is the same — to impose Islamic sharia law in every country of the globe, superseding the Constitution of the United States and all others. Omar Ahmad,[41] co-founder of CAIR, admitted their intent on July 4, 1988, in the San Ramon Valley Herald. "Islam isn't in America to be equal to any other faith, but to become dominant. The Koran should be the highest authority in America."

The stealth jihadists are depending on our tolerance of their beliefs, to disarm, infiltrate and defeat us. Tolerance of evil, whether clad in religious or secular garb, is not compassion, but compliance and destructive. Our Founders' intolerance for religious tyranny is what secured the religious freedoms we enjoy today. The denial of religious freedom in England, in the name of God and State, inspired our founders to establish our Constitution in America — our first and last defense against any who would again use the State or God's name to deny us our religious freedom. In America, religious freedom is an inalienable right; religious tyranny is not. It's treason.

So, I call this to the attention of the presidents and teaching staff of the institutions that have been or will be visited by CAIR. You may be asked a subtle, minor request, but it will be a relinquishment of our rights guaranteed by our Constitution. The first accommodation will betray our Freedom of Speech — to avoid words and phrases that "offend" Islam (aka Islamophobia), accept new textbooks, effect a change in curriculum, hire Muslim instructors, allow a modification that benefits Muslim students only, invite non-Muslim students to attend or participate in a religious rite not performed with other religions, permit students to set up an "Israel is Apartheid" rally or invite a speaker who inevitably betrays the sovereignty of Israel, allow a boycott against an Israeli-made product or divest from a manufacturer that trades with an Israeli business. This is a step towards dhimmitude,[42] allowing Islam to force our submission and destroy our mandates of democracy and yielding to Islam the control of the minds of our students, the next generation to govern our nation. This will destroy us from within, by our own hand.

Know this: Islam is a global existential threat. If the accommodation you're asked to make is only for Muslims, but not for Jews, Christians, Hindus, Buddhists, non-Muslims, secularists, liberals, moderates and conservatives, then it cannot be for Muslims only. If their books have not been vetted/reviewed by members of all religions, then they must not be accepted in the school for all students. We know that the new textbooks or study guides, printed by noted publishers, Chelsea House; Glencoe/McGraw Hill; Holt, Rinehart and Winston; McDougal Littell; Pearson Prentice Hall; and Teachers' Curriculum Institute contain a sanitized history and misinformation about Islam, and demean and betray Israel and Western civilization, and they are currently in use throughout American schools. They are used to proselytize and indoctrinate the next generation to Islam and sharia law. Do whatever it takes to remove those books from circulation.

GOODBYE, COLUMBUS

Islam destroys non-Muslim history and usurps the narrative for its own.

Muslims have been the most persistent and pernicious people on the planet for the past 1400 years, with an imperialist belief system designed to destroy Western civilization and progress and force the masses into obeying Islamist ideology. By implementing a methodical, irreversible hate, with lies and propaganda from infancy, into a religious doctrine, Islam demands obedience with earthly torture and heavenly (sexual) reward. It works. Islam's holy books deal more with the infidel, the Kafir, than religion – 64 percent of the Koran[43] and 32 percent of the Hadith cover conquest over non-Muslims, 81 percent of the Sura deals with Mohammed's struggle with Kafirs – a whopping 60 percent relating to subjugation, torture and death. Their "holy books" are bereft of all morality, conscience and compassion, but contain concepts calculated to intimidate their own people into sacrificing their humanity in order to commit violence for the sake of aggressive expansion.

Obligatory prayer and incitement five times daily and sharia laws keep the populace enraged and hair-trigger ready to participate in the most gruesome undertakings for The System. Men use multiple women to produce future warriors and women produce and train their numerous children for martyrdom.[44] Severe social and sexual inhibitions, as well as sexual mutilation of young girls, harness the vitality of the young to replace the natural instincts of courting found in Western cultures. These also provide the boys and young men with the drive to rape women of the conquered culture. Shrouding their own women and covering the men's faces during war games hinders friendship, its cultivation, camaraderie and compassion, sustaining the constant chaos that comes from living under tyranny.

While some warrior-immigrants reside in their host country and use the schools and legal system to destroy the country from within,[45] others seek to demolish and build Muslim mosques over artifacts and edifices, thereby establishing their connection to the land where none existed before. Over time, the ignorant and complacent lose their heritage and take on the identity of the victors.

Buddhism was introduced from India to Central Asia to China through the Silk Road in the second century, but it declined at the collapse of the Tang dynasty in the East and the Arab invasion in the West during the 8th century. Once the Buddhist temples and all artifacts were abandoned or ruined, the entire Central Area basin converted to Islam. The once-fertile Buddhist areas became desolate wasteland — whole cultures were destroyed, populations slaughtered, children enslaved, women forced into harems, centers of learning sacked, and books and scrolls burned. Their history all but forgotten, the survivors united under Islam.

As recently as 2001, the Persian Buddhas of Bamiyan,[46] two huge statues carved into the side of a sandstone cliff along the ancient Silk Road in the Bamiyan Valley, Afghanistan (507 and 554 CE), listed as cultural landmarks by UNESCO, were dynamited and destroyed by the intolerant Taliban.[47]

In Christianity, the St. Sophia Cathedral, St. Nicholas Cathedral, and Church of St. Ambrose in Cyprus; the Pantokrator Monastery and the legendary Hagia Sophia church in Istanbul; the Church of St. John, in Damascus, were all converted to mosques. The Christian Visigothic Church of Cordoba, in Andalusia, Spain (600 AD) became the Great Mosque of Cordoba by conquest, and restored to a Catholic church in 1236 by King Ferdinand III of Castile during the Reconquista.[48] Recent petitions for prayer rights have been refused by the Vatican, but visiting Muslims recently attempted to pray there in defiance and for their own reconquest.[49]

In Jerusalem, Israel, the Al Aqsa mosque that was built over the Christian St. Mary basilica on the Temple Mount, site of the Jewish Temple destroyed by the Romans in 70 a.d., is included on UNESCO's World Heritage list, yet Muslims are conducting illegal excavations with heavy equipment to ravage the holy site along with its archaeological artifacts. A recent report that stressed the preservation of antiquities and prevention of destruction as a public duty recently designated it a Heritage Site at Risk. In October 2000, Palestinian Arabs reduced Joseph's Tomb[50] into smoldering rubble and within two days, bulldozers were clearing the area and Palestinians were painting the dome green to transform it into a Muslim holy site.[51] Muslim destruction is progressing worldwide.

After September 11, 2001, Muslims have aggressively tried to erect a mosque of conquest on Ground Zero, New York; and newer and larger mosques are being erected nationwide to the legal protestations[52] of local residents. An Islamic Circle of North America (ICNA) Islamic Center, in Alexandria, VA, is designed to reach out to non-Muslims and is supported by New Jersey's Gov. Christie's Muslim Outreach Committee,[53] with extensive ties to the Muslim Brotherhood (MB). A former ICNA president[54] was indicted for brutal political assassinations in 1971, and a 1991 MB memorandum[55] declared they are here to conduct a grand jihad to eradicate Western civilization from within.

Along with appropriating land for mosque construction come the revisionist[56] tales by the Council of American-Islamic Relations (CAIR) that Muslims discovered America first. President Obama announced that "Islam has always been a part of America and Muslims made extraordinary contributions to our country." A YouTube film[57] already exists that declares to the world that Muslims reached America before Christopher Columbus did — thereby laying original claim to our territory and our nation. We were wrong to remain silent during the devastation of so much history. Islamists have a patient, long-term strategy of usurpation, and mainstream media and our citizens have quietly accepted the revisionism that defiles our Judeo-Christian heritage and accomplishments.

Goodbye, Columbus.

THE VIOLENCE OF THE LAMBS

Gay activist uses Islamic tactics to delegitimize Israel for a Palestinian state.

Sheep are usually valued as an excellent source of food and fiber, but what about the sheep at Brooklyn College, particularly the psychology and philosophy departments? Although these predisposed, mindless sheep of academia differ somewhat from their quadruped counterparts, they are also of value because, as a veterinarian noted, both can be worked on a year-round basis.

To another anti-Israel forum,[58] add supportive pro-Palestinians who claimed their right to free speech, boot out the non-disruptive pro-Israel students who were denied the same free speech, and we have the makings of a lynch mob. Their head ram, gay activist Sarah Schulman, who was raised to be ashamed of her heritage, takes the rank of herding sheepdog. Although history has proven that no matter how Jews assimilate and harbor hate against their own, they, themselves, will never escape antisemitism.

Following the political science department's BDS rally against the State of Israel, the psychology and philosophy departments are using City University of New York (CUNY)'s Center for the Study of Gender and Sexuality to continue the assault. They will supplement Schulman's claim of "Homonationalism and Pinkwashing,"[59] a bogus assertion that Israel is intentionally promoting her own gay rights to deflect from their violating Palestinian rights, when Israel has long provided freedom for all its citizens, including welcoming gays into the military. But the more bizarre the accusation and propaganda, the more it appeals to the ill-informed, those inclined to blame their lot in life on others, and to an extreme liberal academia whose ultimate intent is to deny America's exceptionalism and her morality born of the Biblical Commandments and American Constitution. These activists prefer dictatorial officials, dishonesty, discord, and divisiveness, and to destroy the pillars of freedom and democracy inherent in Israel and the United States. If Ms. Schulman and her sheep can betray their Jewish heritage of ethics and morality, how long before she'll seek to betray her country, America, a beacon for freedom and opportunity around the world?

The truth has no place in their agenda, for they would then have to confront life for the Lesbian-Gay-Bisexual-Transgender (LGBT) community under Islam. They would have to admit that gays have no rights in Islam, that they're treated as criminals in Iran,[60] that they undergo severe forms of corporal punishment, flogging, imprisonment, and even execution. In any Islamic country, homosexuals are subject to brutal forms of torture and violence, mob assaults, lynching, and even being burned alive.[61]

Schulman and her sheep would be compelled to confront the rights denied Muslims by the Islamic culture — the right to live a happy, creative, productive life regardless of their sexual identification.

To begin with, Islamic women are victims of one of the most hideous, barbaric rituals —female genital mutilation.[62] Treated no better than sheep, these *untermenschen*[63] are forever demoralized and deprived of their sexuality and education, have no equality to men under the law, play no formal role in government, may take no action against spousal abuse or other forms of gender violence, and may receive no medical treatment without a man's consent. Women may not undertake domestic or foreign travel alone, qualify for inheritance equal to their brothers', expect a monogamous marriage to the man of her own choosing, keep her children in the event of divorce or widowhood, drive a car or even sit in the front seat.

The everyday insults to women are to be constantly imprisoned in a shroud, never to feel the warmth of the desert sun or a light zephyr on their skin and confined to wearing clothing that hampers her ability to run from the frequent attacker or rapist. Any breach of the repressive rules may result in her admonishment, a beating, or being stoned to death, because the man's strength and status are deemed divinely ordained. And, adding insult to injury, how best to show the value of their women and children than when they are positioned as shields at a rocket-launching pad to be included in the body-count accusation against Israel's retaliatory efforts!

Because of Islamic decrees of severe segregation for women (apartheid), many older men "of status" engage in homosexual sex while denying their homosexuality — "Women are for children, boys are for pleasure."[64] This is prevalent, and what could be more damaging and frightening for prepubescent young boys ("who do not have facial hair") than having to yield to rape and sodomy by male adults, and relinquish their childhood of play, creativity and independent thinking to an indoctrination of hate and militaristic exercises and shame that may lead to his own death by explosion?

The more females and sexuality are demonized, and the amicable, respectful interaction between the sexes suppressed, the greater the increase of homosexuality between men and the abuse of boys by older men. Gender apartheid[65] fosters a vicious misogyny[66] where men may become physically ill at the sight of women, and rape young boys who experience deep humiliation and emasculation, which explains why terrorists sexually mutilate their male victims and attack women worldwide. Living without harmony, affection or equality, they surrender their humanity and willingly mutilate and violate others as they have been violated, their rage increasing, and they lust for a death that will bestow what was forbidden in life.

Behind the rhetoric and encouraged by her flock of "willing executioners,"[67] Schulman seeks to dissolve the rights of Israelis and delegitimize the sovereign State of Israel. Whatever lies behind her warped thinking, she pursues Israel's destruction by advocating citizens' rights for malevolent non-citizens. She would rather see these murderous Arabs enter Israel freely to continue their deadly stone-throwing Intifadas and bloody slaughter of peaceful families.[68] But just as she hopes that Palestinians will overrun Israel, she agrees to a *Judenrein*[69] Islamic Palestine. Schulman considers one small state for Jews, surrounded by 1.6 billion Muslims in a land mass a thousand times its size, to be one too many. Inconceivably, her plans are also self-destructive when she works for the delegitimization and annihilation of the only country in the Middle East where she could live happily and without fear.

I am reminded and marvel at Yale's Whiffenpoof Song, written in 1909, and the relevancy of its lyrics now, more than a century later (2013), for Brooklyn College:

We are poor little lambs who have gone astray ...
Off on a spree,
Doomed from here to eternity,
God have mercy on such as we,
Baa, baa, bah.

HUNTER IS THE PREY/ *Pastor Hunter, who works to have sharia law insinuated into our American legal system, is himself the prey of CAIR.*

Dr. Joel C. Hunter, senior pastor, Northland Church in Longwood, Florida, expressed his desire to prevent a law that would protect America from insinuating a law that would prevent America from enacting Islamic sharia law into our legal system. I refer to SB 58 Application of Foreign Laws in Certain Cases to the Florida Senate Committee on Governmental Oversight and Accountability,[70] March 21, 2013. The disease is indeed upon us, and we must never be made to accept laws foreign or domestic that are antithetical to those established by our Founding Fathers.

We are under attack by stealth jihadists who understand our governance and the way to circumvent our laws far better than we understand theirs. The Bishop of Canterbury in the United Kingdom also acceptance sharia law to accommodate their wave of immigrants only to learn that Muslims do not assimilate and will never accept British law over the laws that they deem to be direct from Allah. Similarly, in our country, Muslims demand that their decrees be accepted over The Declaration of Independence and Constitution of the United States, to override the laws of the land they've allegedly adopted as their own, ultimately to destroy our Constitution as their process of Islamization unfolds.

Of the multitudes that have come to live in America — the different races and religions, languages, laws, customs — the Muslims were the first and only ones to have ever demanded exceptions to our laws, and to demand that we accept theirs as our own. This is not the assimilation of the masses, but invasion and conquest of a fascist ideology. The willingness to accept Atif Fareed's petition without a complete investigation of the ramifications of relinquishing our rights to life, liberty and the pursuit of happiness, is criminal. Fareed is a former member of CAIR, Council of American-Islamic Relations, an arm of the Muslim Brotherhood, a terrorist organization. How long after this concession will this feigned friendship evolve into demands that Hunter's church acquiesces to Muslim needs, before he loses his congregants, his pulpit, and his church to Islam?

It is time to learn more about Islam.

Islam is an aggressive, political, economic, military, social and legal system, a totalitarian ideology posing as religion. Since Mohammed's first conquest of the cities of Mecca and Medina in 624 AD, cities he called holy after slaughtering every Jewish and Christian inhabitant (or taking prisoner), he and his followers continued to capture, butcher, convert and enslave – 890 million people over 1400 years, and more than 20,666 deadly jihad attacks to date (of this writing), since September 11, 2001; consider the website, Religion of Peace.[71] There is not one country in the Middle East, Africa, Asia, Europe and in the Americas where Muslims have settled and not brought with them demands, riots, threats, conversion, and deadly conflict with the host culture. And, where they have completely swallowed a nation, such as all the countries that were never Islamic before 624 a.d., they have also erased history by destroying the artifacts of that culture.

What is Sharia Law?

Muslims who choose not to live under our Constitution and strive to implement sharia law in their immediate communities and ultimately infiltrate and change our administration are here to destroy our American way of life, just as they've done in other countries in the past. Considering our laws and size, the Muslim Brotherhood determined that the best road to conquest is through stealth — working within our system and deceiving our religious and community leaders. Our spiritual leaders do not have the right to forfeit our way of life to Islam. They owe it to themselves and their co-religionists to be educated before petitioning to relinquish American rights in support of Islam. Muslims do not have the right to force us to infuse their laws into ours; this is usurpation, destruction, and conquest. Sharia is incompatible with Democracy.

The Declaration of Independence clearly stipulates, "We hold these Truths to be self-evident, that all Men are created equal, that they are endowed by their Creator with certain unalienable Rights, that among these are Life, Liberty, and the Pursuit of Happiness." Further, when despotism is introduced, we have the right and the responsibility to throw off such government. Our Constitution empowers us with the duty and ability to reject and combat both tyranny, foreign and domestic. Islam is such tyranny, as their Koran mandates them to unite our country into a global Islamic caliphate, with complete domination.

Islam has rightly been identified as a death cult, where murder is encouraged, honor killings of their own children accepted, suicide bombings inspired by promises of virgins in heaven and gifts and monetary reward to surviving families. Islam-institutionalized slavery[72] justifies rape and enslavement of captured women and children as their bounty. Islamic countries are to this day the leading slave traders in the world.

In most Islamic countries, women are treated as slaves and prisoners: forced into wearing complete coverings (burqas) or subject to beatings; prevented from attending schools; prevented from walking unaccompanied by a male; forced to undergo damaging genital mutilation, facially disfigurement and gang-rape; and have no legitimacy in a court of law. Kidnapped toddlers are forced to be camel jockeys[73] for the pleasure of Dubai's sheiks. Children are forcibly sodomized, used as expendable warriors or human shields in war zones and girls are forced into pre-pubescent marriages with older men. *Fatwas* (legal pronouncements) are issued to find and execute apostates, and Islamophobia was created to curb our speech and prevent the populace from criticizing Islam or learning about their malevolence.

In addition to a recent revelation that the Taliban has approved a new widower's sexual relations with his deceased wife[74] within six hours after her death, it has now been revealed that Egypt's high school curriculum now encourages students to perform ritual human sacrifice and cannibalize apostates[75] and Muslims who have abandoned praying. The more we delve into Islam, the more unabashed evil we uncover.

While the Islamist may claim the First Amendment as his right to impose sharia law on our citizens (such as banning what offends them, special financial accommodations, and taking over streets for outdoor prayers), it actually states, "Congress shall make no law respecting an establishment of religion, or prohibiting the free exercise thereof; or abridging the freedom of speech, or of the press; or the right of the people peaceably to assemble, and to petition the Government for a redress of grievances." Thus, sharia law[76] may not be practiced in the United States. Sharia violates our Constitution, and the Muslims and Dr. Hunter are complicit and guilty of Criminal Sedition, and subject to prosecution by our Federal government.

As an American citizen, clergy are obliged to prevent the Islamization of our country. They are duty-bound to thwart the law that they have been duped into supporting so willingly. Be assured that Muslims do not have the Constitutional right to impose their laws in our land, thereby destroying ours. And Fareed has already shown his hand by being a former chairman of CAIR, the terrorist-supporting front organization. Together they are betraying everything for which America stands.

Dr. Hunter must understand the danger that comes when despotism is accepted in the spirit of multiculturalism, but I fear he has been bought.

SINS CAST LONG SHADOWS/ *Ireland's Teachers Union voted to cease all cultural and academic collaboration with Israel.*

In the words of Kevin O'Neil, "Kindliness combined with unique native wit and the courage to go and do business with the world have been the trademarks of the Irish character. The Irish have never been known, like so many other nations, to retire from the world, to withdraw, to hide." Yet this is the process Ireland has begun.

As the Teachers Union relinquished its freedoms of thought, learning, research and growth in the interest of healing illusory Islamic wounds, they have entered a collaborative effort to destroy their homeland. While violent jihadis pursue the Koranic dictates to kill the unbelievers,[77] stealth is facilely implemented within Europe and the Americas. Stealth, aka civilizational jihad, is a system of lies *(taqiyyah)*, persuasion and incremental restrictions that the invading entity imposes on the host culture by claiming victimization. By insisting that words or expressions are offensive — the very vehicles of thought and ideas — freedom of speech is purloined, and societies transformed.

By "ceasing all cultural and academic collaboration with Israel, including the exchange of scientists, students and academic personalities, and the cooperation in research programs," the Teachers' Union has taken a step backward in time to the 7th century of Mohammed and the evil decrees found in the Koran. Perhaps the Union does bear a deep-seated desire to assist in the Islamic effort to destroy Israel with a fallacious "apartheid" label. Israel, the only Jewish homeland on the planet is, in fact, home to citizens of every race, religion, and national origin, yet no one addresses the Islamic regimes where Jews and Christians are either expelled, converted by force, enslaved or killed — or the communist regimes of China and Cuba where freedoms are considerably limited.

With this boycott, they also betray their teachers' and students' rights to a more complete education and their desire to be part of Ireland's progress in the 21st century. Ireland's history is filled with ancestors who fought bravely for their right to exist, yet the union has joined a war whose goal is to thwart Israel's right to exist as a tiny, sovereign, dynamic nation amid two dozen hostile Islamic states' covering more than six million square miles (plus 80 percent of what was originally mandated for Israel).

Despite Israel's having to defend its estimated eight million citizens within her borders legally designated in 1948 and later won in a defensive battle against seven invading Arab armies, this unique global leader in innovation and entrepreneurship has managed to excel in all fields of endeavor that give purpose to life — science, technology, medicine. Israel also has more museums, orchestras and publications per capita than anywhere else in the world (whose publications are shared with other nations that are dedicated to their own development and progress).

As a leader in offering international humanitarian aid[78] to such as Sri Lanka, Armenia, Turkey, Japan, Kosovo, Haiti, hurricanes Katrina and Sandy, Israel has already rushed to aid the FBI and victims of the Boston Marathon[79] terrorist bombing. Israel is, by virtue of her morality and medical proficiency, a country that should be protected. Palestinians[80] have excelled as the leading producer of suicide bombers and terrorists in the world (note the PLO terrorist movement in Ireland in the link).

By complying with this initial Islamic agenda, it will become increasingly difficult to defend their position later because Ireland is losing her grip on democracy. From this one agreement will come forced subjugation and revisionism, until culture and laws fail to protect, and Ireland will experience what is already prevalent throughout

Europe – violence, riots and bloodshed, changes in the school systems, more mosque construction, burning synagogues, desecrated churches; and danger for Ireland's teachers, citizens, and their progeny.

Wherever Islam is allowed a toehold, freedoms are sacrificed. Sweden and Norway[81] have the highest percentage of rapes in Europe. From Asia[82] to Africa, worshippers are burned in their churches. In Mali,[83] children are kidnapped and sold into slavery. In France,[84] attacks against Jews are increasing. In England,[85] Muslims are patrolling the streets, enforcing sharia law. In Israel,[86] residents live in constant fear of bus explosions and suicide bombers. Now, in Boston, it may be perilous to join crowds or attend an event. This begs the question of whether the Teachers Union complied because of sufficient recompense or fear of reprisal, and if it will be worth the sacrifice of freedom to learn and thrive as a nation. Is it worth trading one's civilization, culture, advancements, ethics and morality — even national character — for tyranny's domination, the worship of death, the abandonment of the creativity and poetry of the Irish soul? Their forefathers knew, "Sins cast long shadows."

In the words of our John Adams to Thomas Jefferson: "I will insist that the Hebrews have done more to civilize man than any other nation." If Adams were here today, he might add that the Muslims have done more to destroy man than any other nation. They have already destroyed most of the cultures in the Middle East and 300 million[87] inhabitants since the emergence of Mohammed, and they have now come to destroy our democracies. Rather than defend their academic freedom and independent thinking, these educators have succumbed to the Islamist demands — surrendered their independence, free will, and access to Israeli ingenuity and progress to the hate-driven, supersessionist culture of Islam. This will be but the first of many concessions. The future of their children have been sold out to the inevitable cult of death[88] and destruction. From here on in, the grip of sharia will only tighten.

How long before Ireland's citizens must adjust to calls of prayer five times a day, and limit their lives to the highly restrictive edicts of Islam? How long before their Saints and Scholars – Patrick, Columba, Brendan, Aidan – are identified by Islam as true Muslims, just as they are now saying that Jesus was a Palestinian Muslim?[89] How long before the revered Book of Kells is labeled idolatrous? How long before these teachers can no longer teach their history before it is deemed antithetical to the teachings of Allah? What one loses is always more than the gain when the pact is with the Devil.

Ireland must take on the task of preservation for herself and for Israel. If the Irish are not in step with their own courageous history and survival, they will not have the fortitude to stand against tyranny's domination. Before another book is boycotted and rejected, know this: "The disappearance of the sense of responsibility is the most far-reaching conquest of submission to authority." – Stanley Milgram, social psychologist.

NOT THE SAME GOD

Until Islam, all American migrants came to America to become Americans.

It was not so long ago, in 2008, that Rowan Williams, the former Archbishop of Canterbury, welcomed Islam into the United Kingdom. He now speaks of adapting further to the growing Muslim population,[90] now numbering two million, with 85 Islamic courts in the UK, women unequal to men and unprotected from the violence of their fathers and husbands. At least one cleric, Suhaib Hasan, is advocating stoning and amputation (which is yet one more adaptation to national acceptance of One Law for All).[91] English law has already evolved and adopted some aspects of sharia, yet Williams now entertains adjustments to achieve a society that works for the ever-popular "common good." Sharia can never be compatible with Democracy.

For what other immigrant society was adaptation implemented? The migration pattern for the UK since 1100 shows that merchants from the Netherlands settled first; followed by the Dutch and French Protestants in the 1500s; enslaved Asians arrived in the 1600s; then the refugees from the French revolution and Chinese sailors in the 1700s; Jews from Poland, Ukraine and Belarus in the 1800s; trailed by Irish settlers escaping the famine, and trading Indians and Chinese. Still, England was recognizably England.

The 1900s brought the Belgian refugees who escaped WW I, refugees of Nazi oppression who arrived in the 1930s, the Poles who came during 1940–1960, Jamaicans who arrived in 1948, followed by immigrants from the Caribbean. All these cultures, yet not one had the audacity to demand changes to the laws of the land! While they maintain their identity and surely a measure of their culture, they have assimilated and consider themselves English, and they abide by English law.

Not so with the Muslims, for they have come not for the same reasons as their forerunners, but with a different purpose, a different mission. They came not to become English, but to transform[92] the English into their own identity, with their Muslim laws and religion. Just as Mohammed and his followers entered and conquered new lands in the Middle East and parts of Europe to implant their religion and course of conduct into the new host country, so their descendants follow the same path and purpose today. And the naïve Archbishop of Canterbury yielded and permitted these newcomers to insist on sharia law, which can only lead to the United Kingdom's downfall. In the interest of showing an acceptance of multiculturalism, or perhaps he was unable to defend himself against accusations of intolerance or narrow-mindedness, the deluded man sold out his country.

No country, once Islamized, has ever been able to regain its previous identity. Centuries after La Reconquista of 1492, Spain is again teetering under the new

Muslim assault.[93] India has been dealing with the presence of da'wa-jihad for about 1300 years, with Muslims now numbering 280 million.

I call upon Cardinal Timothy Dolan to understand that what is transpiring in the United Kingdom has completely overcome the once-non-Muslim countries of Afghanistan, Albania, Algeria, Azerbaijan, Bahrain, Bangladesh, Egypt, Gambia, Guinea, Iran, Iraq, Jordan, Kosovo, Kyrgystan, Lebanon, Libya, Maldives, Mali, Mauritania, Syria,[94] Turkey, and others. Islam is now the predominant religion in the Middle East, the Horn of Africa, northern Africa, and in parts of Asia. Large communities also exist in China, the Balkans and Russia, and in each of these countries, Muslims are imposing their sharia law in increments, until the country will bear no resemblance to its former distinctiveness. The operation of sharia courts in a democracy has nothing to do with religious freedom, but everything to do with political power and the appropriation of the host culture.

In the presence of mosque clergy, Cardinal Dolan thanked them and God for welcoming him as a friend and family member[95] when, in fact, it is they who should have shown their gratitude for this country's welcome, freedom, security, and life without oppression. Dolan misspoke when he indicated they love the same God, for Dolan's God does not command that His followers bring the entire world under Catholic rule, or demand the subjugation of Muslims and Jews, or require Dolan's co-religionists to slay those who do not share his beliefs — such as beheading a Catholic priest[96] or blowing up school buses of Christian[97] and Jewish[98] children.

The Archbishop has chosen to represent his people in an arrangement for which he is ill prepared. He has arrogantly and wrongfully assumed that he alone understands Islamic intentions and can create a harmony that no one had been able to achieve through fourteen centuries of Islamic jihad. He is gambling with the lives of millions!

The goal of Islam is to deal with every aspect of life in every society, to bring its culture to everyone in all the corners of the globe, "until there is no more tumult or oppression and the Religion of Allah prevails," Koran (2:193), although wherever the Religion of Allah does prevail, there is great chaos, oppression, suffering and bloodshed, even among their own people. Muslims must wage jihad, as an all-consuming, divinely ordained endeavor, or they believe they will be barred from Paradise along with the non-believers.

Hasan al-Banna, founder of the Muslim Brotherhood in Egypt, 1922, said,

"We summon you to Islam, the teachings of Islam, the laws of Islam and the guidance of Islam, and if this smacks of politics in your eyes, then it is our policy ... Islam does have a policy embracing the happiness of this world ... We believe that Islam is an all-embracing concept which regulates every aspect of life, adjudicating on every one of its concerns and prescribing for it a solid and rigorous order.

"Islam is a faith and worship, a country and a citizenship, a religion and a state. It is spirituality and hard work. It is a Koran and a sword.

"O ye who believe! Fight the unbelievers who gird you about, and let them find firmness in you: and know that Allah is with those who fear Him" (9:123)

"Then, when the sacred months have passed, slay the idolaters wherever ye find them, and take them (captive), and besiege them, and prepare for them each ambush. But if they repent and establish worship and pay the poor-due, then leave their way free. (This means that idolaters are to be killed, unless they convert to Islam, and begin following Islamic laws, such as paying alms.) "Fight those who believe not in Allah nor the Last Day, nor hold that forbidden which hath been forbidden by Allah and his Messenger, nor acknowledge the religion of Truth (even if they are) of the People of the Book, until they pay the jizya with willing submission, and feel themselves subdued (9:289)."

Islam's double identity[99] takes the form of groups that appear outwardly moderate, but advance the jihadist agenda through various non-violent initiatives — even as the members themselves have ties to violent jihadist organization.

The Ayatollah Khomeini, in true Muslim fashion, stated, "Eleven things are impure: urine, excrement, sperm . . . non-Muslim men and women." (All of us)

The biographer of Mohammad recorded his master as saying, "I have been made victorious with terror." Bukhari. Vol 3, Book 52.

These are just a few of the sacred beliefs of those the Cardinal has befriended. They do not worship the same God or share the same principles with Christianity or Judaism; they lack compassion and virtue.

Islam is a totalitarian, supersessionist theology that demands obedience or uses armed conflict to achieve obedience, and Dolan has an obligation to his co-religionists and to his fellow Americans not to sell them out by bowing and scraping to those who have come to woo and betray his allegiance. If we continue to accommodate, it will be inevitable that we will have bought ourselves a new master, along with irrevocable bondage for ourselves and our descendants.

!SMITCIV

Despite statistics to the contrary, Muslims claim extreme victimhood to slowly enforce sharia law.

This year's Miss World's competitive beauty pageant held in Jakarta, Indonesia, was threatened by Muslim martinets who insisted that too much skin would offend the population. Apparently, no one could defy the devout religionists who had the right not to attend, but the bikinis were indeed replaced by sarongs, and the participants turned into obedient *dhimmis* (non-Muslim subjects).

Not long after that, there was an attack on non-Muslims at the Westgate Mall in Nairobi, Kenya, where at least 70 were killed, 175 injured, and 49 still missing. Apparently, when you rape, severely mutilate and slaughter in the name of religious persecution, skin color is not an issue.

Around the same time, there were torching of Christians and their churches and attacks on Egyptian Copts who failed to vote as instructed. Kirsten Powers, American political pundit, described the scene where Christians in the Middle East and Africa were kidnapped, raped, tortured, slaughtered, and beheaded, while others were forced to flee the birthplace of Christianity.

Then there was the report of a major fire set in a supermarket, followed by the ambush and killing of 46 students who were receiving a western, non-Islamic education in a Nigerian school. Not to be outdone, Taliban suicide bombers killed at least 85 worshippers at the ancient All Saints' Church, in Pakistan. I could go on and on — and, unfortunately, so could they.

Although this was never done for any other religion, the US National Park Service produced, so far, two pro-Islamic videos (denying their use of taxpayer funds) to help students assure their viewing audience that theirs is a religion of peace. The sweet young things in the film claim to have been misunderstood ever since September 11, 2001 and are themselves victims of bigotry. The mantra of victimhood, repeated time and again when Palestinians throw deadly missiles at Israeli vehicles and when Muslims self-explode on well-trafficked streets or in busy restaurants, was also the declared mission of the Million Muslim March planned for September 11, 2013.

At this point, it might be prudent to add something about September 11, 2001, since I've been reviewing current textbooks that seem to employ a considerable amount of whitewash and historic revisionism. One book states terrorists slammed three airliners into the World Trade Center and the Pentagon, with the fourth crashing into a field in Pennsylvania, without identifying the terrorists as Islamic jihadis. Neither is the meaning of jihad provided, a critical omission. According to Justice Mohammed Taqi Usmani, a 20-year sharia judge on Pakistan's Supreme Court, the purpose of jihad is to establish the dominance of Islam, and that aggressive jihad is "obligatory" for Muslims until the domination of Islam is established over all other religions. If there was any misunderstanding, certainly it was cleared with Feisal Abdul Rauf's declaration that he would erect a mosque on Ground Zero.

In the film, the young women claim Muslims to be victims in America, Europe and elsewhere, pleading for their freedom of worship. They are on a mission for human, civil, and women's rights, such as espoused by their faith. Yet, the First Amendment to our Constitution permits them the freedom of worship in America. It stipulates, "Congress shall make no law respecting an establishment of religion, or prohibiting the free exercise thereof..." It also includes the freedom to leave or discontinue membership in a religion or religious group, called "apostasy," a fundamental part of religious freedom, covered by Article 19 of the Universal Declaration of Human Rights. So why the complaint?

My guess is that a good percentage of Americans came to this land for religious freedom, and found America welcoming. Plus, with such diversity already entrenched in this country and throughout Europe, how is it that only these jihadis claim intolerance? This is a device of deception by accusation and denunciation for what they could not acquire by the proverbial sword — or weaponized jet.

Muslims have the right to practice their religion when and as they wish, not prohibited, as they would have us believe. America imposes no jizya taxes,[100] repressive social legislation, or political disenfranchisement as seen in the Middle East under Islamic rule. Our laws do not mandate executing apostates, or stoning or striking adulterers with a hundred lashes, or torturing homosexuals, or assassinating poets, or decapitating, or enslaving women and children, or that husbands beat their wives, yet these women say they are met with hostility.

If they perceive hostility, it is because we understand jihad, and will not yield our freedoms to grant them domination. If they perceive opposition, it is because we will not desist from speaking our minds and conducting ourselves in accordance with our own culture and laws regardless of offense. We are offended by their hate rallies, boycotts, flag burnings, rapes, and killings.

In America, Islamists threaten others on city streets, conduct BDS rallies to intimidate and discredit (particularly on university campuses), deface synagogues, and make special demands. Accusing their adversary of the strategy they use themselves is called "projection." These students are using a passive-aggressive technique, based on a fabricated accusation, to claim they are "VICTIMS," when, in fact, they are the reverse: "SMITCIV," a word I created because we have no such war strategy in our culture.

In truth, the Muslim woman's true victimization comes at the hands of her own people. She holds a far lower legal and cultural status and is denied the dignity of choice. Although both men and women live by sharia law, with every aspect of their lives tightly controlled and both subject to cruel punishment for the slightest infraction of stringent rules, sharia applies more often and more harshly to women. This is evidenced by the proliferation of head scarves and full-length shrouds, a political, not religious, statement. These were rarely seen before September 11, 2001 but instituting the dress code announced the Islamist's arrival and presence in the host country, along with the increased mosque construction, intensified terrorism, and escalated demands.

Sharia, the basis for the totality of the Islamic way of life, provides no human rights or protection. Sharia demoralizes with female genital mutilation before puberty, specific dress, daily prayers, even which hand to use for which purpose and when it may be chopped off. Severe corporal punishment looms for any deviation from the decrees — from leaving their homes, to attending school, to seeking medical care, to any act that a father or husband may declare a state of dishonor, and more.

Above all, sharia determines that woman's purpose is to serve men, and this is their true victimization.

WOOING WYOMING
Islamic penetration into our libraries covertly influence our children.

An invitation was issued to 125 libraries across our nation, a lure for these institutions of learning to participate in a five-part reading and discussion series, titled "Let's Talk About It: Muslim Journeys." I do not use the term "lure" lightly, as this is a strategy of the Muslim Brotherhood's furtive jihad into our society — an effort to provide additional reading material for our public-school students who are already on a steady diet of Islamic propaganda.

Although Shannon Smith, executive director of the Wyoming Humanities Council, assured me of their interest in diversity in a state that has little, too many in her position of trust have little-to-no concept of the Islamic purpose and ideology. I cannot help but wonder whether the libraries will invite other religious communities to share their history and heritage or expose the true purpose of these religion peddlers.

Of the more than 2106 mosques (2010 census) nationwide,[101] I found three in Wyoming and an Islamic center in Laramie raised and ready for the imminent influx, a sign of their offensive. Ms. Smith, an innocent in dealing with the Islamic agenda, is not considering purpose, that of instilling their belief system into every state, and every country on the globe, to present their religion as the paradigm of peace, when, in reality, it is an authoritarian rule requiring submission or torture and death.

When violent jihad proves impractical or counter-productive, as in the US, stealth jihad is employed — infiltration and domination. These cultural enrichers[102] have not come for reading recommendations to learn about America, our history, our Founding Fathers, or how to conduct a smooth assimilation into our society. They have not suggested that others be invited to the discussion table. Quite simply, they have asked for time to tell their own (misrepresented) "journey" and to distribute Islamic books for inclusion into the system, to proselytize, and demand accommodation and acquiescence.

Their lessons are seductive, explaining that their religion was spread across the lands, as though by inspiration and word of mouth, rather than as a political ideology advanced through 1400 years of aggression by the sword — spreading the blood of innocents and the agony of ruin. While killing Christians throughout Africa with the sword, Jews in Israel with rockets or their suicidal offspring, Americans with bombs (9/11, the Boston Marathon), and Russians with explosives — may be expedient, it is through stealth education, in schools and libraries, that they can reach the receptive population in a land the breadth of the United States.

Russian Communist Vladimir Lenin knew what he could accomplish by controlling the minds of children: "Give me four years to teach the children and the seed I have sown will never be uprooted."

Abraham Lincoln recognized the procedures of tyranny: "The philosophy of the classroom today will be the philosophy of government tomorrow."

The introduction of Islamic material, produced solely by Islamists, could be devastating. Consider that the Common Core textbooks have already diminished the importance of American history, our founding and Constitution, and trivialized the role of Christianity and Judaism in favor of a falsified Islamic involvement in US history. The introduction of these books into the library will augment the already present revisionism.

According to the Koran, Muslims are required to impose their theocracy around the globe. They eradicated by any means millions of Zoroastrians, Pharoahans, Buddhists, Hindus, Christians and Jews in the Middle East, and have risen to conquer[103] Africa, Asia and Europe, and America, an estimated 890 million. Muslims are now overcoming their host populations in Great Britain[104] (London bombing, Glasgow International airport, forced conversions, female genital mutilations, terrorist attacks, a beheading), France[105] (Marseilles a hotbed of Islamic violence, Jews killed on the streets), Belgium[106] (growing radicalism, violence, increased Muslim control), Sweden[107] and Denmark (burnings and rapes rampant), Norway[108] (100% rapes[109] by Muslims; terrorist group demands breakaway nation),[110] and Spain[111] appears to be losing her identity. The deteriorating condition of these nations should be understood as a warning to the United States.

Because Muslims are not yet a sufficient percentage of our populace to physically oppress all Americans, they have implemented changes through other venues, including education. They are aided by Pearson, Houghton Mifflin, and other book publishers without conscience who fill their coffers with Saudi funds, grants from socialist/communist groups, the Bill Gates Foundation, Annenberg Foundation, and many more. Their huge investments will be reimbursed through ever-increasing state taxes.

As we've noted in other libraries, their books depict Islam as an enlightened society rather than the third world, tribal, murderous civilization that has seen no communal advancement since its inception in the 7th century. Under laws that destroy democracy, coexistence is nonexistent. Briefly, sharia laws enforce severe punishment (enslavement, whipping, stoning, amputation, hanging, and beheading) to keep the population under total control, reinforced by ritual prayers five times daily. Islam is exquisitely designed to overtake and convert, or else to annihilate. Its treatment of women[112] is infamous.

They have no Ten Commandments and no Golden Rule. By allowing these visitors access to our libraries to communicate an acceptable, but deceitful, version of their doctrines to the public, the libraries become complicit in destroying our way of life — and woe to the descendants.

The heart of the matter is the Muslims[113] who are not here to become Americans.[114] Just as they are not assimilating in Europe, so they will not assimilate here. Their intent is to establish the caliphate to impose Islamic rule. Mohammed was a warlord and his disciples a warring people in his image, not discoverers or inventors. Their books provide a falsified history, fictitious innovations, and tales of victimhood, yet they are the aggressors. FBI statistics still show that Jews are victims of more than 62 percent of hate crime in America. As Jews flee their current homes for Israel, Christians remain to contend with the hostile immigrants and become the most persecuted religion worldwide. By providing me with book titles, authors and publishers, for research, we may yet be able to stem the tide.

A QUEST FOR COMMONALITY
Outreach programs are stealth jihad designed to win favor of the docile clergy and congregates.

The Adult Catholic Education program, held recently at a local Catholic parish hall, was titled, "Under Abraham's Tent: Jews, Christians, and Muslims in the World Today." The evening, designed to "foster peaceful relationships" of three religions through their shared patriarch, Abraham, attracted about 200 guests.

The first speaker, Rabbi "J," related the story of the biblical Abram, who smashed all but one of his father's idols, leaving a hammer in the hand of the largest. When his father, Terach the idol carver, returned to the store and saw the damage, Abram alibied that a war had ensued among the gods, and the largest idol won. Terach scoffed, saying, "The idols have no life or power," to which Abraham wisely responded, "Then why do you worship them?"

Thus, did Abram show the folly of idol worship and introduce the belief of monotheism into civilization. "J" further explained that the Jews, through Moses, were also the first to bring laws of morality and humanity to an immoral, lawless humankind, laws by which civilizations have since prospered. Regrettably, she ("J") did not offer a definition of Judaism, the role of Jews in world history, or the significance of Israel to the Jewish people.

Although Jews had resided in Egypt, Iraq, Iran, and Mesopotamia, and despite their persecution through the centuries, they nevertheless did not declare these lands as theirs. She might well have dismantled the accusation that Jews are colonialists had she noted the Jewish claim to the land has very specific boundaries[115] as stipulated in the ancient Torah – the same boundaries established by the League of Nations in 1920, and again by the United Nations in 1948. It may be that the rabbi simply forgot these exhaustively documented facts, or that she felt compelled to abandon her religion's survival for the fashionable multiculturalism and diversity.

"J" related an anecdote about the origin of the people that Cain met after his banishment from Eden. The Torah explains that Adam fathered many children before he died at age 930, and Cain may well have met these others in Nod, where he married and built a city. Rather, she responded that she told "our story," and that there could be another's story, thereby unwisely allowing for the invasion of a deceptive revisionist narrative.

She mistakenly added that Ishmael was Muslim. In this, her timeline was inaccurate because it is established that Mohammad was not born and did not agitate for Islam until the 7th century a.d., some two and a half millennia later. Although Ishmael was an Arab, he was not a Muslim. It is known that Mohammed's conquests for an Islamic people began with the slaying of Jews, Christians, and idolaters of Mecca and Medina – beheading the men and raping and enslaving their women and children. Hence, the first Muslims were children of all four groups in the Middle East.

To a prompt about the 1967 origin of "Palestinians"[116] (in quotation marks because before that date, the term meant any Jew or Arab who lived in that geographical area), "J" replied, "I don't want to go there." It is a well-documented reality that Yasser Arafat began using that terminology to provide a false bond for his usurpers to the land, but this rabbi saw it as a threat to multiculturalism and Islamic revisionism when it is, in fact, a threat to Jewish survival.

The rabbi should be reminded that throughout history, Jews have argued that if they abandoned their traditions and rituals, and conformed to their host society, they would be less likely to face persecution. But during the Spanish Inquisition, Jews who embraced their heritage were either converted, murdered, or expelled en masse in 1492. And, of course, during the Holocaust, Jews who trusted the concept in the 1930s and '40s were savagely annihilated. She was ill prepared to contribute to this outreach.

Father "C," the second speaker, also referred to Abram's belief system as the beginning of monotheism, and to Jesus Christ's ministry for the beginning of Christianity. He seemed distressed when an audience member asked, "Do Muslims and Jews need to trust in Jesus to get into heaven?" Whereas the Catholic Church may mandate conversion as an entry to heaven, the Father seemed to abjure an exclusionary viewpoint. He did not reference Catholic Charities' efforts to convert Muslims to Christianity or Muslim efforts to convert Jews and Christians to Islam. Neither did he reveal that the Koran restricts Muslims from designating zakat (charity) to any but Muslims, except for the purposes of outreach and conversion.[117]

Imam "M," the last of the three speakers, stated he would discuss historical accounts, revisionism, the universalism of Islam, and the "pre-Islamists" (Jews and Christians) who rejected Mohammed's message. His claim that Islam's history is akin to Judaism's, and that the two religions "shared ethics," is fallacious. The Jewish Bible exclusively introduced the early Noahite Laws and Ten Commandments that provided God's universal and timeless standard of right and wrong for all civilizations. In stark contrast, Islam's laws contain none of those ethics and morals, and their purpose, as stated by modern-day imams and throughout the Koran, is to require strict adherence to Mohammed's stern teachings of Islam by virtually everyone.

Further omitted was that Islam inextricably links ideology and religion. "M" stated that sharia law is based on scripture, words of the prophet, and human intellect (an ambiguous statement), but failed to inform that 62 percent of the Koran[118] deals severely with the infidel, with other estimates at 81 percent. Sharia laws are meant to regulate non-Muslim as well as Muslim life.

At this point, "M" reminded us of earlier statements — that Jews argued with God (that God must live up to His promise to the Jewish people), that Christians agree with Jesus, and that under the Koran, all people would agree to be one faith, one religion, follow the laws of their prophet/role model, have the same behavior, attitude, and there would be no fighting. A quick check at the countries around the world disproves that easily enough. He also assured the audience that Muslims kill other Muslims more than they kill Jews and Christians — a hardly comforting gen.

He went on to say that Muslims have a high degree of illiteracy. It is a fact that domination and oppression thrive when the masses are kept in ignorance. The importance of education goes back to Biblical times and is inherent in our Constitution.

Before closing, the imam added, "The ethnic people of the Middle East includes Palestinians," yet another invention left unchallenged. The Philistines from Crete are long gone, and the current Palestinians are traceable to Egypt, Jordan, Lebanon, Syria, and Yemen, from which they came to the nascent Israel in search of employment. Adopting "Palestinians" for their appellation was a stealth war tactic to provide a false bond to the region they coveted.

It became quite evident that a mountain of historical revisionism was required to create a very false and tenuous harmony. Only when the Jews diminished their history, when the Christians moderated their beliefs, and when Muslims eluded questions could there be any semblance of sharing and understanding. So, this was not educational, but indoctrinal.

If the church members brought these three philosophies together in the name of harmony and understanding, then at least harmony prevailed for a couple of hours. But the morrow would bring more news of violent Jew-hatred, church burnings, and other catastrophic acts of jihad, and the parishioners would remain terribly misinformed. In the name of multiculturalism, diversity, and political correctness, they were left with dishonesty and self-congratulatory egotism.

FROM HIJAB TO JIHAD

Wonder Woman cast aside, the mayor's Islamic veiling is intended to create an alliance with Somali immigrants.

Did Minneapolis's democrat Mayor Betsy Hodges not get it? This was no game, dress-up playtime or Carnival. Then I wondered if she ever found occasion to dress in the ethnic clothing of her city's other ethnicities — the Germans, Swedes, Norwegians, Danes, English, Poles, Irish, French Canadians, Native Americans. Perhaps she had not done her homework about the Somali immigrants, and it took her only 100 days into office to don a hijab to contrive an alliance.

She had to have heard all the news about the subjugation and severe treatment of women in the Islamic Middle East; the Honor Diaries film that the Council of American-Islamic Relations (CAIR) is trying to suppress; the controversy over Brandeis University's bestowing and then rescinding an honorary degree to Ayaan Hirsi Ali, the pressure applied by CAIR that forced Disney to cancel a movie that Muslims find *offensive,* and more. Then why would she don the quintessential symbol of inequality and bondage — the shroud of the Islamic woman?

The mayor claims to have an increasingly strong admiration for Wonder Woman, the most popular female superstar in figure-hugging, stars-and-stripes regalia, with bracelets that make her invincible. Hodges is a collector of Wonder Woman dolls and has recently hung a photograph of this shining symbol of strength and sexual equality on her office wall. Rather than emulate her heroine, however, she abandoned the image with which she allegedly identifies, this icon of bravery and justice, for cowardice and deceit.

Perhaps she is a lost soul, one without direction, without ties to ethics or principles, unstable in today's culture and society. Unwilling or unable to stand up for American ideologies, she too easily acquiesces to the preferences or demands of the archenemy of humankind. Whether Hodges is clueless and diplomatically inept or has emerged with a heretofore-concealed agenda remains to be seen, but both choices do not bode well for the office she holds.

What began as the 7th century Bedouin woman's attempt at privacy and protection in the desert, these shrouds have become a symbol of woman's indignity and servitude. As Nonie Darwish so aptly explained in her book, Cruel and Usual Punishment, woman has come to represent the totality of evil and inferiority in Islamic teaching. Considered lacking in intelligence and religion, women are deemed half, and sometimes one-fourth, of man's worth in a sharia court (Islamic law). They may be beaten by their husbands and forbidden to leave the house unless accompanied by a male relative. They may be killed by their father if the parent deems his honor compromised. In the oppressive Islamic society, women are the ones who preserve the honor of the male, so that he may avoid responsibility and disrepute for any unpleasantness or trouble.

The hijab and burqa serve the purpose of enforcing obedience to sharia and to men. With the obligation of defending their enslavement under constant threat of their own destruction, they may become very self-justifying when challenged. Some may even try to earn honor and respect by joining the radicals for violent jihad (holy war against the infidel).

To cultures that relish freedom, these hidden women are deemed victims of sadism, forced to endure the insufferable heat of the subtropics under layers of clothing, and prevented from enjoying the summer sun and cool breezes. In fact, medical experts have noted that women so covered in northern climes, with limited sunshine, are suffering more from osteoporosis from the lack of Vitamin D,[119] and experiencing an increased risk of pelvic fracture during childbirth. Their newborn babies are more prone to seizures from the same deficiency.

Islamic law is concerned more with raping, beating, flogging, and stoning women than it is in honoring them. The sharia demand that women be veiled, some covered from head to toe, along with Female Genital Mutilation,[120] is also the Islamic way of solving the problem of male sexual temptations. Rather than teach the men self-restraint and respect, the onus is on the woman to hide herself, her sexuality, her body, her shame. Tragically, because there are women who want to appear obedient to their god and faith, it becomes the burden of other women to withstand being hated, ridiculed, or becoming targets of *fatwas* (legal decrees). Women face divisiveness or derision at every turn, and their society discourages, and even hinders, women from establishing friendships, particularly where polygamy is practiced.

To have surrendered her dignity, self-esteem, pride in her American heritage and culture goes beyond Hodges' courtship of a voting bloc or fulfilling a promise to constituents. She is responsible for having her female police chief and city council representatives wear the hijab on February 28, proclaimed Hijab Day at City Hall. Rather than guide these new immigrants in becoming Americans, as previous ethnic groups have done, she is accepting the newcomers' customs and laws over our own. When the intruder or invader makes demands (no matter how subtle) that are met with compliance and submission from the host culture, it is submission to the invaders.

I am deeply concerned about how Hodges and her administration will address future demands, as they will surely be forthcoming — whether for Islamizing children in the classroom, serving only halal foods in the cafeterias, observing Islamic holidays on the city calendar, or all manner of accommodations in everyday life. Hodges' decision may well have been meticulously planned. Her hijab is aiding and abetting stealth jihad.

CAIR VISITS FRANCISCAN SISTERS

CAIR provides low-information religious personnel with Islam's historical revisionism, theology and doctrines — a false, pleasing narrative for acceptance to the newly conquered.

The Franciscan Sisters of Little Falls were visited by the Council on American-Islamic Relations, aka CAIR, an arm of the Muslim Brotherhood (MB). These trained public relations groups reach out to the accommodating, low-information citizens in political and religious institutions, public libraries, schools and universities, and government security forces, to present a whitewashed history, hide their intent, inhibit discussion, prohibit news coverage of acts of violence, and control language[121] that exposes the truths about Islam.

CAIR and ISNA (Islamic Society of North America) were unindicted co-conspirators of the Holy Land Foundation,[122] a front organization for Hamas, a designated, chartered terrorist group. They are no different than the Muslims who are killing Christians and Jews throughout the world — the Boko Haram that kidnapped, converted and killed the female students in Nigeria; the jihadis who burned to death male students just weeks before; the Muslims who recently destroyed entire villages in Nigeria,[123] burned down 200 homes and butchered 16 while intoning Allahu Akbar. They differ only in their attire.

Among the many strategies of Islamic conquest[124] is the use of a grassroots network of social and charitable organizations to expand their membership base. Their god demands conversion or death to infidels and Islam is responsible for the slaughter of 890 million people over fourteen centuries — with more than 23,000 deadly jihad[125] attacks since 9/11/01. Eighty percent of their Koran incites and advocates death.

Their claim of victimization is bogus; they are the aggressors in today's world. They do not live the Gospel of tolerance and peace, or the Biblical Commandments or Golden Rule. Rather, they advocate the cruelest set of laws, sharia, on the planet. Behind a façade of Mohammad's earlier writings and their five pillars of faith, the later writings in their Koran, Hadith, and Sura contain a doctrine of hate and commands to kill Jews and Christians[126] primarily, but also Hindus, Buddhists, all infidels and apostates. Sexual slavery continues in Islam. This is a political ideology, couched as religion, to globalize Islam. They have made continents unsafe; Jews are fleeing for their lives[127] and Christians with nowhere to run are beginning to experience the crimes of Islam – riots, no-go zones,[128] rapes, terrorism, honor killings, and a loss of their native identity.

I ask the Franciscan sisters to research the matter themselves and perhaps obtain the documentary, "Honor Diaries,"[129] to understand how women are severely mistreated in Islam. I also urge them and all their coreligionists to go to www.memritv.org[130] and download a cross-section of weekly Islamic sermons translated into English, for an analysis of political, ideological, intellectual, social, cultural and religious trends in the Middle East. Books by Nonie Darwish[131] or Brigitte Gabriel[132] or Ayaan Hirsi Alli[133] would also provide a truthful exposé of life under Islam.

The Sisters were told that Muslims and Christians need to come together to stop the violence, but it is the Muslims, not the Christians, who are committing the violence against five religions in dozens of countries. CAIR's purpose is to soften their history and temper any possible resistance against their imposition of sharia.

The Sisters were told that individuals commit violence, not religions, but it is the Islamic individuals who are commanded by their religion/culture/ideology to commit the violence – not only against other religions but among themselves, particularly against their women. It is the Muslims who are taught to hate in their schools, mosques, and television programs and their Koran that promises heavenly reward for carrying out jihad.[134]

The Sisters were told to return to their moral compass, but where is CAIR's moral compass when it shields the Muslims deeds from exposure — deeds that include rape, beheading, dismemberment, castration, gouging-out eyes, flogging, stoning, hanging, blinding women with acid, enforcing genital mutilation on young girls, enforcing their marriage to considerably older men; and keeping many women enshrouded, unable to drive, socialize, or attend school? Their god advocates murder and destruction in at least 109 Koranic verses.[135]

The purpose of CAIR's visit was to indoctrinate the sisters on how to think, what to do and what to say. Today CAIR is challenging Oklahoma to not show a film about Muslims and the Oklahoma bomber; not show the film "Honor Killings," and not show the film being used by the 9/11 Memorial Museum. They also have control over our American schools' textbooks, which some parents are attempting to fight.

We must not be misled by the Islamic propaganda or by the evaded answers to citizens' questions. Consider if CAIR's intentions were indeed as honorable as those of the immigrants who preceded them, would they really need these image-management teams to define themselves? Rather than integrate and become Americans, they require American acquiescence to their demands, and changing history lessons in our schools. This is not assimilation, but conquest. It is they who hate[136] all others, and our tolerance of their intolerance is not tolerance, but civilizational suicide.[137]

The Sisters have many sources for information about this scourge that has insinuated itself into our public schools, places of worship, businesses, and government. We must all become aware of how we might be instrumental in protecting ourselves and our country.

JEWS DON'T BEHAVE LIKE MUSLIMS

A Muslim apologist equates violent Islamists with their Jewish victims.

Lorna Salzman, author of "Jews Behaving Like Muslims,"[138] featured in the New English Review, claims "Zionists and observant Jews" complain like Muslims, regarding The Death of Klinghoffer, an "opera" to be produced at the Met. Mr. Leon Klinghoffer, a wheelchair-bound stroke victim, known to be Jewish, was thrown to his death off the cruise ship, MS Achille Lauro, by attacking Palestinian terrorists who boarded it on October 7, 1985. Disregarding the spirit of the complaint, Salzman, an anti-Zionist and self-hating Jew, used moral relativism (trickery) to equate disparate cultures, events and reactions, villains with victims. Jews don't behave like Muslims.

She knows that Islam, the harshest death cult on the planet, metes out severe punishment for minor behavioral infractions to maintain total control over its people — antithetical to Jewish law. She understands that Islamists invented Islamophobia to quash free speech and hide Islamic history and current activities from the masses — not so in Judaism. She grasps that the Council of American-Islamic Relations (CAIR) was formed to enforce the prohibitions; Jews have no such organization. Salzman can research the hundreds of millions of converted, enslaved, or slaughtered under Islamic law — a phenomenon unheard of among the Jews. She knows that the purpose of jihad is to establish sharia law over all the world. Jews do not impose Judaism on others. Jews don't behave like Muslims.

The opera's producers provided the murderous terrorists with justification for their evil and expunged the humanity from their victim. The conscientious Jewish community is trying to prevent a libelous, fabricated interpretation of an historic event from poisoning the minds of naïve viewers. Salzman is discombobulated.

Similarly, Salzman has rewritten the death of Rachel Corrie, again blaming "Zionists and observant Jews" for objecting to a performance that distorts the truth, without researching evidence that is a matter of record. Therefore, I will lay bare the proof that she ignored.

Contrary to Salzman's claim, Rachel Corrie, an American student, was not killed by a tank; this was not a battlefield. She was killed in an area where an earth-moving bulldozer was operated by a worker who sits high off the ground, in a cage with limited visual range. It would be obvious to even the most naïve that this was a hard-hat area, restricted to a labor force.

Why was Corrie in Rafah, in Gaza[139] during the Second Intifada?[140] Why should any American student have been in Gaza around construction equipment? After intense investigation, it was learned that Corrie was a frequent activist and a member of the International Solidarity Movement[141] (ISM), who took a year off to join in Palestinian unity. She was one of seven who acted as human shields[142] to impede IDF-led bulldozer demolition of illegal housing on the border between Egypt and the Rafah refugee camp, in order to destroy a lethal maze of guerilla hideouts and tunnels[143] used for smuggling weapons to kill Israeli citizens.

Nevertheless, on this day, the IDF was conducting only routine operations — leveling the terrain and clearing debris. The investigation divulged that Corrie was standing behind the debris, an area out of visual range by any driver from his elevated protective cage and was pushed over with the debris by the Caterpillar D9 bulldozer. Corrie's autopsy confirmed that the cause of death was falling debris, and not from the tractor's rolling over her.

Rachel Corrie was "a rabidly anti-American and insidious opponent of the Jewish state," reported attorney and former prosecutor Ari Lieberman, in Frontpage Magazine.[144] He described photographs in which this woman, consumed with hate of America, the West, Israel and the Jews, was shrouded in black Islamist clothing in the midst of an Islamist demonstration. The illegal and traitorous conduct of Rachel Corrie and her fellow activists was directly responsible for the successful smuggling of explosives from Egypt into Gaza – explosives that were later used to kill children in southern Israel, six of whom had been named Rachel.

The query of why her friends did not reach out to save her resulted in the discovery of the experiences of other female activists[145] — that in all likelihood, Corrie was one of many female activists who are used by Palestinians for their sexual gratification — routinely harassed and raped[146] not unlike the "comfort women" of the Japanese during World War II. Unexpectedly, rabid anti-Zionist Norman Finkelstein also confirmed that female internationals serve as comfort women for Palestinians. Jews don't behave like Muslims. Therefore, it is possible that Corrie was raped, betrayed by her fellow activists to maintain silence, and depressed enough to act irresponsibly in front of the bulldozer.

Returning to the Klinghoffer opera, Lorna Salzman wasted no time referencing the Met's financial woes and its need of donor money from "wealthy Jews." Why not add "successful and wealthy Jews," although Jews, in general, have long been known for their participation in the arts (consider the names in opera: Jan Pierce, Beverly Sills, Richard Tucker, Robert Merrill, Rise Stevens, Roberta Peters and more[147]), and their strong financial support, all legendary and disproportionate to their number. Jewish commitment and generosity are also known in medicine, science, education, technology, and their bounteous spirit is evident when Israel is among the first responders to victims of disasters. Jews don't behave like Muslims.

The Hebrew word, *tzedakah,* meaning justice and righteousness,[148] aptly describes the Jewish obligation to contribute to the welfare of others. However, in Judaism, the benevolence is considered an obligation rather than a mere act of goodwill. Do the Salzmans not share their good fortune with others? The Arabic word, *zakat,* one of the Five Pillars of Faith, allows for alms-giving by Muslims based on accumulated wealth and is obligatory for all who are able. However, it is designed to ease economic hardship for other Muslims only. Muslims don't behave like Jews.

Salzman appears to be psychologically damaged, bearing a deep resentment of her heritage. How else might we comprehend her belief that the authors were not expressing their own views, but those of the killers — jihadis who are taught to hate Jews, Christians, and Western civilization from toddlerhood on. Had the Muslims been as compassionate as she insists, they could not have killed the defenseless, wheelchair-bound stroke victim.

Islamic jihad cannot be assuaged. It began in the 7th century and it is eternal until Muslims refute their Koran's directives to enslave, murder, and plunder with the end purpose of establishing a caliphate over the world. Mohammed: "I have been ordered to wage war against mankind until they accept that there is no god but Allah and that they believe I am His prophet and accept all revelations spoken through me. When they do these things, I will protect their lives and property unless otherwise justified by sharia, in which case their fate lies in Allah's hands."

The opera's purpose was to promote the Islamic narrative — to hate the Jews and to temper American acceptance of Islamic violence and sharia law. The sooner we grasp the Islamic ideology and methodologies, the sooner we might save our country and civilization. Muslims are not like Jews.

TRAINING FOR TREACHERY

A network of training camps for terrorism exists in America, protected by our own laws.

"May you live in interesting times," an expression (a curse) that may be traced back to post-World War II England is apt today, when times have become all too interesting —

chaotic and troubling. We must be reminded of the July 7, 2005 bombings of a bus and three tube trains that killed 52. More recently, May 2013, when a Muslim beheaded a soldier[149] on the streets of London; and September, 2014, when a Muslim sodomized a dog and stabbed two women, beheading one of them;[150] and October, 2014, when Scotland Yard captured four Muslims[151] who admitted their mission to terrorize and decapitate ordinary people on city streets, and another four who were plotting to kill police officers or soldiers on London streets — a total of 218 arrests in the past 12 months alone. Britain identified a "complex web" of 60 Muslim Brotherhood organizations now operating from London, Istanbul, and Doha, Qatar.

In Turkey, in August, Islamists shelled, beheaded, crucified and shot seven hundred[152] of the Shaitat tribe because they dared to rise up in their own defense. Over the past week, a recent convert to Islam ran down two Canadian soldiers[153] in a Quebec province, and was shot while preparing to stab a woman police officer. A Canadian soldier was shot and killed by another convert at the National War Memorial in Ottawa; the suspect was killed. A Muslim terrorist ran his car into a crowd in a Jerusalem railroad station,[154] wounding six adults and killing a three-month-old baby. This was followed by a rock-throwing session on a kindergarten and PA leader Mahmoud Abbas's praise of the killer's heroics. Two hospital guards at a Philippine hospital were murdered by a Muslim group. A suicide bomber killed another person in Libya, and six young people were executed and then hung, by ISIS, in Iraq.

America surely needs repeated reminding of 9/11, about which Islamist apologists persistently dismiss with a shrug of the shoulders. Major Hassan's Allahu Akbar was cast aside with a flimsy "workplace violence" designation, and the stabbing and beheading of an employee at a meat-packing plant in Oklahoma was lost in the media amid all the other excitement of the times, including crimes called "scandals." But earlier today, a hatchet-wielding, self-inspired terrorist purposely targeted four New York police officers,[155] perhaps in keeping with the new Islamic directive discovered by Scotland Yard.

In fact, the Jihad Report[156] shows Islamic terrorists were responsible for 78 deadly attacks during the week of October 11–17, fifteen Allah Akbars, 630 dead and 828 critically wounded, bringing the total terror attacks since 9/11 to 24,184 (when this essay was penned) — a number that changes with increasing rapidity.

Walid Shoebat[157] cautions in Why I left Jihad[158] that Muslims have come here for one reason only — to physically act out their hatred for Jews and Christians, until their "enemy is obliterated." Muslims are attending universities only to infiltrate the student body and train and indoctrinate new jihadis. The extremists win over the moderates with campus events that incite the naïve Americans who have already been taught to accept multiculturalism, moral relativism, and contempt for the West. Spoon-fed Islam as an alternative culture by leftist professors, the students are motivated to collect huge sums of money and support the branches of the Muslim Brotherhood whose missions are to kill Jews, take over Israel, and conquer Western civilization.

Crimes are on the rise in the US, such as the recent stabbing and beheading of an employee at a food distribution center in Oklahoma,[159] an ex-convict who had converted to Islam while in prison. When the crimes are reported, they remain unconnected to any common denominator, yet there have been kidnappings, assassinations, and arson or firebomb attacks that are attributed to the homegrown Islamic terrorists, Muslims of America (MOA)/Jamaat ul-Fuqra, (aka Soldiers of Allah). Their connection is terrorist communes that are fully established and operational in rural America, Canada, and the Caribbean.

Beginning in 1979, there were attacks on eastern houses of worship — Hare Krishna temples, Iranian (Shi'ite) mosques, an Islamic Cultural Center, an Indian-owned hotel, an Ahmadiyya Center, the Integral Yoga Society and two Vendanta Societies, a Laotian temple, and more. Physicians of Hindu and East Indian origin have been kidnapped and killed, as were mosque leaders.

Tom Gallagher, of the Bureau of Alcohol, Tobacco and Firearms, describes the MOA, specifically, as a "violent, black Muslim extremist sect that acts out jihads against perceived enemies." The group provides firing ranges and paramilitary and guerilla-warfare training to spread Islam and destroy America through violence. Trained in camps in America, they are sometimes sent to Pakistan to become a new generation of jihadis.

Their activities in Colorado (1989) have included fire breakouts at a power station. Law enforcement officials also discovered a large, well-equipped arsenal, documents and photos of the Jewish Community Center and Hare Krishna Temple in Denver; and an illegal collection of checks. Four of five MOAs were arrested. An MOA arsenal was discovered in 1992, with plans for targets in Denver, Tucson, and Los Angeles.

Five MOAs were arrested in New York in the 1990s for conspiracy to bomb a Hindu temple and Indian theater in Toronto, with an expected death count in the thousands. The FBI and local police discovered a cache of weapons to be used across the Canadian border. The NYC Dept. of Investigation uncovered an Islamic compound a year before the World Trade Center attack (arresting some for mixing explosives) and one year later, learned that this had been a training compound for 9/11. Eight men were arrested from another group with a plot to bomb the UN, FBI headquarters, and the Holland and Lincoln tunnels. A gang of ten who were arrested in three New York boroughs for selling illegal weapons was also linked to MOA.

Other camps in the network were discovered in South Carolina, Pennsylvania, Virginia, and California, all controlled by the group's founder, a Pakistani Sufi mystic, Sheikh Syen Mubarik Ali Gilani. Although general reports claim more than 3,000 members — many ex-convicts who had been convicted of violent crimes — the cleric and known international terrorist asserts to have as many as 15,000 followers, 35 "villages" in 22 states, ranging from 33 acres in South Carolina to 300 acres in California.

En route to interviewing Gilani about shoe-bomber Richard Reid, journalist Daniel Pearl was kidnapped and beheaded because Gilani thought that he (Pearl) was a secret service agent. Although Gilani's original purpose was to recruit mujahedeen to fight the Soviets, Gilani's ideology is the purification of Islam through violence — meaning, the obliteration of all infidels. And, recruiting American citizens makes it is more difficult to stop their activities. Not only are they protected as citizens by state laws, the US Constitution, and our climate of political correctness, but they formed a legal, tax-exempt church. As such, they can conduct banking transactions, launder money; purchase land, buildings, lodging and safe houses, communication equipment, weapons, and lethal substances/explosives, all without having to pay taxes or report expenditures or income.

The U.S. State Department has known of these training camps since 1993. Former FBI Director Robert Mueller admitted their existence; special FBI agent Jody Weis declared the homegrown terrorists to be more dangerous than any known group; and Ryan Mauro, national security analyst and political analyst, exposed the camps in the Counter Jihad Report.[160] Sean Hannity (Fox News)[161] reported on the status of these camps in 2009.

Law enforcement officials believe Gilani hides terrorists, as the "Beltway Snipers"[162] were probably hidden during their 23-day shooting spree in Washington D.C. Christian Action Network (CAN) urges the U.S. to designate Muslims of America a "Foreign Terrorist Organization" (FTO). Sheikh Gilani operates from Lahore, Pakistan, and that connection would make illegal any support to his group and restrict their funding and expansion. CAN also asks that we contact our political leaders and demand that Muslims of America be placed on the State Department's Foreign Terrorist Organization watch list and demand that each State and Congress outlaw any Islamic communities, organizations and mosques that preach Jihad against America.

There exists a real and present danger to the survival of our country and our civilization, and a few phone calls might work to protect us. After all, daily life is interesting enough under the best of circumstances.

A PACK OF WOLVES

Each Islamic terrorist acts distinctly to form an alliance against the common enemy, mankind.

Britain's Prime Minister David Cameron responded to the terrorist attack in Sydney, Australia,[163] in which two of more than 17 hostages were killed by an Islamic extremist. Referring to "lone wolf terrorists," he reminded the British that these dangers will come to the United Kingdom.

It appears that we have had enough lone wolves to constitute a substantial wolf pack, and enough "extremists" to consider them "conventional." How many people must die before heads of state concede that the crimes worldwide are not extreme, not unusual, and not lone wolf? This is Islamic-style warfare against the West, without the sophisticated weaponry, khaki uniforms or tanks. It is time to connect the dots that are quite identical between the burnings and beheadings in 624 a.d. and those executed today.

We naively call them self-starters or lone wolves when, daily, thousands of individuals are inspired and encouraged by an imam in a mosque to be a Soldier of Allah, eagerly awaiting his turn to immerse himself in the blood of infidels. Perhaps the designation helps the West cope with the 1.3 billion Muslims who have unleashed their millions into the world. Perhaps the singular terminology keeps the West from considering war against the multitudes, or courageously declaring the Koran and sharia antithetical to Western beliefs, or fear of inciting the so-called moderates to reach their full barbarous potential.

Must someone remind PM Cameron of the infamous 7/7 bombing of 2005 in London's underground,[164] or the new convert to Islam who beheaded British soldier Lee Rigby on a London Street? Consider America's Major Nidal Hasan, the psychiatrist who killed 13 and wounded 28 at Fort Hood, Texas; the Tsarnaev brothers, who killed two and injured more than 260 athletes and spectators at the Boston Marathon; the Itamar brutal massacre of five members of Israel's Fogel family, and the more recent beheading of four rabbis and a policeman during religious services in Jerusalem.

It is time to admit the truth — that self-radicalization is a myth to befuddle the reality of the demonic cult, where the lone wolf is not alone but a product of Islam, trained from birth or conversion to hate and kill. The West has chosen to disbelieve the incomprehensible because this is an army unlike any we have fought, with different rules and means of carrying out their depraved agenda of oppression, torture, and destruction. Not clad in khakis or camouflage, these demons may be disguised as normal humans in street clothes, prepared to strike with the simplest and smallest of weapons — a knife or a vial of acid.

While the situation is deteriorating rapidly, the West is turning out students who are ignorant of the truth of Islam. Taught by the left, liberals, Marxists, and Islamic apologists, from revised textbooks, our students are indoctrinated to believe that Islam is a religion of peace, when in fact it has been a religion of cruelty and conquest for fourteen centuries. The revised history books paint and polish Islam while tarnishing Judaism, Christianity, Israel and America, omitting or changing facts that might expose the malevolence in our midst. Our media aids and abets these efforts with the accusatory "Islamophobia" to keep the crimes underreported or swept under the rug. Ask the average college students about Islam's history and they will probably respond with a dead stare followed by an uncomfortable giggle at their own ignorance.

No, the murderers are not lone wolves. Whether they come as one or as nineteen, they are still part of a larger pack, each with his duty — one bullet fired by the machine gunner. Whether the Muslims rush a synagogue or church to behead people in prayer;[165] or behead hundreds who refuse to pray to Allah;[166] or throw acid at girls;[167] or beat Jewish youths on the streets of Paris or Brooklyn;[168] or explode themselves or ram an auto into a crowd of pedestrians[169] or kidnap girls for sale or marriage/enslavement,[170] or rape women on the streets of Sweden and Norway;[171] or burn or stone women,[172] or behead their own daughters[173] for "honor," they are One. Whether they are ISIS, Hamas, Hezbollah, Boko Haram, Taliban or any of a formidable number of terrorist groups,[174] they are Islam, with a serious disregard for life.[175]

Each new generation is taught from toddlerhood to hate[176] and aspire to Islamic greatness by killing kafirs – Jews, as well as Christians, Hindus, Buddhists and other Muslims – and becoming a Shaheed (martyr). There are Muslim parents who eagerly raise their babies to be suicide bombers for Hamas.[177] From their earliest school days, children learn that life has no value. They must kill for their god and state and accept their own death and martyrdom while parents encourage and applaud the loss of their children's humanity. There is no hope for a life of beauty, music, creativity and career, of courtship and love-marriage, the joy of caring for a devoted pet, and discoveries of Western civilization. They are robbed of everything we value. Young kindergarteners are trained to behead dolls[178] and toy sheep that ooze red,[179] as they sing songs that include the bleating of a wounded, dying lamb.

As the older child is taught to kill and hold a victim's severed head,[180] he poses for a photo taken by his proud father. Young adults, no longer queasy about death, can play soccer with decapitated heads[181] on the grounds of the Temple Mount.

By the time they reach adulthood, they have no respect for life — animal or human. These deranged sadists who achieve sexual satisfaction from causing pain or degradation to others are able to inflict agony and suffering on defenseless animals throughout the year and celebrate Eid by torturing livestock[182] (the worst animal cruelty in history is in Gaza[183]), allowing them to bleat and bleed out until they lose consciousness and finally die. Muslims consider the torment, fear and excruciating agony of animals to be Halal.[184]

Finally, despite the singularity perceived by some, there is organization, the inevitable mob or herd mentality.[185] Although not a single Muslim had seen the "blasphemous cartoons" in 2005, demonstrators went to the streets, burned buildings, injured and even killed people throughout Europe. Not taught to examine facts, they take their leaders' directives and follow the pack. A recent survey showed that eighty percent of Palestinians support murder. I would propose that the remaining twenty percent are, as Marco Polo is alleged to have said, "... the moderate Muslim who holds the feet of the victim." Where there are Muslims, there is violence with the express objective that Islam will rule the world, with sharia law imposed on all mankind. If it cannot be done peacefully, it will be done sadistically. They are raised in a teamwork environment, faces covered for guilt-free anonymity.

The reality is that all the terrorists are indoctrinated from childhood to sacrifice their individuality for an organization and are probably psychologically incapable of acting as lone wolves.

DESTROY THE HISTORY, DREAD THE FUTURE
Stealth jihad that replaces history is now being waged against our Native Americans.

They present themselves as the Religion of Peace, but they are intensely intolerant, eager to crush truth and the noncompliant. They will force their peace upon you. Their methods are usually violence beyond one's imagination, so that the only ones who achieve complete peace are those who have been killed quickly, not burned, hanged, crucified, beheaded, made to endure hundreds of lashes, buried waist high and stoned to death, thrown from a cliff, succumbed to pain and infection from acid or barbaric Female Genital Mutilation, having one's limbs chopped off, or kidnapped for a short lifetime of sexual slavery. Add to these, Boko Haram's[186] cooking or burying people alive, and realize what has been done to perhaps 890 million innocent victims over 1400 years.

Although most of this brutality remains prevalent in the Middle East and Africa, a new conquest has appeared on the horizon. In an interview with Radio Free Europe/Radio Liberty, Nurat Nazarov, aka Abu Kholidi Kulobi, a jihadist under the Islamic State, said he will build mosques in Native American territories and "live with them under the laws of Allah" (sharia).

What can we expect to happen with American Indians? I believe we can predict their fate. Through their successful strategy of deceit, Islam will replace one culture with another, and the proud Native American will become a craven servant of Allah. If there is no violence, then Islamic holy war will be waged against their holy sites. As we learned from the Israeli experience, Muslims will create a false narrative to delegitimize the people from their land. Their historic sites will be destroyed, as were the tombs of Biblical Jonah, Daniel, and Joseph, and the numerous layers of Jewish civilization, still producing artifacts that bear witness to the Hebrews' centuries of connection to the Temple Mount in Jerusalem. Natan Sharansky described the excavation as "the largest archaeological catastrophe to mankind." The Dome of the Rock atop Judaism's holiest site was built by Caliph Abd al-Malik188 to commemorate his conquest of the capital and, most importantly, to erase Jewish history.

For the same reason, the Taliban have demolished the thousands-of-years-old Buddha in Afghanistan and mausoleums in Timbuktu, Mali (all UNESCO World heritage sites), as well as tens of thousands of Hindu temples together with tons of artifacts, the annihilation of a people's history. Islamic jihadis are also bulldozing and looting Iraq's world-famous ancient cities of Nimrud and Hatra, with their ancient stone relief carvings; Assyrian statues; artifacts in a Mosul museum; and thousands of books and manuscripts in Mosul's library, to eradicate all pre-Islamic civilization. This mindset was also the motive behind the 9/11/2001 bombing of the World Trade Centers — to destroy the symbol of American achievement and reverse Islam's trend of decline since their defeat in the Battle of Vienna, 9/11/1683.[187]

This modus operandi was noted in a traveling Islamic exhibit that claims "1001 Inventions"[188] as Islamic in origin, of which one portion, The Silk Road, was presented at the Cleveland Museum of Natural History. The unmentioned truth is that the faith and cultures of the inventors were victims who were forced to convert to Islam; hence, the credit for any invention was purloined by Islam from the rightful people. Over the fourteen centuries of Islamic history, Muslims have produced inestimable suffering and bloodshed, while expropriating every creative, innovative, groundbreaking invention of their victims, claiming them as their own.

Re-education is a vital weapon in creating a new past to replace the one eradicated. As Vladimir Lenin was known to say, "Give me four years to teach the children and the seed I have sown will never be uprooted." Therefore, Muslims will create a faux Muslim identity for the American tribes, as they have done in the past: that Jesus (Jewish) was a Palestinian,[189] Moses (Jewish) was the first Muslim liberator,[190] and Albert Einstein (Jewish) and others of note were converts to Islam.[191] Turkey's President Erdogan maintains that Christopher Columbus (a practicing Catholic of probable Jewish descent) was preceded in Hispaniola by Muslim explorers,[192] which may be the first step to another Islamic foothold where none existed before.

In addition, our government has implemented the Common Core educational system with a staff of teachers compelled to disregard our American heritage and our Constitution and replace them with whitewashed Islamic history and faith-based studies. This stealth infiltration is supported by Bill Gates, Arne Duncan, et al.; a 45-percent investment interest by Dubai World/Istithmar World[193] Board of Directors (EMPG) in the publishing companies that provide 52 percent of American textbooks; and a perplexing, but unswerving, commitment by presidential candidates, Governors Jeb Bush, Mike Huckabee and John Kasich. (Huckabee has since changed his thinking.)

"Eagle Sun Walker," who describes himself as a Muslim Cherokee-Blackfoot American Indian, is yet another indication of Islamic aggression and forced conversion on American soil. As more Muslims enter our country, they may well move closer to Indian country, and begin to insinuate their beliefs, rules of Islamophobia, and demands on the naïve, obliging populace. With the construction of the first mosque,[194] it may take but one charismatic recruiter to sell his bill of goods to the youth, telling them they will be the vanguard of a new Islamic movement — perhaps even convince them that they are the descendants of "early Muslim settlers." Islamists have the psychological and financial wherewithal to entice and intimidate new recruits who may not yet have found their life's direction. I can see nothing in the Native past that would prepare them for prevailing over the all-consuming deception named Islam.

JIHADIS OF TOMORROW

Muslim-German students, exempted from Holocaust educational programs, are the future jihadis.

Anti-Semitism is growing among German Muslim students. Following Koranic teachings, the early childhood brainwashing, and school books rife with politically biased indoctrination, these students openly declared that they will kill Jews. They specifically threatened Max Moses Bonifer, student spokesman for the school system in Offenbach, Germany, a city of more than 16,000 Muslims. Teenage students in Landsberg, near Leipzig, were reported to be using Nazi slogans, greeting "Heil Hitler," and some sporting Hitlerian moustaches. Yet, despite the increase in anti-Semitism, Muslim and other immigrant students were exempted from partaking in the concentration camp visits required with the Holocaust educational programs.

"Severe intolerance and hatred does not happen overnight," explains Dr. Tawfik Hamid,[195] himself under threat from his co-religionists for teaching a peaceful understanding of Islam. "The indoctrination process, incremental and subtle, occurs in three stages — hatred, suppression of conscience, and desensitization to or acceptance of violence." It is completed when the formerly young and innocent are capable of violence without remorse, no different than the Muslims who attacked synagogues in Germany after Israel's "Operation Protective Edge" against Hamas, or the Nazis who participated in the Kristallnacht pogrom of November 10, 1938.

The hate and intolerance of the Koran is reinforced during prayers five times daily. Beginning in early childhood, toddlers are taught to behead dolls, and young men delight in the worst animal cruelty that Australians say they had ever witnessed being done to their exported cattle. Films from Gaza show Palestinians "kneecapping" the cattle, stabbing their eyes, and hacking their throats open on the streets. Severe animal suffering precedes the slaughter of animals for the celebration of Eid Al-adha or Feast of Sacrifice (it also generates an extraordinary cash windfall for some of Pakistan's most dangerous militant groups).

These Muslim-German students, along with their agitating professors, should be learning about the Holocaust through newsreels, books, and visits to the concentration camps. The excuse that their culture had nothing to do with this period of history is both untrue and irrelevant; history shows that many Arabs were in lockstep with the Nazis. Islam, like Nazism, is an ideology that teaches superiority and subordination; consigning slaves, women, Jews, Christians, Zoroastrians and others to various levels of humiliation and wretchedness. It is their theological imperative that Jews (and Christians) be subservient to Muslims; the success of infidels is an insult to Allah. Therefore, the chants and false accusations of "settlements," "apartheid," "colonizers," "occupation," are diversions and key words needed to trigger hatred and violence against Jews and Christians worldwide, as they have throughout their history (Muslim 001,0031; (Bukhari 4,52,1412).

Mohammed's wrath began with the Jews who remained faithful to the Torah and rejected the Koran — with its more than one hundred verses advocating the use of violence to spread Islam and 123 verses about killing and fighting. It continued when Muslims encountered the formidable Christian opposition in Eastern and Western Europe. Massacres were conducted when Christians primarily (but Jews, as well) earned "too much" wealth and power in Granada (1066), and when Christian communities in Middle Eastern countries identified with Crusaders. Muslims killed the Mongols, who had earlier destroyed their caliphate, together with their Christian and Jewish collaborators. Envy was a consequence of their teachings, causing Muslims to rage and slaughter when they noted the superior economic status of Christians in the 18th and 19th centuries.

Therefore, in 164 verses, the Koran encourages jihad and looting from their victims, so that they may own what belongs to their perceived enemy. True to character, Muslims are unable to tolerate Israel's superiority, the achievements of a mere 67 years of statehood. It is not about settlements or deeds but a deep-seated envy, exemplified by the Khomeinist International Union of Resistance conference held in Beirut (May 2015). Resentful Muslim scholars came together to formally accuse Israel of all Islamic nations' failures. The attendees admitted that they wished to "counter the arrogant world," a reminder of their shame for not achieving the greatness of the West, the greatness they'd been promised in their Scriptures.

In a warped attempt to reverse their feelings of inadequacy, Muslims destroyed the World Trade Center in New York, as well as antiquities, artifacts and shrines worldwide. To overcome their deficiency, they produced an extensive, extravagant museum exhibit that lays claim to "1001 Inventions, the Enduring Legacy of Muslim Civilization," many of which (perhaps all) may be traced to the ingenuity and industry of their conquered and forcibly-converted victims.

Islamists called Israel "arrogant" for being first responders to people who suffer from natural disasters (earthquakes, tsunamis, fires, famine) and for providing medical care to the victims of Islamic unrest (including surgery for Mahmoud Abbas's wife and medical treatment for the sister of an Hamas leader). Islamic countries sent no humanitarian aid to the infidel victims, but accused Israel of harvesting organs of the dead in Haiti when, in fact, families showed their gratitude for Israel's care by naming their newborns "Israel."

These desert people, whose sharia law, ironically, is named for "the way of water," have just witnessed Israel's new capability of recycling water, producing enough to make their land flourish with food, and having more than enough potable water for themselves and a generous supply (more than required by the Oslo Accord) for Palestinians. California has already used Israeli water technology to combat its worst drought in history. Muslims are seething with resentment, yet the achievements that earn praise in the Islamic world are terrorist attacks. They cannot stand being upstaged but hope only to be the best after everyone else is gone.

In a letter of June 1938, the Syrian Alawites told the French prime minister that the new Zionists "brought prosperity over Palestine without damage to anyone or taking anything by force," and American historian Walter Laqueur noted, "No one doubted that the Arabs had benefited from Jewish immigration." (The Arab population almost doubled between 1917 and 1940, wages increased, and the standard of living rose higher than anywhere else in the Middle East.) Still, Israel's contributions made some Arab leaders become increasingly hostile to the Jewish community. Many affiliated with the rising Nazi movement, incited and instigated mob attacks (pogroms) against the Jews in 1920, 1921, 1929, and 1936-1939.

The connection between Islam and Nazism is undeniable. Palestinian Arab leader Mufti Haj Amin al-Husseini, an admirer of Adolph Hitler, recruited a Bosnian-Muslim Waffen SS unit, the notorious "Hanjar troopers," that slaughtered 90 percent of Bosnia's Jews and burned countless Serbian churches and villages. SS Chief Heinrich Himmler favored the recruits and established a special Mullah Military school in Dresden.

Anti-Semitism among these German-Muslim students has become critical and life-threatening and continues as they fail to integrate into their host society. German Chancellor Angela Merkel said, "It is absolutely necessary to counteract religious and political indoctrination among Muslim youth." These words should have been spoken and acted upon yesterday, because the Muslim children of today have been groomed to become the jihadis of tomorrow.

A la Fiorina
Carly Fiorina's assertions about Islam's civilization are counterfactual.

"There was once a civilization that was the greatest in the world."
And so began a mythical, deceptive tale by Carly Fiorina, when she spoke in praise of Islam[196] within a mere two weeks of their bombing of the World Trade Center. My

concern is not that she was deceiving others, but that she, a person who aspires to the presidency of the United States, was herself deceived regarding the true nature of Islam, and that she has never retracted her statements.

"[Islam's] armies were made up of many nationalities . . . [Islam] was able to create a continental super-state . . . within its dominion lived hundreds of millions of people, of different creeds and ethnic origins," and "the reach of this civilization's commerce. . ."*

As a religious leader, Mohammed converted few followers. He was far more successful as a political and military leader, torturing and beheading 700 stalwart Medinan Jews, raping and enslaving their women, and conscripting the survivors for jihad (holy war). Thus, he dominated different creeds and ethnic origins, replenished his army with many nationalities, and increased his wealth with booty.

"Within its dominion" is Fiorina's euphemism for "living under domination." All non-Muslims, slaves and women were treated with contempt, unequal under the law but economically necessary. Although specific enmity was directed against Jews and Christians, the severe *"jizya"*[197] tax was imposed on "infidels" as humiliation and punishment for rejecting Mohammed. This tax and many other discriminatory laws extended through the centuries to Nestorians, Syrians, and Romans and their empires, and further to animists, Buddhists, Hindus, Mongols, Greeks, and Armenians (the Armenian Genocide), who suffered considerable torture and death.

Jews held trades and occupations that Muslims judged inferior — including "this civilization's commerce," diplomacy, banking, brokerage, espionage, working in gold and silver, and cleaning cesspools. The inevitable deterioration of relations between Muslims and the outside world meant more restrictions and social segregation for non-Muslims (dhimmis), but the subservient and useful survived.

"... Its military protection allowed a degree of peace and prosperity that had never been known." "Peace," as the absence of discord, existed, depending on the beneficence of the ruling caliphate and internal/external changes, but from the twelfth to thirteenth centuries onward, tolerance decreased; intellectual, social and commercial life depreciated, and ever-increasing restrictions and deprivation for dhimmis were imposed.

"And this civilization was driven more than anything, by invention. Its architects designed buildings that defied gravity."

The inventions and contributions were made by the victims of the Muslim jihadis who invaded the "infidel" world over 1400 years, enslaving, slaughtering, and plundering. Creativity flourishes in peaceful conditions; Islam is antithetical to creativity but based on envious resentment of the accomplishments of others. Their greatest achievement was their ability to expropriate every creative, innovative groundbreaking device of Islam's victims and to fraudulently claim each as their own.

Fiorina's reference to "buildings that defied gravity," as in "air-borne," surely defies logic, but she doubtless refers to the arches[198,] which were already in use in prehistoric times by ancient Egyptians, Babylonians and Greeks. With the help of concrete made from lime and volcanic sand, Roman arches could support huge weight, and were soon adopted by Byzantine and Romanesque architects, evolving into the groundbreaking inventions of the Gothic arch and flying buttress in northern (Christian) Europe. Meanwhile, the Muslims also adopted the Syrian styles, following with Greek, Byzantine and Persian, and later Chinese and Indian, architecture, to develop pointed, scalloped and horseshoe arches for mosques and palaces. Even the vaulted and hemispherical (domed) ceilings were invented by the non-Muslim Romans.

"Its mathematicians created the algebra and algorithms that would enable the building of computers, and the creation of encryption."

The first positional numerical system was developed in 2nd millennium BCE Babylon, over 800 years before Islam. The first true "zero" was developed by mathematicians in the Indian Subcontinent. Persian and Arab mathematicians are believed to have adopted the Hindu-Arabic numerical system in India.[199] The work of Italian scholar, Fibonacci,[200] "as crucial in bringing them to Europe and the world. Francois Viete, a French lawyer, mathematician and privy councilor to Henry III and Henry IV, provided the step from "new algebra" to modern algebra.

Only an Islamic steeplechaser could leap from working with numbers to creating computers[201] and encryptions centuries later. English polymath Charles Babbage, mathematician, philosopher, inventor, and mechanical engineer, conceived the first programmable computer (1830). Alan Turing[202] laid the groundwork for computational science; Korad Zuse is credited as "the first freely programmable computer."

The earliest form of cryptography is on stone in Egypt[203] (190 BCE), long before Islam. Ciphers were used by the Spartan military and in the 2000-year-old Kamasutra of India. It wasn't until the 9th century that Arab mathematicians and polymath Al-Kindi worked with cryptography.

"Its doctors examined the human body and found new cures for diseases."

Arabs had no scientific traditions. Their scientists were largely Jews who were forcibly converted as a result of Islam's rampage throughout the Near East, Egypt, and Libya. As a typical example, Jews and Berbers, who lived together harmoniously in North Africa, were overcome by 60,000 Islamic troops in 694, and the descendants of those who survived the massacre became "Arabic" philosophers and scientists.

A great physician, Egyptian Jew Isaac Israel of Kairouan, immigrated to West Africa. His surviving works on logic, Aristotelian physics, and pharmacology became the standard for medical history, and it was from him that the greatest of "Arab" scientists,

Avicenna[204] (980-1037) drew inspiration. Known as the Aristotle of the East, Avicenna wrote in Arabic and became a vizier in Persia, but he was born near Bokhara, then heavily populated by Jews, and was probably of Jewish origin. Even so, the physicians who attended lords and kings of Islam and Christendom were largely Jews.

"Its astronomers looked into the heavens, named the stars, and paved the way for space travel and exploration."

Jewish savants were largely responsible for the invention and development of instruments and astronomical tables that facilitated world-girdling sea voyages. The Jerusalem Talmud (Tractate Avodah Zarah, Ch.3, fol.,42c) strongly implies the spherical nature of the earth. The astrolabe,[205] used by Islamic astronomers as a guide to the sky and to tell time by the position of heavenly bodies, was introduced into the Arab-speaking world by a "remarkable Jewish genius, Mashala of Mosul,[206] the phoenix of his age." Astronomical tables, compiled by the Jew, Joseph ben Wallar at Toledo (1396), and in Aragon by Judaic specialists, including Emanuel ben Jacob (aka Bonfils de Tarascon), were used with the astrolabe.

The Jews were among the most notable cartographers, the most advanced being a Jew forcibly converted to Christianity. Christopher Columbus's cartographers and other companions may have been conversos. The most reputable astronomer of the day, Abraham Zacuto[207] (1452-1515), instructed Columbus on using the perfected astrolabe, which was also used by Vasco de Gama and Amerigo Vespucci.

In all these areas, Fiorina makes the absurd leap from recognizing Muslims as merely a people who used a product to being an innovative people who "paved the way" for the future. She made a similar leap of dissonance when she made corrupt trade agreements[208] with Iran in violation of US trade sanctions, resulting in 30,000 workers laid off at Hewlett-Packard, and jobs shipped to China. We could remark in passing that, at the same time, her salary and perks also leaped — they more than tripled.

"When censors threatened to wipe out knowledge from past civilizations, this civilization kept the knowledge alive and passed it on to others."

How much creativity, ingenuity and innovation might we have had from those 890 million people slaughtered by jihadis over 1400 years? What greatness is Islam passing on to civilization now, beyond a high illiteracy rate, boundless intolerance and aggression? Their history is one of perpetual massacre, encouraged in their Koran and taught from early childhood. Their culture is one of unrest, riots and wars; and women's fears of female genital mutilation, forced marriages, rape, and death for male honor. Their homes are microcosms of the greater tyrannical regimes.

Had Muslims the knowledge to be kept alive, how might it have been done? Of the 1.3 billion Muslims, 750 million are illiterate (60 percent cannot read). In Christendom, the adult literacy rate stands at 78 percent. Of the ten most literate countries, not one is Islamic. Muslims are the world's poorest, weakest and most illiterate.[209] The US's GDP in 2016 was $18.7 trillion. Muslims are 22 percent of the world population, yet produce less than five percent of global GDP, and diminishing all the time.

Over the past 105 years, 1.3 billion Muslims produced eight Nobel Laureates (only two won for physics and chemistry); compare this with a mere 14 million Jews (0.23% of the world population) who produced 170 Nobel Laureates.[210]

Islam's militaristic, super-sessionist ideology that began 1400 years ago has remained unchanged. We know of no event that sparked the glory they claim, and no catastrophic event that might have forced a decline. Carly Fiorina is severely misinformed about the civilization that embraces our death and destruction and she confuses politically-correct theories for hard facts — no point from which to hold the highest-ranking position in the United States of America.

MOSQUITOES IN THE MOSQUE

Religions differ, as do their adherents and the laws they follow.

The guidelines for Letters to the Editor of The Chautauquan Daily include warnings that libelous, demeaning or accusatory statements are unacceptable. This also means that the truth must be curtailed, for it is the truth that supremacist Muslims find inappropriate and offensive, even by those who perpetrate the acts.

Nevertheless, I refer to guest speaker Hussein Rashid, who denied the intensity and frequency of religious violence, citing that Muslims kill a mere 17 Americans per year (surely, not in the year 2001), while mosquitoes kill an average of 750,000. This is the new Moral Inversion – that sharia law is now moral and mosquitoes immoral. Are we to flick a wrist at jihadis and the growing body count? (According to Muslim historian Firistha, Muslims killed ~600 million Indian people[211] during invasions and occupation of the Indian continent alone, bringing the worldwide total to more than 890 million victims since the birth of Mohammed.)

Are we to disregard the religious bigotry, sadistic cruelty, kidnappings, rapes, lifelong captivity, persecution of women, and worldwide brutality, and arm ourselves with cans of repellant and netting? This may well be the Enlightenment that Rashid attempted to explain —that we misinterpreted the Middle East, that the wretched mosquito kidnaps young girls for sexual slavery, burns churches, and espouses destructive propaganda in America's universities.

Rashid did eventually declare religions to be violent, but I submit that all religions cannot so be classified. Religions are not equal; their doctrines differ greatly. Buddhism promotes peacefulness, loving-kindness, compassion, sympathetic joy, and equanimity.

Hinduism's many philosophies prescribe honesty, patience, self-restraint, and abstention from injuring living beings. Judaism and Christianity are commonly guided by the Torah, Ten Commandments and the Golden Rule, the law of reciprocity. In the positive: treat others as one would like to be treated, and in the negative: don't treat others in ways that one would not like to be treated. Islam's guide is the trilogy: Quran, Hadith and Sira.

Compare one Commandment, "Thou shalt not kill/murder," with the Koran's 109 verses that call Muslims to war with nonbelievers, to kill infidels wherever they hide, to chop off heads and fingers, threatening Hell if they do not slaughter.

Unlike the Old Testament's verses of violence that are explained in context of history, those in the Koran are open-ended, as relevant today as in the past. Islam's ideology prescribes and promotes violence until the nonbelievers accept humiliation, convert to Islam, or are killed — a history of bloodshed and suffering.

ICELAND'S MELTDOWN

Ignoring their history of the Barbary pirates' raid of 1627, their kidnapping of 400 to 800 natives into slavery, Icelanders are again defenseless against Islam.

Perhaps the earliest known example of Muslims' coming to Iceland occurred in 1627, when the Dutch Muslim Jan Janszoon and his Barbary pirates raided portions of Iceland, including the southwest coast, Vestmannaeyjar, and the eastern fjords. This event is known in Icelandic history as the *Tyrkjaránið* (the "Turkish Abductions"), when an estimated 400-800 Icelanders were sold into slavery.

The city council of the capital city, Reykjavik, Iceland, has fallen under the spell of a small, but toxic, Muslim population. Because of the customary Islamic narrative against Israel, the capital's outgoing councilwoman, Bjork Vilhelmsdottir, declared a boycott against all Israeli products, citing oppression of Palestinians and the "wall"; she is also planning a mission to "help Palestinians." Iceland's interior minister, Ogmundur Jonasson, led an anti-Israel protest complete with "blood-soaked" Israeli flags and accusations that Israel is committing a holocaust against the Palestinian people. Contrary to the Islamic narrative, Jews are the indigenous people[212] of Israel, Gaza and Judea/Samaria (West Bank), and the constant target of Palestinian aggression, who require the wall,[213] one of innumerable similar barriers in the world, including Europe, to protect themselves from their barbarian neighbors.

The administration appears severely uninformed of Palestinian aggression that refuses to make peace[214] with the Jewish state. Although Iceland's Foreign Ministry clarified that the boycott decision "doesn't match the foreign policy of Iceland," this small uprising could portend further discrimination as Islam gains a stronger foothold on the island nation — and Iceland's own history should serve as warning that Islam is no friend of democracy.

Iceland's first encounter with Muslims began with two raids in 1627, The Turkish Abduction – one led by a Dutch Muslim and his Barbary pirates[215] from Morocco and Algeria, the other by the Barbary corsairs from Algiers and Salé. The Muslims captured and sold into slavery an estimated 400 to 900 prisoners, and plundered livestock, silver, and a nearby English sailing vessel. Barely assisted by Dano-Norwegian naval patrols and having no standing army, Icelanders remained unarmed and vulnerable to Barbary corsair attacks, kidnappings and murders.

Muslims were also skilled in overland conquest. Through 1400 years of Islam,[216] the marauders have kidnapped people for military or administrative power, for converts, wives, concubines and personal slaves and others to replenish their relentless slave trade. They have tortured and slaughtered 890 million across continents.

Nurtured in hate and usurpation, the hordes today bring with them animosity, incendiary riots, property destruction, hate crimes and death to Europe – Germany, France, Belgium, the Netherlands, England, etc. Muslims have turned Sweden's third largest city, Malmo,[217] into a twilight of social chaos and increasing violence, earning it the title "Rape Capital of the West" and Germany's Munich into "Europe's Biggest Brothel,"[218] The explosive Islamo-fascism has caused the majority of Jewish citizens to flee.

When Palestinian Arabs realized that their many war tactics[219] — centuries of deadly pogroms, terror tunnels[220] (18 tons of concrete, with a cost of $3 million and the death of 160 child laborers[221]), an estimated 20,000 rockets[222] and mortar fired on Israeli civilians since 9/11 – could not conquer the Jewish state, they opted for war against Israel's economy and culture by convincing a cooperative world that the Palestinian Arabs are the victims, their David against the Israeli Goliath. Their boycott-divestment-sanctions (BDS) campaign is designed to defame Israel as an apartheid state,[223] reduce her support, and enlist corporations, churches, associations, and academia in the international community to deny Israel's right to self-defense and her very existence.

And it is now that Iceland has awakened. But it was not to speak out against Islam's perpetual war against Iceland's democratic ally; not to rally against the devastation in neighboring Sweden,[224] with its Muslim youths rioting and burning hundreds of cars and buildings in 200 ghettos, raping countless women, and murder; not to condemn Muslims' igniting or pelting emergency vehicles with rocks; not to address the epidemic increase in rapes and calls for beheadings and a Muslim state in Norway; not to denounce the murder of Jews in France, the ruinous riots in southern Italy, or increase in terror worldwide. Rather, Iceland was stirred awake by the lie of Palestinian victimhood and, as a result, seeks to isolate Israel and inflict upon her financial damage.

What these Scandinavians fail to realize is that they, too, are at the beginning of a growing Islamic population and that chaos is certain to follow. They fail to recognize the use of propaganda to unite the citizens in a common cause. And if Icelanders will not protest to save others, they will be unable to save themselves from the Islamic menace that festers in every multicultural paradise. *Nei*, they spoke out to condemn Israel, the only Jewish country in the Middle East, herself a victim of Islam. This appears to be the only courage they can muster.

The process has begun and Icelanders will now get their first mosque,[225] with "foreign donors" funding its construction, and naïve taxpayers providing Reykjavik's prime landmark location for its Ground Zero, selected and approved by Mayor Jon Gnarr, a self-described anarchist. The mosque, although far too large for the current Muslim community, will be built to accommodate the projected tens of thousands, complete with minarets and a muezzin whose voice will be heard through the land five times a day.

The Islamic community, now a mere one percent of the city's 300,000 today, is growing exponentially due to immigration and conversion. More than 11,000 foolish, perhaps suicidal, Icelanders[226] have offered to share their homes with incoming new immigrants, welfare recipients, rioters, rapists, and jihadis. At five percent, the Muslims will exert influence inconsistent with their numbers, become more aggressive and push for sharia law. At ten percent, they will become more lawless and violent, and at twenty percent, they will bring rioting, murder, jihad militias, and destruction of non-Muslim houses of worship. Beyond forty percent, Icelanders can expect massacres and attacks, and at fifty percent, genocide, persecution of infidels and apostates, and then, sharia will triumph.[227]

To paraphrase Sir Winston S. Churchill, "You were given the choice between war and dishonour. You chose dishonour and you will have war."

As Iceland may slowly slip from being a constitutional republic to lawlessness and totalitarianism, we ask the government of Iceland to enact legislation, such as was done by the United States of America, to oppose politically motivated actions that penalize or otherwise limit commercial relations specifically with Israel, such as boycotts, divestments or sanctions, and to recognize that such actions against Israel are anti-Semitic aggression against the Jewish State.

Update. Only two of the 1,700 mosques in Britain today (September 2015) follow a modern interpretation of Islam, the rest being fundamentalist. London now sports 423 new mosques, replacing 500 closed churches, and 100 official sharia courts; since 2001, 500 London churches of all denominations have been turned into private homes. London, is a cultural, demographic and religious hybrid in which Christianity declines and Islam advances.

TAKK FYRIR

("Thank you very much" in Icelandic) Only one city will boycott Israel, and only one Islamic mosque will be constructed, to accommodate only one thousand worshippers, for now.

An Open Letter to the Honorable People of Iceland

To the good people of Iceland, I offer our sincere appreciation for choosing righteousness over hate and the growing Islamic totalitarianism, and for voting against the Palestinian proposal to boycott Israel. I confirmed the low-key news announcement with a call to your Washington Embassy on the morning of September 30, 2015.

However, to my letter of concern to the Islandic Ministry of Foreign Affairs, I had received a reply assuring me that "only one" city was boycotting Israel. Following the logic device of where the slippery slope would lead, I feared that it would not be long before there might be "simply two," followed by "merely three." In my lifetime, I have seen many "only ones" that have led to mass destruction, inconceivable carnage, and unimaginable misery. It continues to this day, in the Middle East, Africa, parts of Europe, and the current perpetrators are always fascists who commit unspeakable crimes to spread sharia to the world.

Recall one of the final scenes in the film, "Judgment at Nuremburg," when Dr. Ernst Janning (Burt Lancaster) tells Judge Dan Haywood (Spencer Tracy) that he had intended to declare the death penalty on "only one."

We understand that Iceland is anticipating the construction of her first formal mosque, supported by foreign (Saudi) funds, just as we in America welcomed our first formal mosque one hundred years ago,[228] We now have upwards of 2,100 mosques, eighty percent of which were funded by Saudi Arabia. These edifices serve not as prayer rooms, but primarily as jihadi recruitment and training centers, and Reykovic's prime location for their "Ground Zero" roots will further embolden your aggressors.

In the words of an Islamic poet, oft quoted by Turkey's PM Erdogan, "The minarets are our bayonets, the domes our helmets, the mosques our barracks and the faithful our army." In addition, Col. Myuammar al-Gaddafi (Libya, 1969-1977) proclaimed, in 2006, "We have fifty million Muslims in Europe. There are signs that Allah will grant Islam victory in Europe – without swords, without guns, without conquest — will turn it into a Muslim continent within a few decades."

How will Iceland respond to the next demand for boycott of Israel or some other targeted country, when the Muslim voices, population, and mosques are increased? Germans and Swedes are already subjected to violence and rape and commanded to relinquish their homes to the illegal, violent "asylum seekers" (jihadis). Assuredly,

Icelanders are no less vulnerable than other Nordic countries, mainland Europe, or Israel, when they will be forced to relinquish their inalienable rights, homes, and property.

This is the time to teach your children and inform and prepare the adults about democratic Israel and her battles with the scourges of fascism and Islamism and reaffirm your own history and future. Your citizens should learn that Israel is a leader in innovations, science, technology, agricultural and medical advancements, and cultural progress; a First Responder to world emergencies. The essence of Judaism is Torah, life and kind deeds.

By contrast, Islam, guided by their Koran, is a leader in the world's most brutal laws, total and unqualified submission to the will of Allah, under penalties of whipping, stoning, limb amputations, and decapitations. It is a super-sessionist ideology that encroaches upon its host country in small increments and sets down roots to ultimately overcome and supplant the indigenous population.

Israel became a state in 1312 BCE,[229] two thousand years before Islam, yet the conquest-driven Islamists continue to re-write history to promote the concept of an historically non-Jewish Jerusalem. Interestingly, the Koran clarifies that neither Allah nor Mohammed ever intended Jerusalem for Muslims. From the beginning, Mohammed appropriated much of Jewish and Christian tradition for inclusion in his own religion, but never denied Jewish authority over Jerusalem.[230] When he fretted that Islam had no Holy City of its own, Allah, according to Islamic tradition (Surah 2:144-147-235), directed Mohammed toward Mecca. But because hard facts are meaningless to Islamists, there is no doubt that Iceland's own history will also be rewritten unless you act now.[231]

In modern times, the Balfour Declaration declared the legitimacy of Syria, Lebanon, Iraq, and a Jewish state in Palestine. As defined before the creation of Transjordan, they all derive from the same binding San Remo Resolution that was approved unanimously and signed by the League of Nations on April 25, 1920, which has never been abrogated. The Resolution recognized the exclusive national Jewish rights to the Land of Israel under international law, on the strength of the historical connection of the Jewish people to the territory previously known as Palestine. Above all, the San Remo Conference gave Title to the land to the Jewish people. Except for a mere nineteen years, when Jordan ruled Eastern Jerusalem, following its war of aggression in 1948 (until another attack ended in loss), Jerusalem had been a united city for millennia. When Israel recaptured it in 1967, this ancient unity was re-established.

It was only then, in 1967, twenty years after the birth of modern Israel, that Arab refugees in Israel began identifying themselves as the "Palestinian people."[232] Not capable of militarily conquering Israel, they developed another war strategy — convincing the world of original inhabitance, and victimization and expulsion by the Jews. In fact, they were never expelled; some chose Israeli citizenship, while others fled the war begun by their co-religionists, their number being less than the number of Jews who, during the same passage of time, were compelled to flee the dangers of residing under Islam. Icelanders should be taught that Jerusalem has never been the capital of any Arab or Muslim land, and mentioned 700 times in the Jewish Holy Scriptures, never in the Koran. Perhaps they should also learn now that Reykovic was never an Islamic capital.

Sir Winston Churchill wrote in The River War: An Account of the Reconquest of Sudan,[233] "How dreadful are the curses which Mohammedanism lays on its votaries! Besides the fanatical frenzy, which is as dangerous in a man as hydrophobia in a dog, there is this fearful fatalistic apathy. Improvident habits, slovenly systems of agriculture, sluggish methods of commerce, and insecurity of property exist wherever the followers of the Prophet rule or live. A degraded sensualism deprives this life of its grace and refinement; the next of its dignity and sanctity. The fact that in Mohammedan law every woman must belong to some man as his absolute property — either as a child, a wife, or a concubine — must delay the final extinction of slavery until the faith of Islam has ceased to be a great power among men ... No stronger retrograde force exists in the world."

Before the next boycott is attempted and you lose your freedoms and land to the foreign entity, step to the fore and invest yourselves in saving both Israel and Iceland from Islamic conquest. It is time to enact laws that protect your people (the children! the women!), your land and your constitution from foreign influence and safeguard your principles from compromise. As Iceland may slowly descend from the high ground of a constitutional republic into a morass of lawlessness followed by totalitarian sharia, the window of opportunity to do so is closing by the day.

A VERY SYRIOUS MATTER

The Hijrah was Mohammed's journey to conquer Mecca and Medina. Today's Muslim hijrah is conquest of Western civilization.

The Jewish Community Federations of North America have come together to provide humanitarian aid for Syrian refugees. The organizations, paid contractors who are identified in the Jewish Coalition for Disaster Relief, are too numerous to mention here, but include AIPAC, AJC, B'nai B'rith Int'l, HIAS, ORT America, and National Council of Jewish Women (NCJW), who further the cause of population redistribution.

Refugees, unlike migrants, are defined as those who flee their homes because of persecution. President Obama authorized the State Department to admit 85,000 refugees[234] fleeing humanitarian crises worldwide in 2016. Just as these Muslims have invaded Europe, so our multiculturalists are funding their invasion into America, and despite Saudi Arabia's air-conditioned tents that are ready to accommodate three million for an annual pilgrimage to Medina, no Syrians are welcomed within the Islamic world. By definition, not only are these Syrians not refugees, but the Department of Homeland Security[235] (DHS) has confessed that they have no screening process for the migratory Syrians.

ISIS promised a "sea of chaos" to flood the West with 500,000 refugees[236] — not merely to create a humanitarian crisis and strain our resources, but to also include jihadis to force Islamic conversion and establish sharia as the law of the land. Islamic countries claim to have rejected the Syrians because of terror risks, and the Jewish Federations have turned a blind eye. Historian Serge Trifkovic[237] wrote: "The refusal of the Western elite class to protect their nations from jihadist infiltration is the biggest betrayal in history."

And who are these Syrians? The Federation's announcement contained a particularly deceptive photo of a wide-eyed, blonde toddler complete with Teddy bear in hand, but the colonizers are primarily able-bodied young men, weaned on anti-Semitism and hatred of the West and democracy, who are seen stomping on or burning our flags, brandishing rifles, hurling fire bombs, and wielding swords for decapitation. These are Muslims who have waged wars against Jews and Christians for centuries, and brought their savagery to Europe, complete with their methods of intimidation — riots and rapes of children and women. The rape count was more than 5,000 in 2008 and more than 6,000 in 2009; Muslims account for fifty to seventy-five percent of all rapes of women in Norway, Denmark, and Sweden,[238] and these are the men who are designated to receive Federation funding.

The BBC's website of two hundred images is also dishonest in its refugee presentation —providing a 53 percent focus on children, 36 percent men, and 10 percent women, whereas the United Nations Refugee Agency[239] revealed that 75 percent of refugees were young men.

Interestingly, the largest Muslim charity, with its link to terror financing and settling refugees from terror-torn Syria, has an operating budget of $240 million in more than 30 countries. The charity is part of a network calling for the settlement of thousands of Syrian refugees[240] into "rich countries." Indeed, this is Barack Obama's 2008 promise to fundamentally transform America, and the Islamic State's threat to flood the West. Jusuf Al-Qaradawi of the Muslim Brotherhood declared their mission "to free the occupied lands of the laws and the tyranny of disbelievers." It is undoubtedly a case of jihad for Allah. Are we to believe that the Federations (and the BBC) are *unwittingly* complicit as they aid and abet those who would bring their misery to the West?

Crain's Cleveland Business reported that David Fleshler, chair of the board of directors of Global Cleveland, seeks to invite 100,000 foreigners to Ohio. Is it possible he is also unaware that Ohio is one of eleven states[241] that already have more people on welfare than are employed, and that the Koran prohibits Muslims from assimilating into kaffir[242] lands? He alleges that immigrants will integrate and be employable, while Darrell Hamm, director of the non-profit The Refugee Response, claims to assist refugees with their adjustment.

Judicial Watch's Corruption Chronicles[243] states: "Conveniently omitted is the devastating impact of illegal immigration like the billions of dollars American taxpayers spend annually on their education, healthcare and incarceration," as Germany[244] is now experiencing. They bring with them greater demands for tolerance and accommodations, destruction of the existing cultures, rioting and violent crime, as they perform the Koranic edicts to establish jurisdiction in lands of the infidel.

Judicial Watch's report of September 29, 2015 shows that 1,519 foreigners with terrorist ties were granted special exemptions and residency or asylum through a Department of Homeland Security (DHS) program, to which President Obama appointed Fatima Noor[245] to the post of assistant director for US Citizenship and Immigration. Where prior to 2014, they would have been banned from entry, these 1,519 are currently in the US with the same rights and benefits afforded legal residents. At a time when restrictions were being eased during an asylum fraud of February 2014, the administration unilaterally altered the Immigration and Nationality Act while also announcing our projected acceptance of refugees to 100,000 yearly by 2017. NumbersUSA[246] quoted a new Pew study that cited immigration will account for 88 percent of US population growth over the next 50 years.

The Frankfurter Allgemenie and international statistics show that these foreigners are not "refugees," but "migrants" who are not under threat of war or persecution. The migration is their hijrah, a 1400-year-old strategy of Islamic expansionism, which, coupled with violence and military conquest, will subvert and subdue the host and begin the complete transformation of that country. These are migrant warriors.

Hungarian Prime Minister Viktor Orban wisely warned that the wave of mostly Muslim refugees[247] coming to Europe threatens to undermine the continent's Christian roots. "They represent a profoundly different culture." All too obvious is the dearth of Christian and Jewish refugees who truly need asylum from the jihadis.

Meanwhile, the International Rescue Committee[248] (IRC), headed by former British Foreign Secretary David Miliband, Labour politician, praises the intake of Muslims into Germany (as the Germans citizens march and rebel against Islamization), Iceland and Sweden, and demands that Obama admit 65,000 mostly Muslim Syrians to the US. Miliband, who is affiliated with George Soros, Hillary and Bill Clinton, and Samantha Power, reminds us that more than 11 million Syrians have been made homeless by conflict and Syria is host to 33,000 asylum seekers and refugees from Iraq, Afghanistan and Somalia. Miliband will not admit that Arab states refuse their brethren, but he is sure to remind us that no matter how many we take in, the number will be "unacceptable."

The very lucrative refugee-resettlement programs are used by those who hate non-Muslim countries and wish to replace their laws with sharia. Breitbart News[249] exposes that the US already admits more than a quarter of a million Muslim migrants each year. Obama wants to add 10,000 Syrian migrants to that number. The Jewish Federations, Catholic Charities, World Council of Churches, and other "altruist" counterparts are conspiring against democracy, unintentionally or deliberately, to destroy Western civilization. To support them is to hasten some very Syrious and irreparable consequences.

CHELM

The Wise Men of folkloric Chelm* (khelm) were unique, thoughtful philosophers, able to analyze and solve every question. Their descendants walk among us.

Chelm* is a real industrial town in Poland,[250] once home to about 18,000 Jews (60% of the population) until they were annihilated in World War II. Rather, what has come to mind of late is the Chelm of Jewish folklore, penned by Elijah Ba'al Shem of the real Chelm, and commercialized by Isaac Bashevis Singer in the 1900s — because I believe there are Chelmites among us today.

Chelm the legend began when God's angels inadvertently overlooked an area while they were populating the earth with a reasonable assortment of foolish and wise souls. As one obliging angel, armed with the two bags of souls, made his way back through the clouds to correct the omission, he snagged one bag on the jagged point of a particularly high mountain peak, causing all the foolish souls to float down to one area. Thus was Chelm created with foolish, like-minded people, although there were always a few citizens who deemed themselves above the rest, clever and capable of discovery, analysis, and problem solving for the community.

It was on a snowy, wintry night, that the Wise Men of Chelm were seated around a wood-burning stove, trying to explain why winter was cold and summer, hot. As they sat in the firelight, watching the sparks and smoke moving upward through the chimney, one of the philosophers reasoned that as people throughout the world were burning wood to keep warm, all the heat was rising into the sky. After months of buildup, the air became warm enough to provide summer. Then, of course, when the stoves were idle and the air cooled once again, winter would return. Little did these *Chachamim*[251] (geniuses, scholars) know that their thoughts would become the "big question" of the 21st century – Climate Change.

Despite the difficulties of migration, the Chelmites managed to leave their village, travel and spread their wisdom to others. One such is Al Gore, who presented his whole apocalyptic vision in his 2006 film, An Inconvenient Truth," judged to contain *nine significant errors.*[252] His lifestyle defies his preaching against carbon emissions, he opposes serious debate, and he calls "denier" anyone who challenges.

During the first Democrat debate of 2015, we heard Bernie Sanders, without hesitation, respond to what he deemed the greatest threat to national security — "climate change." Challenged by the moderator about terrorism, he continued, "Of course, international terrorism is a major issue that we have got to address today, but climate change is directly related to the growth of terrorism and international conflicts." Can Sanders explain why only Muslims, specifically, are so imbued with the desire to kill because of the climate? If the syndrome has not yet been identified, we might consider "Thermocide."

Another intellect, Director of National Intelligence James Clapper, said, "Empirical evidence alone — without reference to climate models — suggests that a general warming trend is probably affecting weather and ecosystems, exacerbating the impact on humans." Again we might ask why only the Muslim humans are so influenced as to increase the rapes[253] in northern Sweden by more than a thousand fold since they first began arriving in the 1970s, or to detonate themselves while killing others.

Oblivious to the fourteen centuries of Islamic carnage, our sages pursue a climate change issue that is scientifically constant, and not "change" at all. Climate is used by the Left to distract us from Islam's complicity in drastically changing America. They would sooner discuss climate than the current knifing of Jews, beheading of Christians, and killing and injuring holiday revelers. Sanders and his like-minded sages should explore meteorology.

Secretary of State John Kerry,[254] unquestionably a Chelm descendant, legitimized the Charlie Hebdo massacre and the murder of Jews in Israel as understandable, reasonable, and warranted. He proclaimed that terrorists are encouraged by poverty, despite the oil wealth and strong financial support from the Muslim Brotherhood. He denied our American exceptionalism and pledged to appoint ambassadors based on their sexual orientation.

Another intellectual of the Chelm mindset is Hillary Clinton, who declared: "Let's be clear: Islam is not our adversary. Muslims are peaceful and tolerant people and have nothing whatsoever to do with terrorism." She further offered, "These Muslims over here are just peaceful, faithful people living their lives, whereas those Muslims over there are radical and seek to impose a toxic strain of their faith via terror and violence." It may be that she envisioned arrowed road signs, "Terrorists this way to Europe" and "Moderates this way to America," or she had them posted during her many trips to Islamic countries. Unfortunately, signs are no solution for the high illiteracy rate, which could account for the 900 Islamic terrorist cells in the US, as disclosed by the FBI. They could not have discerned which sign to follow. Of the infamous act of terrorism in San Bernardino, Hillary blamed the inanimate weapons themselves.

Remember that James Clapper said to Congress, "The term 'Muslim Brotherhood'...is an umbrella term for a variety of movements; in the case of Egypt, a very heterogeneous group, largely secular, which has eschewed violence..." In fact, the Brotherhood was a co-conspirator in the trial of the Holyland Foundation, the largest terrorism-financing ever successfully prosecuted in American history. A major financier of the terrorist organization, Hamas, is dedicated to jihad, the destruction of Israel, and to turning America into a Muslim nation, to "eliminating and destroying the Western civilization from within."

The politically correct are inclined to say that a majority of Muslims loathe violence, but surveys prove that the majority of Muslims[255] want violent sharia law to prevail over the host country's laws, and a Fox News poll indicated that one in four admitted that violent jihad against America is justified. The Koran commands Muslims to engage in holy war (Jihad) in order to impose Islam and sharia on the entire world. Sharia demands support of terrorism and suicide bombings, and conversion to Islam or death.

To say that President Obama was also from Chelm, inexperienced and naïve, would in itself be naïve. He followed a specific agenda[256] to bring our country off course. If he were inexpert and bungling, he could not have so thoroughly hidden his background, divided us into opposing factions and causing chaos on our streets, rejected and rewritten laws, dispatched the CIA for secret operations, created a runaway government, trivialized our Constitution, reduced our personal freedoms, so thoroughly changed the schools, and conspired to change our national identity and endanger our existence with tens of thousands of unvetted, Koran-inspired "immigrants."

Now, if the incoming Syrians exhibit no violence, we may conclude that climate change is not a threat. If, however, we recognize that Islamic violence in the Middle East also occurs in northern climes, we would have to ascertain which changes actually result in the atrocities or identify their teachings and laws as the true link to violence. President Obama, however, was not from Chelm. It was his "dark impulses," the same dark impulses of which he accused Americans who sought to close our borders to jihadi invaders, that were failing us. We have faith that President Trump will continue bringing us out into the light.

MUSINGS OF A MUSLIM FATHER

A new father from an Islamic country wants his baby daughter safe, but rejects the laws that will keep her free from tyranny and violence.

Raising American Muslim Kids in the Age of Trump was a meditative essay penned by Wajahat Ali[257] in the *New York Times*. During these years of Obama and Hillary, he was comfortable knowing that no one would question his allegiance to Islamic law (sharia) over the American Constitution. Despite Islam's record of subversion and violence, he and his coreligionists need not have been overly concerned if their children were caught rioting in the name of Allah, damaging or looting property, or burning tires or American and Israeli flags. For eight years, this has been a Land of the Freedom to Run Amok and cause damage; to join the Muslim Student Association in boycotting Israel and terrorize the Jewish students; to march and rally against an emasculated police force; to brazenly masquerade an ideology of conquest as a religion of peace, and to be believed!

As Ali ruminates about his toddler son and new baby daughter, he shares his concerns about the possibility of Donald J. Trump's presidency, and the extreme vetting that could restrict others' entry to America, regardless of possible aggression. He fears that his friend's son might be deported, and he muses that his daughter could be sent to a "concentration camp" by the only presidential candidate who expresses his intense loyalty to American laws! Has Ali not studied the Constitution and Bill of Rights? Has he not heard Mr. Trump iterate that he wants America restored and that his favors cannot be bought? Ali fears a president who upholds the Constitution but would be comfortable with a Clinton-Kaine administration that would continue to promote the Muslim Brotherhood and Iran, endanger our homeland security with additional hordes of unvetted immigrants, betray Israel, and grant positions of power in exchange for compensation, resulting in the stealth imposition of sharia into government.

With pensive reminiscence, he speaks of the beauty of celebrating Eid-al Fitr, an elaborate dining festival that ends the Islamic month of Ramadan and suggests that he could be denied his celebrations and food preparations under new leadership. This is pure fantasy and fear-mongering, as no other religious group has ever been thus denied — unless, of course, he misses the cattle preparation of his co-religionists, the men who walk in the streets with their cattle purchases and intentionally stab and torture the docile, defenseless creatures with picks and knives until they bleed out and bleat their last breath. Does he fear being questioned about his loyalty to the Constitution? Does he fear the prospect of living in a country that does not countenance the torture and abuse dictates found in the Koran?

If, indeed, this new father truly hopes his daughter will grow up in a safe country, why not demand and relish the extreme vetting[258] to verify the identity and ideology of the applicants who will walk our streets and encounter our daughters? Under Hillary and Kaine's continued penchant for multiculturalism from Islamic lands, we might well become an Islamic-majority nation, where no girl or woman is safe — perhaps as Sweden,[259] now titled the rape capital of the West; or Australia and Canada,[260] which share the title of kidnapping capitals of the world; or Germany,[261] where Angela Merkel's news that one hundred women were raped on New Year's Eve, 2016, was finally admitted to be as many as 1200 women raped by gangs of 2,000 Muslim men (do the math to realize these are gang rapes). We could also become as Israel, where knifings, car jammings, explosions and rock-throwings that cause deadly car accidents, along with rocket launchings, are a daily threat. Add to these, the boycotts and legal tactics to delegitimize her very existence. Trump has announced his goal of increasing and strengthening our police forces to ensure that our communities are safe, and that America's daughters will never have to cover themselves from head to toe, see the world through a hole in her mask, and require a related male escort to leave the house — or the latest assault on women, muzzles![262] Does he not find this troubling?

With babe in arms, the writer added a fear about Trump's extreme vetting that might include a database, but there is already an established database of our school children as part of this administration's imposition of the Common Core curriculum, contrary to the wishes of their parents. American law, rooted in the Judeo-Christian heritage, protects the welfare and security of our citizens, constantly adjusted so that security is never sacrificed for humanity, and vice versa. A good example is the suspension of naturalization proceedings, and the addition of registration requirements and restricted mobility for Italian, German and Japanese immigrants a day after the Japanese attacked Pearl Harbor. Islam is at war with America, on par with Nazism and communism. Its declared aim is to destroy Western civilization from within and to ultimately establish a global Islamic caliphate.

Not to be ignored was Ali's subtle accusation of "bigotry" against Americans for their reaction to 9/11 — a bona fide reaction, I might add, to the sudden, spectacular, tragic death of three thousand people and the ineradicable pain of loss to their families, when 19 Muslims crashed planes into Pennsylvania, the Pentagon, and Manhattan's World Trade Center, the personification of financial success resented by the backward Islamic nations. Is it also "bigotry" when we see and hear the adherents of Islam proclaim their intent to destroy America, when we see them stoning or hanging or burning people alive, and when we recoil in horror and grief to learn of the 29,065 (8/21/16) Islamic attacks on Americans and the world since 9/11. Is it bigotry when polls show that the majority of Muslims prefer the ideology and laws of Islam over the laws of the land to which they have made the al-hijrah,[263] the Islamic doctrine of immigration?

Ali took this opportunity to enhance the controversy surrounding Khizr and Ghazala Khan, parents of US Army Captain Humayun Khan who was killed in Iraq in 2004, twelve years ago. Why the choice of this man, and not a more recent military loss, has become clear: Khizr Khan[264] has strong ties to the Saudi government and its huge donations to the Clinton Foundation, and he received $375,000 to his immigration law firm for the political tribute he paid his son at the DNC. We are also aware that Khan's former employer manages the Clintons' taxes and has a patent on Hillary's infamous email-filtering program. Khizr's son's heroism is not in question, but the father's integrity is.

A self-described "spiritual nomad," our new father is nevertheless investing in a project, "Make space" in Virginia, to introduce selected aspects of Islam to their children. We might wonder what the unmosqued adherents will use instead of the Koran, with its 109 open-ended verses of commands to violence. America has been home to people of all nations who practice their many religious rites, but being religions, not ideologies, they have been able to assimilate and become part of American society, something that Islam's ideology cannot do by its very nature. American law and sharia law are profoundly antipathetic to one another and will bring incurable division to America. "A house divided against itself cannot stand," and we will lose America if Clinton and Kaine, academia and the media continue their efforts to negate Christianity and Judaism, and further deprecate our freedoms of speech, assembly, and the right of self-protection.

The BBC reported that 95 percent of its viewers admit that multiculturalism is a failure, and a "leaked German intelligence document" described by The Gatestone Institute says: "We are importing Islamic extremism, Arab anti-Semitism, national and ethnic conflicts of other peoples, as well as a different understanding of society and law." British police are monitoring more than 3,000 homegrown Islamic extremists willing to carry out attacks on the UK, and eighty percent of the 3,000 mosques in America are known to have deep ties to extremism, including to the Muslim Brotherhood.

If this caring father hopes to safely raise his family in America, he has to live and vote so that all may celebrate the holidays of their choosing and be suspicious of the mother of three who espouses "Islam has to trump them all." She is not raising her children to be loyal Americans; rather, she is imbuing them with Islamic supremacism — to inspire them to jihad. Muslims are safe here, but statistics prove that Jews and Christians are now targets in America and throughout the world.

It is neither bigotry nor unconstitutional to enact laws to promote national security[265] and national interests — to keep our citizens safe. Article Four, Section Four, known as the Guarantee Clause, states, "The United States shall guarantee to every State a republican form of government and shall protect each of them against invasion." Therefore, even if the federal government chose to exercise no other power, it must, under the Constitution, provide for the common defense.

ENGRAVED IN STONE

Johnson City prefers no culpability and no memorial to the World Trade Center bombings.

The Children of Abraham of the Southern Tier, an interfaith organization in Johnson City, has taken offense at the 9/11 memorial raised in the nearby Town of Owego, New

York. This association of misguided multiculturalists and Muslim moderates allege that identifying the perpetrators of the worst individual act of aggression on American soil would encourage Muslim hatred. If naming the perpetrators will encourage Muslim hatred and another attack of aggression, what was it that encouraged the first attack of aggression? The alliance never once excoriated the very act that resulted in the death and injury to the roughly 3,000 American victims and 453 responders, and the boundless grief for their families and all Americans. The moderates made no effort to apologize for the horrific crime that forced people to jump to their death rather than burn alive; never expressed their sorrow for the victims and heroic rescue workers or atoned with deeds to benefit the families that suffered such tragic losses. Do they even acknowledge that Islamic terrorists continue their march of evil, Islam's perpetual holy war, against every living being on the planet? No. And the city manager's overtures were also snubbed.

The Muslim residents of Johnson City may be moderates who never take up a lethal weapon for Allah, but they are engaging in a subtle act of civilization or settlement jihad. Such people are comparatively discreet in Western society, going about their lives inconspicuously, but effecting regime changes in gradual increments. By their refusal to acknowledge the obvious links between Islam and 9/11, they shield those who spew hatred against America, Israel and democracy; they empower the academics and students who vilify Israel and Jewish students on campus, and they facilitate the crossing of borders for hijrah (conquest by population). Under the guise of injured sensibilities, they insist on the removal of anything that may identify those who pursue our destruction and conquest with Islam, hoping to erase the ugly truth that fourteen centuries of barbarism continue unabated in every country where Islam is found.

They would have us believe that a tiny minority is to blame, but a recent Pew Research poll[266] shows that 51 percent of American Muslims choose to be governed by sharia; 30 percent believe it is legitimate to use violence against those who insult Mohammed, the Koran, or Islam; 25 percent believe violence against Americans can be justified as part of the global jihad; and nearly twenty percent believe the use of violence in the US is justified in order to make sharia the law of the land. Presented with a choice when sharia conflicts with the US Constitution and Bill of Rights, 33 percent say sharia should be sovereign. That's some minority! Politically, 48 percent are Democrats, 19 percent Independents, and 19 percent Republicans.

Islam already regulates our speech through our government, our media, and the constant hazard of being damned as Islamophobic to those who dare to speak out. They cover their tracks through leftist academics, a strong BDS movement, and textbooks crammed with indoctrinal and fallacious material. Continuing along those lines, the Johnson City assemblage is working to remove from future knowledge the history of 9/11 that was carved into the granite. If we fail to yearly observe events as significant as the bombing of the World Trade Center, the signing of our Declaration of Independence, our victory in World War II, and more, our youth will be robbed of their identity, their heritage, and America as we know it. Wisdom is defense. Ignorance of our journey through history is the greatest threat to our survival.

It should be noted that this interfaith group's complaint was not that they, too, should have paid homage to America's fallen or, specifically, to Owego's citizen, Derek Statkevicus, who lost his life that day. Neither were they inspired to erect a monument in their own city or to join Owego residents in a fight against the greatest scourge of mankind with its unspeakable crimes done in the name of their religion. Rather, they express a phony outrage that the criminals have been identified with Islam! Often enough, other Islamic groups attempt to blame 9/11 on American citizens, on Jews or Christians, but this one is working to eliminate the obvious first, to claim that the 19 were unknown, came out of nowhere, and bombed America for no specific reason. Removing the offensive truth from the monument will leave room for revisionism later, just as Major Nidal Hassan (Fort Hood Massacre) was called anything but what he was, and his jihad massacre was officially named "workplace violence."

Instead of condemnation or owning up to the demands for death inherent in the Koran, these individuals hope to gradually erase the event from our memory and from generations to come — just as Islamists have obliterated or renamed many artifacts and historic tombs to create their own narrative, just as their counterparts in Israel are trying to stop archaeological excavations from revealing more Jewish history. We have seen violent youths destroy selected historic statuary and groups changing the names of our commemorative holidays. These Children of Abraham may well be the Islamic families that escaped tyranny but, unfortunately for the rest of us, they nurture their children with intolerance and harshness, creating a new, young generation of jihadis. These offspring may become the young men enticed online to join ISIS' executioners, or the young women lured to sexual slavery for the Palestinian cause.

We need to be reminded of the anger, the tears, and the patriotism that were triggered that day of September 11th, fifteen years ago, and realize that there is more danger now than ever. The Middle East has grown bolder and more violent. Islamists are acquiring newer, deadlier weapons, and more of their number are making their way into Europe, North and South America, bringing with them new plans to terrorize and infuse their way of life into ours. Islam has been at war with the world since the seventh century. Their holy book is a dedication to brutality and conquest, so that even their own people are condemned to grope in the darkness of oppression and poverty. In the name of their god, they must erase the past to support their own supersessionist narrative, and we must never oblige them. The more that Americans accommodate such requests and attempt to correct or crush our own speech, the more power we will relinquish. Unless we weigh the long-term ramifications of the growing adjustments we make to our lives for the sake of theirs, we will lose our freedoms to their tyrannical sharia laws.

In the words of Hassan al-Banna, creator of the Muslim Brotherhood (1929), "It is the nature of Islam to dominate, not to be dominated, to impose its laws on all nations and extend its laws to the entire planet." If the hate feared by the Children of Abraham does arise, it will be from Islamists' deeds, not the attribution on a memorial stone.

THE FEMALE JIHADI

Women suffer greatly under Islam, and the psychological and physical pain they endure can take them in many directions.

If one needed a convincing example of the damage done to the female psyche by a strict Islamic upbringing, look no farther than to Linda Sarsour.

The treatment of women[267] is brutally degrading within Islam; they are raped and harassed daily, and "not worthy of protection."[268] Traditional gender roles provide that men are superior to women and the female is responsible for the family's honor; hence, they must be obedient to the many prohibitions or punished — even murdered.

Islam is a shame-honor religion as Arab and Muslim cultures are shame-honor cultures that provide a means of manipulation and control by the family or group. It allows for no creativity and no autonomy. When shame becomes a destructive force, it leads the victimized family member to seek revenge and spill blood. It is brought by the families who migrate to the West, and further exacerbated if they observe traditional rigid regulations of surveillance,[269] a key concept that leads to tension and crippling development.

The daughter (and the son up to age 7) spends her time with the devalued mother who was herself a deprived, distressed child who grew into a troubled adulthood, unable to nurture healthy children. The girls especially do not develop independently but understand that they are like their mother and any other women who serve as wives to the authoritarian male head of household. The women[270] live in dread of losing favor, of being beaten, abused, kept naked in isolation, or even annihilated. If the husband divorces her, by simply repeating the divorce mantra thrice, she is left with only the dowry provided by her parents at the time of her arranged marriage.

The child is injured by their strict sharia laws,[271] and by the disharmony, rivalry and envy that exist within the Islamic household, not to mention the fear and anger caused by the intense political hatred found in the Koran[272] and repeated in their prayers five times daily. The pre-adolescent girl is further traumatized and degraded by the physically and psychologically painful Female Genital Mutilation[273] (FGM) that is performed on her without anesthesia, under non-medical conditions, that may well cause lifelong infection.

Children living under circumstances of neglect, abuse, and trauma grow up with defective bonding relations and stay forever connected to the mother in a painful traumatic bonding or terror bonding. When the daughter is ultimately given in marriage to a man of any age, not of her choosing, she is programmed to replicate the life of her devalued mother.

A young Muslim in Gaza or Judea and Samaria (West Bank) would have experienced enough shame to be overwhelmed by rage and aggression, resulting in never developing empathy with others. They are treated as objects from an early age and, therefore, treat as mere objects real people with real needs. Boys who are radicalized at an early age bond violently and aggressively to females, including to the mother; girls internalize that same male rage, also directing it against the female and eventually become pawns of male extremist groups.

So now we have Linda Sarsour, the oldest of seven children born to a Muslim family from Gaza and living among people of the same background in Brooklyn, New York. She promotes herself by championing "cool issues," but seeks leadership roles to promote Islam and Palestinian self-determination. She professes to stand for the feminist movement but rejects all who support Israel and silences any who speak of Islam's severe cruelty to women.

She spoke briefly of her ties to her mother when she said she had to attend the local school, her mother's choice. No doubt, her spare time was spent assisting with the care of her six younger siblings at the expense of a typical American childhood and the effects of westernization, thus denied the opportunity to play and work through fantasy life.

Steeped in the Islamic ideology and the Palestinian narrative, Sarsour admitted to having endured FGM, but not the severity, and shuts down all who criticize the practice. She was limited to meeting young men and women of her own heritage and shared mentality and chose the hijab for further identification. Given in marriage at age 17 to her parents' preference, she bore three children by the time she was in her early twenties. Where she is duty-bound to repress her anger against her family about her own personal abuse, she directs her rage outwardly against Americans, women, and the President of the United States.

She joined several Muslim organizations and labeled herself a "radical activist," that is, a civilizational jihadist, an Islamic supremacist who, through multicultural coalitions, seeks to curry the favor of the public to accept Islam. She has joined rallies of Nation of Islam, Black Lives Matter and, more recently, the Women's March. She is deeply involved with community, may seek a City Council candidacy and ponder the idea of mayor of New York City.

Islam is democracy's sworn enemy because their belief system, their raison d'etre, is based on envy and hatred.[274] The Koran contains 109 versus that decree war with Jews and Christians, commands all manner of torture and extermination,[275] and warns that non-fighters for Allah will go to hell, because Mohammed was offended when the Jews rejected his religion. One of many such commands is "Fight against those to whom the Scriptures were given. 9:29"

A subtle proponent of the prescribed terrorism, Sarsour is a jihadi. Pew Research estimates that 330 million Muslims believe in violent jihad, a number that exceeds the Nazis. Although not trained in armed warfare, Sarsour conducts her own war with lies and propaganda, and her cries of Palestinian injustice and suffering through social media and the Women's March.[276] She bears a strong odium for Israel, and was proud to share a stage with a convicted terrorist murderer of two Jewish university students.

As she thwarts all comments about women's oppression under Islam, she extols the benefits of FGM, explaining it as a mere "cut." And it is here that we find her not trying to free her oppressed female co-religionists, but sanctioning their position of submission, their bondage, and the pathology of her severe jihadi hatred of women. She warns American Muslims not to assimilate.[277] Of Brigitte Gabriel,[278] Sarsour tweeted, "I wish I could take their (female sexual organs) away; they don't deserve to be women." Of Ayaan Hirsi Ali[279] she tweeted, "Brigitte Gabriel=Ayaan Hirsi Ali. She's asking 4 an a$$ whippin'. I wish I could take their vaginas away — they don't deserve to be women."

Sarsour is pathologically fused to, dependent on, and smothered by her mother. While male jihadists attempt to cleanse and release themselves from the maternal bond by killing others, she has exposed a similar malignancy in her desire for bloody violence against her despised enemies, which include all women, Israel, and President Donald Trump. Unable or unwilling to join the physical war, she will continue seeking to inveigle the public through her multicultural activism, spewing hatred and finding her own path of perpetual rage as she works to make the misogynist sharia law, Islamic violence and destruction, legally part of our American way of life.

(Acknowledgment: Kobrin, Nancy Hartevelt, PhD, (2016) The Jihadi Dictionary; Mamaroneck, NY, Multieducator Press.)

PART TWO:
ON ACADEMIA

JIHAD AT KENT STATE
Tenured professor violated code of conduct with inappropriate behavior and anti-Semitic rant.

An anti-Semitic situation occurred at Kent State while Ishmael Khaldi, a Bedouin-Muslim Israeli, former diplomat and current advisor to Israel's Foreign Minister, was speaking about life in Israel from a Bedouin-Muslim perspective. Against all rules of procedure, tenured professor Julio Pino had first distributed literature to students and guests, advocating the boycott of Israel, and then challenged the speaker with propagandist lies and hate speech, shouting "Death to Israel."[280] (He didn't want to hear that life was good in Israel.)

Such behavior is not only unethical, but completely unacceptable by any instructor employed at any institution of learning. He advocated hate and death to the Jewish people, and, in so doing, flagrantly crossed the line of appropriate behavior. Imagine if someone were to yell death to Arabs or Muslims, or a word against Allah, that would have CAIR and allied organizations descending upon the school with accusations of Islamophobia and unimaginable consequences. Contrary to the irrational comments by Associate Vice-President Thomas Neumann, this incident has nothing to do with freedom of speech, but with inciting and advocating to kill.

A background check shows Pino to be an avowed communist who honored Castro's revolution in Cuba and his dictatorship. At UCLA, he blamed the United States for the poverty and deaths of Latinos. After a "crisis in faith," he became an alcoholic, left Christianity, and turned to Islam – in fact, the most extreme wing of the most violent religion/culture on this planet, which carried out more than 17,900 jihad attacks since 9/11 (to date). In their war to conquer the west, Islamists are changing the face of Europe and America and using many methods to delegitimize and annihilate Israel.

Even if his behavior were controlled, it is implausible that Pino could have been considered a trustworthy instructor of history and government at Kent State. Islamists consider Israel the "Little Satan" and America the "Big Satan," and because he has already been outspoken about our country, his views and teachings seditious. Is it not a policy for school management to sit in on classes to grasp what their instructors are teaching to their innocent students, children of parents who support democracy and pay for what enters the young, impressionable minds?

A review of Kent's employee code of conduct indicates that Pino violated several. He failed to maintain a professional demeanor and integrity; deceitfully distributed anti-democratic political material; was discourteous and disrespectful to a visiting speaker; may well have scared any Jewish students in attendance; and indulged in discrimination, disrespecting the differences of people, ideas, and opinions.

Contrary to KSU's operational procedures, Pino's behavior was not the exercise of free expression or speech, but a way of fomenting hate and uprising had the Muslim Student Union been in attendance. Campuses of the University of California have already experienced rioting, with some students injured, a level of instruction that bodes danger to the students.

Although the university's president was critical of Pino's behavior, maintaining him on staff shows an acceptance of the evil he espouses. Pino and his ilk should be immediately dismissed from all current and future positions, and a thorough investigation be made for all similar positions because hiring such jihadis shows a serious error in judgment.

HARVARD: THE HIGHER MADRASSA

Harvard deviates from its lofty mission statement to follow Islamic propaganda and BDS.

Harvard's mission statement contains words such as: open the minds, respect ideas, critical thought, productive cooperation, developing full intellectual and human potential — not to mention explore, advance knowledge and promote understanding.

Under the direction of anti-Semitic activist Paul Beran, a product of supersessionist Presbyterianism,[281] Harvard has become a hotbed of boycott, divestment, and sanctions (BDS) against the one country in all the Middle East, Israel, the only voice of compassion and justice. The assigned readings and visiting speakers have been entirely pro-Palestinian (pro-totalitarianism and anti-democracy), such as Ilan Pappé, Noam Chomsky, and Richard Falk (among the most infamous in their category), influenced by the works of no less than the epitome of evil, George Soros[282] (a very disturbed, but wealthy and influential, man), with representatives from one of his many nefarious organizations, Jewish Voice for Peace.

In so doing, Harvard has negated the intent of its mission, as there can be no opening of minds if they're taught Islamic propaganda; no respect if those who speak do not respect even themselves; no critical thought if the minds are closed in hate; no productive cooperation if only the Palestinian narrative is presented; no exploration, no knowledge, and positively no promotion of understanding. How does the college justify accepting fees for a thorough education while reneging on its contract with the students, except with deception.

Harvard's undergraduates are to be broadly educated in seven areas considered indispensable: Foreign Cultures, Historical Study, Literature and Arts, Moral Reasoning, Quantitative Reasoning, Science, and Social Analysis. There is no doubt that the Palestinian bias instilled in the minds of staff and students has already betrayed at least five of these principles, and the immorality of betrayal to an entire Jewish people — again.

When much of the world is already familiar with taqiyyah, lies encouraged by the Koran for 1400 years of warfare, and the spread of Islamic propagandist war waged by Muslims worldwide for the purpose of acquiring all lands and the conversion or death of people of all five major religions for global jihad, how is it that Harvard's administration is not investigating or in control of the libelous textbooks and other means of incitement to hate and destroy? Harvard appears to have joined the war against Israel and, by extension, all democracies including our own. "All that is required for evil to prevail is for good men to do nothing." – Edmund Burke.

Harvard's silence is indicative of complicity and encouragement of Beran's plan to destroy the Jewish state, Israel,[283] the only haven and homeland of the Jewish people (compared to 57 Islamic nations and 19+ official Christian nations), and the cessation of all of Israel's accomplishments and gifts to the world (verified by Nobel prizes bestowed). The school is also emboldening a very violent people to persist in their destruction of churches, Christian antiquities, and Christians themselves; to continue receiving the major share of all UNRWA (United Nations Relief and Works Agency) funds to increase their supply of weapons, and to help spread the inhumane sharia law within the Middle East, into Europe, and into the United States. Harvard is supporting the ideology of George Soros, the Muslim Brotherhood, and CAIR (Council of American-Islamic Relations) — despotism.

Harvard's heavily funded Saudi Outreach Center has been a shock to the Massachusetts education officials who've seen the distorted political agenda enter the minds of the teachers and K-12 students. The textbooks have been declared absurd and fundamentally flawed,[284] with their promotion of a totalitarian dogma.

Beran is responsible for severe anti-Israel activism, untrue defamatory accusations against the enrollment into a Harvard Business School course (2007) of Israeli Chief of Staff Dan Halutz, and demonizing Israel and her security wall that has successfully kept many fervent terrorists from killing more Israeli citizens (many countries have walls for isolation and protection). His "Cores of the Conflict" slides ignore Israel's security concerns in a most dangerous position as one/one-thousandth of Arab land, while showing only Palestinian demands and deceptions. And in-house activist Sara Royle extols the virtues of Hamas, acknowledged as terrorists on the Secretary of State listing, which is tantamount to subversion.

Despite available facts, the Harvard Outreach Center continues its ideologically-driven incompetence and unscholarly dissemination of hate. Why does the president permit this activity at the university? Are there plans to support bona fide scholarship righteously, or to dismiss Beran's influence? Are there plans for additional Saudi financial influences in the school's future? Where does Harvard's administration intend its future outreach for truth and justice and do they even consider saving Israel and America from the planned stealth destruction?

UP ON THE DECLINE

Gutman is gutless, allowing BDS to delegitimize Israel and embolden the enemy of democracy.

Dr. Amy Gutman, president of The University of Pennsylvania, while disclaiming sponsorship, endorses the PennBDS conference of hatred with her silence. The purpose of PennBDS (boycott, divestment, sanctions) is the delegitimization of Israel, the destruction of the only homeland for the Jewish people. Wittingly or unwittingly, but surely acknowledging Saudi[285] funding totaling millions, the University is an enabler of a militant ideology whose ultimate goal could also destroy America, because Islam and democracy are decidedly incompatible.

Contrived issues of housing and "occupation" are merely the tools of destruction. Islam's ideology uses jihad to wage brutal wars to conquer vast expanses of land and subdue millions of indigenous people across the continents: Asia, Africa, Europe and the Americas. Muslims do not assimilate[286] or live in peace with others, and the surviving vanquished join forces with the murderers — a unique, permanent Islamic institution.

The Koran instructs its followers to kill Jews and Christians to expropriate land for Islam.[287] When their numbers are insufficient to win by violence, Muslims use psychological warfare, beginning with inculcating intense hatred into each new generation. Since 1993, the Abu Mazen/Arafat regime of the Palestinian Authority has indoctrinated an entire generation with terrorist-driven hate education and incitement via their schools, mosques and media. Unconcerned with the destruction of the childhood of their innocents, adults use their children to wage a revisionist historical offensive against the Jewish people. They are aided and abetted by scholars, religious and political leaders, journalists from the Saudi-funded media and psychologically-damaged, self-despising Jews.[288]

These jihadis and their accomplices conspire to discredit thousands of years of authentication from Jewish, Muslim, and Christian scriptures; archaeology, Assyriology, Egyptology; ancient, medieval and modern historical sources, all of which prove the immutable historical Jewish connection to the land of Israel. They openly accuse Israel of myriad false human rights violations, which serve to deflect from the inhumane treatment that Muslims[9] foist upon their own.

Concurrently, Muslim Brotherhood and CAIR[289] work to curb freedom of speech, thereby inhibiting the media and the masses from exposing the worldwide conquest perpetrated by Muslims. In this way, the uninformed rarely learn the full extent of when Muslims kill millions worldwide, and the masses are blindsided and remain deceived about Israel.

The pseudo-history and poisonous fabrications that steal the past are designed to ensure that the Jews will have no homeland of their own. This is conceptual genocide on the Jewish people, and there is no one in the university to stand up and reject the material as malicious and factually incorrect — and potentially injurious to Jewish/ Israeli students. With the administration's silence, propaganda masquerades as scholarship, and the facility is complicit in working to destroy an entire nation and her people.

What the Christian population fails to realize or acknowledge is that Islam is a replacement theocracy.[290] If the Muslims succeed in delegitimizing the history of the Jewish people, they will have also destroyed the foundation of Christianity, and Islam will proceed on the road to world domination.

These are the facts: The majority of today's Arab population of Israel, the West Bank and Gaza, can be traced back no more than 150 years. None other than the Israelites ever left a record that survived into the modern era. The earliest reference to ancient Israelites in extra-Biblical history is the appearance of the name "Israel" in the Mernephtah stele,[291] a granite slab created circa 1200 BCE, referring to the Egyptian King Mernephtah's military victory over an "Israelite people" living in the north-central Israel highlands. And, ironically, there are a number of well-known Koranic references to the high antiquity of the Israelites!

Beginning in the 1880s, Arab nationalists repudiated the term "Palestine" because the area was Southern Syria. The Grand Mufti Hajj Mohammed Amin Al Husseini, the most vitriolic voice of his day, opposed the British Mandate because it created "Palestine" separate from Syria, and Syria's President Hafez al-Assad concurred in 1974. PLO member Zahir Muhsein was quoted in the Dutch newspaper Thouw: "The Palestinian people does not exist. The creation of a Palestinian state is only a means for continuing our struggle against the state of Israel for our Arab unity ... Only for political and tactical reasons do we speak about the existence of a Palestinian people, since Arab national interests demand that we posit the existence of a distinct 'Palestinian people' to oppose Zionism."

The entire endeavor to steal Israel's history and replace it with a fictitious Palestinian narrative is war by any means, and, as with all wars, the first casualty is the truth.

Is there no moral obligation to teach truth and save the democratic State of Israel, which ultimately translates into saving our own United States? History proves what the scourge of Islam has done to the previous peoples of the Middle East and Africa, and how it is now changing the face and character of Europe. Does Dr. Gutman believe that we Americans are immune if we only acquiesce to forfeiting Israel to Islam, the same way Neville Chamberlain forfeited Czechoslovakia to the Nazis? Wherever Muslims have migrated, bringing their destructive culture with them, eschewing assimilation and making demands to Islamize their host countries, concessions have only helped to strengthen their resolve and achieve their goal of conquest. Spain was the only one to reverse the process, but it took them from 711 to 1492 to do so, and now they may be succumbing once again.

The mission of America is to be the leader of the free world, and the University's mission should be to teach the purpose of our nation; to imbue our students with American ideals; to establish, support and defend freedom; and deny submission, subjugation and religious tyranny.

Dr. Gutman was entrusted by the parents to teach the truth and America's democratic ideals to their children, yet she welcomes the enemies of those ideals, those who destroyed the Twin Towers along with the lives of 3,000 Americans and their families. What type of mindset permits one to join forces with those who demonize democracies? I urge the president and personnel of the University of Pennsylvania to rethink their position as Americans and stand against the religious tyranny that is taking root in the schools and in our land.

Be reminded: Those who would give up essential liberty to purchase a little temporary safety deserve neither liberty nor safety. — Benjamin Franklin (1706–1790), Historical Review of Pennsylvania, 1759.

BDS – BIGOTED, DECEPTIVE, SHAMELESS
BDS was implemented for Israel's destruction — jihad without the sword.

The BDS movement (boycott, divestment, and sanctions) is spreading like a pestilence across our country and in Europe, infecting the young and vulnerable in universities.

The background:
On April 1, 1933, a week after he came to power, Hitler ordered a boycott[292] of Jewish shops, banks, offices and department stores. Nazi Propaganda Minister Joseph Goebbels defended it as a legitimate response to the anti-German "atrocity propaganda" being spread by "international Jewry." Signs were posted, "Germans, defend yourselves, buy only at German shops!" In 1945, the Arab League[293] initiated a boycott of Jewish Palestinian businesses. A year later, it was extended to prohibit contact with "anything Jewish."

The BDS movement began in earnest at the UN's Durban Conference Against Racism[294] in the 2001 NGO (often government-supported "non-governmental organizations") forum, when Human Rights Watch (HRW) presented the strategy to advance the "complete and total isolation of Israel" and called for the "imposition of mandatory and comprehensive sanctions and embargos, the full cessation of all links (diplomatic, economic, social, aid, military cooperation, and training) between all states and Israel."

The Organization of the Islamic Conference (OIC) of Arab and Islamic countries (only) held in Tehran was led by NGOs and linked to "war crimes" cases against Israeli officials (lawfare). From this, the pro-Palestinian groups promoted economic and cultural boycotts of Israel (2002), supported a boycott of Israeli academic institutions (2003), and worked to deny the right of the Jewish people to national self-determination (2005).

The purpose of BDS is to reverse the events of 1948 — the creation of the State of Israel, which led to the "Palestinian refugee tragedy," and to demand the return of those Palestinians and their descendants to their former homes inside the Green Line,[295] allowing for no homeland for the Jews. This political anti-Semitism calls for the removal of an existing state (unique in international politics), based on human rights abuses and military invasions that are never considered for the Indonesian presence in West Papua, the Chinese takeover of Tibet, the Russian brutality in Chechnya, or the American presence in Iraq and Afghanistan. The distinguishing characteristic of Israel is her Jewish nationality and identity, and Israel's supporters — irrespective of their varied political views, class background and level of ethnic or religious identification — as the enemy. Targeted are Israel's 80 percent Jewish population, not her 20 percent Arab population.

The hate-filled BDSers gather throughout America and Europe, their campaigns finding favor on campuses, some labor unions, churches, media, and cultural institutions, and base their accusations on lies. Relying on the ignorance of their audience, they accuse Israel of apartheid. South Africa's apartheid allowed no blacks in white hospitals, white universities, or participation in parliament, while Israel's democracy allows for all races and religions to work side by side, Jews and Arabs as both physicians and patients in hospitals, as professors and students in universities, and as parliamentarians in the Knesset. When Israel was among the first to help at international disaster zones, they did so without respect for race or creed, such as to Turkey (1999), Kosovo (1999), the Congo (2008), and Haiti (2010).

The BDSers spread their unsubstantiated, unjustified charges that demonize Israel under the guise of freedom of speech, but it is they who are purveyors of bigotry and hate. Their purpose is to highlight the many inventions and merchandise produced in Israel in order to destroy her economy, undermine freedoms of expression and tolerance. They represent an immoral punishment of a nation by prohibiting dialogue, cooperation, and peaceful ties between Israel and Palestinians, and promote an impossible one-state solution with Muslims as the majority and Israelis as the new "desaparecidos" (political Argentineans who disappeared).

Boycott:

The BDSers coerce companies to refuse to buy/sell Israeli products, demand that artists decline to perform in Israel, and insist that academics not cooperate with Israeli institutions. They analyze which methods work best and which need tweaking to improve effectiveness.

Divestment:

NGOs accuse companies that trade with Israel of war crimes and international law violations, and push banks, investors and pension funds to remove developing countries' access to financial support from Israel's stable and advanced economy.

Sanctions:

BDSers demand that the international community treat Israel as a pariah state, enforcing arms embargos on baseless war crimes, and legal proceedings for defensive actions for survival. And because the campaigns single out Israel explicitly, they violate the EU Working Definition of Antisemitism,[296] denying the Jewish people their history and the right to self-determination, using the classic anti-Semitic symbols, and drawing comparisons of Israel with Nazism. While these haters champion the rights of many minorities to self-determination, they deny Israel those very same liberties.

BDS against Israel only is gaining traction in The United Methodist Church,[297] the major mainline Christian denomination in the US. Its current plan is to encourage divestment from Motorola and Hewlett Packard. The Italian movement for BDS, recently held in Bologna,[298] is targeting Teva, the world's largest pharmaceutical company (est.1901); L'Oreal, located in pre-1967 Israel; Delta Galil Industries, the largest textile manufacturer; and Sabra, Israel's second-largest food company that supplies food for the IDF (Israel Defense Forces).

The BDS mission is not about borders or Israel's size. It is about her very existence. The meeting at the University of Pennsylvania concluded with a commitment to intensify the movement in Italy, in Europe, and around the world.

BDS — AGENTS OF DESTRUCTION
The speakers, their credentials, and their recommendations to annihilate Israel.

The Palestinian Civil Society Call for BDS[299] was launched in July 2005, with a staggering 170+ Palestinian organizations representing themselves as refugees in exile, living as subjugated citizens under occupation, in Israel. The campaign is based on the Palestinian narrative that Israel has gone against international law; the truths of Israel's universal suffrage, social services without discrimination, and free press are dismissed.

The Muslim and self-hating Jewish students are sharia-compliant and willing to abandon democracy. The following are some of the regular BDS speakers.

Badil, (campaign national committee[300]) hosted the first Palestine BDS Conference in Ramallah, November 2007, out of which emerged the BDS National Committee (BNC) to coordinate the international campaign. BDS has an unparalleled organization of boycott worldwide. The website delineates the Palestinian victimhood and formulates strategies and programs of action worldwide aimed at destroying Israel's industry and commerce.

Ali Abunimah, frequent popular speaker at BDS events, is a Palestinian-American journalist and co-founder of Electronic Intifada, part of The Third Jihad,[301] said to contain a treasure trove of highly antagonistic writings against the Jewish State. Born in Washington DC to Palestinian refugees from the 1948 exodus, he is a graduate of Princeton University and University of Chicago and contributes articles to many publications. A member of many Arab-American activist associations, he proposes the one-state,[302] civilizational jihad and seeks to extinguish Israel by overpopulation.

Ahmed Moor,[303] a Palestinian-American journalist born in Gaza, writes regularly for Al Jazeera English, the LA Times, the Huffington Post, and anti-Zionist website Mondoweiss, etc. A graduate student of public policy at Harvard University, Moor questions Israel's right to exist as race-exclusive, thereby denying Israel's multi-racial citizens. As noted on his blogspot, he sees Israel as a Netanyahu-engineered "economic miracle" due to "cash injections," and BDS as a means of terminating Israel's successes. He seeks the right of Arab return, and uses allegations of disproportionate warfare to corroborate their victimization, accusations against Israel's military defense, deflection from Palestinian leadership to blame non-productive lives on "others," and creates situations for which the adversary is blamed in court (Lawfare project).[304]

Helena Cobban,[305] born in England, is a veteran writer and columnist in several pro-Palestinian newspapers and the BBC. A founder of Just World Books (Mid-east focus), she praised the Penn BDS conference and its successes in boycotting Israeli products Ahava and Sabra. She admires the PLO and Fatah. Daniel Pipes,[306] upon reviewing her books, stated they are factually wrong, fraught with lies and glaring omissions regarding the UN partition plan in 1948 and Arab attacks on Israel.

Harvard graduate Philip Weiss shares an anti-Zionist blog, Mondoweiss,[307] with Adam Horowitz. Dedicated to the BDS movement, it includes praise of international boycotting of Israeli products.

Anna-Baltzer, host of Jews sans Frontieres, an anti-Zionist blog site, is the national organizer of US Campaign to End the Israeli Occupation, which encompasses over 200 member groups through its partnerships with Friends of Sabeel-North America,[308] one of the driving forces behind a campaign by mainline

Protestant churches to divest from Israel; UFPJ, the anti-war coalition with anti-Israel messages; and the Council for the National Interest (CNI),[309] an anti-Israel organization behind many inflammatory anti-Israel ads in major national newspapers. She has also participated in occupations in Oakland, Wall Street, Chicago, San Francisco, Atlanta, and beyond.

Rebecca Vilkomerson, as covered by The Huffington Post, is executive director of Jewish Voice for Peace.[310] She has spoken at J Street and other anti-Israel groups to divest from TIAA-CREF, financial advisors and international investors with ties to major companies that conduct business with Israel. JVP and New Israel Fund are among the many George Soros-funded organizations. Research uncovered a connection between these groups and Rabbi Richard Jacobs, newly appointed head of the Union for Reform Judaism.

Hannah Schwarzchild, Philadelphia attorney, has a blog site, "Occupied Gaza: News, Comment, and Analysis," on which she responds to the global call for BDS until "Israel ends its illegal occupation of the West Bank, Gaza, and East Jerusalem." As head of American Jews for a Just Peace,[311] the method is to de-shelve Israel products; advocate for enforcement of the US Arms Export Control Act and other US international laws; raise awareness of the Jewish National Fund's tree-planting, and support the planting of olive and fruit trees in "Occupied Palestinian Territories."

Abraham Greenhouse[312] has a blog on which he self-describes as a longtime Palestine solidarity and BDS activist based in New York City, and focuses on theory and practice of Palestine solidarity activism, boycotting, and proper disposal of targeted products (General Electric, Motorola, Ahava cosmetics).

Dr. Dalit Baum, professor of gender studies and world economy at the University of Haifa and Beit College, holds a Ph.D in mathematics. Northeast Intelligence Network[313] describes her as a radical member of the Coalition of Women for Peace, primarily lesbians for jihad, and a member of Soros-funded New Israel Fund. She teaches anti-Israel subversion worldwide, including at UC Santa Cruz and UC Berkeley, where, for one course, her reading material requires students to plan and carry out an activist attack, preferably on Israel.

Ilan Pappe is a radical left Israeli academic who earns a good living lecturing in Europe about the evil of Israel, his place of birth. A Jewish-Israeli historian and professor of history at Exeter (UK) and former senior lecturer in political science at Haifa University, he is the author of Ethnic Cleansing for Palestine.[314] He is also known for fabricating the story of a "massacre" at Tantura, proven in court to have never occurred.

This is not the absolute end of the list — merely some of many, but enough to provide a picture of the evil that infects our schools and our country

BDS — A CASE OF MYTH-TAKEN IDENTITY

Islam fights archaeological and scriptural verification of Israel with repeated, but refuted, myths.

When one's history is so vile and violent that tolerance would be impossible, change it! But how does one change a 14-century history that has already occurred? Conceal it. Lie about it. Accuse others of being offensive if they utter something that bares the truth, that any allusion to Islamic law and history will be considered an insult and crime against their religion. Accuse the media of indignities if they expose any abhorrent Islamic behavior. Replace old textbooks with whitewashed Islam.[315] Create films for PBS to spread the fallacious material. Usurp another's history and take its identity. Lay claim to other religions' prophets and artifacts and rename areas to substantiate new myths.[316] Promote, publicize, and train the youth to relinquish their lives so that they may spread the word "for the greater good."

Muslims annex and destroy places of worship[317] to validate their new myths. Their historical revisionism uses ideology, policy and strategy to completely refute any connection between the original people and their previous homeland, such as of Zoroastrians,[318] Buddhists,[319] Hindus[320] and Coptic Christians,[321] and are now killing Christians[322] and burning churches to the ground in Africa, the Middle East, and Asia, an increase of 309 percent from 2003 to 2010, and destroying artifacts unearthed under the Temple Mount.

As Muslims work to eradicate the history of Israel and the Jewish people, they supplant with a myth of Palestinian antiquity. Despite volumes of scripture from Jewish, Christian, and their own Muslim sources, along with archaeological substantiation; ancient,[323] medieval and modern historical documentation that verifies the Jewish connection[324] to Israel; Muslim leaders, enabled by Western anti-Semites of all stripes, have launched an offensive to deny Israel's legitimacy and existence. New Islamic myths hold that Judaism's Adom, Moses, Kings David and Solomon, and Christianity's Jesus were Muslim, thereby identifying Islam's conquest and occupation as the "recapture and liberation of their lands." In their own words, the Muslim Brotherhood is engaged in a "grand jihad" with the intention of "eliminating and destroying Western civilization from within."

But how can the claims be realistic if their culture bears no resemblance whatsoever to the Law of Moses, the Torah,[325] or the teachings of Jesus?[326] Certainly, Judaism and Christianity do not demand the inhumanity — torture, enslavement, amputation, decapitation, stoning — that Islam exhorts!

As Islamists target the smaller prey, Israel, with the assistance of the larger prey, Western civilization, we remember Winston Churchill's words, "with the hopes that if he feeds the crocodile enough, the crocodile will eat him last," but eat you he will. Denying the past includes re-identifying and renaming areas (Judea and Samaria[327] as the West Bank); claiming Jerusalem as theirs (although Jerusalem is mentioned 792 times in the Hebrew bible[328] and not once in the Koran); adopting antiquities and Jewish tombs as their own; and destroying all evidence of Jewish history,[329] just as they did with the previous cultures.

Myth: The Palestinians are the indigenous people of the area.

Repudiation: The terms Palestine, Philistia and Palestina all refer to defined areas inhabited by different peoples and cultures. There was never a political entity with defined borders and national identity known as Palestine[330] until the British Mandatory Palestine, 1922. Arabs migrated to the area for work; most of today's Arabs cannot trace their ancestry before 150 years ago. Zahir Muhsein (1977) of the PLO said, "Today there is no difference between Jordanians, Palestinians, Syrians and Lebanese. Only for political and tactical reasons do we speak today about the existence of a Palestinian people..." to oppose Zionism.

Myth: Palestinian people were the ancient non-Israelite peoples referenced in the Scriptures in the Holy Land.

Repudiation: The non-Israelites were the Philistines, Moabites, Edomites, Ammonites, Amorites, Arameans, Amalekites, Midianites and Canaanites of ancient Canaan. "Palestinians" did not exist in antiquity and there is no demonstrable connection between the Muslims of today and the ancient non-Israelite people of Canaan.[331] The Israelites were the only ones to leave a record that survived into the modern era, and Egyptians and Mesopotamians left almost nothing.

Myth: Zionists invented ancient Israel history.

Repudiation: Extra-Biblical evidence of Israel's existence is on the Mernephtah stele[332] (Israel Stela), a granite slab created circa 1200 BC, referring to the Egyptian King's victory over an Israelite people in north-central Israel highlands. Continued references to Israel and Judah are seen in Assyrian, Babylonian, Aramaic and Persian texts from the 10th century BCE onward — including Koranic references.

Myth: The Temple Mount, holiest site in Judaism, never existed. Muslims claim it to be the location from which Mohammed ascended during his heavenly flight, and always Muslim.

Repudiation: The Supreme Muslim Council published in 1925 that the Temple Mount dates back to the ancient Israelite kingdom, and is identified beyond dispute with the site of Solomon's Temple. Sheikh Abdul Hadi Palazzi[333] says, that according to the Koran, it existed as a Jewish refuge at the conquest of Jerusalem by Titus, 70 AD.

Myth: Palestinian chief judge, Tayseer Tamimi, alleged that Israelis are excavating and destroying the Al-Aqsa Mosque and injecting chemicals into its foundation to dissolve the rocks.

Repudiation: The Islamic Waqf,[33]4 which exercises religious sovereignty over the Temple Mount, has been carrying out destructive excavations beneath and alongside the Mount since the late 1990s, damaging archaeological artifacts in Solomon's Stables, including First Temple remains, transferring 13,000 tons of excavated material into the municipal garbage dump to erase every sign, remnant and memory of its Jewish past. In the Islamic Sunnah, Mohammed's first bow in prayer was directed at Jerusalem, but because of the Jews' rejection, Mohammed changed the direction to Mecca, thereby nullifying any religious significance that Jerusalem might have had for Islam. Jerusalem's insignificance was changed after Israel's victory in the 1967 Six-Day War as another war strategy. Other archaeological cleansing eradicated Hebrew inscriptions at the tomb of Ezekiel[335] now a mosque; Rachel's tomb[336] in Hebron, now a mosque; Joseph's tomb337 in Nablus was incinerated at the start of the Second Intifada.

Myth: PM Salam Fayyad of the Palestinian Authority declared The Dead Sea Scrolls to be Palestinian de facto because they were found on territory over which Israel held no sovereignty and were stolen by Israel during 1947-48.

Repudiation: The Dead Sea Scrolls[338] are a thousand years older than any Old Testament manuscripts ever found, dating back centuries before the Second Temple (70 BCE). Some have been identified as 19 copies of the Book of Isaiah, 25 copies of Deuteronomy, 30 copies of Psalms — including new ones attributed to King David and Joshua. The Palestinians did not exist before 1967 and therefore had no legal sovereignty over the Dead Sea region where the scrolls were found.

Myth: Another self-hating-Jewish collaborator, Karen Friedemann, falsifying history for the Khaleej Times, wrote that analysis of Jewish DNA indicates males were of Eastern Europe and non-Levantine Southwest Asian origin; females, of Eastern Europeans.

Repudiation: Recent genetic research[339] shows Jews of Israel (except Ethiopians and Indians) trace back to Middle East origin; an NYU study links them to the Near East (Syria, Lebanon, Israel). Researchers from eight countries examined 600,000 genomic markers, and descendants of fourteen Diaspora Jewish communities. The Palestinian assertions are thoroughly contradicted.

For their goal of genocide against Israel to work, they must continue their lies and jihad to "regain" the land. They need to deconstruct Israel; disconnect Jews from Judaism, their homeland and their history; and continue with their fictional Palestinian lie, reflected in their Boycott-Divestment-Sanctions message of deceit, "End the Occupation." We must continue to refute them intensely and forcefully.

"If you tell a lie big enough and keep repeating it, people will eventually come to believe it." — Joseph Goebbels, German Minister of Propaganda, 1933–1945

TEXTBOOK TAQIYYAH

Islamic indoctrination is stealth jihad in today's classroom.

American children are being taught from textbooks that contain revised Islamic history, hatred for Jews and Christians, and respect for sharia law over our Constitution. The jihad (war) strategy of falsehoods, taqiyyah, hides Islam's violent history and distorts the truth for stealth conquest and for the future jihadist generation — our children and grandchildren.

Act! for America[340] created a full report revealing the historical revisionism, omissions, and biases in teaching Islamic doctrine in our schools, the religion, dogmas, their supersessionist role in the world, innate anti-Semitism, and unending war to conquer Western civilization. Islamic instruction is on the increase in accredited schools, teaching hate and diminishing the values of Christianity and Judaism, and are beginning to raise some parental indictments[341] of proselytization and indoctrination. The following samples were taken from treacherous textbooks, authorized for all grades in American classrooms nationwide.

History of Early Islam, Mohammed and Jerusalem
"The Koran tells the story of the Night Journey in which a winged horse took Mohammed to Jerusalem." Teachers Curriculum Institute, History Alive! The Medieval World and Beyond, 2005, p. 87.

Correction: Jerusalem, the holiest city to Judaism since the 10th century BCE[342] is mentioned 823 times in the Hebrew Bible (including 154 times as Zion); and 161 times (including 7 times as Zion) in the Christian Bible; and never mentioned in the Koran. By contrast, Jerusalem had no connection to Islamic prayers, Mohammed, or to its being a cultural or political center. It wasn't until 715 a.d., when the Umayyad sect built a second mosque on the Temple Mount in Jerusalem and called it the Farthest Mosque (Al-Aqsa) that a strategic connection was given to Mohammed, a century after his death, and the Koran.

Mohammed and Medina's Jews
"In Medina, Mohammed displayed impressive leadership skills. He fashioned an agreement that joined his own people with the Arabs and Jews of Medina as a single community. These groups accepted Mohammed as a political leader. As a religious leader, he drew many more converts, who found his message appealing." McDougal Little/Houghton Mifflin, World History — Patterns of Interaction, 2007, p. 265.

Correction: The books revise history with fabricated, deceitful statements. When Mohammed tried and failed to convert the Jews from their centuries-old beliefs, he was outraged, exiled two Jewish tribes and destroyed the third, beheading the men and selling the women and children into slavery. He decreased Judaism's influence by changing prayer direction from Syria (Jerusalem) to Mecca, changed the prayer day from Saturday to Friday, and renounced the Jewish dietary laws (except for the prohibition on pork).

Status and Treatment of Christians and Jews under Islam.
"Sharia law requires Muslim leaders to extend religious tolerance to Christians and Jews." Mc Dougal Littell/Houghton Mifflin, World History — Patterns of Interaction, 2007, p.268;

"The Muslims were extremely tolerant of those they conquered, as long as they were 'People of the Book.' The Muslims allowed Christians and Jews to keep their churches and synagogues and promised them security," Houghton Mifflin, Across the Centuries, 2003, p.66.

Correction: The "Religion of peace and tolerance"[343] is neither. The Koran calls for Muslim submission to Allah, to subdue and oppress people of other religions, inspiring an aggressive history of Islamic conquest. The Arab and Muslim world is obsessed with a virulent, genocidal hate against Jews and gives no rights to Jews within any Muslim-ruled land. The Koran refers to the People of the Book as apes, pigs, dogs, farther astray than cattle, and imposes countless restrictions and obligations on the conquered. Religious minorities diminished under Islam by persecution, discrimination, conversion, or escape. The vanquished were prohibited from building or repairing their houses of worship, from bearing arms, riding horses, wearing shoes in town, giving testimony in court. They were required to wear distinctive clothing and hairstyles to show their inferior position, and either pay a poll tax or relinquish their children to conversion. Tens of millions of conquered Hindus, Buddhists, Baha'i's and atheists faced death when they did not convert. Islamists in Somalia are beheading Christians now.

Jihad and the Early Islamic Conquests: The Meaning of "Jihad"
"An Islamic term that is often misunderstood is jihad. The term means 'to struggle, to do one's best to resist temptation and overcome evil.' Under certain conditions, the struggle to overcome evil may require action. The Koran and Sunna allow self-defense and participation in military conflict but restrict it to the right to defend against aggression and persecution." Houghton Mifflin, Across the Centuries, 2003, p.64.

Correction: Jihad[344] means "struggle" in Arabic, but "holy war" in Islam. The Koran insists on warfare to make Islam and Allah supreme: Surah 9:5: Muslims to "fight and slay the Pagans … seize them, beleaguer them … lie in wait for them …. *Surah 9:29: Muslims to make war upon 'People of the Book'… until they pay the Jizya with willing submission." Muslim armies forcefully invaded, persecuted, and conquered lands that were once non-Islamic.[345] Twenty nations account for over 95 percent of the world's Islamic terrorist activities, with the top four, Iraq, Afghanistan, Pakistan and Somalia, accounting for over 75 percent of the world's total. Armed with weapons and tools of destruction against ancient shrines, Islamists are destroying antiquities in Timbuktu,[346] endangering rare texts on science and mathematics, some dating back to the 13th century. Palestinians are demolishing the understructure of the Temple on the Mount.[347]*

McDougal Littell/Houghton Mifflin, World History — Patterns of Interaction, 2007. In every textbook reviewed, Islamic imperialism is diligently omitted. Issues of Muslim aggression are avoided, and early conquests are presented in a positive or (at worst) neutral manner. Criticism is never expressed or implied. Many textbooks express approval and/or offer false justification for Muslim wars of aggression.

The Role of Women

"The Koran granted women spiritual and social equality with men. Believers, men and women, were to be friends and protectors of one another. Women had the right to the fruits of their work and to own and inherit property. ... Islamic teachings did account for differences between men and women in the family and social order. Both had duties and responsibilities. As in most societies of the time, however, men were dominant in Muslim society... The Koran allowed Muslim men to have more than one wife, but no more than four... Women had the right to freely enter into marriage, but they also had the right of divorce under some circumstances..." Glencoe/McGraw Hill, World History 208, p.203.

Correction: The paragraph is blatantly spurious, as women have no social or legal equality[348] with Muslim men in their society. Under sharia law, women must cover themselves head to toe, sometimes including faces; are subjected to restrictions and legal disabilities; may be genitally castrated; may not leave the house unescorted; may be abused and beaten by their husbands; must accept polygamy and child marriage; may be whipped or stoned to death if men declare them deserving, may be disfigured or killed by her father for his honor. A woman's testimonial value in a court of law, her rights to divorce and own and inherit property are valued at half the man's, often less.

Islam and Slavery: Early Muslim Slave Trade, Muslim Role in the Atlantic Slave Trade, and Slavery Today

"With rising prosperity in the Middle East and Asia after the 700s, slaves came into demand. Some African states exported slaves. Between 1200 and 1500, about 2.5 million Africans were taken across the Sahara or the Red Sea bound for slavery." Houghton-Mifflin, Boston, MA, Across the Centuries, 2003, Unit 3, Chapter 5, Lesson 5.

Correction: Muslim complicity in the slave trade is either denied or the extent and magnitude are vague, yet they continue their fourteen centuries of African enslavement of 140 million, with 80 percent lost en route. Slaves were not exported, but kidnapped and taken by slavers. This is based on port and ship logs and eye-witness reports. The Islamic slave trade[349] began nearly eight centuries before the Atlantic trade. The Mohammedans enslaved two women for every man (sex exploitation and military service), while the Western slave trade, lasting three centuries, enslaved two men for every woman (for agriculture and household employment). Aided by their converts, the Mohammedans institutionalized, refined, and religiously sanctioned their jihadi wars to plunder, slaughter, subjugate, and rape, and legally permitted heinous treatment. The Koran devotes more verses to the right to have sex slaves than it does to daily prayers.

The Holocaust

"The Zionists wanted the land of ancient Israel to be a home for the Jewish people. Many people had been shocked at the end of World War II when they learned about the Holocaust, the deliberate killing of 6 million European Jews in Nazi death camps. As a result, sympathy for the Jewish cause grew. In 1947, the United Nations (UN) resolution proposed that the Palestine mandate should be divided into a Jewish state and an Arab state. The Jews then proclaimed the state of Israel on May 14, 1948." Glencoe/ McGraw Hill, World History, 2008, p.996.

Correction: The material is misleading, omitting historical information about Zionism and the continuous Jewish presence on this land since Biblical times. It implies that the UN resolution resulted from the Holocaust rather from an historic bond and because Britain chose to end the Mandate.

"Zionist leaders worked with the Nazi government to establish training camps in Germany to prepare immigrants for their futures in Palestine." Chelsea House, the Palestinian Authority (a volume of The Creation of the Modern Middle East), 2003, p.82

Correction: This suggests that Jewish Zionists collaborated with and caused the Holocaust against their own people, murdered them to drive them out of Europe to overtake Palestine. Holocaust denier Mahmoud Abbas's The Other Side: The Secret Relationship between Nazism and the Zionist Movement (1983) wrote: "...the Holocaust was 'the greatest of lies' perpetrated by the Jews and, if there was a Holocaust, the Zionists were behind it." This follows a trend of lies and accusations, just as Imam Rauf blamed Jews and Americans for the destruction of the Twin Towers, at times also blaming President Bush and the Mossad.

Correction: The textbooks are insinuating Islam into Western culture, using taqiyyah — their own misinformation for their own purposes. Jihad is omitted or incorrectly defined; women's rights are mischaracterized; the slave trade is attributed to Europeans;[350] Mohammed's character is elevated above accepted historical facts; Muslims are painted as peaceful or victims instead of the vicious conquerors they are, with their invasions and imperialism minimized; Islam's historical tolerance of Christians and Jews is false; the application of sharia law to non-Muslims is altered; the Crusades narrative is false. The British Mandate and UN Resolution 181 are omitted, as are the Peel Commission and the Arab rejection of every peace proposal. The historical development of the three major religions is chronologically revised, with Islam presented as best. Islam's new claims are that Moses and Jesus were Palestinians. Israel's origin is attributed to world guilt, thereby completely discrediting the Jewish people's ancient ties to their homeland and the creation of the Jewish State, and maps often exclude the Jewish State. The Arabs' refusal to accept partition is omitted; claims of terrorist organizations' roots in the Arab-Israeli conflict are inaccurate, and much more.[351] The books portray Muslims as superior to Jews, Christians, and the United States, and seduce the students away from their duty to their own country, their Constitution, and proper conduct. The books prevent critical thinking, prevent freedom of speech, and they are seditious.

Correction: These textbooks are produced by Chelsea House; Glencoe/McGraw Hill, Holt, Rinehart and Winston; McDougal Littell, Pearson Prentice Hall, and Teachers' Curriculum Institute. Citizens and school boards must reveal the schools, deactivate their accreditation, stop the Saudi funding, and immediately replace these books with new to reclaim the minds of our children.

In addition, new relations are established between Arab groups and US universities, such as the recent connection between Northeast Ohio Consortium for Middle East Studies (NOCMES) and several Ohio universities, Oberlin College and private girls' Hathaway Brown, all funded by the Carnegie Corporation and a Muslim Brotherhood affiliate, and certain American public schools are mandating Arabic studies in lower grades.[352] Financed by Qatar Foundation International (QFI) and the Global Language Project, and affiliated with the Research Center for Islamic Legislation and Ethics, all Muslim Brotherhood affiliates, the program is an immersion in Islam[353] for American children. Bolstered by Channel One Network,[354] it reaches far beyond mere language. Another recent report publicized the more than 120 Islamic Fundamentalist Gulen charter schools[355] throughout the US. New teachings include that Moses and Jesus[356] were Palestinians.

Post script: On July 5, 2012, Rep. Keith Ellison (D-MN) and Rep. Andre Carson (D-IN), both Muslims, told their audience at the -ICDNA-MAS convention (Islamic Circle of North America) that madrassas should be the paradigm of American schools. The goal of the ICNA and 29 other like-minded organizations, according to a 1991 Muslim Brotherhood document, is: "...their work in America is a kind of grand jihad in eliminating and destroying the Western civilization from within and 'sabotaging' its miserable house by their hands ... so that ... God's religion [Islam] is made victorious over all other religions."

Islam is at war with America and we are in the throes of sharia compliance, endangering the very existence of our nation. As American citizens, we must be sure that our schools do not now and never shall use this material as their textbooks.

BROKEN COLLEGE – OFFICE OF SUBMISSIONS

The college campus has become an Islamic base with BDS its first strategy.

Brooklyn College's Political Science Department was planning a BDS Movement against Israel in February 2013.[357] How could sharia law, so antithetical to our democratic principles and the school's own mission statement,[358] be accepted at the beautiful institution I attended so long ago?

How does spewing bigotry and propaganda against the only democratic country in the Middle East, by representatives of Islam who rally and burn our flags, conform to the educational welfare of BC students, alumni, and the community? How does Islamic intolerance on campus lead to outstanding achievements and the furtherance of education? How does permitting the accusatory lies against Israel, the only country in the region that does NOT practice apartheid, further democratic values? They clearly contradict the learning environment as they rationalize their irresponsibility and treachery to so many.

Dr. Martin Luther King, Jr., stated, "The purpose of education is not just a tool to enable people to trample over the masses. Education is an opportunity to learn, to develop skills, and to improve themselves and society." Can we expect to improve our society by closing the minds of our students?

How can the school ignore the attempt to spread Islamic ideology[359] worldwide, as Islam's 1400-year history is replete with conquest, conversion, enslavement, usurpation, and slaughter of hundreds of millions of people in the Middle East? The current Muslim countries were once other cultures. While it may appear that these Islamists are here to discuss only one issue, they seek to conquer the sovereign nation of Israel, to deny her 4,000-year history, destroy her economy, and intimidate and manipulate non-Muslims into joining their war. BDS is a war strategy to master the minds of Americans who will then join the fray in delegitimizing Israel so that the Muslims may then absorb the 8,000 square miles into their Islamic caliphate, while their counterparts are killing and overcoming the citizenry of Africa, France, Spain, England, Sweden, Norway, and the Benelux countries.

The administration is not absolved because they do not preach; it is sufficient to grant permission to such an event on college property. Whether of their own volition, or the PoliSci Department submits to persuasion or riots, it is complicit. If this rally is not held as a bona fide debate with equal time for both sides (sans the infamous Student Union disturbances and interruptions[360]), then it is not constructive dialogue or an equal exchange of ideas. If there is no attempt to instruct the students about the true history of Islam and Judaism, the true rise to power of Islam with full disclosure of sharia law and the true history of Israel and its laws, then there is no free exploration of ideas. Instead of academic freedom, there is tolerance of intolerance. Where there is one group that must acquiesce to the other, the school no longer represents liberty and security for its students; rather it allows mob rule and submission. If the president has lost control over her constituents and the administration cannot govern or adhere to its mission (a constitution), then the school has surrendered to totalitarianism.

Further, if this Islamic evil is permitted to flourish unimpeded, the College will be guilty of accepting tuition under false pretenses and failing the students who attend this institution in search of an honest education in a safe environment. Rather, BC is conspiratorially promoting the will of the Muslim Brotherhood[361] and permitting the destruction and replacement of our culture by theirs.

The Islamic catchphrase is "First comes Saturday, then comes Sunday." Their ruse is apartheid (non-existent in Israel) and "settlements" (housing for Israel's people in Israel's capital); their dogma is jihad. If the school bends to Islam now, how long before the Muslims demand all of New York for Islam – followed by all the United States? Recall their continuing determination for Ground Zero[362] and there are now YouTube videos showing Muslims' contentions that they preceded Christopher Columbus, thereby laying claim to the entirety of America as they have already done in the Middle East.

By permitting the BDS groups[363] to indoctrinate the students on campus, they facilitate the work of illegal associations and terror organizations, such as the Council of National and Islamic Forces in Palestine, a coordinating forum for all terror organizations in their war against Israel. This includes Hamas; the Popular Front for the Liberation of Palestine; the Democratic Front for the Liberation of Palestine; the Palestinian Liberation Front, acknowledged a terrorist organization by the U.S., EU, and Canada; and Palestinian Islamic Jihad, acknowledged a terrorist organization by the U.S., EU, UK, Japan, Australia, and Canada; and many others that do overseas fundraising and money laundering for the Muslim Brotherhood and Al Qaeda figures here and abroad.

BDS is economic warfare[364] and the campus has become a battlefield. When students continue to level false accusations against Israel, slander and propaganda are the weapons on the frontline. Brooklyn College is failing in the teaching process and allowing students to fester in the closed environment of Islam. I implore President Karen Gould to implement a pre-emptive strategy to uphold

Judeo-Christian values, and not permit an Islamist community with all the hate and violence for which Islam is known.

OBERLIN'S ONUS

In lockstep with the Leftist ideology's acceptance of Islam, Hillel fails its Jewish students and humanity.

Oberlin's Hillel Rabbi Shimon Brand's response to the Palestinian students' boycott against the American companies that do business with Israel ("Oberlin rabbi downplays divestment resolution impact," Cleveland Jewish News, May 10, 2013) was feeble. He acquiesced to sharia law, and trivialized, rather than dealt with, the bigotry and propaganda spewed against the only democracy in the Middle East.

How does Islamic intolerance on campus lead to outstanding leadership and organization skills, as noted in Oberlin's mission statement? How do their lies contribute to teaching democratic values? The school's allowing the Islamic students to damage the learning environment with their irresponsibility and bigotry is treachery to Oberlin, to Israel, and to our own republic; the will of the most violent culture on earth was permitted to spread throughout the school and into the community. Contrary to the rabbi's dismissive statement, this is of great concern because it is merely the bourgeoning continuation of the Islamic conquest begun in 623 a.d., when Mohammed enslaved and slaughtered Jewish and Christian inhabitants of Mecca and Medina, and why Jews are fleeing Europe yet again.

Islam is a socio-political concept camouflaged as a religion, and the Islamic false narrative of victimhood has been allowed to gain momentum; the entire school is complicit. The truth is the Arabs displaced the Jews — a hidden, major Arab migration (now recognized as hijrah[365]), and immigration took place into areas settled by Jews in pre-Israel Palestine. Most of the Arab refugees had foreign roots, and the number of Arab refugees from Israel in 1948 were fewer than the number of Jewish refugees who fled persecution from Arab lands. Oberlin and Hillel should have conducted a seminar for Jewish students — for all students — because Christians will suffer equally if Islam is permitted to flourish in America. The Muslim mantra is, "First the Saturday people, then the Sunday people."

The college should be obliged to teach the truth — inform the uninformed that Israel became a nation in 1312 BCE, and a modern State in 1948. In 1964, the PLO[366] renamed the Israeli Arabs "Palestinians" to be a thorn in the side of the Jews, to provide a manipulative link to the territory, in order to steal the land that they could not win militarily.

The land has been Jewish since 1272 BCE, but Jordan's for only 19 years, with Jordan never disputing Jerusalem's heritage. Founded by King David, Jerusalem is mentioned more than 700 times in the Jewish Holy Scriptures, but not once in the Koran, and Mohammed was never there. Sixty-eight percent of the Arabs fled on orders of their armed forces, without ever having seen an Israeli soldier. And the Arabs who stayed at Israel's invitation, now 20.4 percent of Israel's population, enjoy a far better life than their brethren ever have in the despotic Islamic countries.

Still, Israel relinquished the West Bank to Palestinians who, rather than forming a viable, peaceful state, turned it into massive launching pads, using their own women and children as shields to increase the casualties and evoke sympathy — again, their perverse victimhood strategy. They have never attempted to establish their autonomy, even when the land was barren and population sparse, and never showed signs of wanting peace. When given a chance at self-governance, the Arabs throughout the Middle East choose sharia over democracy — obedience to strict, oppressive Islamic law, violence. They have destroyed Jewish and other holy sites, and continue their rocket fire and bombs against Israeli citizens even after announcing a truce.

The students should also know that under Israeli "occupation" (which was discontinued with the Oslo Accords in 1993), Palestinian life improved greatly — with modernized infrastructure, increased manufacturing facilities, and seven new universities. Israelis taught them modern agriculture, set up medical programs with more than a hundred health clinics, instituted freedom of the press, and introduced a Palestinian administration heretofore unknown to these people who originated from oppressive Egypt, Lebanon, Syria, Jordan, and Yemen. Unemployment fell, birth rate survival increased, life expectancy soared, and the population nearly doubled from 1967 to 1993. The West Bank and Gaza became the fourth fastest-growing economy in the world, ahead of such wonders as Singapore, Hong Kong, and Korea, and ahead of Israel itself.

On May 22, 2013, the official PA daily news reported that PA Minister of Health, Hani Abdeen, visited Israel's Hadassah Hospital in Jerusalem and the Palestinian children who represent 30 percent of the child patients. The hospital also has a special program to train Palestinian doctors to treat cancer among children. On the other hand, Palestinian leadership continues to proclaim they will have a Jew-free state.

One should also note that Palestinians receive more funding from the UN than any other peoples, with no oversight for distribution. Severe mismanagement of funds contributes more to deadly violence than to humanitarian needs. Funds for 700,000 Arabs in 1948 has now increased to billions of dollars to support millions of their descendants!

Students for a Free Palestine are terrorists doing the work of the Muslim Brotherhood and advocating for Israel's destruction. Muslims have been the most persistent and pernicious people on the planet for fourteen centuries, with an imperialist belief system designed to destroy Western civilization and progress and to force the masses into obeying Islamist ideology. Their holy books are devoid of all morality, conscience and compassion, and contain concepts that force their own to sacrifice their humanity in order to commit evil for aggressive expansion. Not only do they slaughter, but they burn Christians in their African churches, amputate limbs, decapitate victims, kidnap toddlers for camel races,[367] condone adult males' engaging in sex with prepubescent boys, toddlers, and with newly deceased wives.[368] One jihadist was recently seen on YouTube eating the heart pulled from his dead victim. Such is the culture of Islam, the culture to which Oberlin is capitulating. This is Jihad.

Of the eight types of Jihad identified, the following two apply to Oberlin:

Intellectual Jihad, propagandizing to spread acceptance of Islam. Speakers in universities, libraries; interruptions and filibustering; forcing boycotts against Israel's books and products; and Religious Jihad (using freedom of religion and tolerant religious leaders to advance Islam) while other religions are forbidden theirs. Destroying antiquities; building mosques.

These students should be focusing on freedom for Muslim women who are victims of one of the most hideous barbaric rituals — female genital mutilation. Treated no better than animals, these *untermenschen*[369] are enshrouded and forever demoralized and deprived of education, have no equality to men under the law, play no formal role in government, may take no action against spousal abuse or other forms of gender violence, and may receive no medical treatment without a man's consent. Women may not undertake domestic or foreign travel alone, qualify for inheritance equal to her brothers, expect a monogamous marriage to a man of her own choosing, keep her children in the event of divorce or widowhood, drive a car or sit in the front seat, among the many other restrictions.

What does Hillel propose now that we can no longer dismiss the boycott as a simple, inconsequential matter? Our schools and students have been inducted into the Islamic war against Israel and the West, whether we wanted it or not. We have already been invaded, and there is too much history behind us to assume that we will be immune to Islam's history of intolerance, slavery, war, conquest and destruction. If we allow Islam to take control, we forfeit our religion, independence, our country and our civilization.

CARY'S CANARDS

A propagandist professor supports and teaches the falsehoods of a warring nation.

Cary Karacas, assistant professor of political science, economics and philosophy, teaches global and regional studies at the College of Staten Island. His course deals with "Palestine and Israel," a propagandist title using fallacious terminology to provide credibility. The term "Palestine," which never appears in the New Testament, existed only as a Roman slur to taunt the Israelites whose enemy was the Philistines,[370] an Aegean people. Today's "Palestinians" are the Syrians, Jordanians, Lebanese, Yemenites, and Egyptians who sought work in the new, growing nation of Israel, beginning in the late 1800s. Genetic analysis suggests that most of the area's Muslims, including Israel's Arab citizens, are also descendants of captured Christians and Jews.[371]

The exchange of facts and responsibility is a moral inversion of events in the Middle East, a technique that Karacas favors, as his name is also tied to "an ongoing project to build a digital archive dedicated to the international dissemination of information about America's air raids[372] against Japan." Is Karacas dismissing Japan's first attack on Pearl Harbor, in 1941, to discredit the American raids that brought Japan's final surrender in 1945?

There are many paths to Islamic world domination, provided in both the Koran and the 1928 Muslim Brotherhood doctrine, espoused by imams and teachers in the classroom. When five Arab armies lost their aggressive 1967 war against Israel, they took the name, Palestinian, to establish a false identity and storyline of victimhood. In the case of America, when rioting, violence and bloodshed (such as used in Africa and Europe) would be less effective due to America's immense area and population, the strategy is to vilify the Jews to the impressionable students and their uninformed parents; the ever-present bigots would produce the needed attitudes and pressure. Working in tandem with the Obama administration that seeks Islamic favor and the complicit mainstream media are the schools, the teaching staff, and severely biased, pro-Islamic Common Core textbooks.

So, Karacas teaches that Jews are terrorists and colonialists and the Arabs are victims of aggression. After spending a considerable sum of money and time for their education, the students are being deceived and robbed for goods (education) not delivered.

Judaism has its roots in the land since the Creation, shown by the Jewish calendar to be 5774 years ago — 3,671 years before Christianity and about 4,361 years before Islam. Israel became a kingdom with Jerusalem its capital and with an ancestral religion. Jews were the first people to reject idolatry, sacrifice and polytheism, and to introduce monotheism and moral codes (the Torah's commandments), featuring logic and order, ethics, justice, equality before the law, loving-kindness, social welfare, ideals of peace, political freedom, and the dignity of humankind.

The "Promised Land"[373] was deeded to the Jewish people in the Bible 3,200 years ago. The land designated is very specific, verifying that Israel is neither colonialist nor opportunistic. It is therefore ludicrous to label Jews colonialists for demanding to keep their only Jewish state in the world, when Muslims have 22 formal Islamic states, are a majority in 49, and continue to invade and persecute the nationals of Europe, Africa, Asia and the Americas.

The Jews are recognized as the indigenous people of the area, reinforced by Article 80 of the UN charter, and have been a continuous presence on the land and a majority since the 1800s. Jerusalem appears 2,834 times in the Bible, but not once in the Koran, and Mohammed's "ascent to heaven" was added to counterfeit the Arab cause for world domination. Britain and the League of Nations created the Palestine Mandate as the Jewish national homeland, 80 percent of which was acquiesced to the rioting, violent Arabs, and another 22 percent later ceded to form what they now call the West Bank and Gaza. The Palestinian state was established in 1922, and it was called Transjordan.

The Jews thrived, built and created a rich culture. Syria's Bashar al-Assad's grandfather al-Alawi's notable letter in 1936 said, "Those good Jews brought... prosperity over Palestine without damage to anyone or taking anything by force." What have the Palestinians brought to Western civilization besides terrorism and carnage? And what have the Arabs brought to themselves but subjugation, unrest, destruction and death? Even today, the number of Muslim-on-Muslim deaths in Egypt and Syria is staggering.

The Jews won the land during Israel's defensive wars of 1948 and 1967, so using the term "occupied" for the Jews, but not for all the conquered once-non-Islamic countries, is immoral. The marauding Muslims usurped nearly the entire continent, destroying the cultures and the people — Zoroastrians, Buddhists, Pharoahans, Sumerians, Babylonians, Assyrians, Copts, etc., and are continuing their deadly destruction through Northern Nigeria (burning people in their churches), Vietnam, Burma, Indonesia, Egypt, Iraqi Kurdistan, India. They have also invaded, occupied, and are slowly changing the faces of Sweden, England, Germany, Spain, Greece, Turkey, Belgium, Norway, and the Americas, but are not termed "occupier?"

If Karacas claims Jews must return land they won, especially in a defensive war, then he must also demand that Muslims return all the land they won over 1400 years of expansionism and bloodshed. Writing to the College of State Island yields no reply, and the propaganda continues. "The philosophy of the schoolroom in one generation will be the philosophy of government in the next," – Abraham Lincoln.

ASA: ACADEMICS SURRENDER TO ALLAH

American Studies Association abandons integrity for Islamic jihad against Israel.

Five thousand members of the American Studies Association (ASA) would be better identified as Academics Surrender to Allah (ASA) because they have declared jihad against the State of Israel. ASA president Curtis Marez admitted that there are worse countries than Israel but, he added, "One has to start somewhere!" Imagine Marez as part of a firefighting team, sent to extinguish a blaze in Southern California but starting in North Dakota because he has to start "somewhere." So, they're boycotting Israel's universities, which are also attended by Palestinian students, rather than boycotting Palestinian universities that were established by Israel but prohibited to Jewish students — perhaps a study in reverse psychology.

If you ever wondered how Nazism took hold in Germany or if the masses really knew what was happening in their country, look at America now. There have already been 50 court cases in 23 states decided according to Islamic, not American, sharia and the actions of the ASA clearly expose the many judges who are willingly sharia-compliant, eager to abandon civility, justice, and integrity, to join forces with tyranny. Just in: Another 1,000 academics have joined the crusade*.

Israel's universities are listed among the top 100 world universities[374] in mathematics, physics, chemistry, computer sciences and economics, with the world's highest per-capita rate of university degrees and the world's highest ratio per capita of scientists, technicians, PhDs, and physicians, with contributions in every aspect of life, while being only .02 percent of the world's population. Israel contributes to advances in water shortage, agriculture, space travel, solar power, DNA, and more, for all the world's benefit. Her advanced methods of Intelligence benefit America's security.[375]

Despite attacks from warring Arab neighbors, Israel is the only vibrant, liberal democracy in the Middle East, with the highest average living standards and per-capita income, exceeding the UK. Israel is the largest immigrant-absorption nation on earth relative to its population, and a trustworthy first responder to countries in peril caused by natural disasters. Foremost in humanitarian program,[376] there was marked improvement when Israel entered Gaza — the Arab population rose from 360,000 in There was progress in social welfare. The Palestinian mortality rates fell by more than two-thirds between 1970 and 1990; life expectancy rose from 48 years in 1967 to 72 years in 2000 (when the average for Arabs in the Middle East and North Africa was 68). The infant-mortality rate[377] went from 60 per 1,000 live births in 1968 to 15 per 1,000 in 2000. Under Israel's inoculation program, childhood diseases of polio, whooping cough, tetanus and measles were eradicated. The Palestinians' standard of living increased with electricity, running water, gas ranges for cooking, refrigerators, TVs, and cars. Such was Israel's brutal occupation.

On the other hand, Arabs as a whole, and Palestinians in particular offer no scholastic advantage, so we must conclude that the ASA is guided by other advancements — the "cutting edge" by the People of the Sword. Palestinians must prolong their false victimization to further demonize Israel for the purpose of delegitimizing, weakening, and destroying Israel altogether.

Israel is not an apartheid nation with its Arab population of 20.7 percent,[378] despite Arabic rhetoric, so the only conclusion for boycott is unabashed Jew-hatred. These professors were schooled by leftist instructors to hate the West, democracy, organized religions like Christianity and Judaism, and are discontinuing school study of our Founding Fathers and documents, destroying our Constitution and Bill of Rights, our proud history and, indeed, the exceptionalism that President Obama denounces.

The ASA claims a commitment to social justice, against racism, while aware that Israel is home to every nationality and religion, and Palestinians welcome no such mix of people and brutally mistreat their own women[379] and children. In the name of equality, the group acts to invalidate the indigenous Jews[380] of the land, and support the usurpers who lay claim to land that was never theirs; they teach their children to hate and detonate themselves for the sake of land acquisition. With demonic inspiration, the ASA withholds condemnation against Muslims who kill Christians and Jews worldwide, slowly diminish the rights of Jewish students nationwide, and who would eagerly demolish our American republic.

They are fascists who have already implemented the use of Common Core textbooks to encourage the hatred of Jews, Israel and the American values derived from Judaism centuries ago.[381] The first monotheistic belief system to appear when barbarism reigned, the Jews introduced 613 Commandments[382] of morality and ethics, creating and offering a civilized society of respect for all life and property to those willing to accept it. Yet those who uphold these laws are the first victims and scapegoats of tyranny — the despised conscience of the world.

The ASA prefers totalitarianism, assuming they will be in the surviving top strata to rule the others; Jews and Christians are as unwelcome as the cultures that disappeared before them. The ASA upholds the rights of Islamic jihadis who wage war against Afghanistan, Algeria, Bangladesh, Bosnia, Congo, Cote d'Ivoire, Cyprus, East Timor, Egypt, India, Indonesia, Iran's Kurdistan Arabs, Kashmir, Kazakhstan, Kosovo, Kurdistan, Libya, Macedonia, Christian Maronites of Lebanon, Middle East, Nigeria, Pakistan, Philippines, Russia-Chechnya, Somalia, Sudan, Syria, Tajikistan, Thailand, Tunisia, Uganda, Uzbekistan and Yemen. They endorse the rights of the Muslim Student Union to intimidate, threaten and harm the Jewish students on university campuses. They employ the Common Core textbooks and their revisionist history, where Islam is whitewashed with a kindness quite alien to their culture, and credited with the achievements of others. How contrary it is for Muslims to be recognized for inventing the Arabic numerals[383] originated by the Hindus, to be held blameless for the death of 890 million innocents over 1400 years, and for their history Judaism has been in the crosshairs of many warring civilizations, but was never the only one. Just as no nation was considered safe from Hitler, no nation will ever be safe from Islam, yet the boycotts are against the Jews, the first begun by Arabs before Israel became a nation. If we don't band together to recapture our nation and fight the forces that produce groups like the ASA, we will all fall separately.

Criticism was issued by the American Association of University Professors, the Anti-Defamation League, the Simon Wiesenthal Center, Zionist Organization of America, American Jewish Committee, Scholars for Peace in the Middle East and StandWithUs. Penn State Harrisburg and Brandeis have officially withdrawn their membership from the ASA.

COMMUNIZING COMMON CORE

Common Core closes the education gap by reducing expectations, limiting literary and cultural knowledge, and de-emphasizing Americanism, and more — in the name of social engineering.

Patrick O'Donnell's Plain Dealer articles of April 17 and 20, regarding Common Core, stated that our educators were surprised that Common Core tests were tough. The people in positions of trust accepted the new curriculum before evaluating the complete package and its potential damage because the payoffs far outweighed all other considerations, including the children's maturity levels and welfare.

Despite the Constitution's Tenth Amendment that prohibits a federally controlled education system, President Obama's American Recovery and Reinvestment Act[384] (stimulus package) bribed cash-strapped states with $4.35 billion; the Bill Gates Foundation added $200 million more, and states will be heavily taxed (Ohio: $10 million) to cover operational costs of this program that spells disaster.

A research company, Achieve, Inc., and Gates selected non-academic people to design the standards, without the input of educators, parents, and professionals in the disciplines. A 24-member team headed by David Coleman, who also lacked experience with English instruction, signed a non-disclosure agreement, keeping parents and school boards entirely in the dark. The standards, although accepted, violated three federal laws — Elementary and Secondary Education Act (1965), General Education Provisions Act, and Department of Education Organization Act.

Common Core mandates prohibit teachers from lecturing for more than 15 minutes per day per subject! This "Type #2" agenda is student-centered learning, where the teacher is reduced to the role of facilitator, unable to provide history, purpose, and background for comprehension. How does one grasp a Constitutional Amendment without its foundation and purpose — or find the essence of a speech without the events that inspired it? America's founding, exceptionalism and achievements are de-emphasized; Islam is whitewashed and accentuated in great detail.

The program is designed to close the education gap by reducing expectations, and emphasizing skills over literary or cultural knowledge. Their perception of college readiness is not academic preparation but abundant test taking that takes time from learning, creativity, and developing the imagination. Great literature and fiction are sacrificed for new sexualized novels that emphasize social activism. Fifty percent of the reading material, comprised of informational texts and instructional manuals, discourage the desire to read.

The test material given for Test I, Grade 3, deals with trickery, disappointment, feelings, social engineering — not resourcefulness, achievement, success. Test 3, Grade 11, deals with aloneness, divisiveness, social issues, and the errors in word usage and punctuation confirm the carelessness that also permeates the history books. Imagine being tested about the Declaration of Independence and speech by Patrick Henry before disambiguating, studying and analyzing them. A brief video would have no value.

English and Math courses contain social concerns. Students are being taught what to think — that America is a nation of bigots, poverty-creating capitalists, intolerant war-mongering imperialists, anti-immigrants; and segregating, discriminating, disenfranchising racists; and that they should want big government that relies on redistribution of wealth, globalization, etc. Key concepts of America are negative or openly hostile.

The math places students more than two years behind their international peers by eighth grade. High school students will have to pass college exams on faulty information. Reform math is fracturing our society — teachers cannot help the parents and parents cannot help the children with homework, leading to frustration and anger. Our education establishment is alienating them from a desire to learn.

Highly degreed and qualified professionals, Dr. Sandra Stotsky[385] (developer of one of the country's strongest sets of academic standards for K-12 students and the strongest academic standards and licensure tests for prospective teachers), Stanford University professor Dr. James Milgram[386] and New York University professor Jonathan Goodman[387] refused to sign off on Common Core, citing the damage to education posed by its methods.

Microsoft and Achieve's State Longitudinal Database System will capture, analyze, and use students' personal and confidential data from preschool through employment. Through functional magnetic resonance imaging, skin-sensitive equipment and cameras that judge facial expressions and posture, data about student frustration, motivation, confidence, boredom and fatigue, plus private family statistics will be available for workforce development in this German model system. Does this sound like a democratic government or an all-powerful tyrannical regime?

Pearson publishers are responsible for the textbooks and tests, apps, international media, business information, and more, although their books are shoddily assembled and written. Most notable are the history textbooks that present history out of time context, a smokescreen for what has been intentionally excluded. Our high school students are being deceived and brainwashed so that they will be intellectually incapable of dealing with the subversive threat to our country coming from the Muslim Brotherhood and its supporters in the American Islamic community and the Left.

Today's students will be tomorrow's teachers and leaders, obedient to the state, robbed of their freedom to thrive. Common Core is destructive, and it is up to the parents to recapture our educational system from the grip of the current Obama administration.

ASA, AN ANTI-SEMITIC ORGANIZATION

They have chosen socialism and Islamism over democracy and our Judeo-Christian values.

The American Studies Association (ASA), allegedly a scholarly association ("our nation's oldest [1951] and largest association devoted to the interdisciplinary study of American culture and history"), has abandoned its scholarly pursuits for the boycott of Israel, and banned Israel's university representatives' participation in a forthcoming academic conference at a California hotel/resort. The hotel chain subsequently declined. Why would a once-respectable organization depart from its stated mission, and take on a jihadist agenda? Moral bankruptcy. Clearly and definitively anti-Semitic, they have chosen Marxism and Islamism over democracy, virtue, and veracity.

Jihadi professors want to isolate Israel for the "Palestinian cause," a deflection and façade for the greater global threat of Islamic world domination. A blood-thirsty lot, Mahmoud Abbas has openly called for the murder of Israelis. The reign of terror has begun on the Jewish state, just as it is underway in other countries. This is the group that ASA supports; this is the group that ASA has become. They will boycott Israel's universities, which are also attended by Palestinian students, but not Palestinian universities, which were instituted by Israel but prohibited to Jewish students.

All but the comatose know that Israel has won more Nobel prizes per capita than any other country; has more laureates in real numbers than China, Mexico and Spain; publishes more books translated from other languages, and Israelis read more books per capita than any other nation. She leads with the number of scientists and technicians in the work force (exceeding the U.S. by 63%) and most physicians and engineers per capita, ranks third in producing the most scientific papers per capita, and her Israel's contributions to medicine and agriculture[388] are beyond miraculous. With Israel's dedication to ethics and improving life, she appears as the moral conscience that Islam and ASA resent. The association has chosen tyranny over democracy, using Palestinian propaganda to trash Israel, while also harming America and the entire non-Islamic world. We are all Islam's despised infidels.

An estimated nine million Christians martyred by Islam,[389] another 50 million killed in jihad,[390] and still another million African Christians killed in the 20th century, total 60 million Christians. Between the 8th and 19th century, 10 to 18 million Africans were brought by Arab slave traders from Africa. An estimated 80 million Hindus were killed in 500 years of jihad against India,[391] counted among the world's greatest genocides. India's mountains, Hindu Kush,[392] is called "funeral pyre," where Indian women first self-immolated to escape Muslim rape and enslavement. Tamerlane,[393] one of the most violent jihadis (and after whom a Boston Marathon bomber brother was named), devastated 700 villages, killing 90,000 Indians in a day, enslaving 180,000. His son destroyed temples, forced conversions, and built two towers of human heads "so high that men on horseback could not see over them."

About 10 million Buddhists were killed[394] by jihadis in Turkey, Afghanistan, along the Silk Route, and in India.

Jihad was 100 percent effective against Jews in Arabia. Lacking political power, Jews submitted to dhimmihood, and Persian Zoroastrians were all but destroyed.

After constant wars between Persia and the Byzantine Empire, followed by the Black Plague, Islam's apostles invaded and slaughtered Christians and Persians, destroyed Egypt (the breadbasket) and Syria (heart of the law), and annihilated all classical civilization in Europe within 25 years. Over 1400 years, Muslims brutally killed 890 million, new estimates by historians. Since 9/11, this "religion of peace" has carried out close to 25,000 deadly terrorist attacks against five religions (the number, 32,454, an update for January 2018)

In every measurable area of civilization, the Islamic world finishes last or next to last, but their people among the highest in illiteracy and in producing terrorists, suffering and bloodshed. Islam glorifies memorizing the 7th century Koran and poverty, which go hand in hand with backwardness, frustration, jealousy, anger and war, with which ASA is seeking "deeper engagement." And, because the Koran teaches that Islam is superior to all other religions, the Muslims must annihilate those who stand between them and their supremacy — advanced Western civilization — whether by sword or social, political, and economic destruction for conquest.

Islamists obstructed early Mediterranean commerce, forcing traders to the Silk Road, increasing expenses, hardships, and travel time by months; and continued to kidnap, rape and behead, to intimidate and frighten, and enforce Islamic sharia law. Today, they use less violent means to demand "religious" accommodations, infiltrate government and academia, boycott to foil international cooperation and tourism, create no-go zones to control cities, but violence as needed. The war against Israel is most publicized, but Sweden also holds the world record for number of rapes and school fires set by Muslims — one per day. They are versatile, determined and persuasive to entice the unprincipled.

In her incoming speech, ASA's president, Lisa Duggan, identified her Neo-Marxist radicalism, citing "American imperialism" as their focus. Novelist Giannina Braschi, mocking the 9/11 attacks, advocated holy war against capitalism and individual achievement. They deliberately displayed their moral impoverishment when abandoning their founding tenets, and of 5,000 members, 2,200 libraries and other institutions, only 200+ universities rejected the bigoted boycott of Israeli and US scholars. Only four universities withdrew their membership. Jihadi professors and academicians are collaborating with pure lethal hatred against Israel (national origin) and Jews (religion). This is not a Palestinian issue, but a religious war, with a national and international campaign against Jews, as existed in Germany, 1933 — to be followed by books banned or burned. ASA should be deprived of its tax-exempt non-profit 501(c) organization, since it has become a political advocacy group.

This is religious war, jihad against "infidels" by other non-Islamic "infidels." Duggan does not address Islam's legacy to the world, the history of brutality that changed entire continents, North Africa and the Middle East, from Christian to Muslim. Rather, she has joined the (at least) 63,035,000 jihadis[395] responsible for financing the Munich Massacre of Israeli Olympic athletes,[396] refusing the many peace efforts; inciting riots, throwing stones, butchering innocents,[397] using Muslim human shields to increase their blame tactics; the terror tunnels,[398] and the current car and knife intifada.[399] Duggan has joined the Muslims who have invented nothing, created nothing, and given nothing to civilization's betterment.

Today, ISIS (wealthiest terror group) demolishes shrines, temples and tombs, relishes decapitation and burning people alive. Hamas (second wealthiest group) uses Muslim children to dig tunnels through which they will reach and slaughter Israeli children (and have been killed during the construction). Boko Haram kidnaps, rapes, and enslaves innocent young girls for profit in the slave trade. Palestinians are malevolently slaughtering Israelis and firing rockets from occupied schools and hospitals.[400] And ASA is deliberately showing solidarity in religious discrimination with these savages for a "greater Islam." Muslim Brotherhood operative Mohammed Akram and the Brotherhood knew to appeal to different strata of the American population; advancement of the Islamic movement includes, among many others, the world of education. Ties exist between the Muslim Brotherhood, ASA, and Georgetown University professor and member of President Obama's National Advisory Board, Dr. John Esposito.

"Show me just what Mohammad brought that was new and there you will find things only evil and inhuman, such as his command to spread by the sword the faith that he preached." — Manuel II Palaiologos, one of the last Christian rulers before the fall of Constantinople to the Muslim Ottoman Empire.

"Israel has proved that for fifty years, its real power is in its democracy, guarding the rights of citizens, applying laws to the rich and poor, the big and small ... and in the participation of the nation in the development of institutions according to ability and efficiency..." —Columnist Dr. Talal Al-Shareef, Palestinian newspaper Al Quds, May 27, 1999.

PURGING ISRAEL FOR PROFIT

Profit leads Harper Collins to removing Israel from Geography Atlas.

Collins Bartholomew, the map-publishing company of world-leading publishers Harper Collins, removed Israel from its Geography Atlas to accommodate "local preferences." To wit, in the interest of selling maps to an enemy that hopes to wipe

America off the map, the company was willing to erase Israel, as well as dispense with scruples, integrity, conscience, ethics, and credibility. Let's take this a step further.

Muslims cannot abide truth. Thus, they invented the accusatory term of Islamophobia — to suppress all things that expose their essence. Islam has been at war with the world and reality since the seventh century. Their culture is a dedication to war and conquest, so that even their own people may not grow and prosper. From the moment their children are born, they are robbed of the human spirit — freedom, creativity, imagination — and are twisted into becoming hardhearted "weapons of mass destruction" against their perceived enemies. In the name of their god, they attempt to erase the past by destroying ancient artifacts, refute history to support their own supersessionist narrative,[401] and call "offensive" all actions that lay bare the true nature of their barbarism – Muslims cannot tolerate their failure.

Islam teaches hatred of Jews as well as of Christians, Buddhists, Hindus, Zoroastrians, idol worshipers and animists — but the Jews above all.[402] Because Mohammed could not convert the Jews in Mecca, he beheaded all the Jewish men, took women and children for slaves, and passed his intense umbrage and rage to his descendants and disciples. Yet, Muslims claim a tie to Judaism through Abraham — and perhaps resent it. Muslims also need the Jews to blame for their failures and adversities, and while they also claim Jewish successes and world contributions for their own, it has been said that they also feel the shame[403] of having to do so. Why else would there be a traveling world exhibition called "1001 Inventions,"[404] for which they claim scholarship and ingenuity, but whose originality may be traced to Jews and other captives forcibly converted to Islam? Why else have some Muslims begun claiming Moses, Jesus, Christopher Columbus, and Albert Einstein as Palestinian or Muslim, even if there were no Muslims or Palestinians during those Biblical times?

Each defeat in wars begun by the Muslims against modern Israel was yet another intolerable humiliation, particularly when seven Muslim armies (Egypt, Lebanon, Syria, Iraq, Jordan, Saudi Arabia and Yemen) attacked, but were defeated (1948) by what they thought would be a defenseless, fledgling, ragtag army of starved, beaten Jewish survivors from Europe. Failing in conventional warfare, Islamists began a psychological war with the help of the uninformed, the envious, the angry, and those who are eternally predisposed to hate for their own reasons. This war includes the influential propaganda that Jewish achievements have been at the expense of others and that Jews are therefore the cause of every earthly ill.

Islamists have discovered that what they, themselves, do, may readily be blamed on the Jews and accepted by the masses. Muslims have broadcast their plan to create an all-encompassing world Caliphate, but they peddle the idea that it is the Jews who rule the world. It suits the Muslims to keep their brethren in a constant refugee status in Gaza and the West Bank to garner world sympathy (and the steady flow of funds) and to lay claim to territory illegally occupied by Jordan and Egypt, although the land is both legally and historically Jewish. Through the centuries, Muslims were never interested in working what was then a desolate wasteland,[405] but now insist that flourishing Israel is theirs.

In the surrounding Muslim lands, the majority continues to live in age-old poverty and ignorance under tyrannical regimes; this is blamed on Israel. If the rainfall is inadequate and unequally distributed through the year in this sub-tropical zone, Israel is liable for not supplying water. If their women and children die because they were placed among jihadist rocket launchers, Israel is impugned. They accuse Israel of Palestinian genocide, when, in fact, the Palestinian population has dramatically increased, doubling in size with each new generation; and of apartheid, when the reality is that Muslim citizens live as other Israeli citizens in Israel, but Jews are forbidden from living in Islamic countries.

The war is also against pluralism, individual rights and freedoms, liberal democracy, and Western ideas of progress, which have become a collective Islamic obsession. Yet the horrific crimes that Muslims commit against their women, their fellow Muslims and Christians are swept under the prayer rug, withheld by the media, and not addressed by world leadership. If the Jews cannot be incriminated for these crimes, then the mere mention of kidnappings, beheadings, honor killings, rape, and assorted acts of cruelty are impermissible topics.

This is also where our schools and teaching materials fail us. Except for a perfunctory early timeline on which one might find a designation for Ancient Israelites along with Assyrians, Babylonians and other defunct civilizations, world history studies begin with Ancient Rome and Greece, although the Jews had substantially contributed to human development during those earlier years. The Fathers of our US Constitution derived their morals, ethics and standards of behavior from Cicero and English Common Law, which drew from biblical law[406] given to the Hebrews by God. Exodus reveals that the Hebrews had a representative form of republican government, not unlike the system created in the Constitution. And while appropriate credit is given other countries, Israel's contributions in medicine, science and technology to society at large has been overlooked, as is her eternal capital, Jerusalem, which is referenced 823 times in the Hebrew Bible, 161 times in the Christian Bible, and never in the Koran.

Many history textbooks now devote a disproportionate number of chapters to Islam. Jerusalem is cited as the city where Mohammed ascended to heaven on a winged horse, but rarely as Israel's eternal capital. Mohammed has been praised for "impressive leadership skills," but not for his methods of rapine, brutality, and slaughter. There is never mention of Islam's butchery of 80 million Hindus in India,[407] their skulls piled to mountainous dimensions and their cities burned to the ground;

of the all-but-complete annihilation of Iran's Zoroastrians; or of the trickery used to enslave Iran's Sogdiana, taking their healthy men to replenish their Arab army, and annihilate the masses. Neither is there word about Muslims' killing perhaps more than 890 million infidels over fourteen centuries.[408]

If today's publishers have made a small correction on a map or two when it was called to their attention, is that sufficient? Have they reviewed all their products (textbooks and maps) for accuracy? No. Absolutely not — not until they are called to task by parents and school boards, and not until the books and maps are thoroughly reviewed by trusted people, replaced, and distributed anew. It takes the indoctrination of only one generation to completely change the nature of our country. Adding Israel and her name to a map, which can then be defaced by another "offended" student, will not bring enlightenment to a world that is plummeting into darkness.

VEILED PURSUIT

An American high school is influenced by CAIR and bends to Islam.

January 29, 2015, was Hijab Day at NP3, a public charter school in Sacramento, California. One student who is interning for the Council on American-Islamic Relations (CAIR) gave a presentation on Islamophobia and in no time at all, the befuddled faculty, staff and students were "encouraged" by an uninformed principal to wear a hijab — a veil that covers the woman's head and chest.

What began as the seventh century Bedouin woman's attempt at privacy and protection from the desert has become a veil symbolic of a woman's indignity and servitude. As Nonie Darwish so aptly explained in her book, Cruel and Usual Punishment,[409] women have come to represent the totality of evil and inferiority in Islamic teaching.

Considered lacking in intelligence and religion, women are deemed half the worth of men in a sharia court; in the case of rape, her accusation has no worth without four witnesses. Women may be raped for wearing "indecent" clothing and beaten by their husbands for leaving the house unaccompanied by a male relative. If her behavior further irritates, he may imprison her without food and clothing, and arrange for stoning until dead. In this despotic society, women bear the honor of the male, so that girls and women may be killed by a father who fears his esteem has been sullied.

The hijabs and burqas serve to enforce women to obey sharia and submit to men. Women are also compelled to defend this life of bondage or risk their own destruction at the hand of their families. It is because of such constant fear, that many women are defensive when challenged by non-Muslims. Some may even try to earn honor and respect by joining the radicals for violent jihad (holy war against the infidel); case in point, Linda Sarsour.

To cultures that enjoy freedom, these concealed women should be regarded as victims of sadism, forced to endure the insufferable heat of the subtropics under layers of clothing and prevented from enjoying the summer sun and cool breezes. In fact, medical experts have noted that these covered women in northern climes, with less sunshine, are suffering disproportionately from osteoporosis due to the lack of Vitamin D,[410] and experiencing an increased risk of pelvic fracture during childbirth. Their newborns are more prone to suffering seizures from the same deficiency.

Islamic law is concerned more with raping, beating, flogging, and stoning women than with honoring them. Sharia law demands that women be covered from head to toe as a way of solving the male's sexual temptations. Rather than teach the males self-restraint and respect, the woman shoulders the responsibility of hiding herself. Tragically, because some women want to appear obedient to their god and men, other women bear the burden of ridicule and targets of fatwas (legal opinions that often lead to threats of death).

The school principal, and the president of the Board of Trustees of the Natomas Unified School District, appear to be gullible and ill-informed. Whether somehow compelled or naively eager to please, they have, albeit temporarily (thus far), aligned the school to Hamas and the Muslim Brotherhood — both recognized as terrorist groups by the United States government. The usual claims are trumpeted, that this is to promote a deeper understanding between different faiths, but the interchange will predictably be in one direction only. The Muslims will not be required to don a Jewish kippah or a Catholic Sister's habit on this side of Paradise.

Rather than guide the new immigrants in becoming Americans, as previous ethnic groups have done, the school has accepted the customs of those who refuse to assimilate. No matter how subtle, when an intruder or invader makes demands that are met with compliance and submission from the host, it is not assimilation but conquest. How will the school handle future requests, such as having an entire class visit the local mosque, installing footbaths in the restrooms, removing and replacing "offensive" foods with halal foods, removing "distasteful" animal pictures, erasing Israel from a map, eliminating all historic information about the Ancient Israelites, allowing a room and time for Muslim prayer, replacing American school holidays with those of Islam, and demanding sharia law for school and country? These are among the many incremental adjustments to result in a gradual change of America as we know it.

The student is a representative of CAIR, whose motto is, "Islam isn't in America to be equal to any other faith but to become dominant."[411] A discussion on Islamophobia ensued, a term used to curb our freedom of speech by teaching non-Muslims to refrain from language offensive to Muslims, including the violent history of Mohammed and Islam, the brutality of sharia law, the truths about the treatment of women and sexual slavery, the 1400 years of Islamic savagery against all others, jihad and terrorism, democracy and Israel. By curbing our children's free speech, behaviors, and dress choices, they are destroying America's cultural thoughts and conduct, producing submissive adults and their future army. They have eliminated from the history books all record of Islamic violence, and the history and founding of America, including our Constitution and Bill of Rights. As our freedoms of thought and discussion are eroded, so are our cultural enthusiasm and growth. They are working to transform Americans into their image — one of a backward, destructive desert people.

CAIR has "engaged in more than 100 political influence operations[412] on behalf of foreign principals in the United States." It is very concerning that the school authorities knew that the student was an intern for the Hamas-linked terrorist CAIR, the worldwide organization that is linked to the Muslim Brotherhood, supports terrorism, and seeks to implement sharia-based governance globally — and why the authorities could not or would not protect themselves and their students from the stealth cultural onslaught.

Therefore, in all fairness and in the interest of equality and mutual understanding, the school administration should schedule days of honor for other religions, and detail precisely how they'll equalize the programs. In that way, all the students may learn to appreciate each other and grow to be proud Americans with their rights to life, liberty, and the pursuit of happiness intact, each in his/her own way.

THE MODERATE VANGUARD

The vanguards are stealth moderates who quietly change every facet of our culture to destroy America.

Just when everyone's attention has been directed toward ISIS and some of the most despicable crimes ever committed, and our government is loath to war with our planet's unequalled brutality, Jordan's King Abdullah assumed the role of world leader. Such activity continues to distract us so that we may ignore the evils unfolding within our own country — the war of the Moderates who exploit children in incalculable ways.

ISIS and Boko Haram, who hope to establish a shared Muslim empire, have lured thousands of American and European children to join their jihad against Western civilization. The UK Mirror[413] reported that, within a single two-week period alone, the Islamic State kidnapped about 3,000 Yazidi women and children,[414] and Boko Haram kidnaps young girls by the hundreds from private schools for sexual slavery. European teenage boys are persuaded to join ISIS with cash offers, rap videos, and tales of adventure.

Young women[415] are enticed by adventure and romance, only to be underfed and forced to live in the nude as sex slaves, beaten, shared among friends, and raped to bear the next generation of jihadis. The International Labour Organization estimates 1.2 million children are trafficked for exploitation each year.

Chechen Muslims, with their violent history, were responsible for the 2004 Beslan school hostage crisis,[416] when they captured 1,200 people (including 777 children), terrorized and raped their captives. The death toll of 331 included 186 children. Palestinian Muslims have bombed Israeli school buses and built terror tunnels that led to children's dormitories and classrooms.

In America, boys and young men are brainwashed in mosques to join ISIS's fight for Allah. Schools, such as the Universities of California, have become a hotbed of anti-Semitism not seen since the 1930s. Given a diet of Islamic propaganda in textbooks and videos, the public schools are now "encouraging" and praising Allah (which leads to wearing complete burqas and forced conversion).

Girls are not born with a sense of modesty. They are taught to feel unsuitable, inadequate and subservient, beginning in the Islamic home environment, where the man dominates the loveless marriage, and continuing through their schooling, From this environment, the young women will readily accept the burqa and its quality of escape and invisibility. Encumbered by these portable tents, they will also be prohibited from the joys of being American, from all forms of sports and social activities (even friendship between women), and they will learn to accept their captivity. Following these forms of conditioning, or being forced to lie (taqiyyah), they will assert their right to the restrictive dress code.

There is yet another consequence of burqas. In Islam, the idea of modesty is warped into becoming the woman's shame of her womanhood, which undermines her security and self-respect. This results in an increase in female genital mutilation, and facial disfigurement by acid (which I already noted in our local upscale shopping mall when a young woman's face covering slipped). Those not covered in burqas will be at risk of being raped; the risk in Islamized Sweden,[417] Norway, and Germany has reached epidemic proportions, comparable to Islamic countries. The more subjugated the women, the higher the overall crime rate in a tyrannical regime. When news reporters state that we must defeat the Islamic ideology to win against ISIS, be reminded that we must also defeat the ideology's permeation into our own lives.

Of the 1.3 billion Muslims in the world, an estimated 25 percent may support violent extremists, with the majority of Muslims in most Islamic countries favoring sharia law.[418] Within the populace are the traumatized, fearful and irrelevant women, as well as the mentally challenged (from a high consanguineous rate), both invariably disposable and "volunteered" for suicide mission. Another group, a courageous handful that speaks out against parts of the Koran and for Islamic reform, has undertaken a daunting and dangerous mission.

Finally, there are the "Moderates," the comparatively discreet in Western society, who go about their daily lives inconspicuously, never speaking out against terrorism, all the while effecting changes in our land in gradual increments. They are the non-violent who nevertheless seek to establish a tyrannical regime here, in America. While citizens are battling the ACLU's attempt to allow Muslim laws in Oklahoma, a sharia court[419] has been established in Texas. New school textbooks are crammed with indoctrinal material about Islam, with little about America and the other major religions, leaving alert parents in Massachusetts[420] and Florida[421] furious about the deceitful programs inflicted on their children. It is the Moderates who surreptitiously prepare proselytizing films and school excursions to mosques without prior parental notification, all changes that are meant to create a new generation of devotees and jihadis. Only recently, did Florida's parents expose to the media the textbooks that contain several chapters on a glossed-over Islam, with a hundred pages of Judaism and Christianity missing.

Moderates are also the college students who, now brazen and empowered by a quiescent, ignorant, leftist administration, defend terrorist organizations, vilify and call for the annihilation of Israel, and unite to attack Jewish students. Encouraged to invite outside speakers from terrorist groups (Hamas, the Muslim Brotherhood), the Muslim Student Union (MSU) and Students for Justice in Palestine (SJP) work together to impose their ideology and establish sharia laws and restrictions on their host population. Their leader, Azka Fayyaz, is now openly promoting violence[422] and Israel's destruction. A dedicated anti-Semite, she announced that Hamas and sharia have taken over the University of California and is no doubt responsible for recent Nazi-style graffiti at a Jewish fraternity and Hillel House.

The families that allege to have come to the West to escape tyranny raise and nurture their children in their home culture of intolerance and harshness. These Moderates are fast becoming the jihadis of tomorrow, eager to replace our way of life with theirs. They are the new devotees who celebrate the Islamic Eid[423] with animals that are ruthlessly tortured and slaughtered for sacrifice, and demand particular accommodations from the public schools. They are the bystanders who cheer while non-moderates behead, torch, or throw their fellow human beings off cliffs. They are the ones who danced in the streets on 9/11 and celebrate suicide bombings by one of their own. They are the parents of young women who leave home to join a Palestinian cause and become comfort women to Islamo-fascist barbarians and are ultimately killed. They are the ones who believe that every punishment meted out in the 7th century Koran is acceptable today, against homosexuals, women, apostates, infidels, and more. These are the Moderates who are working to influence and change our children.

Their clothes may remain unsplattered, but we may be assured that their hands are soaked in blood.

DAWA* AT CHAUTAUQUA

The Chautauqua Institution provides a pseudo-intellectual atmosphere to indoctrinate the unenlightened about Islam.

The Chautauqua Institution, considered an adult education center, is less education than indoctrination to the world of the Left. In an idyllic setting in July, the Institution invited Islamists who spoke of "Love and Justice in a World of Suffering," hiding the truths of the suffering caused by Islam – both the harsh sharia law already in effect for its adherents and to establish sharia in Dar Al-Harb (House of War), the countries not yet under sharia but targeted to writhe under Islamic oppression.

Omid Safi, appointed director of Duke University's Islamic Studies Center in July 2014, spoke in terms to please the underinformed. He and they would prefer that hideous acts of violence, such as perpetrated by ISIS, ISIL, Boko Haram, Hamas, Hezbollah and countless others with like purpose, be removed from the news media and replaced with stories of compassion. In so doing, he would silence the reporters and critics and destroy our freedom to speak, report, and apprise the masses about the evils perpetrated by Muslims, so that we would remain oblivious to Islam's stealth control over our media and our minds. He would then pursue and obtain legal accommodations without obstacle, enforce sharia law over our Constitutional laws without hindrance, and threaten all our freedoms through influence, treachery, and force.

The "pain and suffering" he referenced in Ferguson, Baltimore, and Staten Island, were shown to have been largely incitement encouraged by outsiders who represent Islam and the Left — conquest is best accomplished during turmoil and disorder. The mayhem forces the unprepared, unarmed victims into appeasement mode, to cede their rights and ability to speak and defend in favor of assuaging the unmanageable horde that cries victimhood, and peace at any cost. The chaos allows the aggressors to dominate and, under the guise of "love and justice," impose its law on all nations – thus implementing the laws of Allah through jihad.

Safi was also sure to remind that there was insufficient money for social issues but a glut for our military — an inverted fabrication to which the unaware nod in assent because Chautauqua provides no discussions, no debates, and no visitors with opposing views. The rhetoric that passes for intellect remains unchallenged; the audience is never encouraged to analyze and grasp that the narrative undermines America's very survival.

In fact, the growth in national health spending and welfare programs has accelerated to levels that, unchecked, will bring our country to bankruptcy.[424] The federal government's centers for Medicare and Medicaid Services have expanded to cover additional and improved services for 200 million people;[425] and an average of 46+ million people receiving food stamps on the Supplemental Nutrition Assistance Program during 2012, with more illegal aliens and "new Americans" still coming to our shores — unvetted for physical and mental illnesses, crime, or productivity. The programs thwart the incentive to strive and inhibit growth and achievements, and cut back funds for investments, new jobs and opportunities for the many — boding a future of indigence.

He advocates cuts to our military budget, already at a pre-World War II low,[426] when the threat to our national security is at an all-time high. Severe cuts in defense spending have already subjected our nation to accumulating strategic risks to such as crisis-readiness, sustaining pilot skills with sufficient flying hours, and maintaining a Naval presence in key regions. Our military must continue diplomatic, economic and intelligence elements for preserving trade routes and stability in vital regions, and to serve global interests. Financial support is crucial for military infrastructure and civilian and contractor defense workforce. Safi instigates his audience to desire further increases in social expenditures (higher taxation and prices, shrinking wealth, increased poverty, and compounded national debt) and to diminish our self-defense and military superiority against Islamic or any tyrannical expansionism. Disarmed, submissive subjects are easier to rule and more likely to provide the revenue and manpower needed for further conquest.

Safi reminded his audience of the human condition, always to plead for Muslim suffering, the perpetual offender becomes the eternal victim. In my previous essay, Mosquitoes in the Mosque,[427] I mentioned Islam's expansionism and the slaughter of hundreds of millions of victims since its inception in 824 AD, unparalleled by any other people, and ongoing. The FBI has reported that ISIS exists in "every single state,"[428] and Chautauqua has its numerous visitors from the Muslim Brotherhood, including the notorious Imam Rauf, who failed to develop his Cordoba Mosque on Ground Zero but is planning one for this vacation spot in southwestern New York state.

While Safi urged his audience to love and empathize with "the human condition everywhere," he fails to address those who have fallen prey to Islam. An ardent champion for the end of a Jewish Israel,[429] this corrupt jihadist has written fallacious articles[430] that blamed Israel for atrocities against Arabs, using Holocaust-era photos of bodies from Buchenwald concentration camp! Who invites these speakers to so misinform those who presumably come to learn? How are they vetted and allowed these opportunities to propagandize against our liberties, our nation, and against Israel?

The Chautauqua Institution, originally designed to bring culture, hope, and promise during the Great Depression, now presents a façade of scholarship, intellect, and critical thinking, its attendees duped at a critical time in American history. Alas, idealism does not protect one from ignorance, dogmatism, and foolishness.

Dawa: proselytizing Islam

PRECARITY

Overwhelmed by all of life's insecurities in a free society, the women prefer ritualization, and boycott Israel.

Precarity is a neoliberal term with which I was unfamiliar until I researched the theme of the National Women's Studies Association (NWSA) conference. It means precarious, hazardous, risky, and it focuses mainly on the alleged "evils" of capitalism. Although life's uncertainties have existed since the beginning of time, these women had come together to discuss the insecurities of living, focusing on the drawbacks of being ill-prepared for functioning in today's workforce. Where previous generations sometimes stayed with a company from hiring to retiring, today's employees change jobs frequently and must keep up with the ever-changing technology. Thus, these women fear the problems that arise within a free society, changing economy, other unreliable coworkers, and all that freedom and free enterprise offer.

Risk is the very essence of freedom and of life, and yet this is their anxiety. They spurn those gifts bestowed upon us by our Creator and cited in our Declaration of Independence — Life, Liberty and the Pursuit of happiness, all of which involve risk. It is the freedom to pursue our chosen path and our own happiness that helps us to accept failures and overcome hindrances, and to continue chasing our personal dream. Rather, these women are overwhelmed by responsibility, regarding the challenge as simply "misery" generated by capitalism, since they view that the sale of one's abilities for profit may also result in failure and unemployment. Resistant to change and diversity, they yearn for their vision of a more secure and simpler life of the past, which, of course, is remembered without the discomforts, diseases, poverty and squalor that free enterprise and success have reduced!

Their dreams of the utopian past erase the men's long hours of hard labor, the women who were bound to a life of raising more children than they could manage, illnesses that have since been eradicated, few kitchen appliances to ease daily chores, and a labor force of children to help families make ends meet. Blaming capitalism for their current difficulties, the NWSA members want more entitlements and government intervention in exchange for the joys of innovation, growth, and the dignity of achievement.

Taught by today's academia to rely on their feelings and to redefine right and wrong, they wallow in comfortable discomfort and, significantly, decide to boycott Israel, her harvest, inventions and medical innovations. Could it be because Israelis treasure life and produce advantages and benefits not previously known, while the Palestinians desire to acquire Israel without the labor? Arab leaders had allowed the barren, sparsely populated, impoverished land[431] to become malaria-ridden over centuries before the Diaspora Jews returned to their historic homeland to cultivate the soil and recreate a flourishing democracy.

Precarity is the cost of living! It is the cost of charting one's own course with all the possibilities of turning the unsure into opportunities. The Universal Declaration of Human Rights declares that "all human beings are endowed with reason and conscience and shall act towards one another in a spirit of brotherhood," but the new liberalism distorts the vision of brotherhood into a nightmare of sameness, none better or worse;

the goal of certainty without triumphs or failures; and a less educated population reduced by chaos, abortion, sterilization, euthanasia, and incurable diseases. And for political correctness, with their minds distorted and freedom of speech eradicated, these souls will no longer recognize friend from foe, good from evil, excellence from mediocrity, or even female from male.

Although we know that eighty-one percent of mosques in America advocate violence,[432] Germany appears to be losing its autonomy to the invaders, Sweden is losing its heritage, Belgium went on lockdown, Angola banned Islam, and France is actively closing mosques but suffering militant no-go zones, but the NWSA denounced Israel. Despite the legal documents to verify that Jews, not Arabs, hold rightful title to the land,[433] and under whose direction diverse people within flourish, these women choose Islamo-fascism, where a clear majority of its people favor severe sharia law and terrorism.

As technology (much of it from Israel) provides us with a front seat to the world, we have seen Muslims destroy 3,000 people in the World Trade Center; Muslims behead or burn Christians alive; Muslims turn their young children into knife-wielding murderers; Muslims kill groups of revelers in arenas and weddings and schoolchildren in classrooms and school buses; Muslims car-attack or knife Jewish pedestrians, but these women are boycotting Israel. Muslims are harming girls with Female Genital Mutilation, followed by enslaving, torturing, and imprisoning women in lifelong domestic/sexual servitude in the Middle East, Africa and Asia, but the NWSA women ignore where they could be truly useful. Islam is overtaking and creating havoc in Europe, and our national intelligence-gathering agencies (FBI and DHS) have long terror-watch lists of dangerous Islamic jihadis, but the NWSA is boycotting Israel.

What the NWSA will not accept is that the Jewish people have moral, historical, religious and legal claims to the disputed lands in Israel, yet Israel has been willing to forego some claims for the sake of peace. The State of Israel was built on land purchased by Jews, and Jews have been a presence in Jerusalem for 3,000 years,[434] with a majority-Jewish population for more than 250 years. Israel already ceded land to the Palestinians, who, in turn, destroyed prospering businesses and use the land for launching rockets. In truth, the occupiers are the Arabs who took the name "Palestinian."[435]

Morally, Israelis are first responders who have helped numerous countries,[436] from Albania to Turkey, after floods, fires, earthquakes, bombings, tropical storms, hurricanes and cyclones, providing emergency humanitarian and medical personnel and assistance. Israelis helped Boston after the Marathon Bombing and California with its fires and water shortages. America benefits from this valuable partnership,[437] including intelligence; the UK benefits from Israeli technology in protection, jobs, medicines and more.[438] Israel is a global leader in bio-technology and defense, agriculture, water innovation, medicine, book publishing, and more. Increasingly,

Israeli entrepreneurs are attracting more foreign banks' investments in their innovative technology.[439]

IsraAid, in cooperation with Israeli NGOs FIRST and Operation Blessing-Israel, launched a social-worker training program in the new African state of South Sudan,[440] one of the most undeveloped countries in the world. They are addressing the country's violent misogynistic culture of rape and forced marriage. The women of NWSA could be involved, but show no interest and do nothing.

How will these work-shy, incompetent women defend themselves when the soldiers of Allah fill our streets and execute their many forms of violent jihad on our citizens? Will they open their homes and crumble into submission when the young Muslim males wreak havoc on the most vulnerable? Will they merely stand by and watch the migrants join forces with their brethren in the terror mosques to create battalions beyond the control of our diminished police and armed forces? These women are either terribly ignorant or filled with a fanatical evil — how else to explain this mindset?

Perhaps it is then that the National Women's Studies Association will finally achieve its goal. Their insecurities will be gone because their future will be ritualized to the letter. All the laws of Islam are clearly defined for women in the Koran. Independence and security will be as amputated as the limbs of Islam's thieves.[441] They will be guaranteed equality to all other women (devalued by men), and their tomorrows will be precisely as their yesterdays — that is, of course, unless they are accused of some minor Mohammedan infraction. Then their morrow may never materialize.

Final note: With all the ignorance shown by NWSA, they also appear to be unaware that Israel boycotts are illegal. Under corporate law, an organization, including nonprofit, can do only what is permitted under the purposes specified in its charter. Boycott resolutions that are beyond the powers of an organization are void, and individuals can be sued and board members liable for damages.

THE ART OF WAR

York university's social justice and responsibility are a jihadist picture, empty words and absent deeds.

York University, a public research university in Toronto, Ontario, is Canada's third largest university, with 52,800 students, including 5,462 international students, and 7,000 faculty and staff. The Mission Statement is grandiose and appealing, claiming "excellence in research" with a goal of cultivating "the critical intellect." There are assurances that the University is "open to the world: we explore global concerns," accompanied by ensuring "social justice" and a commitment to teaching "social responsibility." The President's Message further confirms that the

University is "proud to be one of Canada's most socially responsive and engaged Universities," yet the president, Dr. Mamdouh Shoukri, is unwilling to test those very ethics.

If the University welcomes the diversity from 157 countries, it should be prepared to suppress conflict and injustice. If it prides itself on social responsibility, it should discourage irresponsible behavior and the incitement to isolate one people, one country. If excellence in research is encouraged, then it may be time to thoroughly research both the irrational Islamic hatred and culture of violence and the validity of the Jewish bond to the Land of Israel.

Affixed to a wall in the Student Centre is a mural that features a Palestinian youth preparing to throw two rocks at an Israeli structure. More than 4,000 incidents of rock throwing against Jews are reported each year in the West Bank, causing severe injury and death. The "art" expresses the Arab demand for a Palestine that includes Israel along with Gaza, Judea and Samaria (Jordan's West Bank), without border definitions, without compromise. The violent elimination of the State of Israel and the Jewish people define the words beneath "Justice" and "Peace."

Having initiated four military wars against Israel, suffering utter humiliation with each loss, the Muslim Brotherhood chose the course of psychological warfare, propagating lies on which to base another intifada (uprising), days of rage or boycott, and it is on Israel specifically that Muslim students maintain their focus — for the time being. The mural is propaganda meant to provoke, to deny Israel her 3,000-year history of Jewish presence[442] (Muslims appeared in the 7th century CE), and the legal deeds held by the Jewish state since 1948. The mural supports the invented history of Jordanian, Lebanese, Syrian, Saudi and Egyptian Arabs who deceitfully took the Latin name of Palestinians to fabricate a bond between themselves and the area they invaded and then lost in 1967. The concocted history and accusations of "occupation" are part of the Islamic aggression against the world,[443] one of many battles in which Muslims are engaged — in Africa, Asia, Europe and the Americas — to establish a global Caliphate.

Yet despite voiced disapproval by students and citizens alike, University President Dr. Mamdouh Shoukri assured us of their commitment to a safer environment, but that this instance is off campus and beyond his jurisdiction. The claim to be cultivating "critical intellect" in the students and "social responsibility" rings hollow, for these are York students, and the building is the York University Student Centre. There is no responsibility to maintain an apolitical, non-threatening environment. The mural is encouraging violence, perhaps worthy of emulating, climate permitting. Dr. Shoukri knows such incidents in American universities have resulted in terror and bodily harm inflicted on Jewish students. Who is charged with overseeing student welfare, or is this disengagement meant to perpetuate the narrative? Is this considered "free speech" until legally challenged, or slander and incitement to violence? It is certainly advocating one political viewpoint while suppressing another.

Therefore, to fulfill his aim of "social justice," I would ask the president to consent to five more murals to enhance the Palestinians' objects of glory or mission on one wall, and an equal number of similarly sized murals to express the objects of Israel's glory or mission on the opposite wall. Thus, both groups could legitimately present their ideas of justice and values to students, faculty and staff, and allow "critical intellect" to prevail.

A second Palestinian mural should show the stoning of Islamic women who are accused of adultery or simply owning a cell phone. Siddqa,[444] age 19, was dressed in a full blue burqa, buried up to her waist in the ground, and pelted with stones. When she collapsed, covered in blood but still alive, a Taliban fighter shot her three times in the head with an AK-47. This photo is of her 19-year-old lover who, trying to flee, was captured and stoned to death. Justice was equally served.

The third is the Jordanian pilot from the US-led Coalition, Muath Al-Kassasbeh,[445] who was deprived of food for five days, displayed in front of armed terrorists, caged, soaked with petrol and set afire as an offering to Allah. Watching and listening to the screaming and melting is considered justice to the "religion of peace."

The fourth, death by decapitation, is not as commonplace as stoning or being buried alive and left exposed to the elements and animals. Beheading,[446] mentioned twice in the Koran, instills fear into those who watch, and it attracts more publicity than car bombings and suicide bombings. The killers achieve a sense of justice. Children are taught to behead at an early age,[447] using dolls and live animals.

A recognized Australian victim of rape.[448] In Saudi Arabia, rape victims would receive 100 lashes for committing adultery, followed by incarceration for a year. Australia lacks such rules of "justice." Sweden is the rape capital of Europe, since welcoming Muslim migrants.

The sixth is justice for women. The Muslim woman, mother of three, walking in the street, was stopped, pronounced guilty of wearing a red jacket over her black burqa, and told to kneel. She was summarily shot in the head.[449]

This new discovery is worthy of inclusion because of the enormous pride and occasion for celebration. Samir Kuntar,[450] Palestinian superhero, smashed the head of a four-year-old Israeli girl with the butt of his rifle.

The opposite wall should display a like number of murals to acknowledge the interests and commitments of the Israelis.

Haiti's devastating earthquake of 2010 attracted many rescue teams, including from Iceland, China, Qatar, South Africa, Columbia, Cuba, Japan, Florida, and New York City's experienced 9/11 personnel. Israelis brought a rescue team of 200 and a field hospital.[451] An Egyptian-Jewish Haitian supplied his factory's grounds and trucks to bring in tents, medical equipment, communication hardware and all supplies. Within eight hours, the field hospital was set up and operational, and became the model for the future. Israelis treated broken bones and traumas, performed surgeries and births; the first baby born was named Israel Michel.

An Israeli company's water purification systems deliver safe drinking water from almost any source, including contaminated water, seawater and urine. Following a major earthquake in Taiwan in 2009, Israeli humanitarian aid workers brought locally made WaterSheer products[452] to ensure a steady stream of potable water for the survivors and wherever it was needed. Within 48 hours, Taiwan had 4,227 gallons of pure water per day.

Dr. Amit Goffer, an Israeli, developed ReWalk Robotics,[453] an exoskeleton system that enables the paralyzed to walk. Facilitated by computers and motion sensors, it allows independent, controlled walking. It helped Clair Lomas to complete the marathon course at the London Paralympics in 2012, and assisted a groom to walk down the aisle. It also provides dignity, mental health, improved cardiovascular health and bowel function, loss of fat tissue, and building of lean muscle mass. Users have less pain, take fewer medications, and require less hospitalization.

Israel has become the fastest growing laboratory for innovative technology, following US and China in creativity and entrepreneurial leadership. Some innovations are responsible transportation using batteries, not oil; drip irrigation that allows farmers worldwide to grow 40 percent more crops using half the water. Tahal Group[454] has technological solutions to make wastewater treatment processes more efficient and relevant. LifeStraw[455] is the water filter chosen by leading NGOs for humanitarian relief worldwide since 2005, meeting or exceeding EPA standards for efficacy. It removes most of all the waterborne bacteria and parasites and it filters a maximum of 1000 litres of water, enough for one person for one year.

Israel's breakthroughs are too numerous to mention. Here are a few recent ones:

♦ Researchers at Hebrew University of Jerusalem developed a molecule (NT157) that targets metastatic human melanoma and colon cancer.

♦ Israel's Oramed gives China the right to its oral insulin capsule to treat the large, growing numbers of diabetics in China.

♦ A new arthritis treatment reduces high blood pressure.

♦ Japan turns to Israeli tech to treat radiation disease.

♦ Voice technology Voice ITT translates speech of people with communication disabilities.

♦ Israel's Enopace performed first implant operation to treat patients with congestive heart failure.

♦ Israel developed a plastic material that repairs itself.

It is insufficient and irresponsible for the University to blithely state that it is concerned with "social justice" and yet be unprepared to equalize information for unprejudiced "critical intellect" of the students to make their assessment. Dr. Mamdouh Shoukri, an Islamist, failed to reply or re-align himself and the University with the pursuit of true "excellence in research" combined with intellectual honesty and fairness.

MORALITY AT MISSOURI U

The person who assumes the presidency during peacetime must nevertheless be able to preside during wartime.

The University of Missouri has been the location of several anti-Semitic acts that its President Tim Wolfe appeared reluctant to address. The final vile act, which included the formation of a swastika in excrement,[456] was enough to encourage thirty-six Jewish and civil rights organizations to demand the president's resignation. Concurrently, Black graduate student, Jonathan Butler, heroically began a hunger strike, and within days, both Wolfe and Chancellor Loftin stepped down from their positions.

In her unusual response, Tammi Rossman-Benjamin said that Jewish students will likely find themselves facing an even more hostile, threatening and unsafe environment because administrators are either too busy or too scared to address anti-Semitism, thereby leaving Jewish students more vulnerable and unprotected. So, should the inmates continue running the asylum? Acts of bigotry are occurring throughout America's campuses and worldwide. Anything can trigger another "moderate" to becoming an active aggressor, whether the bully is motivated by the relatively unobtrusive prey or others' acts of intolerance and violence. Being busy or scared is hardly an excuse for the head of a university to be allowed to shirk his responsibilities.

Rossman-Benjamin suggested that a president may fear appearing to favor Jewish students. Does she think it wrong to favor any victimized students or just the Jewish students? What if there were a second group of victims? Would the administration feel more comfortable and legitimized if a non-Jewish group were imperiled along with the Jewish? In fact, is it not moral to protect and care for the students who are attacked? An administrator must be both ethical and courageous to govern such an institution and use the event as a teaching strategy and warning.

As hate is permitted to fester on various campuses, without administrative interference or penalties, the number of hostilities and kinds of depravity may be expected to increase. These establishments are microcosms of countries around the world, where the hatred and violent behavior may well reach unmanageable proportions to the point of taking complete control — unless they are stopped now.

The U of M must be administered by people who may not remain ignorant, cowardly, or indifferent, no matter the alibi. We do not remove our cities' police forces or our country's armed forces because of how we might be viewed as pandering to one side over the other. If the administrators are too busy or fainthearted to address the growing animosity, they are ill-equipped to perform the duties of their position. Their stated duty, after all, is to "work together on behalf of all citizens."

All positions change, whether because of a political climate, improved technology or fluctuating needs, and while it is regrettable that terrorism has become a grave issue for the schools as it has for the world, a candidate who assumes the position of leadership during peacetime must be able to adjust his skills and responsibilities accordingly during wartime.

The United States Department of State has adopted a definition of anti-Semitism, which includes advocating the murder of Jews, Holocaust denial, accusing Jews of fabricating the Holocaust, accusations of dual loyalty (loyalty to both Israel and their country of birth), denies Jewish people's right to self-determination (one-state solution), using symbols associated with anti-Semitism (swastikas and Nazism), holding Israel to standards not demanded of other countries or criticisms not leveled at other countries, harassment (verbal, graphic, electronic, written; offensive, harmful or threatening conduct). Know your rights and reach out for help: EndBDS.com.

There is a new interim president at the University of Missouri, Michael Middleton. It appears that he has the will and resourcefulness to protect the school's citizens, regardless of race or creed. If anti-Israel or anti-Black groups threaten to harm students on campus, we trust they will face expulsion. The university administrators need to display the qualities of integrity and valor, attributes that our students should acquire during their formative years in order to be the fine, upstanding American citizens required to restore America to its recognized level of greatness.

CHANGING MINDS

From Kindergarten to our highest institutions of learning, radical social engineering is changing our students.

Columbia and Cornell, considered two of the finest institutions of higher education in the United States, have been identified as leading the list of "most anti-Semitic," as they continue to host Jew-hatred[457] events on campus. By the time our students enter this new phase in their education, they have been well primed for the venomous climate, having been molded into frustrated, resentful, disrespectful, demanding, angry young adults, ill prepared for anything, unwilling to accept responsibility, and ripe to lash out at others. These young people have already been activated, prepared to join any group that uses "social justice" language, warranted or not.

The K-12 classes provide the first toxic element. Education is being restructured according to a radical political ideology promoted by President Obama's White House, Bill and Melinda Gates,[458] and other supporters of a federal takeover of education.[459] Their purpose is to produce workers for a Global Economy (aka Agenda 21). The major players are Valerie Jarrett's mother, Barbara Taylor Bowman, a member of the Muslim Sisterhood; native-born terrorists Bill Ayers and Bernardine Dohrn Ayers (Weather Underground)[460] who support a radical network to defeat America; and Secretary of Education (ret.) Arne Duncan,[461] who promoted the Common Core Standards, with its drastic, untried curriculum overhaul that has lowered school standards to ensure that no child is left behind or excels at the expense of others. This is accompanied by the disturbing data mining that profiles the children (from cradle to grave) and their families.

Classical literature, known to improve vocabulary and foster creative expression, thinking, speaking, and writing skills, has been jettisoned in favor of dry, uninspiring informational texts and Dystopian, sexualized, disheartening novels[462] for children whose pre-frontal cortex is insufficiently developed to cope with dark situations and mature content. The result is depression. Mary Calamia,[463] licensed clinical social worker and psychotherapist in Stony Brook, NY, has reported that children have come to hate school, cry, wet the bed, experience insomnia, and engage in self-mutilation — an increase of 200 to 300 percent more children with serious trauma than before the new curriculum's introduction.

Math problems once solved in a few steps now require a convoluted system. Karen Lamoreaux, mother of three and member of Arkansas Against Common Core,[464] presented a simple 4th grade division problem to the Board of Education that one could solve in two steps, but now requires 108 steps to completion. In New York, principals have reported that some students are severely stressed — even vomiting during testing.

History has become another endangered learning experience. A popular textbook is Howard Zinn's "A People's History of the United States,"[465] which focuses on "the exploitation of the majority by an elite minority," designed to inspire a "quiet revolution" against America. Historians heavily criticize the book's concentration on slavery, racism, and colonialism while omitting America's enormous achievements for life, liberty, and the pursuit of happiness. Students do not learn America's founding documents — The Declaration of Independence, The Articles of Confederation, the Constitution, The Bill of Rights, or the Ten Commandments. A new vocabulary is in use to give new meaning to old ideas, including "framers" for "founders," indicating a flexible and distorted view of our history and heritage, and a turn to global governance.

True history has been replaced with a counterfeit version, introducing the second toxic element,[466] another oft-used textbook that contains multiple chapters on Islam (whitewashed of its 1400 years of ongoing bloodshed and conquest), without equal time for Judaism and Christianity. Such studies may also include unscheduled trips to mosques, simulating a hajj[467] (pilgrimage) to Mecca, girls' donning traditional Muslim clothing, learning Arabic calligraphy, memorizing the Five Pillars of Islam and the Shahada,[468] the testimony required to convert to Islam. And, as if these approaches were insufficient, political indoctrination is included, using the Palestinian narrative to vilify the State of Israel and world Jewry.

To what do we owe this new development? America's educational institutions receive significant donations to create Middle Eastern and political science study programs that ensure the installation of anti-American professors. The students are besieged by Islamic and leftist indoctrination[469] that demonize Israel, Jewish and American history, and disallows opposing views. The hate agenda is presented as scholarly and the West is blamed for Islam's self-imposed or invented ills. Scheduled anti-Israel events are designed to promote the narrative of Israeli colonialism, and to delegitimize and erode support for Israel by advocating a boycott-divestment-sanctions (BDS) effort.

The propaganda campaign is global, well-financed and well-organized but the biggest focus is college campuses, where Students for Justice in Palestine (SJP) and the Muslim Student Union use the rhetoric of social justice and human rights, historic Palestine, genocide, apartheid and oppression, to motivate the boycott movement and support the Islamic ideology of conquest. Jewish children are harassed and harmed. Our colleges are breeding grounds for future jihadis who are turned against Israel and will one day soon turn against America.

The groups within the colleges are well-funded arms of the Muslim Brotherhood, menacingly delivering their accusations and claims of apartheid, maltreatment of women, death to homosexuals, etc. against the Jewish state, when, in fact, these are descriptive of the Muslim cultures. Islam allows homosexuality[470] (despite severe outward condemnation and murder), pedophilia[471] (sexual pleasure with pre-pubescent boys and infants), kidnapping for sexual slavery, polygamy, wife beating,[472] stoning women, disfiguring their daughters with FGM[473] and acid, chopping off hands[474] and feet, death for apostasy, murder of Jewish and Christian civilians — and, quite recently, beheading a 15-year-old Iraqi boy for listening to pop music.[475] With the complicity of liberal instructors, a crisis is being nurtured for acquiring power, diminishing freedom of speech, and promoting an increase of immigrating non-integrating Muslims who, through hijra,[476] will irretrievably transform our Western countries.

The situation has become so critical that schools are providing "safe spaces,"[477] a concept similar to Islamic "sacred space,"[478] an aggressive territorial system that holds all land on earth as given by Allah to Mohammed in perpetuity. Kent State University invites students and community to a safe environment for ongoing interaction and conversation on "diverse," but "approved," subjects. The University of California Berkeley has adopted a policy requiring all "Caucasian" students to purchase mandatory Free Speech Insurance[479] at $1,000 per semester "to cover the cost of therapy and rehabilitation of victims of unregulated, freely expressed Caucasian ideas." Thus, the schools encourage a mentality of victimization, anger and vengeance along with feelings of shame and White Guilt.

This is social engineering, a force that is being cynically employed to restructure the soul of an entire generation of young people and render it vulnerable to the globalist one world order, in which none of the traditional values will have survived. With value and context stripped from books, a generation is being deceived and denied the aptitude to discern fact from fiction or right from wrong. Thus deprived of the ability to think critically, they are ripe for joining any number of hate groups on campus, the Occupy movements, Black Lives Matter, and those that favor a Palestinian state and the destruction of Israel. But, most significantly, they become easily malleable by and for the ruling class.

The pathway to the final destination goes by the Orwellian term, Agenda 21, the schema that indoctrinates to retrofit our children for future global citizenship, to overtake properties and communities, and to transform America with the enticing promise of social and economic development in a competitive (not free) marketplace. The all-powerful government will determine the equitable distribution of the fruits of all labor, meaning the successful countries will distribute its profits to third world countries until they run out of other people's money — the only things left to share would be destitution and illness. Only then will the elite bask in a society in which thinking has been obliterated and every spark of creativity trampled into the dust.

We are standing at a crucial time in history and working against the clock.

MOBOCRACY IN ACADEMIA

Unprotected by a weak college president, a Jewish professor was victimized by Islamic students and militant teaching staff. (Names have been replaced for security reasons).

An incendiary atmosphere of hatred, divisiveness, intimidation and lies is filling today's schools across America, with 73 percent of Jewish students admitting they've experienced some sort of anti-Semitism. Taking full advantage of America's liberties, a captive audience and with the full knowledge of faculty, militant Islamic professors[480] use the liberal campus environment to spew an anti-American and anti-Israel agenda to effect changes and recruit new Jew-hating Muslims.

Pursuant to the activities of Students for Justice in Palestine (SJP) (an aggressively anti-Israel organization) and Conn Students in Solidarity with Palestine (CSSP), along with some teaching staff, Connecticut College[481] is no more the school described in its professed ideology. Founded in 1911, the school was to be a "vibrant social, cultural and intellectual community with an enriched diverse perspective"; to prepare "responsible citizens, creative problem-solvers, and thoughtful leaders in a global society." It boasts of a "long-standing Honor Code," with "students expected to monitor their own faithfulness to the principles of honesty and moral integrity." It declares, "The principles of justice, impartiality and fairness — the foundations for equity — are paramount."

Yet, in early 2016, an incident was allowed to escalate in direct contradiction to the College's lofty aims, with the Honor Code's becoming a Code of Silence.[482] It involved Dr. Andrew Pessin, distinguished philosophy professor of Connecticut College, during the tenure of President Katherine Bergeron, who is responsible for internationalizing the curriculum, although not objectively; and David Canton,[483] who paradoxically holds the title of Interim Dean of Institutional Equity and Inclusion. Pessin had posted a Facebook entry during the Fall 2015 semester, wherein he described the situation in Gaza as "a rabid pit bull trying to escape." His student, Miya Khan, an active member of SJP in high school, knew of the entry, and admitted she'd never felt victimized in his class. Yet in February 2016, under the tutelage of her student advisor, Sophi Yu, director of Global Islamic Studies, Miya decided to become offended and issued a complaint that the entry "condemned Palestinians."

Pessin explained that he referred to Hamas, an acknowledged terrorist organization, apologized for any misunderstanding, and removed the Facebook entry, but the unrelenting student, obviously encouraged, intensified her attack, accusing him of racism and conspiring to annihilate the Palestinian people. This was her opportunity to create a crisis where none existed[484] to suppress speech in order to control the narrative, and specifically to target the Jewish professor who speaks favorably of Israel. Khan gathered her forces to malign his reputation. Concurrently, Lea Land, editor of the Campus Voice,[485] published articles by Mitchell Rait and Kate Barge, who wrote that Pessin condoned the extermination of a people, and other students' anti-Semitic comments. Lea's column also exposed her own lack of journalistic ethics and the anti-Semitic agenda of History Professor James T. Downs and others whose intent it was to create a hostile atmosphere for Dr. Pessin.

Dr. Pessin was denounced, he and his family threatened, and the hostility worsened, forcing him to leave the college. For her achievement, Khan was granted the Scholar Activist award by the Dean (he of "Equity and Inclusion") in May 2015.

Vitalized by success, CSSP students, under the direction of faculty advisor Eileen Kane[486] who heads the school's Global Islamic Studies program, launched a poster campaign to vilify Israel, Jewish and Israeli students and faculty, including an attack on Israel's Birthright program[487] The placards contained propaganda meant to mischaracterize and discredit Israel, Jewish historic and legal rights to their land; to intensify the fabricated accusation of Palestinian victimhood; and to motivate new students to the cause. A typical lie consists of their allegations of seven million Palestinian refugees today, while even the United Nations Relief and Works Agency for Palestine (UNRWA), no friend to Israel, puts the number at five million and admits that no other group in the world but the Palestinians includes succeeding generations in their refugee status, thus establishing an entirely new definition of "refugee." Adding insult to injury, the somewhat larger number of displaced Jews (refugees) during the same time is never articulated.

In view of such developments, it is beyond ironic that in December 2005, the Organization of the Islamic Conference (OIC) endorsed a Ten-Year Programme[488] of action for global governance and human rights and called for a UN resolution to protect Islam's image and combat "Islamophobia." They complained that racism and the defamation of religion lead to human rights violations — of Muslims, specifically. They advocated the limitation of expression — in print, audio-visual and electronic media, and the Internet; and that xenophobia, intolerance and discrimination — even implied — were intolerable. An EU Monitoring Centre, renamed Fundamental Rights Agency, committed to freedom of expression, was, instead, committed to Islamophobia. Thus, are people threatened and their rights limited, and students wage wars of words with threats of violence against other students and teaching staff. These young fascists shout down visiting speakers[489] with whom they differ, forcing their departure from campus.

Khan was thus encouraged and given authority to defy Israel›s validation and Pessin's tenure. The College condoned Pessin's sacrifice toward establishing sharia law, in which there are no freedoms of speech, thought, artistic expression or equality. Islam teaches that the Creator, Allah, granted people freedom of speech and yet, in contradiction, limited it by defining what constitutes acceptable and unacceptable speech. Evidently, Pessin dared contradict the Palestinian narrative and fell afoul of what Allah permits.

Students were further empowered to wage a war on campus because of visiting speakers invited by Eileen Kane. One was Remi Kanazi,[490] who gives poetry performances on boycotting Israel. Another guest, although cancelled, was to be Rutgers University's Jasbir K. Puar,[491] a disturbed "queer" woman who, at Vassar, spewed proven-false and libelous accusations that Israelis harvest Palestinian organs and conduct scientific experiments. Pro-Israel speakers are never invited.

Connecticut College is yet another college that has relinquished its God-given and Constitution-guaranteed rights by complying with Islam's sharia. It is time to restore American rights to the American campus, with a strategy in place to counteract jihadi conduct. Why was there no official supervision to protect a valued teacher or to schedule a hearing by responsible peers? Why were Dr. Pessin's fellow-instructors silent? President Bergeron was quick to condemn Pessin based on the allegations, but now owes the Professor an apology.

The students need to learn about being an American, and understand Dr. Pessin's rights to speech and press, regardless of their own opinions. Khan should be made to apologize to the professor and the school for creating the chaos and return the ill-gotten award or be free to leave the school.

Student advisors must know their boundaries, and inciting to discriminate, causing harm or rewarding jihad and BDS, do not fall within their job descriptions. A sincere apology is due Dr. Pessin for creating their detestable incident, waging a discriminatory campaign of falsehoods in an institute of learning, endangering Dr. Pessin and his family and causing his loss of income. These advisors deserve to lose their positions and income.

Dr. Akron was weak and unable to govern under the circumstances. Failing the task of ensuring that justice and peace prevail on campus, he must stand down — as others have done in similar circumstances (Missouri University[492] A leader is required to maintain civility on campus according to our Constitution, and in keeping with the implied promise that parents have the right to expect a safe environment and an honorable education for the tuition fees.

Intelligent classes on the true history of the Middle East and of Israel and Palestinians should be mandatory. History associate-professor and faculty advisor, James T. Downs, who uses his classroom for his anti-Semitic agenda, and Lea Land, who admits to lacking journalistic ethics for the smear campaign, should be dismissed.

American students are owed a balanced and unbiased international curriculum as well as a promise that Connecticut College will never cede their authority to sharia.

THE JOY OF WITLESSNESS

The Ayatolla Khomeini says Islam counsels war and that deniers are witless. Unable to face certain truths, an Oberlin College professor champions revisionism.

Oberlin College's assistant professor Joy Karega teaches Rhetoric and Composition. Whether pitifully ignorant of Islam or intentionally following a path of rhetoric and propaganda, a typical selection of her Facebook posts blames the Jews for both 9/11 and the Paris massacre, and asserts that ISIS is run by Israel and America.

Not only is this untrue, libelous and offensive, but it is also amoral and dangerous. Her lies could incite impressionable students to jihadi violence, thereby endangering Jewish and other American students. Lacking scruples, Karega has responded to reasonable criticism with vitriol and defiance, choosing instead to ignore facts and engage in revisionist history. She further exacerbates the damage by assigning readings to her class that explore the hazy realm of social justice, rejecting accuracy and true justice. How can an instructor so focused on accusations and mischief-making be expected to positively inspire the student writer's creativity?

At the heart of her illogical behavior one might well find the seeds of envy and resentment. Her contempt reflects the Jew-hatred that is found in the Koran. The Jews were the ones who brought ethical and intellectual monotheism[493] to the world and continue to create, invent, and make improvements to our everyday lives in innumerable ways, earning Nobel awards out of proportion to their small number, while Islamists remain fixed in the seventh century, continuing their offenses, bloodshed, destruction, looting and enslavement wherever they go.

The Islamic Arabs started the African Slave Trade.[494] "The greatest tragedy is that most of the descendants of the African slave trade are totally ignorant of the actual facts. The worst, most inhumane and most diabolical institution of the black African slave trade was initiated, refined, perpetrated and implemented by the Mohammedan Arab and later aided and abetted by the Black Congress to Mohammed and Islam ... Slavery was not created by the white races; the very word slavery comes from the Arab word Ab, meaning 'slave of Allah,' as in 'Abdullah.' All blacks are called abi, feudal or forced slaves ... Arabs institutionalized, systematized, and religiously-sanctioned slave trade on a global scale — more than 600 million over fourteen centuries (and still not abolished). The Koran allows taking of slaves as booty. Holy wars, jihad, are not holy; they are designed to plunder, slaughter, rape, subjugate and rob other humans of their wealth, produce, and freedom."

Karega may be conflicted championing those who would have enslaved her merely for her skin color, and must opt for a change of narrative, a fictitious one in which she lays the responsibility on the Jews. The following solid facts about Israel's acceptance of Jews worldwide, without regard to superficialities, may help her to escape from her self-fashioned the fictitious world.

"Operation Moses"[495] was Israel's mission to rescue the Ethiopian Jews who had long dreamed of returning to their ancient homeland. Once recognized as Diaspora Jews in 1975, and despite being forbidden to leave Ethiopia and encountering the hardships, dangers and violence along the way, they stealthily trickled their way on foot to the Sudanese border between 1975 and 1984, where they were held in camps until Israel could covertly retrieve them and fly them to a better life in Israel. Eight thousand Ethiopian Jews, 1500 of them parentless children and youths, were resettled and are now living life as Israeli citizens. The operation was halted when the Sudanese government feared Arab reprisals. This week, the last of the Yemenite Jews (19 of 200) were saved from a war zone and covertly brought to Israel.

Offering no evidence whatsoever, Karega openly denies that Islamists are responsible for the 9/11 attack. A psychologist may suggest that being subconsciously ashamed of the Muslims, she projects their depravity onto Israel, but Karega's naïve efforts to transfer blame are derided by the Muslim leadership and ISIS, who proudly distribute films for world recognition of their beheadings, burnings, and tortures. She cannot face the ugly truth that Islam is a religion of war.[496]

Omar Abdel Rahman, the "blind Sheikh," has proudly taken ownership of his successful attack on the 1993 World Trade Center. No ordinary terrorist, he holds a Juris Doctor from al-Azhar University in Cairo, with a specialty in Islamic law, sharia. He has quoted Islamic scripture precisely, proving that Allah commands Muslims to wage jihad worldwide. There are 164 similar verses within the Koran that mandate Muslims to "fight those who believe not in Allah . . . fight and slay the pagans wherever ye find them."

The foundational statement of the Muslim Brotherhood's Hamas Charter says, "Our struggle against the Jews is very great and very serious." Hatred for the Jews supplies the reason for Hamas's existence, continuing the age-old struggle of evil against good. For every Israeli innovation[497] in medical advancement; improved technology for communication, water, agriculture, etc., and Israel's outreach as First Responders[498] to countries in adversity, there are hordes of Muslims who are torturing, enslaving, raping and killing in the name of their ideology.

Mohammed Sa'id Ramadan al-Buti, Egyptian scholar from al-Azhar University, wrote, "The Holy War (Islamic Jihad) ... is basically an offensive war."[499] We are in the midst of jihad, when a Muslim fights an infidel without treaty to make the word of Allah ... forcing him to fight or invading his land ..."

Hasan al-Banna, founder of the Muslim Brotherhood (1928), wrote, "It is the nature of Islam to dominate, not to be dominated, to impose its law on all nations and to extend its power to the entire planet."[500]

The Ayatolla Khomeini, leading Muslim of the 20th century, said, "Those who know nothing of Islam pretend that Islam counsels against war. Those who say this are witless.[501] Islam says: Kill all the unbelievers ..."

Karega is either quite witless or she has taken the path of civilizational jihad, joining the bloodless propaganda war. Spending her time writing hate material, leading a life without joy and compassion, she is fulfilling the Islamic principle of preferring death over life — preferring the lives of illiterate, violent males and emotionally and physically imprisoned/shrouded females, over life as we value it. Compare their ideology with the life lived by Israelis, the advanced little country that recently earned the title of Top 5 Happiest Countries in the World[502] according to the new Better Life Index report by the Organization for Economic Co-operation and Development (OECD). (Under Obama's watch, the US dropped to 13.)

It is reasonable to suggest that Karega is more than just witless. Her hate mongering and abuse are reserved only for Jews and Israel, accusing them of imagined crimes and absolving Muslims of actual crimes. Her immaturity, malice, bigotry, and fanaticism do not conform with freedom of speech, as specified by the Supreme Court's established complex framework on the rule of false statements of facts, which can be subject to civil or criminal liability. Common limitations on speech relate to libel, slander, obscenity, incitement, fighting words, public security, public order, public nuisance, and oppression, under the harm principle, all of which appear to apply to this instructor. (Others are pornography, classified information, copyright violation, trade secrets, non-disclosure agreements, right to privacy, right to be forgotten, campaign finance reform, and perjury.)

Neither is Karega alone in her witlessness. College officials who ignore the enmity and fail to protect the Jewish students from their abusers are complicit, as well as supportive of the advancement of sharia over America's democracy. The College's President Kislov has passively submitted to the Islamic ideology that demands supremacy. He remains a spineless failure, inept and silent, allowing the invectives to proliferate unchecked, which will encourage the "moderates" to join the ranks of the jihadi oppressors in their abuse of an unprotected prey. If he cannot defend his position of leadership and protect the students from Jew-hatred, he should step down. If he lacks the integrity and courage to safeguard the school's citizens from verbal or physical discomfort, taking tuition fees from parents who believe their children are in a safe and scholarly environment, and if he cannot control a vicious renegade instructor, then he is not the man for the job.

Post script: Joy Karega has been terminated.

OF VILLAINY AT VASSAR

Vassar permits discriminatory events that sustain the perpetual Islamic war against civilization. Names have been changed for their security.

Vassar College, a private, coeducational college in Poughkeepsie, NY, has gone from prestigious to pernicious by reason of its support for the Islamic invasion of the West (America and Europe) and its biased programs against Israel and Jews. Complicit are eight of the college's 54 academic departments (including "Jewish" studies) that invite radical speakers, such as the left-wing Jewish Voice for Peace (JVP)[503] and others who advocate the BDS movement (boycott, divestment, sanctions), against Israeli products and American companies that conduct business with Israel.

Jashir Puar, Rutgers' infamous professor of women's and gender study, who is herself conflicted with her own gender identity, among other things, was a recent guest speaker. She vigorously demonizes Israel, the only Middle Eastern country that would permit her, a lesbian, to live. Without a shred of evidence, she employed the vicious, centuries-old blood libel and accused the Israel Defense Forces of harvesting Palestinian organs, adding that Israelis are poisoning Palestinians with elements, such as uranium, to stunt their growth. Curiously, she did not mention a Michigan State University report in 2014 of about two dozen Syrians who ate the hearts of their victims and died of Kuru, a neuro-degenerative disorder associated with cannibalism.504 Two others were hospitalized for treatment in Germany.

Puar is one of several who present preposterous indictments against Israel to academia's captive audiences — the unwitting students who listen raptly and the spineless faculty who remain mute during these hate-mongering sessions. Puar, who had been declared a "crackpot" by the NY Daily News, is a dangerous crackpot, who now disallows recordings of her lectures.

Psychologically at odds with her gender and consumed by animosity, Puar favors tyrannical Islam, whose police patrol the streets to enforce sharia on all and would likely condemn her to_*500–1,000 lashes*[505] and imprisonment, or execution. (The highest number of lashes recorded by Amnesty International was 40,000 for murder.) However, the rich and powerful are explicitly permitted to practice pedophilia,[506] citing supportive versus from the Koran and the examples of Mohammed.

If Palestinian growth is indeed stunted, as the professor contends without substantiation, blame may rest with the *Koran,*[507] which declares that Allah made marriage with first cousins acceptable and lawful because Mohammed seduced his first cousin and children as young as 9,[508] and endorses other sexual activities with infants.[509]

Further, consanguineous marriages — those between blood relatives — are an integral feature in Islam, accounting for more than half of all marriages in some nations and leading to a higher incidence of offspring with genetic disorders. Perhaps Islam produces these impaired children to be sacrificed to war and suicide, with a double purpose of culling out the defective results of inbreeding and assuaging the revulsion that accompanies incest and rape.[510]

In 2014, Vassar's Hillel Union, part of a 100-year-old network of Jewish students, professionals and leaders dedicated to enriching the Jewish campus experience, chose to re-define itself as "Open Hillel."[511] This is nothing less than abandoning their rules that are meant to protect Israeli and Jewish students, and showing their willingness to host anti-Semitic speakers (including Students for Justice in Palestine — SJP) who advocate to boycott, divest from and sanction (BDS) Israel.

On February 17, 2016, after several years of discriminatory events and adverse publicity, one outspoken alumnus, CAMERA Fellow Jason Storch, succeeded in bringing Palestinian Human Rights Activist Bassem Eid to speak in condemnation of Students for Justice in Palestine (SJP) and the BDS campaign, and to reveal some truths about Israel. Nevertheless, the Vassar Student Association, motivated by the SJP and forty faculty members, enacted their BDS Resolution 30-x.

Vassar Student Association Resolution 30-x294 declares Israel guilty of racial and gender inequality and oppression, using known biased sources for its condemnations. Israel is home to all races and religions and just recently brought some of the last remaining (19) Yemeni Jews to Israel in a clandestine operation. The 50,000 Yemini Jews who arrived since 1949 are now an integral part of Israeli society.[512]

Israel's Declaration of Independence states, "The State of Israel will maintain complete equality in social and political rights for all citizens, irrespective of religion, race, or sex." Equality is nonexistent in Islam, where women are subjugated and imperiled by many prohibitions, imprisonment, torture and death. Then why are these Vassar jihadists not concerned about freeing the Muslim women? Because their Koranic purpose is death to Jews and the Islamic conquest of Israel and all other lands for a global caliphate.

Citing Vassar College's mission to provide an education that promotes "analytical, informed, and independent thinking and sound judgment" and nurtures "intellectual curiosity, creativity, respectful debate," these qualities appear to be limited in application.

We are informed that students will not attend classes or lectures by pro-Israel scholars on the history of Israel or the 1967 creation of Palestinians; neither will they accept comparative analyses of Jewish, Christian and Islamic cultures and laws. So much for the "informed" and "respectful debate." Some Stanford University students are finally decrying the near extinction of Western civilization studies that began in 1964, realizing the necessity of their reinstatement if we are to remain a nation of free people.

The College naively cites the Palestinian civil authorities' call for "people of conscience" to impose broad boycotts and implement divestment initiatives against Israel, falsely accusing her of apartheid. The facts stand stubbornly against these lies and confirm that there is no apartheid in Israel. The companies to be boycotted include Sabra, Tribe, Ben & Jerry's, Hewlett-Packard Company, Ahava, General Electric, Eden Springs, and Motorola; and to divest from Caterpillar, G4S, and Elbit Systems. By opposing these companies, the BDS campaign is also opposing the survival of Israel and her people.

Yes, Israel has barriers, to protect them from Palestinian terrorists and suicide bombers who would continue to enter Israel and commit unspeakable crimes against innocent civilians. Israel is but one of many countries that need fortification from marauders and murderers. Most notably, in 2015, the Saudis began a 600-mile-long "Great Wall," as protection from the Iraqis.[513]

Although it suits the Palestinians to claim that barriers, fences, and bunkers are a means of segregation, no citizens within Israel are segregated, regardless of gender, country of origin, race or religion. The barriers exist to deter those non-citizens of Israel who ascribe to hijra and jihad.

Like the general silence about the Saudi "Great Wall," and seldom mentioned, is Mahmoud Abbas's occasional oath that any future Palestinian state will forbid entry to Israelis.

The Resolution cited three goals of the BDS campaign: (1) ending Israel's occupation and colonization of all Arab lands and dismantling the Separation Wall; (2) recognizing the fundamental rights of the Arab-Palestinian citizens of Israel to full equality; (3) and respecting, protecting and promoting the inalienable rights of Palestinian refugees to return to their homes of 1948.

(1) For 1400 years, the Mohammedans conquered, colonized and continue to occupy lands from other nations throughout the Middle East.[514] The Jewish people have a 4,000-year connection to the land of Israel,[515] including Samaria and Judea (from which is derived the name "Jew"). Israel won Judea and Samaria in a defensive war from Jordan, which had held these territories illegally for 19 years. There are no people, but the Jewish people and Jewish State of Israel, with a stronger legal and historical claim to this land. New *archaeological evidence* has again verified King David's united monarchy from the 11th to 9th centuries BCE[516] in Judah, its capital in Hebron, later moved to Jerusalem.

(1,2) Israel was reestablished as a modern state, recognized by the community of nations in May 1948. Israel began with a Jewish majority that purchased and settled the land and accorded full civil, political and cultural rights to all its minorities. Israel has the right to build a wall on her land to prevent Palestinian savagery.

(2) Israel is neither racist nor "intersectionalist." Vassar students need to learn the truth of Islam's history, the conquests and death of more than 890 million people over fourteen centuries (600 million Hindus alone).[517]

(3) The Arab refugee crisis is artificially maintained by Arab rulers to exploit their own people's "victimhood" to acquire the land they could not conquer by war, and for using acquired land as staging ground for anti-Israel propaganda and jihad. *UNRWA admitted*[518] that the Palestinian refugees are the only refugees in the world who maintain and bequeath refugee status to successive generations; their "law of return" is deception.[519] Arab apartheid laws prohibit even Jewish tourists from entering some Arab countries. The 170,000 Arabs who stayed in Israel are flourishing in Israel's free society and number more than 1,400,000.

(3) No more than 650,000 Palestinian Arabs became refugees; the UN Mediator on Palestine claims 472,000. The number of Jews fleeing Arab countries was 820,000, of which 586,000 were resettled in Israel at great

expense and no compensation from Arab governments that confiscated their possessions. Any compensation for Arab "refugees" must include the same for Jewish refugees, although very few true refugees remain since 1948.

(3) Palestinians still live *in refugee camps,*[520] even when the camps are in Palestinian Authority-controlled areas, because the PLO opposes and prevents refugee resettlement, except to Israel, as a means of conquest by increasing population. Arabs who inhabit a vast land mass of 8,368,272 sq. mi, charge the indigenous Jewish people, Israel, on 12,877 sq. mi. with colonialization[521] and the absurdity is supported by the United Nations.

It is time for President Catharine Bond Hill to evaluate her role at Vassar, where she has allowed the school to become a platform for propaganda in the Islamic war against Israel and the West (Europe and America are also targeted). By ceding control of the school to one of the most backward and immoral cultures on the planet, she has reduced the quality of education and the school's integrity. These actions encourage further submission to sharia law, with increased censorship, FMG (female genital mutilation), rape, beheadings, chopping limbs, burning people alive, brutal lashings, death by stoning, and enslavement of her fellow human beings. She has surrendered the school to agents of Islam whose sole existence is to destroy civilization – Kurds, Yazidis, Copts, Christians, Shia and Sunni Muslims, and Israel, one of the most advanced cultures on the planet, from which we benefit greatly in medicine, technology, science, agriculture, water conservation, and more.

If President Hill does not grasp this and Vassar maintains this path, how is she qualified to preside over the college and how does the college continue to qualify for Accreditation? Surely, it is time for her to bring visiting pro-Israel speakers to all the students, to present factual, accurate information about Israel and Palestinian Arabs — speakers such as Professor Alan Dershowitz, Ambassador Michael Oren, Nonie Darwish, speakers from StandWithUs, CUFI (Christians United With Israel), and others. Vassar had been designated an education institution and it is time that Vassar took the obligation in earnest. If American students are not taught the truth, we will surely pay a heavy price.

"The only thing more expensive than education is ignorance."
— Benjamin Franklin.

OFFENSE BY DESIGN

A Muslim student in hijab's stealth assault on her fellow students is defended by student editor of school paper. (Names were changed to protect their privacy)

"Opening Your Eyes to Other Cultures," was written by online Editor-in-Chief Della about Ayla an American teen born to Lebanese parents. In a high school with students who enjoy their myriad inherited differences as much as they do their mutual accomplishments, Ayla asserts that she is not entirely comfortable with her hijab and blames her classmates. The newsletter of the small midwestern high school proudly presents stories and photographs of students of all ethnicities, levels and types of achievements, who have found friends and camaraderie from among the substantial school population. And how can we forget other brilliant, famous women from the Middle East - ACT! for America's Brigitte Gabriel, Nonie Darwish, Ayaan Hirsi Ali and many more — who have assimilated, achieved, and are widely applauded in every setting?

Integration is often slow for new immigrants, particularly when they must master a new language, find employment, and adapt to a new culture. It is the human condition, even for a child who must change to a new school within the same state, but Ayla has few of these disadvantages. This country offers the freedoms to reside, to work, to attend school, to worship, to dress, to speak, but there is no right to not be offended, as that would limit another speaker's freedom. We have all experienced being offended at least once in our lives, but we have the right to express another opinion, leave the premises, and seek and court new friendship elsewhere, if necessary.

Ayla made the revealing suggestion that her scarf may be intimidating others. Surely, the Tignon scarf originally worn by women in the slave era and present[522] and the Tichel scarf worn by orthodox Jewish women[523] are among many kinds of headwear and not intimidating. Ayla appears to be projecting her own attitude to the inanimate hijab,[524] or she might be using it to support a complaint of victimization to the school authorities. She did specify that it reminds her of who she is, and I would ask "Who is she?"

The hijab ("veil" or "covering" in Arabic) that she has chosen to wear meets the requirements of sharia,[525] whose harsh, excessive laws come directly from the founder of Islam. Likewise, Mohammed himself laid down the extreme punishments and policies, which, unlike the Judeo-Christian laws, rob people of their dignity. Islam's brutality is antithetical to the US Constitution, and if Ayla believes the Koran to be Allah's literal words, then its many passages direct her to wage even a non-violent war on non-Muslims. Is the obligatory hijab symbolic of her personal jihad (holy war) worn to intimidate others and bring them to silence and submission?

Dr. Tawfik Hamid, a self-described, former-Islamic extremist and a fellow at the Potomac Institute for Policy Studies, declares a relationship between wearing the hijab and so-called "passive terrorism."[526] Does Ayla heed the ethic that promotes Islamic supremacy and conquest? Is she learning the commands to wage war against non-Muslims? to be anti-Semitic? to chop hands and feet from thieves? to kill homosexuals? to relegate women to full obedience to their male guardians? Does the hijab help her identify with these doctrines and does she secretly relish the belief that her headwear does indeed "intimidate" others?

It is plausible that Ayla agrees with the concept of "Our Mission,"[527] penned by Hassan Al Banna in Egypt, 1928, which declares that Islam is all-embracing to regulate every aspect of life, and that Muslims are obligated to use jihad to combat the decadent West, to control "offensive" language, to control others and make them submissive to Islam. The Muslim Brotherhood has been active in the United States since the 1960s. The movement's first long-term strategy, crafted in 1975, focuses on proselytizing efforts for youths and newly arrived Muslim immigrants. Seeking state and federal political influence, the Brotherhood formed multiple religious organizations, such as the Muslim Students' Association (MSA), the Islamic Society of North America (ISNA), the Islamic Circle of North America (ICNA), and the Muslim American Society (MAS) (among many others). In 1991, they issued a programmatic memorandum, "The General Strategic Objective[528] for the [Brotherhood] in North America," highlighting its goal to penetrate the heart of American society — that all Muslims had to "understand that their work in America [was] a grand jihad in eliminating and destroying Western civilization from within and sabotaging its miserable house by their hands so that God's religion [Islam] is victorious over all religions."

Islamic religious authorities tell us that loyalty to Islam is incompatible with loyalty to America, so that Ayla must choose between identifying with her laws or with her fellow students. She may not realize that by wearing the hijab and identifying herself with Islamic scripture, she is displaying her disloyalty to America and offending her classmates. Ayla paints herself as a victimized minority in this land of more than 2,000 mosques and an increasing flood of Muslim immigrants by the tens of thousands. According to FBI statistics, 48.5 percent of hate crimes are race-based, with 66.2 percent of those being anti-black; 18.7 percent of crimes are religion-based biases, of which 62.4 percent against Jews and Jewish institutions; 11.6 percent were anti-Islamic.[529]

Victimization is a recognized, essential strategy of Islam. The best way to justify hate is to assume the role of victim; one cannot hate unless one feels oppressed and victimized. Hitler came to power based on Germany's defeat in WW I and her victimization. Similarly, Muslims are taught from toddlerhood that their miseries are the fault of Israel, America, and the West, and it is the job of the Council of Islamic-American Relations (CAIR) to identify anything on which to base accusations of hatemongering and villainy.

Islamic terrorism is reality. A review of the past fourteen centuries exposes the bloodshed and beheadings begun by their prophet and continued by his followers into the present. Today, the largest persecuted religious group is Christian, but let's go back in time. Mohammed invaded Medina and Mecca,[530] beheaded 800 Jewish men, took women as slaves and booty. Muslims conquered the Indian sub-continent 1400 years ago,[531] and began destroying the world's greatest of civilizations — every Hindu man, woman and child, for a total of 100 million Hindus. Muslims slaughtered millions of Armenians during World War I. The 3000-year march of terror against Copts continues in Egypt, and 2,000-year-old Syrian-Christian towns are today being destroyed. Boko Haram kidnaps Christian girls and forces them into a life of sexual slavery. Christians and Hindus are persecuted to near annihilation in Pakistan. Buddhists in Thailand, Hindus in India and Jews in Israel are routinely assaulted and murdered.[532]

Muslim men abuse their own wives and daughters with FGM (Female Genital Mutilation), bans on independence, beatings, and forced restrictive clothing. The Madrid attack (3/04), the London trains bombing (7/07), the Fort Hood massacre (11/09), the Boston Marathon bombing (4/13), the Nairobi Mall massacre (9/13), the Charlie Hebdo/Paris attack (1/15), and the recent horrific Orlando massacre (6/16) are honest examples of the 32,423 deadly terror attacks carried out by Muslims since 9/11, to date. Non-Muslims are the real victims.

Ayla is safe. She may be offended, and she may be conflicted, but she needs to understand what she wants out of life, whether it is Islam and strict sharia law or a civilized life as an assimilated American. She can't have both.

OFFENSE BY DESIGN, Pt. 2

School indoctrination leads to moral equivalency, blindness to truth about the Koran and Islamic history. The thought process is distorted and immobilized. (Names were changed to protect their privacy)

It began when Della, a high school junior and editor of her school newspaper in suburbia, Ohio, championed Ayla, a senior in hijab, complained to school authorities that she was a victim of racial bias. To the disquieting article, I wrote "Offense by Design,"[533] and Della replied in her own defense. In response to my readers' requests and to Della, I submit the following about the severely misinformed product of our deteriorating national educational system.

Della, a first-generation American of a Holocaust-surviving Jewish family, attended Jewish day school as a youngster before entering this public high school, and presumes knowledge about immigrants, irrespective of the individual's personal history, heritage, culture, language, beliefs, needs, aspirations and expectations. By referencing 11 million Nazi victims,[534] she dismissed the conventional number of six million Jews exterminated specifically for their religion, two-thirds of Europe's Jewish population. (New research indicates the number could well be 20 million people in some 42,500 Nazi ghettos and camps,[535] not the accepted 1,500.) Hitler called himself a barbarian,[536] and despised morality; hence, he abhorred the Jews, guardians of ethics and morals, and made them his priority in his race war. Della's Holocaust lessons appear to have been sideswiped and distorted by the Leftist position.

Pursuant to my negating her blaming Donald Trump for America's current racism, Della glossed over the growing divisiveness since 2008, when Trump was absent from the scene. It was President Obama who divided and undermined our country at home and abroad, repeatedly sullying our American history to our enemies, diminishing our exceptionalism, insulting and betraying our allies, and even initiating the teaching climate that increasingly blames white people for all our ills.

Obama snubs the white Christians who left England's monarchy to create a republic; establish our national government, fundamental laws, and guarantee certain basic rights for its citizens. Our US Constitution and The Bill of Rights (the first Ten Amendments) protect the individual from tyranny; and the Republican Party,[537] specifically, instituted our 13th Amendment against slavery; our 14th Amendment to ensure that no State can deprive any person of life, liberty, or property without due process; and the 15th Amendment that guarantees the right to vote regardless of race, color, or previous condition of servitude, against strong opposition by the Democrat party.

By sermonizing to the American people on gun control, gay rights, racial discrimination, our police and armed forces, climate change, transgender bathrooms, immigration, etc., Obama pits one faction of the community against the other. Divisiveness exists in school textbooks because Hillary Clinton ("it takes a village") and President Obama implemented the Common Core curriculum that supports Islam while suppressing Judaism, Christianity, and Americanism. The program, crafted by the unqualified David Coleman and funded by the Bill Gates Foundation and a 45-percent investment interest by Dubai World/Istithmar World Board of Directors (EMPG) in the publishing companies that provide 52 percent of American textbooks,[538] was presented by then-US Secretary Arne Duncan to the National Governors Association with a threat of withholding funds — long before Trump's appearance. This was eagerly accepted by Governors Jeb Bush and John Kasich. Instead of learning the Declaration of Independence, Articles of Confederation, the Constitution, Bill of Rights and the Ten Commandments, today's students study the Five Pillars of Islam, the Hajj, and the Ka'aba.[539] To his credit, during his campaign, Trump promised to return the right of education to the states (10th Amendment) where it belongs.

Ayla, born in the US, may be "just another awkward teen," but she chose to blame her fellow students for her own discomfort. Everyone has differences to overcome, whether in the classroom, social setting, or workplace, and perhaps Ayla did not extend herself enough — demanding, instead of earning, respect. Yet Della, who authored the article, presented the perfect example of Common Core thinking by citing Ayla's and her own feelings. Students are learning affective, emotional outcome-based conclusions instead of common sense/critical thinking or factual verification.

Nevertheless, not so long ago, the hijab provoked only mild interest and curiosity, but today's thoughts align Islamic dress with Islamic violence and destruction of non-

Islamic cultures. Who is to blame? The non-Muslim whose life is under daily threat? or the Muslim who represents the ideology that boasts its intent to dominate the world?[540]

Mohammed Akram, a Muslim Brotherhood (MB) operative in Virginia, understood that a "soft" or "stealth jihad" would be more effective than terrorism in subduing the West. He wrote that their "work in America is a kind of grand jihad in eliminating and destroying the Western civilization from within and 'sabotaging' its miserable house by their hands." This is where the blame lies. If the non-Muslim responds with suspicion or animosity, he/she must not be reproached, but understood.

It is fair to say that we all experience times of ridicule or rejection, and the following three healthy guidelines might be of help to anyone in that common situation:

- Don't criticize, condemn, or complain
- Become genuinely interested in other people
- Join, praise, and appreciate others.

Ayla's donning the scarf of the stealth jihadist appears to be a statement, pushing boundaries and creating a societal discomfort for Islamic gain. Provocation through her hijab and its tie to an oppressive culture brings her victimhood, attention, and reaction, and Della, the writer, should not be assuming the position of Islamic apologist.

If Ayla does not sympathize with the violence and bloodshed seen in New York, Boston, Florida, Madrid, London, Brussels, Germany, Paris, Nice, Calais, Bosnia, Argentina, Mali, Israel, Kenya, (and more), she should be directing her anger at her co-religionists who announce their exclusivity, hate and brutality, and who have virtually destroyed any Islamic claims to being civilized. Towards her fellow students, she should have shown more humility combined with an openness to discuss her values and beliefs in order to gain acceptance. In a civilized society, it is incumbent upon the one who gives offense to apologize, not the one who is offended. Ayla might have chosen to show genuine grace and good manners rather than create a situation of suspicion and animosity. She might also have considered the likely fate of an individual's wearing a cross or kipah in Islamic society.

To Della's offensive defamatory statement of moral equivalence — that terrorism exists among all religions, another sign of her Leftist education — I provide statistics: The number of deadly Islamic terrorist attacks since 9/11, to date (01/22/18), is 32,423; the death count mounting rapidly, with the number of severely injured unknown. Islam is at war with minorities and majorities in 33 countries; 57 percent of anti-religious hate crimes in the US targets Jews and 17 percent targets Muslims. In Europe, the majority of hate crimes against Jews are committed by Muslims, and less than one percent of hate crimes against Muslims are carried out by Jews.

Islam has the unenviable reputation for being the only religion that teaches, as a matter of doctrine, violence against all other people:

Quran 8/60: "Against them make ready your strength to the utmost of your power, including steeds of war, to strike terror into (the hearts of) the enemies of God."

Quran 9/29: Fight against those who (1) believe not in Allah, (2) nor in the Last Day, (3) nor forbid that which has been forbidden by Allah and His Messenger (4) and those who acknowledge not the religion of truth (i.e. Islam) among the people of the Scripture (Jews and Christians), until they pay the Jizya[541] with willing submission and feel themselves subdued.

Islam is a religion of war: its followers inflict death and destruction upon both Muslims and non-Muslims daily, with growing sadism and ferocity. American students are a captive audience to unscrupulous instruction, manipulated to mask the truth and protect the guilty with accusations of Islamophobia. Della and her teachers should be duty-bound to provide the statistics of the Jewish and Christian terror attacks they claim, and other accusations, or apologize for the unwarranted and offensive defamation.

June 2016's statistics alone should have been another warning: 238 attacks, 2055 killed, 2006 injured, in 13 countries, by Muslims. As a reporter, writer, and potential voter, Della cast blame upon Mr. Trump for the thousands of unvetted migrants brought in by Barack Obama and Hillary Clinton into safe "receiving" communities and for the subsequent growing crime and carnage — the honor killings, stabbings, beheadings, mass rape of young women that remain unreported by mainstream media.

Sharia obliges Muslims to engage in jihad worldwide. There is not a country where there are Muslims, where the construction of that first mosque doesn't result in conflict with the host population. Obama's Department of Justice is suing Bensalem Township, Pennsylvania,[542] for refusing their first mosque, the forerunner of unvetted migrants into an unsuspecting community. And more than half the Muslims living in America today say they would prefer sharia law over the US Constitution!

While most Muslims may not follow the directives or engage in jihad, the reality is that the imposition of strict sharia doctrine is followed at various stages across the world, and it includes the repugnant behaviors and crimes. Through our own freedoms of religion and diversity, we inadvertently enforce a tolerance that allows for an unconstitutional agenda. Tolerance of the intolerable is civilizational suicide.

Della bristled at the comparison between Muslims and Hitler. She cited the people killed by Nazis over five years, but ignored the forces of sharia that have warred against non-Muslims for 1400 years, and against America for 220 years — when Thomas Jefferson repulsed the Barbary pirates,[543] beginning with 1778. "Fight them; Allah will punish them by your hands and will disgrace them and give you victory over them and satisfy the breasts of believing people and remove the fury in the believers' hearts (Qur'an 9:14-15).

Jihad destroyed a Christian Middle East, a Christian North Africa, and the Persian Zoroastrians — about 60 million people; annihilated about 600 million Hindus; devastated the first Western Buddhists (Greeks descended from Alexander) and all Buddhists, about 110 million, along the Silk Route; and obliterated more than 120 million Christians and animists in Africa. The Jews became permanent targets throughout Islam. With as many as 890 million[544] killed by Muslims, yes, Islam can be compared to Nazism.

The Muslim Brotherhood (MB) was founded in Egypt in 1928 by Hassan al-Banna, a Muslim who admired Hitler's hatred of the Jews[545] and wrote to Hitler of his desire to collaborate with the Nazi party. With Nazi support, al-Banna developed the Brotherhood into a Middle East ally, complete with spy network and troops in the Waffen-SS Handschar Divisions. Haj Amin al-Husseini, the Grand Mufti of Jerusalem,[546] was another Hitler admirer. The Palestine Brigade that helped Britain was Jewish; the Muslims fought for Hitler and joined the invasion of the new nation of Israel. The MB in Israel created Hamas, which uses the Nazi salute and reads Mein Kampf. Translated into Arabic in 1930 and retitled My Jihad, it remains a bestseller in the Islamic world. And yes, again, Islam can be compared to Nazism.

The Hebrew and Christian scriptures do not command or endorse murder, but the Koran contains at least 109 verses that call Muslims to war with nonbelievers for the sake of Islamic rule, along with instructions to chop off heads, fingers, and kill infidels. They are warned to fight or be sent to Hell, facts omitted from the classroom.

The Left teaches that it is morally superior to accept all religions as peaceful, which keeps the populace blind to the truth that the Koran leads to violence and death. Islam is intolerant: the apostate deserves to be killed; all public expression of ideas and art must submit to sharia's prohibitions; musical instruments are condemned; those who listen to singing will have their ears filled with lead; those who make pictures will burn in Hell (their art is geometrical); all literature must meet sharia's restrictions; those who resist must be killed. The United Nations finally revealed the number of honor killings worldwide (Muslim-on-Muslim crime, men against their wives and daughters) at 5,000 per year.[547] In this Obama Era, we suppress and tolerate criminal behavior in the name of relativism, tolerance, anti-racism, diversity and political correctness, and shroud the truth as they shroud their women, and allow ourselves to be deceived.[548]

Della tried to explain away Islamic terrorism, indulge Ayla's position of feigned victimhood, and to be dismissive of Orthodox Jews who were Hitler's earliest victims as roaming Brown Shirts (stormtroopers)[549] cut their beards and made them clean the streets with toothbrushes, who were gassed along with other Jews, who were ridiculed in cartoons that Muslims now reproduce for their own hate propaganda, and who labored side by side with all other Jews to build a thriving democratic Israel out of barren swamp land. The orthodox were among the Jews who had to relinquish their beautiful city, Gush Katif, with its thriving greenhouse businesses, to make room for Arabs in a failed "land for peace" exchange, as the city was converted into a rocket-launching pad. Her own heritage aside, Della was taught to malign Jews who dedicate themselves to live by the laws of the Torah and Commandments, and who transmit the honesty and morality of Judaism from one generation to the next.

American school children are learning what Palestinian children learn — to disparage Jews and Israel, which could again lead to genocide. Muslim student groups' anti-Semitic activity is eight times more likely to occur on a college campus if one anti-Zionist group exists. The number of anti-Semitic campus incidents increased by 45 percent from last year. Suppression of freedom of speech[550] and assembly for Jewish students doubled from last year. Jews are reminded at every Passover Seder that the enemy rises up against them in every generation, and it is distressing to see how Della and other students are being indoctrinated.

We know that not all Muslims are the same, and we don't know Ayla's perspective, but I think it was fair to lay out the case. I personally wish her well and hope she and this entire generation, which is also my grandchildren's generation, live happy American lives, in security, under our laws and the guaranteed freedoms.

I wrote more than I'd intended, but falsehoods and accusations without proof require fewer words than their repudiation, which requires reason and explanation. Today's educational system has been severely corrupted, and the children are deprived of much. When we return America to her original greatness, I hope that we will be able to do the same with our educational system.

My information comes from several sources, and I recommend the reader avail him or herself of the data within the links provided. I recommend a simple, short book, *Sharia Law for Non-Muslims,* by Bill Warner, Center for the Study of Political Islam, and another, though larger, but also an easy read, Sharia, the threat to America; an exercise in competitive analysis, Report of Team B II.

AN EDUCATION IN CORRUPTION

A teacher of American government, affected by Democrat party bias and revisionist textbooks, can no longer function.

I took the liberty of addressing a form letter, dated October 24, 2016, signed by Carol Meek and "Paid for by the Ohio Democrat Party." An Ohio public school teacher for 33 years, she was distraught about constantly hearing Donald Trump's "mean, cruel, racist, and reprehensible" words. Of course, this has been the persistent smear campaign conducted against Mr. Trump by the Democrat party and mainstream media, which also buries Hillary's scandals.

Meek said, "The 2016 election is no longer an opportunity to teach about American government in real time . . . because of the vile words and behavior of Donald Trump." How askew she is! This is the perfect time to see our government in action, in this age of a despotic ruling class protected by a corrupt media, when one man, not of the establishment, who lives the American dream, wants to work and restore our purloined freedoms. Meek's students would be exposed to revealed "private conversation" as well as to illegal, private, scheming conversation with people who buy and sell favors that harm our country. They would have seen "in real time" the presidential debates controlled by biased moderators, and learned later that one candidate, Hillary, was illegally prepared for the debates with questions provided in advance. We may soon watch "in real time" how justice will prevail in a court of law against a candidate who enriched herself on foreign funds, with a history of corruption that should render her ineligible for office.[551]

We have a larger, empowered government that has eroded our liberties, and children who are reading indoctrinal textbooks that provide a leftist and Islamic agenda — and too little about American government as it is meant to be, should they be required to defend it for future generations.

If Meek will teach about American government, she must overcome the revisionism and expose the deeds and effects of our current administration and how Hillary Clinton intends to carry on in Obama's stead. I compare Trump's vile words (yet unverified accusations) with the following:

Bill Clinton's sexual deviancy and other misconduct while in public office that led to his impeachment by the US House of Representatives on charges of perjury and obstruction of justice.

Exposure of Hillary Clinton's numerous misdeeds courageously reported by "the fixer" who worked for the Clintons for many years and her links to unresolved deaths of 47 acquaintances.

Hillary's "hellacious" verbal abuse to the Secret Service[552] who considered protection of the Clintons punishment.

President Obama is considered the most divisive president[553] in our history. The Black Lives Matter movement endangers police and aligns with Hamas against Jews and Israel. The BDS (boycott-divestment-sanctions) in schools across America victimizes Jewish and white students. Academia teaches that America is immoral. Our First and Tenth Amendments are compromised, and Hillary threatens the Second Amendment.

The Clintons use the IRS and FBI to target political opponents, including subjects of Bill's sexual trysts.

James O'Keefe of Project Veritas is filing a formal complaint against the Federal Election Commission (FEC) and Hillary Clinton's campaign for violence at Republican rallies and voter fraud — willful evasion of federal election law requirements.

Under Hillary's watch, urgent requests from Ambassador J. Christopher Stevens's team at the CIA annex for military back-up during the attack on the US consulate in Benghazi were repeatedly denied. She lied that the attack was due to a video.

As Secretary of State, Hillary travelled the Islamic world, accepting payments in the millions of dollars for "speeches," which were pay-to-play donations for despots to control America's direction and policies.

The Haiti earthquake of 2010 that killed 200,000+ and left 1.5 million homeless attracted $10.5Bn in aid, with $3.9Bn from the US. The Clintons stepped in, controlled construction of an industrial park and posh hotels, and are accused of stealing the citizens' money and resources. The Haitians were never helped.

Muslims are employed in cabinet positions and as close advisors, some connected to the Muslim Brotherhood, working in opposition to our American way of life. Obama's list of Muslims earmarked for high governmental positions has recently come to light, as well as the stealth imposition of sharia law in American courts and unmarked halal foods introduced into our schools and supermarkets.

Hillary's emails are proving to be a betrayal of our country's highest confidential information, and their illegal destruction verifies her awareness. Meek's students should learn why the press was established and how it is failing its obligations by covering up probable sedition. Discuss the First Amendment with the students.

The Affordable Healthcare program, aka Hillarycare, constructed by Jonathan Gruber,[554] and presented to the trusting populace by the duplicitous House Minority Leader Nancy Pelosi, furtively became law because of the "stupidity of the American voter." Premiums will be increased by double digits (with care halved), as Gruber admitted it was designed to morph into a government-controlled system, another departure from democracy.

A note about Israel, our local and beneficial ally because of her strategic location; cooperation on intelligence gathering; unparalleled military support to America; trade of about $15Bn; innovation in medicine, technology, agriculture; assistance during crises (Marathon bombing, California's drought, etc.). Hillary will continue Obama's work to destroy democratic Israel by betraying her borders and ultimately allowing the UN to delegitimize her identity. Hillary continues to condemn Israel's normal housing growth while refusing to recognize Jerusalem as Israel's eternal capital. Trump promises to move the US embassy to Jerusalem.

We have a growing record debt of $20T. Hillary will increase taxes on the middle class and remove our Second Amendment while welcoming untold

156 | TABITHA KOROL

unvetted millions — an existential threat. Our freedoms are under attack and our students would benefit from learning our heritage and the laws designed to protect our civilization.

Common Core Standards[555] is a progressive vision of education, described to "mobilize the nation for excellence and equity in mathematics and science." Mobilization means social activism, social engineering for equity or equal outcome; removing academic knowledge, learning, thinking, creativity, thriving, excelling, and pursuing one's dream, and replacing them with common (equal) attributes for workforce development skills, directing students into a very early career pathway. Common Core suppresses character, creativity, and the pursuit of excellence for the sake of sameness and mediocrity.

Hillary's progressive agenda includes indoctrinating almost all school children in America with a social justice agenda that is based on pure emotion instead of on fact-based reasoning, which is producing violence and rebellion in our young.

National investments in educational technologies resulted in zero improvements in student achievement. Technology enables, but does not drive, high-performance learning. Children are not being taught how to think, but what to think. Grades reflect equality, not excellence; the desires to "learn and go forth" (and follow one's dreams) are quashed.

Contrary to the Tenth Amendment that reserves education to the States or the people (parents), it is now under government control, with a school-to-work (cradle-to-grave) model of instruction that discourages student individuality. Manipulated according to market need, their natural talents and interests are forced into compliance for a dumbed-down workforce.

Emphasizing collaborative learning (discouraging individuality), interpersonal relations (dependency on others), and affective domain (feeling, not reasoning) moves the classes away from individualism to group-think, co-operative learning, and outcomes-based education —repressing this generation's inherent creativity.

History textbooks provide information that is deliberately wrong, fallacious, revisionist, and biased, yet this teacher of 33 years naively accepts them as solid facts.

Deliberately injurious is the removal of classical studies that improve creativity, imagination, writing and speaking skills, and replacing them with corporate data (dry, boring, discouraging the desire to read) and sexualized (shaming and fear-inducing) literature beyond their maturity; removing phonics (phenome awareness, the ability to hear, identify, increase vocabulary); and removing cursive writing (which contributes to cognitive development — conscious reasoning, interpreting sensory input, guiding physical actions, empathizing with others).

Carol Meek claims an extensive educational background, yet she justifies teaching according to Common Core standards that also destroys truth, minimizes the importance of Americanism, Judaism, and Christianity, and misrepresents the Islamic ideology. Selectively, she also chooses the one blight against Trump while hiding the numerous crimes committed by Hillary.

Eleven days before the election, FBI Director James Comey has re-opened the investigation against Hillary. How do the following compare with Donald Trump's private speech?

18USC§201	Bribery
18USC§208	Acts Effecting a Personal Financial Interest (Includes Recommendations)
18USC§371	Conspiracy
18USC§1001	False Statements
18USC§1341	Frauds and Swindles (Mail Fraud)
18USC§1343	Fraud by Wire
18USC§1349	Attempt and Conspiracy (To Commit Fraud)
18USC§1505	Obstruction of Justice
18USC§1519	Destruction (Alteration or Falsification) Of Records in Federal Investigation
18USC§1621	Perjury (Including Documents Signed Under Penalties of Perjury)
18USC§1905	Disclosure of Confidential Information
18USC§1924	Unauthorized Removal and Retention of Classified Documents or Material
18USC§2071	Concealment (Removal or Mutilation) Of Government Records
18USC§7201	Attempt to Evade or Defeat a Tax (Use of Clinton Foundation Funds for Personal or Political Purposes)
18USC§7212	Attempts to Interfere with Administration of Internal Revenue Laws (Call to IRS On Behalf of UBS Not Turning Over Accounts To IRS)

Copies of Carol Meek's form letter have undoubtedly overwhelmed the postal services, encouraging readers to vote for Hillary based on her opponent's negatives, while disregarding Hillary's incalculable crimes. The letter omits Clinton's leftist-to-globalist agenda and her desire to emulate Angela Merkel's flooding Germany and Europe with criminal Islamists, and omits Hillary's resolve for a continuous, borderless Western hemisphere, where the millions may come for our bounty until we are financially destroyed. It is then that the unassimilated, backed by oil wealth, will establish a global caliphate and Hillary may somehow aspire to taking up the sword and scepter. May the renewed FBI actions awaken the voters so that we may not leave a lawless country to our progeny.

A CHOICE OF ONE

This stealth assault was intended to provoke a sense of guilt over western prosperity and breadth of choice, to ascribe to the gullible audience the promise of superior morality when they accept Islam over American decadence.

Chautauqua Institution, originally a cultural center, continues to be a disseminator of Islamic messaging to reach out to uninformed Christians and Jews who are already programmed to accept multiculturalism. Featured speaker Shadi Hamid, a senior fellow at the Brookings Institution's Project on US Relations with the Islamic Center for Middle East Policy, is part of the worldwide movement financed by oil money.

On August 9, he spoke of American anxiety, incongruously blaming occasions such as buying jam at the grocer's, where, alas, so many choices will cause regret that he hasn't purchased the best option. He sees no beauty in the many fruits, flavors or quality, or why, if one manufacturer makes jams and employs and pays a decent wage to improve life for himself and his neighbors, another cannot do the same in another locality. Why must ingenuity be stifled and why can't others enjoy the fruits of their labor?

Blind to possibilities, Hamid is instead guided by Islamic rules, allowing only one jam, or having one of his housebound wives make it. He prefers that leadership dictate one's lifestyle, whether by conversion or force; create one nation, the _Ummah_[556]; one law, sharia; and one goal, world domination. One might even consider one garment for all women, a burqa.

Where democratic nations have excelled in science and technology, medical advances, improvements in agriculture and water technology so that humanity may flourish, the Islamic culture is based on shame and honor, and a high illiteracy rate to impede advancement and dissent. Their greatness will come when all vestiges of forward-looking societies are destroyed.

He described the universal condition as a "struggle," but he meant "jihad," just as Hitler meant "Mein Kampf." Hamid is a "moderate" unweaponed jihadi, hoping to conquer by message, to convince his conditioned audience that his culture is superior, and particularly to reach those who have chosen to worship at the altar of liberalism and forsake Judaism and Christianity, from which derived those freedoms, morals and ethics imperative to happiness and peace. Judaism and Christianity do not struggle for meaning; struggle is a proclivity of all forms of fascism, because authoritarianism provides no contentment.

The divisiveness that Hamid sees in America comes not from democracy, but from those who seek its destruction. Our laws provide respect for human rights, religious freedom, workers' rights, stability, a secure peace by combating international terrorism, prosperity, open markets and economic development, and improvement in the global environment and human health. The enemy hopes to use our laws to defeat us. Arab-American author Nonie Darwish penned a warning, "America must protect its democracy, culture, and sovereignty from nations with aspirations of conquering us from within."

We need look only to the Islamic Middle East to see Hamid's "rich tapestry of traditions and contentment" — the rampant violence that has now created a *"lost generation"*[557] of Middle East men — 30,000 suicides, 35,000 deaths from interpersonal violence, a ten-fold increase of fatalities from HIV/AIDS in 25 years (a side effect of FGM on women), and 144,000 deaths from wars in 22 Islamic nations.

Other twisted threads of this vintage brocade constitute the sharp increase in non-communicable diseases in the Eastern Mediterranean[558] region — depression, anxiety, bipolar disorder, schizophrenia. The death toll from Islamic terrorists[559] since 9/11, at 31,546 (to date), is born of, but also affects, the families from which these terrorists are woven.

The speaker educated his audience that Mohammed, a prophet, was also theologian, politician, head of state, and state builder, but his list was incomplete. His prophet was also a warmonger, conqueror, murderer, beheader, enslaver, rapist and pedophile. Hamid imperiously denounced the Bible as not being the entire word of God, but tells us that the Koran is – (of a god who wreaks pain and havoc on his children).

While also insinuating that the Hebrew Scriptures are superseded by the Christian Scriptures (although the former provides the foundational doctrines for the latter), he added that the Koran supersedes the Christian. In a few words, he has delegitimized the basis for all Western civilization, slighting the world's most compassionate laws by which humans live in comparative harmony.

Interestingly, Hamid acknowledged that Islam is also a political doctrine. He cannot distinguish the role of religion from state because Islam is a theocracy, and their deity, Allah, the sole source from which all authority is derived.

The rule of conquest is carried out by both armed terrorists and self-styled moderates working within the framework of the invaded country to insinuate their laws in increments, gradually and differently, shrewdly modified to suit the invaded host culture.

The speaker closed with the usual feigned victimization, a plea for "peaceful disagreement if there must be disagreement." This is taqiyyah, holy deception, "a strategy to make Islam dominant; a persistent tactic of the skilled to deceive the non-Muslims and downplay the threat of Islam." Yet the reality is that while mosques are being erected throughout the US, Christians and Jews are not demanding churches and synagogues in Saudi Arabia. While American school cafeterias are removing pork from the fare to accommodate Muslim students, Jewish students are not demanding kosher foods anywhere. While our textbooks have been revised to accept whitewashed Islam, Americans are being robbed of their own history.

Of all the ethnic groups that have come to America, Muslims are the only ones who require accommodation, and create neighborhoods[560] and school areas that exclude others. His is the group that will use our laws to enact theirs for dominion.

Dear reader, his was not a neophyte's extemporaneous speech. Hamid's words were judiciously chosen, with a lesson to be derived from his explicit example of achieving contentment from only one jar of jam. He cares not a whit about quality, flavor, or your preference; he wants only one choice of jam and one choice of religion — Islam. In 1400 years, Islam was unable to produce the quality and flavor of Western civilization, but if they could succeed in annihilating Western civilization, ahhh, then Islam would finally be the best and only choice.

This is civilizational jihad. This guest is one of many who come to indoctrinate the uninformed in Chautauqua, that fewer choices mean fewer worries. Life is not made better, but infinitely simpler when you do as you're told, eat what you're given, and dare not complain. It is more than just a "Shadi" deal; it is bondage.

GOOD MORNING, LITTLE COMRADES
A deceptive academia is changing our children to destroy our nation.

Nikita S. Krushchev said, "Comrades! We must abolish the cult of the individual decisively, once and for all."

Vladmir Ilyich Lenin said, "Give me four years to teach the children and the seed I have sown will never be uprooted."

The teachings of the Left include discrediting the Bible and replacing religion with social justice, dishonoring America and family, controlling the schools and curricula, and normalizing promiscuity. The Left has set about "deconstructing" (breaking down) the child's psychology, removing every facet of life that provides the sense of security needed to create a mature, stable, responsible, independent, confident, and productive adult who will contribute to a free society. And it is through today's schools that they are deconstructing our children in order to destroy the free society.

♦ Education reformers are damaging the children's psyche with gender redefinition,[561] creating dysfunctional adults with confused purpose.

- California lawmakers are proposing SB48;[562] radicals, elitists and pseudo-experts are selling corruption disguised as freedom, promoting homosexual lifestyles while reducing morality and responsibility.

- Fine literature that hones our comprehension and creative skills, teaching initiative and courage, are replaced with dystopian literature that adds to the children's sadness, immorality, and overall impairment. Mis-education[563] is becoming un-education.

- Cursive writing,[564] known to enhance creativity, is removed from curricula, and restricts the student's ability to read our founding documents and understand their rights, inducing subservience.

- Common core began with higher standards,[565] intentionally designed to frustrate and cede education control to the *government*,[566] making for unhappy students. Standards were then lowered across the board, to falsely lift self-esteem, reduce achievement and raise grades, but not in keeping with maturity and ability levels.

- Fatherless households[567] lead to irresponsibility, rebellion, and crime; welfare policies encourage unmarried motherhood and incomplete families.

- Schools discredit our Judeo-Christian roots and allegiance to our country, but dwell on Islam and socialism.[568]

- A growing disrespect[569]for police and government is encouraged.

- Limiting free speech[570] and providing safe spaces prevents students from hearing opposing views, and the schools from providing a genuine education. They are fed ideas of Socialism/Marxism, globalism, and Islamism, and cannot reason, understand, or face ideas not within their realm of indoctrination.

- Schools are creating young fascists[571] who are taught to march, rage and destroy, yet cannot articulate their purpose.

- The future workforce is reduced through dysfunctional children and entitlement programs, and open to replacement by migrants who bring their tyrannical way of life with them.

And now, another assault against the children has appeared in the offing, perhaps the most egregious. A mandate that first became evident in some English schools several years ago, now seen in some Canadian and American schools, is that children should be discouraged from having "best friends." England's Thomas's Battersea school[572] has determined, with the agreement of some (but by no means all) parents and psychologists, that group bonding would encourage inclusion of all children and prevent rejection of the few.

The strength one gets from a best-friend relationship, if removed, may be sufficient to create enough despair where the individual will seek comfort in an ever-expanding government (the Marxist purpose). As with any detrimental Leftist concept, this technique is couched as an appeal for sympathy and compassion for those who are slow to bond with a best friend, but its stealth purpose is a means of assuring equalization by removing the securities of friendship.

Of course, not all children will immediately develop warm friendships, but should that be the norm to impose on others? Our schools have already lowered standards to meet the levels of lower achievers. Should we also remove music and the arts with deference to the less gifted, or impose a veritable "eye for an eye" on behalf of those with poorer vision? Would not our population be better served by a sensitive teacher to help all the children overcome their timidity and fears, learn the art of conversation, and develop the social graces needed to negotiate their future? For school personnel to reduce every student to his or her lowest common denominator is a Marxist technique that also exists under Islam. Already implemented in grading, it guarantees equality to the masses with obedience to the authorities, and where equality is imposed, freedoms are sacrificed.

There are many quotes about the value of friends, four of which I thought prudent to include here:

"When it hurts to look back, and you're scared to look ahead, you can look beside you and your best friend will be there" – Anonymous.

"My best friend is the one who brings out the best in me" – Henry Ford.

"Things are never quite as scary when you've got a best friend" – Bill Watterson.

"A blessed thing it is for any man or woman to have a friend, one human soul whom we can trust utterly, who knows the best and worst of us, and who loves us in spite of all our faults" – Charles Kingsley.

The benefits of friendship are many and unique. We are social beings and friends fill a psychological need for survival, to cope with life's trials and to remain inspired. A friend is an eager companion, one who provides praise and kindly given criticism, and a way for us to learn trust and support. Friends are there for comfort and to teach us about respect, sharing, thought, discussion and debate, analysis and problem-solving; simply put, they bring us happiness. Vital for our emotional wellbeing, best friends provide what parents and teachers cannot, particularly because the adults are less than perfect or may have, themselves, been deprived of best friends.

The lack of close friends results in emotional distress[573] — loneliness, sadness, emptiness, withdrawal — which can also take its toll on physical health. It is known to be the leading reason for delinquency, school dropouts, antisocial personality disorder and suicide. In adults, loneliness precipitates depression and alcoholism, and stress with sleep disorders and multiple medical problems. Psychologist John Cacioppo of the University of Chicago concluded that social skills are crucial for mental and physical wellbeing.

In geographic situations that contribute to isolation, but where children may turn to books of imagination, challenge and rewards, achievement and travel, one might anticipate emotional success. But today's educational system has removed such books and replaced them with dystopian novels, where the characters are immersed in loneliness, sadness, defeat, and an environment bereft of reason. The stories provide situations of crises from which the characters may not always extricate themselves. Therefore, with no escape and nowhere to vent, the child can lose his individuality, creativity and the chance to form valuable coping skills, and be drawn to any available group mentality, as well as drug abuse and alcoholism.

Robbing the children of the necessary human encounter and intimacy conforms to Leftist ideologies that intend to destroy all social, economic, and political artifacts of classical liberalism. We see disintegration of the old society and family in the history of the Soviet Union, but, significantly, there are parallels in Islam's jihadi warriors who emerge from emotional solitude and emptiness. The Arabic term, *Asabiyah,* defined in Kobrin's *The Jihadi Dictionary*, is comparable to group consciousness, group-think, and the loss of individuality. By destroying intimacy, empathy and compassion, the group creates the shame-honor culture, using passive-aggressive behavior of intimidation and scapegoating.

The child who is friendless and isolated, bereft of independence and initiative, responds with obedience, guilt, and lying to protect himself from being ostracized. He may then be vulnerable to joining violent Leftist movements or submitting to Islamic radicalization.

A civilization becoming a shadow of its former greatness — this is the gift of the Left.

PART THREE:
THE MEDIA

THE VALUE OF ONE

The reporter cannot grasp the imbalance of Israel's exchanging a thousand Muslim criminals for one Jewish soldier.

The conclusions drawn by Deborah Orr, regarding the value of an Israeli versus an Arab life, are bizarre, yet not altogether unexpected from The Guardian[574] and its staff.

The Israelis have been trying to negotiate for the return of Gilad Shalit since his kidnapping five years ago. Orr appears to believe that Hamas asked for an even exchange and Israel refused so as to increase Hamas's bounty. She seems to indicate that Israel refused a one-for-one exchange until Israel convinced Hamas to accept the return of a thousand of their own. Perhaps Orr thinks Israel relished having a thousand criminal guests to house, guard, feed, and clothe.

The real question is how little the Palestinians value life when they raise their sons to become suicidal murderers. Such is the case of a recent recipient of the *Shield of Resolve and Giving,* Um Yousuf Abu Hmeid,[575] whose four sons were imprisoned for several life terms in Israeli prisons, and a fifth "martyred," in addition to other family members convicted of terrorism and killing. How can they value life if they place such a high value on death, which includes the myth of 72 heavenly virgins, the naming of plazas and streets after their destroyed offspring, and the distribution of candy to celebrate the loss of a child?

Whether Orr sees this asymmetrical exchange as Hamas victory or Israeli weakness, she is offended by the numbers, the exchange of one Israeli life for a thousand Arabs. Mathematically, in 57 Muslim lands containing 1.5 billion Arabs, the ethnic cleansing deaths of Muslims by Muslims is unfathomably high: Sudan's genocide, 2.6 million; Syria's government killing 40,000 citizens; Turkey-Kurdistan, 38,000 Kurds killed and 4,000 villages destroyed; Algeria's Civil War, 200,000 killed; Iraq's an estimated one million killed; Iran-Iraq War, one million killed; Bangladesh, 1.5 million, just to name a few! Muslims are killing Muslims and non-Muslims in up to 135 places worldwide. More people are killed by Islamists each year than in all 350 years of the Spanish Inquisition.

Muslims slaughter their own,[576] decapitate and amputate for deviations from their harsh sharia laws; enshroud and subjugate their women; kidnap and enslave young children; kill their own children under a destructive sense of honor. Rather than plan lives of achievements for humanity, success, marriage, parenthood for their progeny, they proudly raise them for martyrdom while killing others. Of 1.5 billion Arabs in the Middle East, the one thousand terrorists who managed to survive their culture and be released are 1/1,500,000 of the population.

By contrast, Israel, with fewer than six million Jews, has the educational potential to discover a cure for cancer, author a significant book, contribute to the sciences, make further inroads in helping third-world countries, invent something new for the ever-expanding communication technology, or be one of the world's largest number of startup companies in the world. Since life is precious to Jews by virtue of their religious doctrines and their history, these children will first serve in the armed forces to protect their country, continue to higher education, contribute to society, and be expected to marry and raise a family, rather than become a human explosive. As one of 5,800,000, Israel's Gilad Shalit, captured by Hamas and held for five years, is a more significant loss for a small country, and not deemed dispensable.

At the same time, we see that not one of the many Arab children available for martyrdom has attempted to improve the infrastructure of Gaza and the West Bank; they rely on Israel for the simplest necessities. I would have cut their electricity and more, before returning these thousand dangerous creatures into the wild to kill again. But sometimes, irrational circumstances bring irrational decisions.

FOUL PLAY

Page Eight, a propagandist play about Rachel Corrie, misportrays her place in history and the role of activists in Gaza.

At a time when Israel faces an existential crisis by 1.5 billion terror-minded Muslims from a landmass a thousand times her size,[577] must she also be libeled by the UK with a hate so unfathomable since Israel has done nothing to warrant it? Despite the Palestinian propaganda, the rebuilding of Israel represents one of the most peaceful in-migrations in human history. The Jews are the indigenous people and the Zionists' return was uniquely mercantile,[578] not militaristic. The Jews purchased land, farms and houses, with funds from the Jewish National Fund (JNF) that was created in 1901 to assist in the rehabilitation and reclamation of the barren and malarial swamp land.

Although the UK claims not to take sides, the Judeophobic programs and anti-Semitic articles persist, and academics boycott the only Jewish democratic country, but not the 58 totalitarian Islamic regimes that provide a life of misery for their subjugated citizens. England's long history of anti-Semitism is evident.[579] The expulsion of the Jews from 1290 to 1656 was based on their rejection of Christianity and any financial success. England's Queen has never visited Israel, although she has visited her neighbors — Abu Dhabi, Kuwait, Bahrain, Saudi Arabia, Qatar, United Arab Emirates, Dubai, Oman, and Jordan. Perhaps the UK populace prefers their new immigrants, the masses praying in the streets,[580] the rioting that blocks traffic, the brandishing of swords;[581] the voices raised against democracy and for sharia law; the fully cloaked, cringing women; and the multitudes on welfare that guide the BBC and PBS media to have such a strong affinity for Islam and violent opposition to the small democracy of Israel

The case in point is "Page Eight," a play by prominent playwright and anti-Semite, David Hare, which was produced by the BBC and aired on PBS's Masterpiece Theater. The underlying story shows brutal Israelis killing a peaceful demonstrator and causing great suffering, with a grand finale of England's admonishing Israel. The purpose of the play is obvious — to vilify Israel and her people.

The BBC, in an attempt to defend the production, replied and explained that the story was based upon the death of two activists in the Palestinian-occupied Judea and Samaria, namely American Rachel Corrie and English Tom Hurndall, but they failed to identify the two as members of the ISM, the Palestinian "International Solidarity Movement."

A key witness, retired Colonel Pinchas Zuaretz, said Corrie was killed in an accident caused by her own negligence, that her behavior reflected either a very deep ideology or stupidity. Her death took place in the middle of the terrorist *Intifada* against Israel in 2003, and she was the ISM's first line of defense against Israel's Operation Defensive Shield to stop terrorist suicide bombers. The ISM enlisted dozens of internationals to serve as support troops, which are known to serve as human shields for terrorists. Examples are those who holed up at the Church of the Nativity, to be killed if the IDF were to act against the hiding terrorists. Another was known to have met with terrorists before they left to blow up a bar in Tel Aviv. The ISM has been aiding and abetting terrorists, and Corrie was helping to thwart the IDF's ability to protect Israeli citizens where there was intense terrorist activity at the Hamas tunnels.[582]

In the accounts published, ISMers admitted that several internationals had decided to put themselves in harm's way in front of the bulldozer for at least two-and-a-half hours. One activist, Jenny, was nearly run down, when a fellow ISMer pulled her out in the nick of time. That day, the internationals decided to play Russian roulette with the Israeli army, and Corrie lost. Although her parents insist that the driver intentionally drove over her, it was proven that the driver could not have seen her squatting amid the rubble. The operator's obscured view, through a narrow, double-glazed, bulletproof window, and behind pistons and the giant scooper, might well have prevented him from seeing her kneeling. The playwright gave no hint of the true circumstances. Neither he indicate the true nature of Rachel Corrie, who also burned American flags.

Interestingly, several journalists had uncovered the likelihood that the Palestinians had used Rachel Corrie for sexual gratification, as they learned of the experiences of other female activists.[583] Two activists exposed a disturbing phenomenon, an open secret within the peace camp, namely that many foreign women who go to Judea and Samaria to demonstrate against Israel end up being sexually assaulted by the Arab men they'd come to help. They are what the Imperial Japanese called "comfort women"[584] during the Second World War, and the "humanitarian activists" try to conceal Palestinian rape of one of their own.[585] News reporters have learned that representatives of the protest movement and the Palestinian Authority prevent activists from publicizing the story. And Hare is equally complicit.

If Rachel Corrie was thus used and peer pressure prevented her complaints, lest it hurt the Palestinian cause, this may well have been an impetus for her to surrender her own life.[586] We are also reminded that none of her fellow activists counseled her to keep herself safe or pull her to safety. And, the dramatist never explains that the "wall" is primarily a fence that has saved Israeli lives from deadly terrorists.

UK citizen Tom Hurndall was also a volunteer for the ISM, which has been exposed as a logistical front for terrorists. It is now known that the ISM held recruiting and strategy sessions at Ohio State, Duke and Georgetown Universities[587] to get anarchists to the West Bank, to incite riots to hinder the IDF and use the volunteers as human shields. (At one point, the local Arabs asked the IDF to deport the anarchist ISMers because of their behavior.) An anarchist leader explained that Israel is the training ground for the American anarchist movement to eventually bring their tactics over to the US. This strategy was initiated by Adam Shapiro of New York. Regrettably, charges were never brought against him as he continues to endanger our vulnerable students and Israel and America.

Hurndell toured American colleges calling for Israel's destruction and was a human shield in Iraq for Saddam Hussein just before the US and UK troops sent Hussein to his underground bunker.

The playwright, Hare, intentionally withheld the truth about these activists and the ISM, thereby concealing our enemy and their strategies, and not identifying the enemy of our uninformed university students and our citizens.

I protest their continued virulent enmity against Israel, the acceptance by PBS of such programming that continues to protect her enemy and support anarchy with the use of American taxes and donations. I urged them to air a prominent statement that tells their viewers that the events were entirely fabricated and have no basis in fact, and to issue an apology for their negligence in not treating this as journalism and requiring investigation. By airing Hare's play, they became an accomplice in thwarting the British and American citizens' need to understand that this is yet another method of global

Islamic jihad with deception. PBS is not deserving of citizens' donations until they completely reject Islamic propaganda and return to American ethics and values.

NPR, NOTORIOUS FOR PALESTINIAN REVISIONISM
National Public Radio excels in deceitful programming about Israel.

Morning Edition of November 18 (Renee Montagne/Sheera Frankel) produced an unacceptable, biased report "Attacks Target Palestinians in Israeli Towns,"[588] charging that Israel is attempting to ethnically cleanse the state of Palestinians. There were never a Palestinian people, except for the Arabs from Lebanon, Syria, Yemen and Egypt who, in 1967, renamed themselves to create a fraudulent heritage to the land after losing their aggressive war. They live in Judea and Samaria (renamed West Bank) and Gaza and they are not citizens of Israel. On the other hand, Israeli Jews, Israeli Christians and Israeli Arabs are citizens of Israel who chose to remain and become citizens of Israel — and now live with other Israeli citizens. The report is obviously racist and libelous, with misinformation intended to disparage and inflame.

Fueling hatred against the State of Israel, NPR (National Public Radio) reports that religious Zionist Jews will have ethnic-based housing in Jaffa, without also reporting that the Arab citizens will have their own ethnic-based housing in Aviv-Jaffa municipality.[589] Three of the four areas are within the 1949 armistice lines.

NPR is guilty of reporting incidents of Jewish vandalism, never mentioning Arab vandalism on centuries-old Jewish antiquities of the Jewish people who are indigenous to the land with a continuous presence for more than 3,000 years, according to archaeological and historical evidence. Jewish civilization in Israel was already more than 1,000 years old when Rome destroyed the Holy Temple, of which the Western Wall remains, and conquered the Jewish nation in the first century.

The Al-Aqsa mosque was built on the Temple Mount, and the Arabs desecrated the substructure. Beneath the site were Solomon's Stables, where the Palestinians committed a crime of historic proportions against antiquities. Archeological treasures/relics from the First and Second Temples in Jerusalem were found in the Kidron Valley amid rubble dumped by the Islamic authorities. The disrespect and removal of ancient artifacts is an ongoing problem, as Palestinians try to eradicate Jewish history.[590]Among the artifacts were pottery from the Bronze Age and First Temple; coins, arrowheads and figurines from the Hasmonean dynasty[591] and before the destruction of the Second Temple in 70 C.E

Also destroyed were stonework by Jewish artisans of 2,000 years ago — thousands of years of layered Jewish history intentionally trashed.

Christian relics on the Temple Mount are also destroyed, haphazardly chopped, thereby also obliterating centuries of Christian history.

Synagogues of Jerusalem's Jewish Quarter were dynamited and destroyed by Arabs; Israel's policy is to honor all religions and not destroy their antiquities or houses of worship. So, even though the Muslims built a mosque on the area that was once the Temple of Solomon, General Moshe Dayan granted the Arabs access to the mosque as a symbol of good will. The opposite has never been true. Muslims destroy and purposely build over what is not Islamic.

The 2500-year-old Jewish cemetery on the Mount of Olives that contained 250,000 tombstones was destroyed and desecrated by the Palestinians, and 38,000 tombstones were used to pave roads and latrines.

The Christian Holy Church of the Nativity was intentionally defiled by Palestinian terrorists, who purposely used pages of the Bible for toilet paper.

Islam breeds shame and pride, honor and humiliation, and the willingness to riot, burn, loot, rape, kill, and issue death threats. Once the Muslims were in Gaza, they bombed and burned Gazan churches; Jewish synagogues in Jericho, Nablus, and Gush Katif, were torched to the ground.

In violation of international law, Rachel's Tomb in Bethlehem was turned into a mosque;

Joseph's Tomb in Nablus was torched, six Israeli soldiers killed; and Shalom Al Yisrael synagogue in Jericho was torched.

Under PA rule, archaeological sites of Hasmonean kings and King Herod were left to decay.

The Palestinian Administration allowed villages to encroach upon a synagogue on Mt. Hebron, where worshippers and tourists are now not permitted (despite Oslo Accords' guarantee).

There is little doubt that Palestinian authorities are conducting this assault on the Temple Mount to erase any vestige of archeological evidence for Jewish (and Christian) history. In Arabic, this practice is known as Tams al-ma'alem, meaning 'erasing the signs' — destroying the relics of all cultures that preceded Islam.[592]

Frenkel's aberrant report should be corrected. Jews are the indigenous people, and one of the few ancient peoples to have survived into modern times. Judaism is among the world's oldest living religions (Christianity began 2,011 years ago, and Islam began in 624 AD). Rome renamed the Jewish state "Palestine" in defiance of the Jews, and Palestine was associated with Jews and the Jewish homeland until the mid-20th century. The Palestinian brigade that fought with England during WW II was a Jewish brigade; the Arabs fought on the side of the Nazis.

The Arabs are not ready to live with Jews. They had 63 years to stop the attacks, the rockets, the missiles, and the classes and TV programs that continue to nurture a deep hatred of Jews in their children. Muslims killed Jews in Arab lands and they are now killing Christians. NPR's reports encourage the hateful propaganda, favor the Palestinian narrative, and Mahmoud Abbas says they will never recognize a Jewish State.

NPR has become **N**otorious for **P**alestinian **R**evisionism. NPR owes its audience an apology and multiple corrections to reach the same listeners who have been misled on Morning Edition. It is time to truthfully expose their programming as the exceptionally deceitful news report that it is. The listeners deserve better.

RESTRICTED VISION

From a girl who leaves democracy, to the cab of a bulldozer, to the biased journalist, there is restricted vision.

Stéphane Gendron lives in free Canada with the right to hate whomever and whatever he chooses. However, his work shows he has not done the research incumbent upon a journalist on which to base his animosity and partiality. Neither does he even remotely comply with the Canadian Broadcast Standards Council's guidelines. He uses odious language against the people of the State of Israel, one of the most modern, democratic, and magnanimous states in the world. Why was this permitted by CBSC?

Gendron displayed his ignorance, not only of the circumstances surrounding Rachel Corrie's death[593] but also of Israel, making his opinions ring hollow. His bigotry and serious character flaw betray his position of trust. He lied about an event, deceived the public, and wrongly maligned Israel.

One of his more loathsome accusations was a statement that Israel bulldozes Palestinians, obvious slander. It is incumbent upon a reporter to read at least as many reports as I did, in the name of truth and responsibility. Many reports stated why Corrie was there, what she was doing during the bulldozer's operation, the line of vision of the equipment operator, and Corrie's possible frame of mind.

Why had the American student gone to Gaza? She was a frequent activist and American member of the International Solidarity Movement(ISM),[594] who took a year to travel to Rafah, in the Gaza Strip during the Second Intifada. She was one of seven who acted as human shields[595] to impede IDF-led bulldozer demolition of illegal construction on the Rafah refugee camp and Egypt, which included guerrilla[596] hideouts and terror tunnels used for smuggling weapons or for secret passageways to enter Israel and kill Jewish people. However, on this day, the IDF was routinely leveling terrain and clearing debris. The investigation showed Corrie was standing behind the debris, an area obscured to any driver in his protective cage.

Qishta, a Palestinian interpreter, noted: "Late January and February was a very crazy time, when house demolitions were taking place all over the border strip and the activists were not only brave, they were crazy." A British participant had also been wounded by shrapnel. Palestinian militants[597] expressed concern that the "internationals might be spies." Corrie learned some Arabic to overcome suspicion, and she participated in mock trials denouncing the Bush administration and burning a mock US flag, fostering hate against the US (yes, a traitor to her country). In time, the ISM members were taken into Palestinian homes for bed and meals, and the activists sought to engage the military further.

The military investigation of the IDF Judge Advocate's Office concluded that Corrie was killed by debris pushed over by the Caterpillar D9 bulldozer,[598] which has a restricted field of vision with several blind spots, and the soldiers had to stay in their armored vehicles that day because of Palestinian sniper fire. The ISM later claimed that when the bulldozer refused to stop or turn aside, Corrie climbed up onto the mound of dirt and rubble being accumulated and knelt in front of it, but an autopsy of Corrie's body revealed that the cause of death was from falling debris and not from the tractor's physically rolling over her. It was a tragic accident.

Journalist and Middle East commentator Tom Gross's[599] article, "The Forgotten Rachels," referred to six Rachels, other victims of the Arab-Israeli conflict whose deaths received no outside coverage. "With credit to Rachel Corrie and fellow activists, the smuggling of explosives from Egypt into Gaza continued — and were later used to kill children in southern Israel."

A *National Review* editorial argued, "Corrie's death was unfortunate, but more unfortunate is a Western media and cultural establishment that lionizes 'martyrs' for illiberal causes while ignoring the victims those causes create."

The ISM to which Corrie belonged was directly responsible for illegal behavior and conduct in the area of her death and their actions directly led to this tragedy. The Israeli army's report, in Britain's *The Guardian*, said Corrie stood behind a mound of dirt, hidden from view. She had not been run over by an engineering vehicle but struck by a hard object, most probably a slab of concrete. And why did her friends not reach out to save her?

Then a scenario became evident because of the experiences of other female activists[600]—that in all likelihood, Corrie was one of many female activists who are used by Palestinians for their sexual gratification — "routinely harassed and raped" not unlike the comfort women of the Japanese during World War II. Their culture is not like ours; "Palestine» is not safe for women.[601] An Islamic Mufti in Copenhagen sparked a political outcry after publicly declaring that women who refuse to wear headscarves are 'asking for' rape."

In addition, Norman Finkelstein, a rabid anti-Zionist, confirmed that female internationals serve as "comfort women" for Palestinians. It is therefore entirely possible that Corrie had been raped, betrayed by her fellow activists and forced to maintain silence, and depressed enough to act irresponsibly in front of the bulldozer.

This was a lesson in restricted vision, within the bulldozer, by the ISM, by the activist parents who allow their daughters to journey to harm's way, and by the journalist who fails at his craft.

A TWIST OF HATE
A leftist Jewish newspaper rejects protective rights for Jewish college students.

Several years ago, a friend of mine was asked by a Christian, "Why do Jews bury their dead upside down?" The friend proceeded to explain to this innocent that he'd been duped by an anti-Semite, and this was just another malicious canard. If I were to answer today, I'd probably quip, "That's only for the Jews who've been reading *the Forward* and long ago adapted to their inverted view of the world." I no longer subscribe to the periodical, but a recent editorial was brought to my attention.

The Forward, a staple for the Jewish immigrants to ease their way into assimilation and citizenship since 1897, now has staff writers who take an antithetical approach to Israel. Under the pretense of concern that Jews may employ Title VI of the 1964 Civil Rights Act[602] afforded other groups, the editorial provides reasons to dissuade Jewish university students — and only Jewish students — from availing themselves of those rights.

Briefly, Title VI of the Civil Rights Act, 1964, prohibits discrimination on the basis of race, color, and national origin in programs and activities' receiving federal financial assistance. Public funds should be withheld from any program that encourages, entrenches, subsidizes any programs that result in discrimination, and appropriate legal action can be taken by the Department of Justice. The legal manual provides Investigation Procedures and other material helpful to ensure effective enforcement of Title VI.

While the editor superficially agrees with Title VI's morality, he suggests restraint by the Jewish students out of deference to the right of freedom of speech afforded other students. I suggest the editor hopes to inhibit these Jewish students from legally protecting themselves in order to curb or forestall an impending violent backlash. This is intimidation and cowardice, Islamophobia and sharia-compliance, a direct violation on laws that sustain modern civilization and meant to protect its citizens from savagery and hatred — and intended to protect our Jewish students.

Despite the BDS conferences designed to boycott, divest from, and sanction businesses that trade with Israel, the National Students for Justice in Palestine (SJP) or Muslim Student Union (MSU) knowingly and intentionally create an atmosphere of anger and resentment against pro-Israel activists. Their mantra includes accusing Jews and Israel of all the Palestinian propaganda of apartheid, ethnic cleansing, land usurpation, wantonly killing Palestinian children, and more, — in fact, all the deeds for which Muslims have been responsible for 1400 years.

Therefore, with the deep-seated anger for retribution against all who gather to defend Israel or wear articles of clothing and jewelry representing Judaism, the Muslim students have rioted; damaged vehicles belonging to Jewish students; used a cinderblock to shatter the glass door of Berkeley's Hillel building[603] (followed by the severe beating of two Jewish men the following week); set fire to an Israel flag, its flames spreading to the roof; carved swastikas on private property;[604] defaced dorm walls, hallways and doors; distributed false eviction notices in dorms; abused and threatened Jewish students; used International Holocaust Remembrance Day[605] to promote hatred of Israel and Jews; denounced Jews as "Nazi-Jews"; denied the Holocaust; denounced as "collaborators" those Muslims who appear willing to conduct peace negotiations; and blockaded and physically attacked a Jewish professor, Mel Gordon,[606] while he was en route to his class, and he required medical treatment. To add insult to injury, when a Jewish student sued a Muslim student for ramming her with a shopping cart, the sharia-compliant judge ruled in favor of the latter's "freedom of speech." I suggest the *Forward's* counseling restrictions are due to fear and ignorance, but inhibiting Jewish students from defending themselves will only embolden the Islamists to strengthen their convictions and resolve, and worsen the atmosphere considerably.

The Islamic students have already been indoctrinated at home and in mosques by the time they arrive at universities, and are then encouraged to continue their aggression as long as they are not confronted by the administrative body. President Mark Yudof has recognized the severity of the enmity enough to engage outside help; is that not enough proof for *the Forward*? Are the aforementioned scenarios of violence not sufficient to contact the Department of Justice for Title VI's Investigative Procedure? Must the victimized students be severely traumatized and hospitalized before serious action is taken?

How, when and under what circumstances should protection be sought is a matter of some debate, claims the Forward editor. While he agrees there is a somewhat hostile environment, "it is not the rule," he writes. Do we have any idea where the editor draws the line? That he dwells on the majority of campuses that are not "rife with anti-Semites and Israel-haters" is an apologist response. Must we wait until all the campuses have gone to lethal extremes? And shall we wait until more students are hurt and sent along with professors to hospitals to prove a point? Is the student's law suit considered frivolous because she was able to return to class or should we wait until she is comatose or at least wheelchair bound? Should we wait until a professor requires intensive life-saving surgery before considering the harm bona fide? Which students and professors are expendable?

When there is no formal declaration of war against the Jewish people, how many Jews must endure pain and suffering to be counted? How many school buses bombed, pizza parlors destroyed? How many men, women, and children may be slaughtered in their homes before we remind ourselves that we once said, "Never again," but some among us are still saying, "This wasn't that terrible; we can overlook this too." And I must question how the editor would respond if the student were his daughter or granddaughter.

We have gone beyond the acceptance and obeisance to Islam's *muzzlification,* and still we are told to silence our outrage and quash our defenses, just as some Jews remained silent as their neighbors were taken from their homes in Germany. My cousin in Buenos Aires acknowledged his own silence, fearing for his own safety, when his neighbors and his daughter's fellow-law students disappeared in the 1970s in Argentina. There is cause to use Title VI Act, but not if we're Jewish. If we're Jewish, we must impose further restrictions on ourselves and our children even before a dictatorship so decrees. This is dhimmitude,[607] where our progeny will soon understand that they can no longer attend Islamic-controlled universities, and experience terror far beyond the current fear. If we have learned nothing else from our past, we must surely grasp that we must never again succumb to conquest.

HARDTALK, HARD TO SWALLOW

A BBC hate fest, Montague invents help given Israel by Presidents Roosevelt through Obama.

Sarah Montague, of BBC's HARDtalk, tainted the air on May 8, with the prejudices of centuries in the United Kingdom with her opening declaration that American presidents have always been too "in thrall with the Jewish lobby,"[608] and "American Jews influence US policy and that explains Washington's increasing support for Israel."

One must wonder if "all those Presidents" include President Roosevelt, who rejected the bombing of the railroads and death camps that might have saved Jews during the Holocaust,[609] and who forced the return of more than 900 Jews on the SS St. Louis[610] to their imminent death in Nazi Germany; or President Truman[611] who pressured the British to admit displaced persons to Palestine but was still averse to the idea of a Jewish State; or President Eisenhower,[612] who pressured Israel in 1956 to withdraw from areas conquered by Israel in the Israel-France-Great Britain campaign to evict Egypt from the Suez Canal, without obtaining concessions from the Egyptians, thereby sowing the seeds of the 1967 war; or President Nixon,[613] who was known for his intense dislike of Jews and Blacks; or President Clinton,[614] who continued to oppose and withhold recognition of Jerusalem as Israel's capital, blamed the failure of the peace process on Israel, and remained silent when Mahmoud Abbas praised their suicide bombers; or President Obama,[615] and his years of bullying Israelis into signing a suicide pact with their sworn enemies, Muslims.

Montague faults American Jews who favor Israel, the country known for her extraordinary advancements[616] to benefit mankind during her 70 years' statehood, over Islamic countries whose fourteen centuries[617] of enslavement, conquest, amputations, decapitations, and female mutilation are unparalleled, and which have now made their mark on England, with their sights set on Buckingham Palace for the caliphate.[618] From her statement, I can only assume that the native English truly favor the despotic Islamic countries that are now sending their representative citizens to overtake the UK. In fact, as the leaders of the Free World have repeatedly turned their back on Israel while falsely proclaiming a friendship, they must now face their grave error. In the name of securing a peaceful co-existence and economic parity by sacrificing Israel, they must deal with Islam's rise to becoming the greatest threat to Western civilization in human history.

That the BBC could sanction or encourage Montague to tackle this topic is offensive enough, but coupled with hosting the likes of Norman Finkelstein is a move that no doubt necessitated extensive, collaborative, strategic consideration. The psychologically damaged Finkelstein, like George Soros, Karl Marx, Avram Burg, Richard Goldstone, and others, is a self-hating product of centuries of suffering that turned him from victim to aggressor against his own people. The author of "The Holocaust Industry," in which he accuses Jews of exploiting the Holocaust for their own political and financial gain, references other known anti-Semites to give credibility to his bogus work. Finkelstein also claimed the lobby prevented Prime Minister Netanyahu from dismantling settlements when, in fact, Israel had dismantled settlements in the interest of peace, only to be fired upon the next day from the Palestinians' "new launching pad"[619] such as the once-beautiful city of Gush Katif.

Of all the speakers available to explicate on the myriad characteristics of American Jews, their possible influence on Washington or ties to Israel, Montague selected one whose obvious odium, distortion of facts, and damaging assertions resulted in his banishment from Israel. Therefore, one can't help but wonder that this "qualified analyst" was particularly chosen for one reason only. More than mere controversy, this was a premeditated hate fest. Surely, if American Jewry were indeed so cohesive and influential, there would be no Finkelstein, Chomsky, Burg, or J Street. If American presidents were truly so supportive of Israel, President Obama would not be insisting on the dangerous 1967 armistice lines[620] as final boundaries for a Jewish state that is already reduced to a mere one/one thousandth the size of all Islamic land, with a width of nine miles at one point, and he would not have gone against Congress's freeze to gift an additional $192 million[621] of US taxpayer money to Israel's genocidal Palestinian neighbors.

Montague betrayed many of the BBC's "official" guidelines and values:[622]

(1.2.1) This was not an impartial and honest report.

(1.2.2) Finkelstein verbally denounced the Jewish state for multiple transgressions without sound evidence.

(1.2.3) The duo was free to condemn and indict Israel, their animosity uninterrupted and their slander unchallenged.

(1.2.4) The BBC has long lost its integrity by permitting unfair coverage and allegations, and freely influencing the audience, unhampered by impartial discussion.

(1.2.6) In the interest of truly serving the public interest, it should offer a fair and honest story about Israel's 5,000-year history, Jordan's 19-year occupation of the land,[623] the invention of the Palestinian people,[624] the wars Israel had to endure for self-preservation, and the goals of Islam[625] for Western civilization.

(1.2.7) One would expect the BBC to attempt to regain the audience's respect, and provide an in-depth, on-air retraction. To Finkelstein's accusations that Israel has initiated wars with its neighbors since its creation, Montague should deliver the vastly accessible documentation to show that the Arabs began each and every war against the Jewish state.[626]Montague owes the contributors and audience an apology followed by programming to undo the misinformation that aroused suppressed anti-Semitism.

We expect little from the reprehensible invitee, primarily because he is a by-product of Holocaust survivors who, themselves, may well have been severely emotionally and psychologically damaged by their experiences. Nevertheless, it is criminal to have this individual speak to the masses, since he is apparently quite blinded to reality. There have been several studies written on the subject of turncoats (aka The Oslo Syndrome[627]), particularly self-hating Jews,[628] and it is the BBC's responsibility to never give audience to such a broken or intentionally evil man.

(1.2.11) If the BBC would devote itself to being accountable to all concerned, perhaps that lost trust could be restored. If not, only those who wish to believe the lies will continue listening — and the lies will be England›s undoing, as the media continue to do the work of Islam. The more the UK becomes sharia-compliant, the fewer democratic laws will be available to save themselves. With the exception of Spain. no country has ever reversed its course from Islamism, but it wasn't until 781 years later, in 1492, that Spain's "Reconquista"[629] allowed the Spaniards to shed their subjugation to Islam and retrieve their heritage and culture, yet perhaps not for much longer. I can't predict a reversal for England, and wonder if the BBC has the courage to begin its return to integrity and impartiality in future programming. HARDtalk must be included among the many programs that need formal, on-air corrections to comply with their official journalism guidelines — ethics and honesty, above all.

LOURDES OF THE LIES

Skewed news is part and parcel of NPR's reports on the Middle East.

If National Public Radio (NPR) were manufacturing anything other than news, US consumers en masse would be clamoring to return their merchandise for refund, citing shoddy workmanship and inferior quality. This is not so with the media, and NPR and Israel. Reporter Lourdes Garcia-Navarro's (LGN) interview with Palestinian Prime Minister Salam Fayyad is fraught with holes and ripped seams, but prepaid by the taxpayer, it continues to be shipped without complaint to the duped American consumer.

Garcia-Navarro twists Fayyad's words, despite his explanations to the contrary. If Fayyad admitted the Palestinian Authority is not inspiring its people to take on the responsibility of growing the state, LGN blames the Israeli occupation. If Fayyad noted that Arab states have not met their financial obligation to sustain the Palestinian economy, providing only $750 million instead of the $1.1 billion pledged in 2011, LGN lays the bulk of the blame at the feet of the West and the ever-popular occupation (1967-1993) when, indeed, Israel improved Palestinian life in those years.

The reporter intentionally fails to bare several truths: that life improved considerably for Palestinians during Israeli's administration of the Territories.[630] Military barriers were removed, enabling freer travel. Israel helped to modernize Palestinian infrastructure, increased manufacturing facilities, established seven new universities, expanded schools, taught modern agriculture, set up medical programs, opened 100+ health clinics, instituted freedom of the press, and introduced a Palestinian administration heretofore unknown to this populace that originated from oppression in Egypt, Lebanon, Syria, Jordan, and Yemen. Unemployment fell while life expectancy soared, and the population nearly doubled (1967-1993). Historian Efraim Karsh noted, *"During the 1970s, the West Bank and Gaza constituted the fourth-fastest-growing economy in the world — ahead of such 'wonders' as Singapore, Hong Kong and Korea, and substantially ahead of Israel itself."* [631] Lourdes calculatedly omits such facts.

Other truths are also omitted: that the Oslo Accords ended the occupation in 1993, and a Palestinian-elected government was put into place; that Israeli troops left Palestinian towns and cities by 1997; and that Arafat rejected the Camp David proposals and began the Intifada, which required the deployment of Israeli troops against renewed terrorist hostilities toward Israel.

Garcia-Navarro failed to report that Palestinians, more than any other peoples, receive funding from the United Nations with no oversight as to its distribution for either genuine humanitarian aid or weaponry for terrorism, and never refers to Arafat's severe mismanagement of funds. UNRWA was established[632] as a refugee

178 | TABITHA KOROL

organization, granted no power to assimilate the 700,000 Arabs made homeless by the war they began in 1948, but has since bestowed perpetual refugee-victimhood status on all Arab (non-Jewish) descendants.[633] Neither did she stipulate that these people, now numbering in the millions, continue to eschew self-sufficiency, and require ever-increasing funds from around the world. Neither would she mention America's $249.1 million in assistance last year alone (2011), followed by Obama's more recent gift of $192 million, to an astounding $4.4 billion since 1949. Rather than acknowledge the billions of dollars in foreign aid from worldwide sources, the PA's continued irresponsibility for wanton neglect of basic infrastructure; the hundreds of millions that remain unaccounted for under Arafat's leadership; and Mahmoud Abbas's wealth, estimated at $100 million, she continues the myths of Israeli occupation.

Although Fayyad expressed his concerns about the three-year delayed *Palestinian* elections in the West Bank, control of Gaza by Hamas terrorists, and a discordant relationship between Fayyad and Abbas, the interviewer pushed these aside because they are internal problems for which Israel cannot be shown culpable.

She also failed to report the attempt by the Bank of Israel to assist the Palestinians with their financial crisis. Israel applied for a $1 billion loan from the International Monetary Fund (IMF), on behalf of, and aid for, Palestinians. Israel agreed to accept responsibility for the loan, and Abbas would repay the loan directly to the Israeli government. The IMF refused because Palestine is not a sovereign state. It is clear that NPR, aided by this reporter, has a strategy to unswervingly discredit the Jewish nation at all costs, and never report Israel's virtues or blamelessness.[634]

I fail to fathom why NPR continues to support those who threaten to destroy the only democracy in the Middle East and our democracy own in the West, and why it still qualifies for federal funding.

LGN again places the failure of negotiations on Israel for not freezing settlement construction in the occupied West Bank, but Prime Minister Netanyahu did impose a ten-month freeze on settlement construction in November 2009! Abbas waited for the last month to reject all negotiations and, instead, attacked Israel at the UN. Israel also uprooted Jewish families, ceded land — beautiful towns, good housing, viable businesses — for peace, and the Palestinians again turned that land into a missile launch facility. It is a fact that Israel›s construction is entirely legal, and the Arabs have no legal claims to the territories because they were gained by Arab aggression in 1948, yet nary a word was uttered about the Palestinian violations of all previous agreements to end incitement.

There may never be peace as long as the Palestinians do not extend efforts equal to that of the Israelis, and as long as they continue to maintain their ruse of self-imposed victimhood. There may never be peace as long as the Arab world continues to follow the dictates of their Koran — to kill, conquer, and globalize Islam. Islam has attacked nations in all manners, whether culturally or by the sword for 1400 years, succeeding in their subjugation of people in the Middle East, Africa, and parts of Europe.

How truly naïve and haughty — and perhaps complicit — of the Western mind to think that by forcing Israel to cede a few square miles of land, Islam will cease its all-inclusive jihad and become a peaceful and civilized alliance of democratic Muslim nations — particularly when some of our citizens, such as NPR and its journalists, are conspiratorial with the foe.

60 MINUTES OF MENDACITY

CBS's 60 Minutes' reporter Bob Simon hosted a dishonest program of life for Arab-Christians in the "Holy Land," that suggested, but was not, under Israeli rule.

I researched Journalism Ethics to be sure I wasn't demanding more of CBS's 60 Minutes than is reasonable. Although the media is not legally bound, the public assumes and expects it to be honor bound to enforce the rules and avoid irresponsible, destructive journalism. But with this production, *Christians in the Holy Land*, both Jeffrey Fager, CBS news chairman and executive producer, and Bob Simon, host reporter, have betrayed their profession's values, by producing a program that is not only severely slanted, but injurious to a country, Israel, in her current fight for her survival and one we recognize to be our only trustworthy ally in the Middle East. Not only was the report of Christian life in Israel inaccurate because Simon interviewed only Arab-Christian sources with an Islamic agenda, but it was sufficiently twisted to promote the Palestinian narrative to suit the objective of the Islamic global conquest — and it has been removed from YouTube.

Just as Islam is at war (jihad) with civilizations worldwide, so is it also at war with Israel, and the tactics are as varied as the cultures and societies to be subjugated. Among the many strategies are open warfare, destruction, enslavement, and beheading in Africa; conversion, rioting and occupying swaths of cities in Europe; infiltrating and scheming within the administration and media in America; suicide bombings and rocket/missile fire in Israel, and the overall use of propaganda to dupe the Western World. The Qur'an 9:29 commands that the Muslim world fight the *People of the Book* (Jews and Christians), which is obviously the motivation, but the violent and non-violent policies are directed toward the same end: the Islamization of the world and implementation of sharia law over all *kafir* societies.

CBS's objective should have been to remove personal prejudices (in which Bob Simon seems extraordinarily steeped) and objectively report the truth. Rather, the story was complicit with the Arab storyline, deserting the laws of our culture to aid Islam. Instead of producing a factual report on how Christians live in Israel, they interviewed

Arab Christians who live in Arab-controlled cities and who have adopted the Arab grievances. By not accurately describing Christian life among Muslims, they have also continued to endanger those who are targeted for their religion. In fact, this video effort contributes to the suffering and death of Christians who live among Muslims.

An Al-Qaeda bulletin proclaimed that "all Christian centers, organizations and institutions, leaders and followers, are legitimate targets for jihadis."[635] Nearly two-thirds of the 500,000 Christians in Baghdad have fled or been killed. Of the roughly 100,000 Christians who lived in Mosul, only 5,000 remain. Coptic Christians are routinely murdered, or persecuted and prevented from worshipping in Egypt; 200,000 fled and 200 churches were burned. Muslim converts to Christianity are executed in Saudi Arabia. Islamists butcher priests and nuns in Turkey. Christians are menaced by surging Shiites and Sunnis in Lebanon. And, the Grand Mufti of Saudi Arabia declared all churches in the region be destroyed! What would CBS report if the Pope had declared that all mosques be destroyed?

Under Islam, Christians are enslaved, tortured and slaughtered for their religious beliefs, and this might have been the perfect opportunity to inform the world of their plight and perhaps be responsible for a course of action to save them. Imagine the potential of such a story — to save people at risk and earn praise and journalism awards for the effort! Rather, CBS chose to sink to new depths that are recognized by many as fulfilling an Islamic jihad strategy of *projectionism* — blaming Islam's evils on Israel. And has there not been sufficient backlash from this deceptive report to bring CBS to the boardroom for a re-evaluation of its mission and methods?

Christians live well in Israel.[636] Only under Jordanian control of the Old City (1948-1967) were Christian rights infringed, Israeli Christians barred from their holy places, with the Christian population in decline. Muslim Palestinians have attacked Christians in Gaza, defaced their cemeteries, and broken into their monasteries. With the security fence, while Christians may be inconvenienced, they are now protected and have the freedom of access to their holy places. The population of Christians in the Palestinian territories had dropped radically (Christian populations decline worldwide when Muslim populations increase). By contrast, Israel's Arab-Christian population continues to increase. Palestinians also expropriate housing and lands belonging to Catholics, as well as molest young women and attempt to press Christians into their Intifada actions. Christians in Palestinian territories are harassed, have their property plundered and looted, and fear speaking out for their safety to the Palestinian Authority. Not so in Israel.

Brigitte Gabriel, Walid Shoebat, None Darwish, and a host of others who have fled Islamic countries, have written books and spoken at televised conferences in praise of life in Israel for all races and religions. What the staff of 60 Minutes has done is spoken of life for Arab-Christians in Arab-controlled areas! While it may be part of the "Holy Land," it is not under Israeli rule.

The Arab-Christians in the program advocate the unrealistic two-state solution. Although Mahmoud Abbas was the one to rebuff Israel in her quest for peace, such a solution could only have ended in Israel's signing her own death warrant. As Ambassador Michael Oren aptly grasped the motive for this 60 Minutes program, he clearly explained that the security wall and checkpoints against its warring neighbors have saved the lives of Israeli citizens of all faiths. And if some must be merely inconvenienced so that others may live, so be it.

I know that I represent many who insist on an immediate retake — a truthful enlightenment of life in Israel[637] — for all citizens. Israel ranks sixth in life satisfaction, low employment rate of 6.5 percent, seventh highest self-reported good health (81%), and sixth highest life expectancy of 81.7 years, all despite security concerns.

Therefore, if there is an honest, unbiased journalist among the CBS staff to announce the necessary corrections and report the truth to the viewing public, and an executive who will stress honesty and reject Simon's penchant for anti-Semitism, 60 Minutes should apologize and correct its defamation of Israel while exposing the true plight of Christians in the Islamic world. Wouldn't that demand a modicum of heroism!

THE PALESTINE KHOURI DOESN'T KNOW

The reporter wrote a biased, sharia-compliant harangue of malice, myth, and propaganda for a jihad agenda.

Zahi Khouri's opinion, The Palestine Romney doesn't know[638] in the Washington Post, spews the same mantras with the expectation that the falsehoods will become reality. It continues the narrative that the Arabs living in Judea and Samaria were Palestinians for centuries before 1967, so that the world will put a *judenrein* Israel in their control, complete with the beauty, wealth, ingenuity, and successes of its current residences. As Governor Romney stated during the first Presidential Debate in Denver, "I)m used to [my sons›] saying something that's not always true, and they just keep on repeating it and ultimately hoping I'll believe it — but that is not the case."

Jews have been a presence in Sumer and Egypt from the "dawn of history," for 5,000 years to the present — 1,000 years before Islam and more than 2,500 years before Arab nations appeared. They were an influential society with their own identity,[639] a surplus food supply, common language, writing/art, specialization of labor, laws of governance, and a class system. As slaves, they built the pyramids; as free men, they built their own homes, tended their own olive groves and herded their flocks. Ninety percent of the world's Jews lived where there are now Islamic countries, yet they have never insisted that Egypt, Iraq or Morocco be theirs.

Only the Arabs destroyed lands to create their own Islamic regimes through the centuries. They did not accept the land apportioned them at the end of the English mandate, will not live in peace and harmony, and continue to wage war against others and among themselves. The myths to which Khouri and the Palestinians adhere are merely a psychological strategy used in tandem with violence. Muslims killed more than 890 million people over fourteen centuries, throughout the Middle East and from India to Africa to Europe. Muslims have conducted 19,724 terrorist attacks[640] since September 11, 2001, against five religions in 62 countries,[641] all the while claiming eternal victimhood and living as scroungers off the handouts from the rest of the world. Israel may be the cause célèbre, but it is far from being the only target in the Muslim sight.

Overwhelming documentation exists about Muslim conquests,[642] the most authoritative of which being their own, for the purpose of spreading Islam through brutal invasion. Thus, they overcame the Middle East — Syria around 636 a.d.; Egypt, 641; Mesopotamia and the Persian Empire, 650. By the eighth century, Islam conquered North Africa, Spain, lands of central Asia and India; centuries later, Indonesia, Somalia and eastern Europe. The Islamic world's religious duty is to wage jihad until they Islamize the globe.

Khouri insists that Israel stole Palestinian land and culture, when a sovereign Palestine or culture never existed. "Palestine," is a Latin term for the overall territory that was home to Jews and Arabs. Emperor Hadrian replaced the name of Provincia Judea with Provincia Syria Palaestina, after the Jews' biblical enemy, the Philistines, an Aegean people. Most of the Arabs in the area came from the surrounding Arab countries during the late 1800s/early 1900s, attracted by Jewish industry as they restored their homeland, economic prosperity, employment and a higher standard of living. Khouri's family was likely among them, identifiable by his surname: Khouri[643] or Khoury, which is Lebanese or Syrian, and means (Christian) priest. He is not from the country or culture that never existed.

Jerusalem was established in 1000 BCE, 1,642 years before the advent of Mohammed. Hebron comes from "Hebrew." Gaza is Canaanite/Hebrew. Nablus was Shechem, the chief city of Samaria and capital of the kingdom of Israel, renamed Neapolis by the Roman emperor Vespasian, and mispronounced by the Palestinians. Ramallah is Arabic from the 6th century when the Arabs persecuted the Christian occupants and the Christians fled. The Arabs were not indigenous, but colonizers with no national identity. The migrant tribes from Saudi Arabia, Syria, Lebanon, Yemen, etc., use a false Palestinian narrative to establish an identity and history to establish claim to the entire region.

The article contained a fallacious accusation that Palestinian Arabs were forced to leave Israel in 1948. When five Arab nations invaded to destroy the new state of Israel, Israel encouraged the resident Arabs to stay and become citizens of Israel. Those who did and their descendants make up the two million Muslim citizens living well in Israel today. Those who fled did so of their own choosing or at the urging of their warring generals who promised victory. They were not victorious and wound up with less territory than they would have received had they accepted the partition agreement. They were counseled to refuse and became bargaining pawns for the Arabs.

Khouri wrote "as millions flee conflict around the globe to this day," another dishonest statement. Today, the Muslim population is not fleeing, but seeking to take up residency for eventual control in other countries — another jihad strategy, called hijrah. In Africa, the invasions are violent: taking slaves, killing Christians who refuse conversion to Islam, burning churches, and destroying antiquities and replacing them with mosques of conquest. In Europe, the takeover is by numbers, a growing immigrant population demanding accommodations from the host country, threatening the populace, and Jews are again leaving for safer harbors. Muslims are waging a civilizational jihad in the United States, infiltrating and influencing our schools and government, policies here and internationally, to Islamize the laws of the United Nations.

The writer refers to Palestinian Arabs persecuted by their brethren, another way to perpetrate jihad by keeping the Palestinians homeless to enforce a case against Israel. The Muslims did not absorb their own 600,000 who were made homeless to preserve a victimhood status, stimulate pity, instigate wrath against Israel, continue a parasitic existence off generous funding from UNWRA (United Nations Relief and Works Agency for Palestine Refugees) until they crush Israel. The "humanitarian aid" continues long after the refugees are replaced by their descendants and provides financial support for terrorists.

The Washington Post omits information about the 850,000 Jews who faced the Arab countries' program of persecution and oppression,[644] seizing Jewish assets (valued at $6 billion today), their bank accounts, their businesses, and forcing them to flee to safer lands. Most of the Arab Jews were absorbed into Israel and now comprise half of Israel's Jewish population; others went to the US and France. Rather than wallow in self-imposed prisons or receive compensation for their plight and losses, they are part of Israel's productive, thriving society. Although an international fund to resolve and compensate both refugee societies was to be established at the Camp David peace talks, it never came to fruition.

For *The Washington Post* to eschew even minimal fact-checking and balance, particularly for such an explosive issue, is a serious breach of journalistic ethics. Khouri's "opinion" was a biased, sharia-compliant harangue of malice, myth, and propaganda for a jihad agenda.[645] Rather than insisting on the facts to explain the existing situation, The

WP has encouraged and bolstered the Muslim culture to continue its efforts of hate and bloodlust. Not only has the news provider done a serious disservice to its readers and to the democratic State of Israel, but it has also given no encouragement to provide a solution for both peoples. What good could be accomplished when one gives free-reign to jihad, in all its forms, in Israel, Europe and to our own United States, and would it be foolhardy to expect *The Washington Post* to stand on the side of decency and correctly cover the situation in its entirety? It is dangerous, disgraceful and disloyal when American media must shun honor to become sharia-compliant.

OREN ON HONESTY

Ambassador Michael Oren reveals the false narratives and media bias used in reporting about Israel.

The November 23, 2012, Op-ed[646] by Israel's Ambassador to the United States, Michael Oren, concerned the Islamic jihad fought on many fronts, not the least of which are false narratives for Palestinian propaganda and outside pressure demanding equal casualties. The left, usually obsessed with disproportionality, never suggests that Israel return an equal number of rockets and missiles. Hamas, a recognized terrorist organization, uses its youth to throw rocks[647] at civilians and cars, employs rockets and missiles[648] to terrorize Israeli citizens, and engages mainstream media to portray Israel as the aggressor. Unable to win militarily, Hamas is aided by the media's depicting Israel as the invader to delegitimize the Palestinians internationally.

Islam breeds a contempt of women,[649] recognized by their treatment in Muslim societies, including female genital mutilation; prohibiting their public appearance unaccompanied by a male escort and forced enshrouding under threat of rape or death; forbidding their driving cars, attending schools, working; condoning their honor killings by male family members; forced marriages, and more. These beleaguered women and children are also used by terrorists as human shields[650] during rocket attacks on Israel, to increase the number of citizens killed by Israel's retaliatory strikes. Thus, can mainstream media "attest" that Israel has done more damage and killed more people. Hamas can turn world opinion by claiming the higher body count, and boost the Palestinian accusation of war crimes against "innocent civilians," because journalists never report the millions of dollars Israel spends in early-warning systems[651] and bunkers to protect her citizens from frequent attacks.

Granted, Israel's media coverage is second only to England's because her democracy is transparent, whereas the authoritarian Arab regimes strictly control the press corps — what they see and write, and whether they'll travel safely. So, in complete dishonesty, journalists fail to report that Gaza fired more than 2,256 rockets into Israel from January through November 2012, and exceeded 13,000[652] since the beginning of the century, and nurture the enmity for the State of Israel. Because written media and television emphasize visuals over substance, as Amb. Oren proved, news agents eagerly print a story with photos that are often staged, inaccurate, obtained from other conflicts, or are of deaths caused by the Palestinians' own rockets — but quite effective to increase a body count.

Mass media often uses terminology to turn the truth on its head, even as they know that Islamists represent a malevolent society. Under the harsh laws of sharia, Muslims choose to continue their hostilities against women and homosexuals, and incite to murder Jews and Christians alike, worldwide, in the name of jihad, global conquest. The media will not inform that the IDF is known to call the Gazans or drop leaflets to alert of a forthcoming retaliatory effort to warn the civilians to leave the premises or be treated and counted among the obliging combatants.

The *New York Times* and the Post have led the way in implementing enlarged photographs of civilian Palestinians' suffering to play on Western opinions, never showing their sons of all ages dressed in their radical face coverings and belts of explosives, rallying in reverence of death and martyrdom. By contrast, they more often show Israeli soldiers while avoiding photos of heinous crimes[653] perpetrated against Jewish families, housing destroyed by missiles, children trembling in fear of the next attack and having a scant fifteen-seconds to reach a safe bunker. PBS has all too often produced hour-long programming of seriously distorted pro-Palestinian misinformation, hosted by Islamists Christianne Amanpour, Lourdes Garcia-Navarro, Bob Simon, et al. Reuters[654] has frequently been called to task for supplying wrong photos for articles. When discovered and held accountable, a perfunctory correction is quickly replaced by another story, another hour of slander, another deceitful photo.

While the media applies the Islamic disproportionality-tactic for Israelis, Arabs are held to a different standard. Israel's expulsion of four Palestinians earned far more headlines than Kuwait's[655] deportation of hundreds of thousands, or Islam's 2,459 barbaric attacks[656]against five religions in 22 countries during 2012, or burning churches[657] and parishioners, or President Assad's slaughter of 60,000+ Syrian citizens,[658] imprisonment and torture of 37,000. Journalists have taken to calling Gaza the *most densely populated area on earth* to give false purpose to Palestinian "unrest," when, in fact, Tel Aviv has twice the population.

There is no longer any semblance of honor, respect for their craft, their reputation, or for the people the media are supposed to serve. Praise to Amb. Michael Oren for attempting to enlighten us. We must challenge the media, recognize these deceptive Islamic war strategies, and understand that America is no longer even a "stone's throw" away from indoctrinal warfare. It is here.

TIMES UNSQUARE*

There's no square deal or honesty from the New York Times. Reporters continue the Palestinian lie while betraying the truth of Israel's first moral civilization.

The *New York Times* encourages its writers' disinformation to conform to Islamic propaganda. This continuing politicized coverage of the Middle East, is inconsistent with American values and journalism ethics and an assault on Israel by disreputable writers. It is designed to undermine public policy and change our value system, damage our ethics and destroy our morality. Our republic can only thrive in an educated electorate.

Jodi Rudoren used an old, hostile opinion piece to serve as a political message, to rile the uninformed reader and breathe new life into an old conflict. Already cited as a lazy journalist[659] with a poor performance record, she confessed to her anti-Israel bias,[660] to using "imprecise language," and admitted to not using a map for accuracy. Why, then, was this new Jerusalem Bureau Chief chosen for Middle East coverage?

Placing the blame of friction on 44 apartment units, Rudoren calls Israelis "colonizers," while that term, along with "squatters," more aptly suits the Palestinians. Why didn't this slothful reporter contact Jerusalem's city planner about the legitimacy of the housing or cite the 2500 apartments recently built in one city area and 19,000 in another, all for Arabs? Obviously, the apartments are a ruse, not a threat. Israel's many offers to negotiate a peace were rejected long before there was housing.

As often as Israel has offered to negotiate a peace agreement, the Palestinians have refused. The opposition to peace comes from the Arabs who, from the onset, declined the major Mandate offered while the Jews reluctantly accepted the smaller land proposal. Resistance to peace comes from Islamic hate, taught and encouraged from infancy, and from the continued support by complicit journalism.

Why not remind the *Times* readership that the end of the Ottoman Empire brought the British-endorsed Balfour Declaration (1917)[661] that mandated Palestine's new boundaries to re-establish the Jewish homeland, that was then twice followed by Britain's violations of the Mandate, at once granting 77 percent of the land to what became Jordan and granting the Golan Heights to what became Syria? Twenty-two Muslim countries with 400 million warring Arabs surrounding one tiny Jewish state containing about six million Jews and Rudorun and her ilk demand more land for yet another Muslim state!

Overlooking the Jews' historical 3,000-year claim to the land, according to archaeological and historical evidence and biblical text; their formal, legal statehood in 1948; their majority in Jerusalem since the 1860s; their industry and democracy granted to Jew and Arab alike (exceeding anything the Arabs experience in their original homelands); their medical and scientific contributions to the world, Rudoren champions those who never had a state in Palestine or a capital in Jerusalem, who only named themselves Palestinians as a war tactic in 1967, and who never proved themselves capable of self-governance and peace. Rather than inform, her purpose is to propagandize. This is neither sloth nor incompetence, but malice with intent to incite, to fabricate and strengthen tyranny in the Middle East and in the US.

When will the *New York Times* offer fair and balanced journalism and stop encouraging the continued Islamic encroachment on Western civilization? Are the deaths of more than 890 million people over 1400 years, and the current, growing Islamic chaos on every continent, not enough to awaken their conscience?

The second of the *NY Times'* double whammy was the Sunday Magazine's feature, Ben Ehrenreich's "Is this where the third Intifada will start?"[662] Ehrenreich cited Israel's construction plans of 3,400 homes for Israelis as the cause of spreading Arab protests, but no word of the 11,500 homes built for Arabs, against which neither the Israelis nor Ehrenreich protested. Rioting has always been an Arab war tactic, and if they could not gain Western interest with housing, they would find another equally innocent issue. In this case, the author finds the housing ruse appealing.

Ehrenreich visited the Tamimi family when the elder Bassem, responsible for the weekly protests against Israelis since 2009, was due to return home from another stint in prison. Bassem, an activist who promotes hate and violent protests on Fridays, had been found guilty of incitement, organizing unauthorized processions, and soliciting children[663] to pelt Jewish citizens. Supported by the Koran and the Palestinian Authority (PA), he indoctrinates the town's youth to participate in killing Jews by attacking vehicles with deadly missiles, resulting in crashes and passengers killed.[664] Thus the young rock throwers of today are cultivated to be the violent terrorists of tomorrow, to continue their psychological warfare against civilians in the Jewish State — 1,500 rockets[665] fired in November, 2012 alone; more than 13,000 rockets, mortars, and missiles fired into civilian neighborhoods since 2001.

We learn that a brother-in-law died after he was hit by a tear-gas canister, indicating the Israelis' moral choice of safer methods of trying to keep the ferocious Palestinians at bay. When Ehrenreich recounts a Palestinian clash with the army, noting more than half of the 432 injured were minors, he should have recognized the Palestinian use of their own children as weapons and human shields.[666] Hamas Member of Parliament Fathi Hammad had boasted of using civilians for warfare — *We desire death as you desire life* — to increase the body count and elicit the West's sympathy for their cause of the land grab. Ehrenreich admits the Israelis try to contain the jihadis, activists and black-booted anarchists, with tear gas, rubber-coated bullets, water-cannon blasts of noxious liquids, and resort to live fire only occasionally, as needed (more cautious than their parents about the safety of their children.)

How do Ehrenreich and similar reporters envision peace with non-moderate Arabs who cannot live in peace even among themselves, engaging in violence at every turn? They nurture their young to use deadly large rocks, Molotov cocktails, improvised grenades and burning tires against civilians and the security forces, and celebrate severe injuries and death. Neither is there peace within the unstable Egypt, Syria, Lebanon and Jordan; or in any European, African, or Asian country to which Muslims have migrated. These are an inherently aggressive, brutal people who have lived in a constant state of war since Mohammed first set out to spread Islam in the 600s.

Ehrenreich noted, "Little was resolved in Oslo,"[667] blatantly blaming the failure on Zionism, an unsympathetic accusation. Under the Oslo Accord, Yasser Arafat seemed to capitulate to Israeli demands of recognition of Israel, renunciation of terrorism, and a promise to revoke his covenantal call for the destruction of the Jewish State, undoubtedly because of the withdrawn financial support from the collapsed Soviet Union and the growing Islamist presence. Israel's Yitzak Rabin agreed to legitimize the PLO based on a statement and a handshake. So were created Palestinian authorities for internal development and trade, supported by pledges of billions for development from 43 countries (Europe, Japan, Scandinavia, the US and Israel). Nevertheless, the Palestinians broke their promises, escalated the violence against Israel, and Arafat unreasonably promised his people statehood — a mortal danger to Israel's existence (whereas Israel and Jordan have been at peace since 1967).

Bassem seemed to grasp that the heavy wave of suicide bombings was as strategic (and immoral) an error as the persistent rocket fire. The second intifada brought death again — 5,000 Palestinians and 1,000 Israelis. The Oslo Accords could well have ushered in harmony, a better life for all, with no refugees on either side, but one outstretched Israeli hand does not an agreement make.

Does *The New York Times* grasp that its deeply inflammatory and offensive articles thwart the efforts of peace, encouraging that third intifada? I have seen nothing to suggest it. How long will it be before their readers can count on unbiased, fair, balanced reporting?

And the next Intifada?

Has the *NYT* considered the possibility of Times Square, Manhattan?

*Referencing the following definitions of Square: Balance; just, equitable: a *square deal;* honest; direct.

TWO-TIME OSCAR WINNER TWO-TIMES

Emma Thompson, an example of the underinformed and ill-informed, denies the existence of Islamic evil and the eight types of jihad strategies used against Israel and Western civilization.

David Miliband, former Secretary of the United Kingdom, current president and CEO of The International Rescue Committee, said, "Israel is a strategic partner and close friend of the UK," yet there are those in the limelight who use their positions of influence to destroy that alliance. Case in point, "Two-time Oscar-winning actress and director Emma Thompson" is two-timing the alliance, the State of Israel and the Jewish people. She supports Islamic Palestinians who have been occupying the Biblical Judea and Samaria since they lost their war of aggression in 1967, but condemns Israel as the occupier. Thompson's propaganda over historical documentation is either woeful or willful ignorance.

Thompson eschews Palestinian terrorism, the murder and mayhem against Israeli children on school buses[668] or asleep in their beds,[669] and prefers a fabricated Palestinian victimhood that captivates UN and world attention through generations and provides them with enormous financial support — "one of the highest levels of aid in the world."[670] To maintain their free medical care from Israel and financial aid from the US, UK, UN, Europe and Israel, Palestinians utterly destroyed, with "no hope of repair," the extensive greenhouses[671] and infrastructure in the Gaza Strip so generously left them by the departing Israelis in 2005.

Why is Thompson oblivious to the more than 3,400-year-old Jewish Jerusalem, but accepts Mohammed's warring advances in 624 a.d.? Why can she not accept the Islamic wars lost to Israel, but accepts the fleeing Arabs' new identity, "Palestinians," as a means to fabricating a bond to land that was never theirs. Why the disdain for the Jewish Palestinian Brigade that fought with the English against the Nazis, and preference for the Arabs who fought with the Nazis against England? Is this not two-timing?

Thompson concluded that Israel's home construction is illegal without legal evidence. Israel has shown her goodwill by ceding the Golan Heights to Syria, Sinai Peninsula to Egypt, the West Bank to Jordan — all in exchange for the elusive peace. Still the defeated Arabs declared, "no peace with Israel, no recognition of Israel, no negotiations with Israel," so the sacrificed land became another foundation for rockets against the Jewish people. How many more concessions would Thompson demand from a country that is already one-thousandth the size of Islam's landmass, with 1.4 billion combatants ready to die for conquest compared to Israel's eight million citizens who are eager to live?

If Thompson believes "to the vanquished, not the victor, go the spoils," she should then consider offering England to the Nazis, and advocating that Muslims return all the land they conquered over 1400 years. According to Raymond Ibrahim, a Shillman Fellow at the David Horowitz Freedom Center and Associate Fellow at the Middle East Forum, that includes tens of thousands of Arabs in Arabia who were killed or converted in the "Ridda Wars" (Apostasy Wars) that ended in 634; Syria in 636; Egypt in 641; Mesopotamia and the Persian Empire in 650; North Africa, Spain, Central Asia and India by the early 8th century. She would then advocate that Muslims restore other civilizations, centuries later, to Indonesia, Somalia, and the Philippines. This was not the willing conversion that is being taught and glorified in our textbooks, but conquest by warfare — threats, humiliation, enslavement and bloodshed.

Thompson should have investigated Islamic Jihad:

The *Encyclopaedia of Islam*'s entry for "jihad" is the "spread of Islam by arms is a religious duty upon Muslims in general ... Jihad must continue to be done until the entire world is under the rule of Islam ... Islam must completely be made over before the doctrine of jihad can be eliminated." Scholar Majid Khadurri (1909-2007), after defining jihad as warfare, writes, jihad "is regarded by all jurists, with almost no exception, as a collective *obligation* of the whole Muslim community."

Perhaps then Thompson might become aware of Islam's history of war and subjugation of Jews, Christians, Zoroastrians, Hindus, Buddhists, and all the turmoil and danger they present into whichever country they migrated. Islam is at war with the rest of the world in its religious duty to bring all to Islam. These un-uniformed warriors have already invaded the British Isles, stirring up old bigotry and hatred to divide and conquer, using a fallacious plot to convince the English, Irish and Scottish to boycott a peaceful ally, Israel, and support the tyrannical regimes of the Middle East. "First come Saturday people, then come Sunday people." The uneducated have been convinced to turn against their own survival instincts.

Infidelesto has listed seven types of jihad.

♦   **Military Jihad,** using all types of arms — bombings and rockets by the thousands against Israel, burning African Christian churches, local bombings such as New York's Twin Towers, London›s underground, Chechnya›s school children, and the Boston marathon.

♦   **Immigration Jihad,** migrating in overwhelming number to the US, Europe's mainland, and the UK, establishing their own schools and mosques to keep their children from assimilating.

♦   **Population Jihad,** maintaining polygamy and many children to overwhelm the host country, and debilitating the economy by excessive social aid.

♦   **Intellectual Jihad,** using Islamic propaganda machines to spread the acceptance of Islam. Speakers who visit universities, libraries and social groups; using interruptions and filibustering to inhibit the audience's power of reasoning. Forcing groups to boycott Israel's books, theater, and scientific exchanges, etc.

♦   **Economic Jihad,** holding the West hostage through the use of fossil fuels. Profits from gasoline purchases finance the Islamic military and all facets of Jihad.

♦ **Political Jihad,** advancing Islam politically, forcing governments to assert that Islam is a religion of peace; stirring old ideologies and providing common vulnerabilities to revive Jew-hatred, Israel being the first level of a Western delegitimization. Overwhelming a naïve Bishop of Canterbury[672] to gain acceptance of sharia.

♦ **Religious Jihad,** using the host's country's freedom of religion and tolerant religious leaders to advance Islam, while other religions are forbidden in Islamic countries. Destroying antiquities of past cultures[673] on the continent and defacing and Christian and Jewish holy sites and declaring them mosques.

♦ Add to these: **Lawfare Jihad:** using international law[674] to attack or condemn a rival country (Israel) with stealth activities in America. This includes legal battles with UN collusion to claim Judea and Samaria to be Palestinian and claim the Temple Mount to be a mosque since "time immemorial"; to stifle journalists with threats of lawsuits; to force the UK to betray an ally, to erode the will to fight and delegitimize any self-defense; to subvert human rights protections and peaceful coexistence. Using the host's court system to accept the construction of numerous mosques (misinterpreting US Constitutional) and accepting foreign laws (sharia).

These, combined with sheer ignorance, increase the chances of succumbing to Islamic control. When we allow our tolerance and legal system to be used against us — to accommodate Muslims with public prayer rooms and foot-baths, to meet demands by the Saudi-tied Muslim Student Unions to anti-Israel rallies, to oblige terrorists in prison, to call jihad attacks "workplace violence," to fund public madrassas, to bypass noise ordinances and accept prayer calls five times a day, to limit our access to entertainment and scholarship and accept Saudi-vetted books and customs, to sever ties with peaceful partners — we are welcoming Islamic Jihad.

As long as the world continues to look away from evil, allows their news media to misinform and protect Islam and do its bidding, then by their own hand will they change the nature of the United Kingdom to the despotism of the United Caliphate.

Adolph Hitler knew, "Propaganda ... has to accommodate itself to the comprehension of the least intelligent of those whom it seeks to reach." And the friendship between the Fuhrer and Grand Mufti of Jerusalem ensured that the Muslims learned well.

POLLUTED WATERS
Roger Waters testified against Israel at the UN to delegitimize the country and her people.

Roger Waters of Pink Floyd raged when he testified to discredit and delegitimize the State of Israel at the UN, aired on YouTube. He adamantly denied the Jews their only homeland, where they've been a steady presence since 1300 BCE, amid proof of their ancient monarchy, culture, ethics, morality, and religion, established by 1000 BCE.

Waters comes by his biases naturally. He is from the England that blamed the Jews for the Black Plague and expelled them for 350 years, the England that established and then violated the British Mandate in capitulation to Arab pressure, the England that turned thousands of Jewish Holocaust survivors away from Palestine to return to Germany and their death. He is from the England whose Archbishop of Canterbury[675] welcomed oppressive sharia to compromise English law.

Scheduled to speak on April 30, 2013, in support of BDS (Boycott, Divestment, Sanctions) of Israel at Manhattan's 92St Y, financially supported by the UJA Federation, Waters then cancelled. Either he or the Y folded to opposition; surely, it was not his conscience. This four-flusher will not reconsider his position of blaming Israel for the stagnated peace process; perhaps the UJA Federation folded to pressure.

Unable to compete with modernity and modern warfare, the Muslim Brotherhood devised the strategy of keeping their brethren isolated to win global support — this IS apartheid. "To the vanquished go the spoils!" Did the Brits welcome back the vanquished Nazis or the Argentineans to the Falklands? Yet Israel has often returned captured land with the hope of peace, but jihadis cannot acknowledge Israel as a Jewish State.

Waters had been boiling at the security measures for those who travel between Israel and Gaza. Would he react similarly with routine questioning and searches between countries of the UK? Might he have better tolerated discovering the bodies of the Fogel family, the baby's head virtually severed, when Israel's security failed?[676]

He called the security barrier an "appalling edifice to behold," this barricade with a mere 10 percent comprised of concrete, the rest wire, Israel's protection from her lethal neighbors —ignoring the numerous walls throughout the UK, and 44 stone-and-steel "Peace Walls" in Belfast alone; and the numerous thicker, higher, sturdier walls, some electrified, throughout the world.[677]

Waters was also immersed in Israel's housing developments, ignorant that the land was legally obtained in several ways: land purchased from absentee landlords at high prices; the formal birth of the independent, sovereign State of Israel;[678] and winning territory in wars begun by five Arab armies. Great Britain remained a major obstacle to Jewish self-defense, barring entry to new immigrants and refusing the Jews the right to form a militia and removing weapons wherever possible, yet Brits signed a treaty with Transjordan that armed the Arabs. And the US imposed an arms embargo on the entire region. Still, the Arab war to destroy Israel failed and Arabs lost what could have been theirs, had they accepted peace and the partition.

If he esteems the Palestinians, can Waters define them? They are the descendants of Afghans, Algerians, Arabs, Armenians, Bohemians, Bosnians, Bulgarians, Circassians,

Copts, Egyptians, Georgians, Germans, Greeks, Italians, Kurds, Latins, Maronites, Persians, Ruthenians, Samaritans, Syrians, Sudanese, Tartars, Turks and more, regarded themselves Syrians in 1939, and took the name Palestinians to avail themselves of a link to the land they coveted. The Ancient Romans' political strategy was to destroy the Jewish connection to the area by calling it *Syria Palestina*, referencing the Aegean Philistines, the sea people[679] of Ancient Greece, but the connection to the Philistines[680] is mere terminology. Today›s Gaza is occupied by an illegal population calling itself Palestinians, forsaken by a war strategy of their own making.

Never a distinct people, Palestinians have no specific history, language, culture, or antiquities. Their commonality is the Koranic command to usurp a history and dominate the inhabitants. In Britain, there are already 85 sharia courts and an Islamist campaign to turn several British cities into independent Islamic states,[681] the beginning of a UK transformation, with Buckingham Palace chosen for their Caliphate. US Imams are already claiming that Muslims preceded Christopher Columbus and the Native Americans. This is warfare by historic revisionism and propaganda and it feeds on the prejudiced and uninformed. Their assertions hold no water, but revisionism can deceive. Fourteen centuries of persistence and success suggest they need not step into modernity. Hamas is now training students[682] in the use of weapons for killing Jews, and Waters and the UN will have a new generation of jihadist deaths to blame on Israel.

Waters also tapped into the Islamist accusation of Israel's ethnic cleansing, but not Arabs' ethnic cleansing of Jews! According to his thinking, Israel, the size of, say, Wales, is appropriating land from the Islamic landmass a thousand times its size. Is this the same Israel that is home to every national origin, race and color, including Arab Jews who fled the threat of extinction? Israel, of which 20 percent of the population is Arab, with 12 Arab Knesset members? Where is this ethnic cleansing?

Ethnic cleansing creates a decline in population, but the neighboring Palestinians are thriving and increasing due to Israel's improved healthcare. There is now longevity and a decrease in the Palestinian birth-mortality rate. The only "cleansing" appears to be Israel's providing cleaner, healthier environs. The accusation doesn't hold water. Ethnic cleansing was Hitler's deeds, and what the Jews are experiencing from Muslim threats of worldwide genocide, their fleeing Scandinavia,[683] Germany and France;[684] and the constant barrage of Hamas rockets from Gaza. And while Hamas Prime Minister Ismail Haniyeh[685] was calling for Israel's destruction, his relative was receiving life-saving heart surgery in Israel.

Ethnic cleansing is also when Muslims killed seven million black Africans in Southern Sudan,[686] while the UN and Waters maintain silence. Muslims capture, enslave, brutalize and dehumanize their victims as the world looks away. The new Republic of South Sudan has spoken in gratitude for the safety and humanitarian aid offered the children who managed to escape and reach Israel.

The Palestinians declined every chance at statehood; their *raison d'etre* is Israel's destruction. True occupation is the Palestinians in Judea (Judea=Jews) and Samaria, and Muslim control over the entire continent that was once inhabited by non-Muslims.

Finally, the musician, Waters, launched an attempt at accountancy, but battles are not waged for proportionality. He did not dispute seven Arab armies' attacking the new State of Israel or, for that matter, the Muslim multitudes raping, pillaging, killing the unarmed in Africa. England and Germany did not war for congruence. Arabs terrorize, and accuracy is considered inconsequential; the higher the body count, the more pity they elicit. The UN has finally acknowledged that Hamas positions women and children as human shields at rocket sites to increase the death toll for outpourings of compassion. Former British Army Colonel Kemp[687] has time and again testified that the IDF operates in exemplary fashion, with more precautions to safeguard civilians than "any army in the history of warfare." He called to task the lies of the media, the fallacious Goldstone report, and the evil propaganda war waged by the Arabs, the media, and organized supporters. Mr. Waters is "all wet."

Radical Islam is intolerant. Over 1400 years, they extinguished Jews, Christians, Copts, Buddhists, Hindus, Pharoahans, Zoroastrians, and others. That's ethnic cleansing. Where is Waters' voice against this destructive Religion of Peace?[688] Where is his voice against their inhumane treatment of even their own women and children?

Roger Waters needs to begin a true investigation and a return to honesty and integrity. As it stands now, he is drowning in ignorance.

HONOR FOR DISHONOR

The Newseum in Washington DC honored for martyrdom two journalist employees of Al-Aqsa Television who were killed while performing as Hamas operatives.

I had not heard the expression, Moral Equivalence, until fairly recently. I don't believe it was used during World War II, when we could distinguish the enemy from ourselves. But in an era when everything is reversed — truths are interchanged with lies, textbooks spew a revised history with fabrications and omissions, people cannot discern fiction from fact or promises from deeds; and the word "Peace" describes a severely brutal culture — we seem to have lost our moral compass. We have reached a crossroads where we can just as readily show compassion to the abductor as the hostage because, after all, both were confined in the same building.

This same perverted thinking is used to compare the exchange of fire between Israelis and Gazans. The left cannot differentiate between Hamas's firing rockets into civilian neighborhoods and Israeli soldiers firing in self-defense to thwart further attacks. They cannot discern Israeli civilians killed in the offensive assault with Palestinian women and children intentionally positioned at Hamas's rocket sites to be killed from the defensive activity.[689]

Our logic has been warped by a deliberate intent to support a fallacy, an evil ideology, and such is the case at the Newseum, a Washington, DC museum that contains memorabilia of special news events, exhibits, programs, education, and more. It holds an annual Journalists Memorial ceremony dedicated to truth-seeking correspondents who have fallen in the line of duty to gather the news. But the museum's mission statement is somewhat innocuous. While the staff wishes to honor journalists, there is no reference to honorable journalists. They claim to value a free press, but the journalists need not represent a free press. They may just as well be honored for engaging in dishonorable activities and for reporting inaccuracies for a tyrannical regime's political agenda.

MISSION STATEMENT:
The Newseum educates the public about the value of a free press in a free society and tells the stories of the world's important events in unique and engaging ways.

In its prominent location on historic Pennsylvania Avenue in Washington, D.C., the Newseum blends 500 years of news history, up-to-the-second technology and hands-on exhibits for a one-of-a-kind museum experience.

The Newseum is a 501(c)(3) public charity and is funded by contributions from individuals, foundations and corporations. The Newseum does not accept government funds.

Hassam Salama and Mahmoud al-Kumi, were two employees of Al-Aqsa Television (a disreputable, propagandist medium), which, along with the Islamic National Bank (INB) of Gaza, is controlled by Hamas, a global terrorist organization. Executive Order 13224, dated November 2010, froze all assets of INB and Al-Aqsa, and prohibited US citizens' conducting transactions with them.

The men were Hamas terrorists targeted by the Israel Defense Forces during Operation Pillar of Defense (Nov. 2012). These dishonorable photojournalists are now considered martyrs by their Islamic society, a society that burns the American flag and swears "Death to America, Death to Israel" in support of tyranny against democracy. They were killed not as journalists, but as active Hamas operatives, and Al-Aqsa's spokesman, Mohammad Thouraya, admitted his employees were "all part of the resistance."

Nevertheless, The Committee to Protect Journalists, Reporters Without Borders, and The World Association of Newspapers and News Publishers, followed by Al Aqsa, professed that these journalists were killed in the line of duty. Evidence from Israel proved their terrorist involvement and their obvious ties to Hamas.

Fortunately, one need not support unethical museums. Washington has an endless variety of fascinating museums from which to choose and seek honest information.

L'AMERICAINE

French leisure reflects their one-in-four unemployment, increased debt, raised taxes, welfare assistance, food stamps, more austerity. We must recognize this as social engineering.

One of our newspaper comic strips, Pajama Diaries, by Terri Libenson, published October 2013, showed the following headings across four frames: *"There is no doubt our society is kid-centric. But there seems to be a growing backlash. Taking a cue from Europe, families are trying a more laid-back approach to parenting. Still, most of Europe has certain advantages: better work hours, government-mandated childcare, and most of all, no Americans."*

In the final panel, our American mother sees a French couple enjoying a beverage at an outdoor cafe, and asks, *"Who wants to carpool to soccer? Parlez-vous anglais? Art club? Chuck E. Cheese? Bonjour?"* And the French utter, *"L'Americaine stupide."*

Should we take our cue from Europe? While the intensity levels differ, the magnitude of unemployment is the thrust of their financial system, necessitating an austerity program that led to a recession. At this writing, Germany, Austria, Netherlands and Luxembourg's unemployment is below 6 percent; Denmark is at 7.4, the UK at 7.7, Poland at 10.6, Italy at 11.7, Lithuania at 13.3, Ireland at 14.6, Portugal at 17.6, and Spain and Greece at a whopping 26.2 and 27 percent respectively. Portugal, Spain and Greece's unemployment match the US's during The Great Depression, and the general rule is that for every single person unemployed, three others are affected. Therefore, at 25 percent unemployment, everyone is affected. France's rate, close to 11 percent, is concentrated at its north and south poles, giving them the "enviable" leisure time.

With unemployment come lifestyle changes, increasing debt, more welfare assistance, food stamps, and increasing taxes for the workers who must now support the mounting needy. The cartoon mother envisions a couple strolling with their infant, without understanding that this leisure is part of a long-term social crisis — neither parent is working. Americans are also experiencing a shorter work week with a record low of under 30 hours in the low-wage industries, diminished take-home pay, disappearing luxuries and fewer necessities, reduced buying power and more businesses hurting, less productivity, and fewer customers, and on ... "Mom" may soon not be able to send her children to soccer or art lessons.

Would mom welcome government childcare? Studies show that families, not childcare centers, have a greater impact on a child's development when mothers are responsive, sensitive, attentive and provide good stimulation during interactions. Families with organized routines, books, play material, and engaging experiences produce children with better social and cognitive skills. Children fare well in supportive childhood, but most US childcare centers rank between "poor" and "good." Be reminded that we are Americans who do not want our government mandating anything — the more mandates, the scanter the freedoms. "We the People" are citizens; Europeans are subjects. Mom is oblivious to the freedoms she would have to relinquish in order to live as a European. Our capitalist society has flourished where Europe's has not.

Fascism blossomed in Europe because of the high unemployment, as people seized the promise of improvement if only they could find those responsible for the country's ills. And who better to blame than the eternal scapegoats? The Jews — who number about .02 percent of the world's population. We can see this materializing here — the higher unemployment rates, no promise of improvement, government spending out of control, increasing government regulations and domination, worsening divisiveness and, of course, fueled anti-Semitism.

Control comes in many forms, the healthcare mandate being only one. Although our Founding Fathers obstructed the federal government from manipulating education standards and curriculum, the Communists found a way. Common Core Standards was created according to a (supposed) classless, moneyless, Communist social order and provides a way to dominate and indoctrinate schoolchildren without parental interference.

Beginning with first grade, the textbooks are designed to produce a new generation of radicals who abhor the America we knew, and to work for the new Communist world. Authoritarians begin with education and immerse the children in social engineering that delivers an anti-religious propaganda and promotes an equality that discourages individuality, special talents and interests. The program was developed by the leftist Achieve, endorsed by two trade groups, and funded by the Bill and Melinda Gates Foundation, along with AT&T Foundation, the Boeing Company, Carnegie Corporation of New York, Du Pont, The GE Foundation, and allies George Soros and Peter Lewis: ACORN, ACLU, Center for American Progress, MoveOn.org, and many more. Their goal is a One World Order[690] with control over students during a 13-hour day to create the submissive working class of tomorrow.

Islamic revisionism was also introduced to our passive, vulnerable society as Saudi Arabia is funding the historic heresy in American textbooks. Islamic "scholars" have turned Mary into the Muslim Mariam, Jesus into a Palestinian, and Christopher Columbus into the Muslim who discovered America. Students are also taught to memorize Quranic scriptures and how to make prayer rugs.

Mom can forget the soccer games, art lessons, and outings. If more parents don't wake up to Common Core's not-so-subtle damage and fail to contact their state's Parents against Common Core groups, then . . . L'Americaine stupide.

PROBING THE PROPAGANDA

Kristallnacht was a pogrom, prepared, orchestrated, and executed when the propaganda minister found the perfect dupe for the event on 9/11.

"The Kristallnacht was started by one individual," she said, referring to Hershel Grynszpan, a 17-year-old German-born Polish Jew who assassinated Ernst von Rath, a German diplomat stationed in Paris. "It shows how a minor event in history can lead to mass destruction." The Cleveland Jewish News (CJN), Nov. 1, 2013.

The CJN interviewed Roni Berenson, a Holocaust survivor, about Kristallnacht. Born in Berlin, she remembers being pulled out of school on the day after the violence and, with her parents, boarding the penultimate ship to leave Europe. Berenson blames the events of Kristallnacht on Herschel Grynszpan, himself a Jewish victim of the Nazi menace.

Grynszpan, was an adolescent German-born, Jewish refugee of Polish parents. He had been sent to an uncle in Paris to escape persecution, but now his parents were among the many thousands of Polish Jews expelled and abandoned at the German-Polish border only to be refused entry and sanctuary in their native land. Perhaps distraught over their situation and his own, and fearful of the future, the teenager bought a gun and shot Ernst von Rath, a low-level German embassy official who was assigned to assist him. And it was this minor incident, this shooting, that would be termed an assassination and used to justify Kristallnacht and the unspeakable brutality to follow.

History shows that German journalist, Wilhelm Marr, coined the term "antisemitism" in 1879, in his published pamphlet, "The Victory of Judaism over Germanism,"[691] pronouncing it a science rather than the more precise *Judenhass,* Jewish-hatred. After his next pamphlet in 1880, "The Way to Victory of the Germanic Spirit over the Jewish Spirit," he founded the League of Antisemites, the first German organization dedicated to opposing the alleged Jewish threat to German culture and forcing the Jews from Germany.

By 1920, The German Workers Party became the National Socialist Workers Party, aka Nazis. It brought the right's nationalism and the left's socialism together against big business, the middle class and capitalism, shifting to antisemitism and anti-Marxism in 1930. The Party advocated a Master Race to exclude or exterminate Jews, homosexuals, Romani, blacks, the physically and mentally handicapped, Jehovah's Witnesses and all political opponents.

Within a few short years, Germany had lived through The Great Depression, the Weimar Republic's collapse, and the surge of unemployment. The rise of Hitler's Nazism was established by 1921, with Hitler's appointment as party leader, followed by his appointment as Chancellor of Germany in 1933, and establishing his totalitarian regime, the Third Reich. The Nuremberg Laws[692] were introduced at the Party's annual Rally in 1935, when they legally defined who was Jewish in order to legislate against German Jews' basic rights, which eventually extended to other *untermenschen* (subhumans).

Adolf Hitler planned the pogrom for 10 November, Martin Luther's birthday,[693] following Luther's writings of 1543, "On the Jews and Their Lies," and the anniversary of the infamous Beer Hall Putsch[694] of 8 November, followed by a staged march on 9 November 1923. But that was also the day that von Rath died of the gunshot wounds and, not surprisingly, Foreign Propaganda Minister Joseph Goebbels[695] saw this as the perfect opportunity to declare this a Jewish attack on the German people, a way to justify previous anti-Semitic pogroms and carnage in Germany. He announced that the German people were so outraged by the Jew's "assassination" of a German diplomat, that they spontaneously took the law into their own hands.

Ask any American to write the date, and he'll write November 9 or 11/9. Ask any European to write the same date and he will write 9 November or 9/11. You see, the rest of the world always puts the day first, followed by the month; therefore, the date was 9/11. The Grand Mufti of Jerusalem and Islamists were (and still are) great admirers of Hitler and both cultures assign particular significance to special seasons and anniversaries. Kristallnacht began on November 9 (written as 9/11) and the World Trade Center was bombed by Islamists on 9/11. I suspect this was not a coincidence, but a deliberate choice.

Yes, Grynszpan had been distressed about his parents and his own situation, but the shooting of von Rath was merely a pretext for the pogrom. While Berenson accepts the events as reported by the Nazi press, the reality is that the Nazis had entered a new radical level of violence, and the SS (Schutzstaffel)[696] had been created explicitly, months before, as the primary organization [697] to plan and carry out such a large-scale attack.

The Holocaust Encyclopedia[698] stipulates:

The Nazi Party leadership, assembled in Munich for the commemoration, chose to use the occasion as a pretext to launch a night of anti-Semitic excesses. Propaganda[699] Minister Joseph Goebbels, a chief instigator of the pogrom, intimated to the convened Nazi "Old Guard" that "'World Jewry" had conspired to commit the assassination and announced that, "the Führer has decided that ... demonstrations should not be prepared or organized by the Party, but insofar as they erupt spontaneously, they are not to be hampered."

The well-orchestrated, two-day pogrom took place throughout Germany, annexed Austria, and in areas of the German-occupied Sudetenland in Czechoslovakia. Nazi party officials, Storm Troopers (SS) and Hitler Youth (SA) now had their orders.

Armed with weapons and sledgehammers, they flooded the streets on cue. They ransacked 1600 synagogues, setting some afire with their worshippers locked inside; broke windows and doors; and looted synagogues, Jewish homes and businesses — but with commands to support the fiction of outrage at the "assassination"; to remove archives and artifacts before vandalizing synagogues; safeguard non-Jewish German life and property and all foreigners; and arrest young, healthy Jewish men, of which 30,000 were sent to concentration camps in waiting trains.

About 100 Jews were beaten to death in homes and on the streets. Thousands of Jewish homes and about 8,000 Jewish shops were vandalized and devastated. Jewish cemeteries were wrecked, tombstones smashed, and corpses unearthed and defiled. Women were raped, and people committed suicide. Jews were blamed for the pogrom and fined the equivalent of today's $37 trillion for damage and $37 billion for clearing the wreckage. Another 100,000 victims were deported to death camps.

German college students burned censored books written by all Jews and Christians like Thomas Mann and Mark Twain. A century before, German-Jewish poet Heinrich Heine had predicted, "Where they burn books, they will eventually burn people."

Grynszpan did not resist arrest and immediately confessed to the crime. He was not tried or put to death in a country where death was meted out for far smaller infractions, as a trial would have exposed the government's collusion. Rather, he was imprisoned, and spent the rest of his life in German custody and declared dead by West German officials in 1960.

Herschel Grynszpan[700] was the patsy who took the blame for Kristallnacht. He was no more the justification for Kristallnacht than an Israeli apartment building is for Palestinian violence or a videotape for the mayhem and slaughter in Benghazi.

NUREMBERG REVISITED

Compare the 1935 Nuremberg laws with Common Core and Islamophobic changes here, and the similarities are chilling.

A PBS special on Kristallnacht (Night of Broken Glass) showed a series of coordinated attacks against Jews throughout Nazi Germany and parts of Austria on November 9-10, 1938. These were carried out by Hitler's forces and non-Jewish civilians and resulted in the death of hundreds of Jews and thousands sent to concentration camps. A vast number of Jewish homes, hospitals and schools were destroyed, more than 7,000 Jewish businesses devastated, and more than 1,000 synagogues burned to the ground. A review of a transcript revealed the two infamous Nuremberg Laws that Hitler initiated during his rise to power. From those, more than 2,000 anti-Semitic laws were ratified at all levels of government, thereby sealing the fate of the Jews of the Third Reich.

To my utter horror, I realized that these laws survived the Nazi regime and are now being implemented against Jews and Christians here and throughout the world. In the U.S., our students are coming under state control through the Common Core "standards" adopted in the 45 states that succumbed to multimillions in government Race-to-the-Top dollars. When challenged by parents, we see teachers and administrators who are clearly trained in the community-organizer mode and refuting, bullying, and intimidating these critics. I've selected a handful of the 2,000 laws to cite and compare.

April 1, 1933: A week after Hitler came to power, he ordered all Jewish shops, banks, offices and department store closed.[701] Nazi Propaganda Minister Joseph Goebbels defended this draconian move as a legitimate response to the anti-German "atrocity propaganda" being spread by "international Jewry." Signs were posted — "Germans, defend yourselves, buy only at German shops!" The Arab League, founded in 1944, began boycotting Jewish goods, and later rejected all who conducted business with the State of Israel.

Today: We have BDS — boycott-divestment-sanctions — advocated by Muslim students on college and university campuses, and supported by school staff and professors. Rallies are held with Islamist videos and guest speakers who target companies that conduct business with Israel. The groups submit Israel boycott resolutions to The National Council of the American Studies Association,[702] in journals and academic associations worldwide. The director of the Center for Peace and Conflict Studies at the University of Sydney is being sued in the Federal Court of Australia because he refused to sponsor a fellowship application from an Israeli academic.[703] France's Left Party announced its support for BDS.[704] Britain's plans to issue Islamic Bonds would de facto discriminate against Israel.[705] Ireland's BDS activists affix yellow boycott stickers on Israeli products in retail stores.[706] The Methodist Church of Britain consistently targets Israel with criticism while ignoring the sins of her foes.[707] The methods are different; the results are virtually identical.

President Obama uses the same tactics (also defined as Chicago-style brass knuckles) to marginalize and demonize his adversaries, such as with the Republican party, Wall Street executives, Fox News, news commentator Rush Limbaugh, and others perceived as obstacles to his radical agenda.

May 1933: One hundred years after German poet Heinrich Heine said, "Where one burns books, one will soon burn people," members of the right-wing student organization of Wilhelm-Humboldt University in Berlin tossed tens of thousands of books from their library and other sources into a roaring bonfire at the adjacent Franz Joseph Platz. Denouncing the authors —mostly Jewish, such as Albert Einstein, but also Thomas Mann, Jack London, Ernest Hemingway and others — they purged their country of ideas, philosophies, and advancement.

Today: Ireland censors books opposed to Catholic dogma, terrorism and pornography, and in April 2013, Ireland's Teacher's Union[708] relinquished its freedoms of thought, research and growth to collaborate with Islam in banning Israel›s books and choosing to be instructed and indoctrinated by the most illiterate and violent culture on earth, who are as barbaric today as they were fourteen centuries ago. At the same time, Scotland's Clackmannanshire Council[709] announced they would rebuff all economic support for Israel.

Throughout America, a select group of left-leaning executives, with not one academic among them, created the Common Core Standards to completely replace all previous textbooks from which American students learned and subsequently formed our exceptional nation, with its advancements in technology, science, medicine, space travel and more. Historical facts and the best in literature are now purged. The new lessons destroy individuality and disregard the developmental stages, the children's maturity, and ethics.[710] Just as the Fuhrer offered no flexibility and tutored all students to become soldiers for the Reich, these textbooks present a fallacious, whitewashed and glorified Islam while systematically diminishing and distorting Christianity and Judaism. There are key omissions and false premises about America, her founding and her values. They encourage students to learn the Shahada (profession of Islamic faith) and to empathize with terrorists and suicide bombers. The methods differ; the results are the same. Education, because of its impact on future generations, is among the first institutions targeted by despots.

The 1935 Nuremberg Laws[711] and the 1933 Law for the Prevention of Hereditarily Diseased Offspring[712] were introduced to distinguish Aryans from *untermenschen* (subhumans), targeting people for eugenics and to initiate a euthanasia program. The Nazis implemented a vast racial caste system, where teachers measured their students' skulls and noses and recorded hair and eye colors for classification into the Volksliste, choosing Nordic traits over the "racially impure," which often humiliated the Jewish and Roma students. Days after the Kristallnacht, politician and military leader Hermann Goring decreed to remove Jews from German economic life, thereby destroying 30,000 Jewish-owned businesses.

Today: In addition to Obamacare registration, Common Core Standards feature a data-mining system[713] to track test scores, academic progress; information on religion, political beliefs and affiliations, family income, discipline, sexual behavior and attitudes, extracurricular activities, DNA, blood type, psychological evaluations and more, to evaluate the students and entrap them into pre-determined schools and jobs. The private database, inBloom[714] violates our Fourth Amendment rights and conflicts with students' rights to pursue happiness. Paralleling the Nazi laws, students will be prevented from choosing and entering specific careers and trades.

Also under consideration is the use of Galvanic Skin Response bracelets[715] to evaluate skin response to emotional stimuli. Bill Gates admitted the data would enable him to design standards and software to create their steadfast market and train future employees under a socialist system. This is the modern-day social engineering to seek their version of "racial purity."

May 21, 1935: Jews were banned from serving as Wehrmacht officers.

Today: Since 2009, the Obama administration has been weakening our military and reducing our power by dismissing highly decorated military officials,[716] Jewish and Christian, most ranked Colonel or above, in the five branches of US armed forces. The allegations vary, with some notably frivolous, but the effect is the same. Former White House Chief-of-Staff Rahm Emanuel explained this as a way of dismissing those who disagree with this government's ideology.

April 1937: Municipal authorities in Berlin exclude Jewish children from state schools.

Today: College and university administrations across America are currently subjecting Jewish students to anti-Semitic harassment, as their departments sponsor, fund and legitimize BDS events with films and speakers who advocate Israel's economic destruction. Islamists, aided by left-leaning professors, are threatening Jewish students in schools, making life, at the least, distressing, and their pleas for help fall on deaf ears. Parents of K-12 students across America are choosing to homeschool in record numbers, as they see the decline of public schools. But the current administration has taken aggressive steps to stop homeschooling[717] in the United States.

Christian students throughout the Islamic Middle East and Africa have been attacked and killed[718] in their dormitories in the name of Islam. The result is the same now as it was in Berlin, with Jewish and Christian students experiencing exclusion and danger. Palestinians intentionally fire rockets at Jewish schools and school buses in Israel. Islamic separatists targeted the Beslan school in the North Caucasus region of the Russian Federation on September 1, 2004, capturing 1,100 hostages, including 777 children, and killing 380.

July 1938: Jews are prohibited from owning gun stores or trading weapons, enacted within days before Kristallnacht (again proving the event was planned). In 1922, Hitler said, "An evil exists that threatens every man, woman, and child of this great nation. We must take steps to ensure our domestic security and protect our homeland." The Weimar Republic had already legislated gun registration to disarm Nazis and Communists. Hitler reinforced the existing German law, banning Jews from obtaining a license to manufacture firearms or ammunition and then prohibiting Jews from possessing dangerous weapons, including firearms.

Today: After the shooting and mass murder of schoolchildren and teachers in Sandy Hook, CT, in December of 2012, Obama and his minions began demonizing guns and ammunition, and campaigning for the elimination of all guns. Yet the US Federal government and Department of Homeland Security (DHS, named for Hitler)s Office of Fatherland Security) purchased 1.6 billion rounds of ammunition for domestic use.[719] The DHS has national, not foreign, authority, yet it purchased 450 million rounds of hollow point bullets (banned for military use by the Geneva Convention), enough for a seven-year war with Americans. The DHS also purchased $400,000 worth of radiation-protection pills, and thousands of bulletproof roadside checkpoint booths. Might we count on the cooperation of the Occupiers (Wall Street, etc.), the Knockout gangs, and steadfast Obamaphiles to form a domestic army? After all, was it not Barack Obama who said on the campaign trail: "We cannot continue to rely on our military in order to achieve the national security objectives we've set. We've got to have a civilian national security force that's just as powerful, just as strong, just as well-funded."

Senator Dianne Feinstein (D), gun opponent and senior senator from California, introduced the Assault Weapons ban of 2013, to stop the sale, transfer, importation and manufacture of military-style and high-capacity weapons. She is supported by citizens who willingly relinquish their freedom for self-protection. Her requirements,[720] posted on her website, include many rules from the Nazi-era control requirements concerning sale, transfer, importation, manufacture, registration with photo and fingerprints, and specific features of rifles and handgun, including type and serial number. Clearly, the purpose is to weaken political opponents and the masses.

At this writing, I received information that matches Hitler's *Schutzstaffel,* his Protection Squadron or defense corps, aka the SS, of which the *Waffen-SS* was the armed wing. Louis Gohmert, Republican Representative from Texas, exposed Obamacare)s Secret Security Force.[721]

July 11, 1938: The Reich Ministry of the Interior banned Jews from health spas.

Today: The YMCA of St. Paul, in a timely report, explained that the Minnesota police force supports the creation of a one-hour "Muslim girls only"[722] swim time. This reinforces their disconnectedness and non-assimilation in America. Muslims have always had the right to use the facility alongside Americans of all races and religions, but now the sharia-compliant authorities have agreed to reserve an hour during which Jews and Christians will be forbidden from this health spa.

The Constitution of the United States is under attack by forces that are working to usurp our spirit. There is no excuse, and it should not be allowed. America is a step behind Europe in its current efforts to sell out. The details are different than in WWII, but the similarities are chilling — it was a sell-out to tyranny! Had Europe heeded the signs and acknowledged Hitler's plan, rather than acquiescing to Hitler's earlier demands, they might have averted the epic catastrophe of World War II. Now is the time to take back our country and to resist both Islamic and fascist/socialist tyranny. And if not now, when?

WE HAVE MET THE ENEMY (and he is us … Pogo, by Walt Kelly)

Met director Peter Gelb, says The Met's anti-Semitic production, "The Death of Klinghoffer," will go on.

During World War II, a violinist dressed in military uniform went to play for the servicemen in an United States Army hospital in Italy. As he entered a ward designated for young men who had recently lost limbs, he was shocked to see that one patient was attempting to applaud with his only hand. As the musician's face lit up with compassion and sensitivity, he raised his violin and played. His name was Jascha Heifetz, a Lithuanian-born Jewish American whose 65-year career began at age four. He made his Carnegie Hall debut at age 16 and became world renowned for the perfection to which other violinists still aspire.

Seated next to Heifetz at the hospital piano was pianist Milton Kaye. Fifty years later, Kaye recalled that memorable concert when he heard "the greatest violinist of the ages." The following year, pianist Seymour Lipkin beheld that same magnificence when he accompanied Heifetz on another GI tour, stating that the violinist always played his best, no matter the circumstances. Heifetz had been so moved when he entertained the paraplegics, and despite his grueling schedule, he continued to add more such concerts to his tours. Kaye remembers those days as "the greatest privilege" of his musical life.

In addition to an unparalleled talent, Heifetz had what is known as *neshamah*, a Jewish soul — what may be described as an energy and essence of virtue and humanity, passion and compassion, and depth of empathy for others. It was even apparent to his father who saw the four-year-old prodigy cry when he played sad music. No doubt, it is the Jewish *neshamah* (soul) that Israelis have to provide quality medical attention even to Israel's enemies, and the same that sends Israeli first responders to countries devastated by natural disasters. And it is this same quality that appears to have eluded the next generation of Heifetzes, — Jascha's great nephew, Peter Gelb, artistic director at the Metropolitan Opera (The "Met").

It was said of Gelb that he declares himself a man of the people, but that he is out of touch with the prevailing *zeitgeist* (culture of the time). Noted in the Berkshire Fine Arts,[723] "Gelb lacks the qualifications to organize a program and appoint or audition singers and, despite his in-expertise, captured this Met position from the ailing James Levine." But it is Gelb's choice of opera for the 2014 fall season that is most disturbing.

The opera, *The Death of Klinghoffer*, was cited for being anti-Semitic and pro-Islamic terrorism,[724] and Gelb's integrity and moral compass are in question. Instead of eliciting compassion and tears for the murder of Mr. Leon Klinghoffer, a defenseless, wheelchair-bound veteran of WW II, a Jewish fellow-American, Gelb's opera will offer sympathy and apology for the Islamic murderers — who might well have also thrown the Jewish-American Gelb overboard, had he vacationed on the ill-fated Achille Lauro.

Gelb's collaborators were director Peter Sellars and choreographer Mark Morris for concept, with John Adams's music and Alice Goodman's libretto. The opera was commissioned by five American and European opera companies and was first performed at the Brooklyn Academy of Music. And the Met staff decided to cast ethics to the wind and fan the flames of anti-Semitism.

Rather than show concern for the victim and his family and the other terrified, endangered tourists who were taken hostage, although ultimately spared, the *artistes* extol the contrived virtues of the cold-blooded killers. They took a pro-Islamic, anti-American/ Jewish stance in favor of an avowed enemy — Islam, whose adherents repeatedly warn that they will overtake the West and establish an Islamic caliphate on our soil. And the Met's callous staff and cast will provide the venue for the glorification of Islam, thereby softening the eventual conquest of an acquiescent people.

Would these soulless specimens sympathize with these Muslims if the victim were also their own family member or religious compadre? Did they likewise sympathize with the Mahmoud Abbas-financed-and-orchestrated Munich Massacre of 11 Israeli athletes? Or the Muslims who commandeered the planes that killed three thousand in the World Trade Center? Or the Boston Marathon jihadis who killed three and injured/ crippled 264 racers? Or Major Hassan who fatally shot 13 and injured more than 30 at Fort Hood?

Would the Met also consider providing sophisticated entertainment while reproducing the beheading of Jewish-American journalist Daniel Pearl? Or blowing up a school bus of children in Chechnya or Israel? Perhaps Gelb would consider a choral group of 200 young girls for an opera about the Boko Haram kidnappings in Nigeria. What other inspiration might one select for musical adventures into the exaltation of Islam and its adherents for the pleasure of the callous and unenlightened?

Can the Met not grasp that to glorify evil is evil? While the author(s) and producer(s) claim to find motivation for Islamic acts, they do not seek truth. Islamic motivation is hate, envy, resentment, against Jews, Christians, Americans, Western Civilization.

♦ Mohammed bore extreme hate for the Jews because they rejected his new religion and his status as prophet.

♦ In revenge, he beheaded the 800 Jewish men of Mecca and Medina; captured other men, women, and children as slaves (or for slave trade); seized the coveted metal crafts for his booty; and declared the cities holy for Islam. This success became part of the Islamic "religion."

♦ The envy of Islam for Western accomplishments is strong because their lives were devoted to war, conquest, and bloodshed, not learning or creativity. Therefore, their claims to invention come from the creativity of the people in the nations they conquered. Muslims are now asserting that Moses, Jesus, Christopher Columbus, and Albert Einstein were Muslim.

♦ Additional envy and hatred come from their belief that Islam is the best and only religion, yet they are conflicted because their society is beset with illiteracy, poverty, distrust, discrimination, enslavement, pain, vigilante killings and unhappiness. They understand that life is better in the West, yet they are in the West to change our system to theirs.

Just as we must never recreate the atrocities of the concentration camps for our amusement, so we must never recreate any acts of malevolence to minimize their impact on the human psyche. No matter the adversity or personal history behind acts of evil, the acts are nevertheless evil. Although Islamic motivation is the hate embedded in the Koran, taught to the very young and throughout their lives, the motivation is immaterial. Criminals must be held accountable, not excused, for their behavior, and never celebrated, or every felon would be freed, and anarchy would reign.

You see, the Muslims did more than take a man's life. They've stolen the humanity from everyone who is even peripherally involved with this murder. For the sake of our survival as a nation and as a species, our obligation is morality.

THE METROPALISTAN OPERA

Despite its exposure as jihadic, anti-Semitic assault on the American public, the opera, "The Death of Klinghoffer," will be performed on stage.

Canceling the simulcast of 'The Death of Klinghoffer" does not exculpate any of the personnel affiliated with the opera if the show will be presented on stage as scheduled. Because Peter Gelb acknowledged the "genuine concern in the international Jewish community" — he is not oblivious to the impropriety — yet he continues as a psychopath without conscience. He may well be an active partner to the insult, an accomplice to Alice Goodman's rejection of their mutual heritage, or he lacks the capacity to see that this creation should also be of enormous concern to the greater American community. In fact, this may well rank with the Bavarian Oberammergau that continues to inspire antisemitism — but not only antisemitism. This perverted story is of itself an act of Islamic jihad.

For the still uninformed, Jihad is "holy war," or it would be a holy war if Islam were a bona fide religion. Rather, Islam is political ideology, a movement of conquest that is presented as a religion (a religion of peace, no less!), a duty for all Muslims to wage war against the non-Islamic world on behalf of their prophet, Mohammed.

In the 7th century, after 13 years of futile attempts at converting Meccan and Medinan Jews, Christians and idol worshippers to his new religion, Islam, Mohammed began torturing, looting and destroying those who would not accept his god or him as prophet. He beheaded (Jewish) men and prepubescent boys, enslaved women and children, and killed until both cities were inhabited by Muslims only. Thus, he acquired "holy" land and converts to Islam. To this day, his followers must obey the same Koranic decrees. Eighty percent[725] of the Qur'an is devoted to dealing with the unbeliever. Mohammed converted about 10,000 victims to Islam every year, committing violence until the end of his life. Islam is a detailed political system, a demonic doctrine of jihad and the fight to implement Islamic laws, sharia, everywhere.

9:29 Make war on those who have received the Scriptures (Jews and Christians) but do not believe in Allah or in the Last Day. They do not forbid what Allah and His Messenger have forbidden. The Christians and Jews do not follow the religion of truth until they submit and pay the poll tax (jizya) and they are humiliated.

Over these 1400 years, jihad has been responsible for the death of many millions. "The Tears of Jihad"[726] include 80 million Hindus, 60 million Christians, 10 million Buddhists, 120 million Africans, the number increasing with each attack throughout the Middle East, Africa, Europe, Russia, India and China, to where some historians assess the deaths at 890 million. To assume that we Americans are not included in their vision is, at the least, foolhardy. To paint the jihadis as though they might be justified or in need of compassion is reckless. To believe that the violent jihadis went only to Europe but the peaceful Muslims preferred America is preposterous. We cannot turn a blind eye and portray the terrorists with humanity, or we will not be able to defend ourselves as they change our culture and mindset in this slow, methodical onslaught. These cold-blooded killers who are meticulously trained since childhood to revel and celebrate death[727] have been robbed of their humanity.

The opera's purpose is to prime us to be insensitive to the death of a wheelchair-bound American, a veteran of World War II, an inventor and appliance manufacturer, a husband and father, with the smokescreen that he is Jewish and, therefore, responsible for every misfortune known to the Muslim world. It is also preparing us to slowly lose our moral compass, to tolerate their violence, evil, and assume their Koranic mission of hate and bloodlust as "acceptable under the circumstances." These ideas are reinforced with accusations of "Islamophobia," to prevent us from naming and discussing the enemy.

Raymond Ibrahim, associate fellow at the Middle East Forum and author, exposed Islam's war on Christians. There are news reports daily of Muslim killings according to Mohammed's commands — oppressing their women, honor killings, hunting down apostates, kidnapping children into sexual slavery, and converting or killing Christians in Afghanistan, Algeria, Cameroon, Egypt, Iran, Krygyz, Morocco, Nigeria, Pakistan, Saudi Arabia, Somalia, Tanzania, and into Europe. You need only turn on the few TV channels that are still dedicated to reporting the truth. The news reports of killing Jews in Israel and Europe are ignored by mainstream media and, all too often, more reliable news sources.

The opera is an insult to the memory of Leon Klinghoffer and his family and an assault on us and our humanity. We must not be manipulated into this gradual acceptance of the Islamic viewpoint. This is yet another jihad war strategy with the purpose of destroying us — nihilism —to establish an Islamic caliphate in the Western world. There is no greater threat to mankind today than Islam and this opera must not be staged.

THE BOARD IS NAILED

The Daily Iowan Editorial Board has become tolerant of Islamic intolerance.

The Daily Iowan Editorial Board[728] appears to have fallen prey to some very dangerous rhetoric — as though influenced by an un-American entity. Rather than provide an overview or opinion, their editorial presents a plethora of deceitful statements in defense of Islamic sharia law —preaching that it is compatible with religious liberty.

The Board began with an objection to a statement made by Louisiana Governor Bobby Jindal (R), which was, "America did not create religious liberty; religious liberty created America." That is due to our Founding Fathers' understanding about our sacrosanct, *inalienable* rights to life, liberty, and the pursuit of happiness. It was for these rights that they left their oppressive homeland and established a republic in America.

The board's second brainstorm suggested that sharia be included with international law! International law is legal rules, regulations, and guidelines by which countries will interact with each other to solve international disputes. It does NOT mean that every country should cede its individuality and its citizens' rights to a body — the United Nations, no less (or an Islamic caliphate) — that will impose its decisions and edicts over the entire world.

The UN is most often a biased, tyrannical assemblage whose Islamic voting block frequently overlooks the truths in the Middle East. The Organization of Islamic

Conference (OIC) of the UN pressures the rest of the countries to impose worldwide limits on free speech, limits demanded by sharia. Islamic countries are home to harshly dominated, long-suffering citizens who live with poverty, illiteracy, severe restrictions, enslavement, and the most sadistically brutal, barbaric behavior of any classification of creatures. Their sharia must never be imposed on others.

The Board submitted that opposition to sharia law is in opposition to religious freedom — twisted propaganda. Under sharia, there is no freedom of religion, speech, thought, artistic expression, press, equality of people or equal justice for different classes. Sharia is the antithesis of democracy and its purpose is to ban laws that conflict with dictatorial Islam. Sharia would destroy our American Constitution.

Because of Islamic sharia, traditional invocations at Friday night high school football games were banned in Santa Fe, Texas;[729] a science teacher in Ohio was fired for having a classroom Bible;[730] a New Jersey high school coach was banned from praying before a football game;[731] prayer around a school flagpole was banned in Clay County, Florida;[732] the Ten Commandments were removed from schools in Muldrow, Oklahoma;[733] some Texans were told that flying their American flags was offensive[734] — in America! Some schools are yielding to removing lunchroom foods that Muslims find offensive.[735]

Sharia succeeds when citizens of the host country do not speak out. Islamized textbooks are used to indoctrinate students;[736] jihad is being taught in California;[737] schoolgirls are forced to wear full burqas in some states;[738] some students were required to "become Muslims for two weeks and learn prayers";[739] and Ohio and Tennessee students were taken, sans parental permission, on a field trip to pray in a mosque.[740]

Because of sharia, our children are being taught that Moses and Jesus were Muslim;[741] that Muslims, not Christopher Columbus, discovered America;[742] that the Qur'an is the final revelation and Mohammed the prophet; that when Muslims kill and take land, it is "building an empire," but when Christians take their land back, it is "violence" and "massacres"; and when Israelis protect their country, it is "massacres" and "apartheid." If 9/11 is mentioned at all, the terrorists remain unidentified.

The board has declared unequivocally that sharia is more concerned with the laws of personal religious observance than national policy and concluded that opposition to sharia is unnecessary. This appears to be more than rhetoric by the *ignorentsia*, but a willful denial of the truth about Islam with the intent to create an ill-informed, malleable population for easy subjugation. (Read *Sharia for Non-Muslims,* produced by the Center for the Study of Political Islam.)

Islam, as defined by Hasan al-Banna, founder of the Muslim Brotherhood, "is an all-embracing concept which regulates every aspect of life ... a duty incumbent on every Muslim to struggle toward the aim of making every people Muslim and the whole world Islamic, so that the banner of Islam can flutter over the earth. By their own admission, the ultimate goal of Islam is to "establish an Islamic government on earth," by the sword, if necessary, to eliminate Western Civilization. The "extremists" are following standard mainstream Islamic doctrine.[743] There is no "fringe" of intolerance, hatred and violence against non-Muslims. This is Islam.

Jihad (war, by violence or stealth) is part of sharia, and it means war against Kafirs (non-Muslims) to establish Islamic law in the land. It is a universal, eternal, and communal obligation for all sane able-bodied men. In their own words:

Koran 4:89 They would have you become kafirs like them so you will all be the same. Therefore, do not take any of them as friends until they have abandoned their homes to fight for Allah's cause [jihad]. But if they turn back, find them and kill them wherever they are.

[Muslim 0010031] Mohammed: "I have been ordered to wage war against mankind until they accept that there is no god but Allah."

[Bukhari 4,52,142] Mohammed: "To battle kafirs in jihad for even one day is greater than the entire earth and everything on it."

The Board implements the accusation of Islamophobia, which is a recognized means of restricting speech, intimidating criticism and withholding knowledge about the ferocity of Islam. The Human Rights Council does likewise to keep the Western world from grasping that most atrocities are committed in the name of Islam, including female genital mutilation, stoning women to death, chopping limbs and heads, enslavement of women and children, and much more, and that since 9/11, more than 23,260 terror attacks to date were committed by Muslims.[744]

Islamophobia also inhibits the FBI from monitoring suspected terrorists, the media from revealing criminal activity, and the masses from grasping that although only a "small percentage" will admit to being Muslim, the "moderates" are changing the nature of America by stealth —through our schoolchildren; through restrictions, accommodations and legal channels; through the indoctrination spewed in the growing number of mosques, and through the uninformed apologists who try to insinuate foreign laws into our courts.

Despite population percentages reported, Muslims in the West are increasingly demanding that Americans adapt to their culture and activities. With their persistence, the accommodations increase, so the "moderates" are making inroads without violence — for now. They could also be quietly plotting the next disaster.

As noted in Andrew C. McCarthy's *The Grand Jihad, How Islam and the Left Sabotage America,* of Islam's approximately 1.4 billion adherents worldwide, there could reasonably be hundreds of millions globally with the potential of becoming radical

212 | TABITHA KOROL

as needs arise. The Pew Research Center found, in 2007, that 13 percent of Muslims in America believe suicide bombings against civilians to be justifiable.[745] If there are perhaps a mere three million Muslims in the United States, that percentage equates to a half-million people — and it took only 19 to kill 3,000 on September 11.

Cultures are not equal, religions are not equal, and our tolerance of Islamic intolerance will lead to our destruction. Under the guise of acceptance and accommodation, we are being asked to change and lose what keeps us free Americans. When the stranger adjusts to the host culture, it is adaptation and assimilation; when the host changes for the stranger, it is conquest. We may be welcoming to a point, but the door must swing both ways.

Finally, the board was *offended* that a "community center" to be built on Ground Zero was called a "symbol of Islamic conquest." The label is appropriate; the Muslims insisted it be erected at the point where their co-religionists killed Americans. In fact, Imam Feisal Abdul Rauf intended to name it the Mosque of Cordoba, an attribution to the "Golden Era," when Muslims ruled Spain cruelly, until the Imam was silenced. This would not be a community center, and the board expressed no offense at the slaughter of our three thousand.

So what is the takeaway from their Idiotorial? This board has been influenced by the Council of American-Islamic Relations (CAIR), an arm of the Muslim Brotherhood that was named an unindicted co-conspirator in a terrorism case involving funding for Hamas. Sami al-Arian, considered a moderate professor at the University of South Florida, pled guilty to conducting stealth operations and to a charge of conspiracy to aid Palestinian Islamic Jihad (PIJ) in the aforementioned terrorism case.

They are dedicated to Islamic supremacism and dominance in the US, to be the "only accepted religion on earth." Their goals are to encourage Americans to downplay anti-terror initiatives, accommodate Muslim practices, and make special exceptions for Islamic (sharia) law, while using cries of "bigotry" to thwart resistance.

Can you imagine having Americans' willing to forfeit American values and freedoms in exchange for sharia over our land? This board would! We must never permit foreign laws in American courts. This is a betrayal of epic proportions.

GUARDIAN WITH GUILE

The Guardian reports are replete with lies that protect the Islamists who physically and emotionally harm even their own children.

Notwithstanding England's experiences during World War II and the current informal "occupation" by her own brand of deadly Islamists, The Guardian's views are neither civilized nor rational. In his column, "Gaza: this shameful injustice will only end if the cost of it rises,"[746] Seumas Milne has a willful misinterpretation of the events in the Middle East. His column is laden with stark hatred and lies, and he clearly champions a policy that supports the Hamas Covenant, a Charter[747] that calls for the eventual creation of the 58th Islamic state in "Palestine," and the obliteration or dissolution of the *only* homeland for the Jewish people — as well as the annihilation of the Jewish people worldwide.

The Guardian is often factually inaccurate, its writers insisting on their own type of equity for what amounts to a verbal pogrom against the Jewish state — but not against tyrannical regimes. However, even ISNA (Islamic Society of North America), Syrian American Medical Society, Syrian Relief and Development, Muslim Public Affairs Council and Islamic Relief USA recently condemned Syria's chemical weapons attack of her people (including women and children). When it was revealed that at least 108 people, including 49 children under age 10, were slaughtered in the 15-month Houla massacre,[748] it was explained as *acceptable* that tyrants kill children[749] to intimidate the opposition!

There was no demand for equal justice when Mahmoud Abbas's terrorists slaughtered the 11 Israeli athletes in 1972 Munich,[750] and no demand for vengeance for the beheading of Jewish-American journalist, Daniel Pearl.[751] They expressed no shock at the injustice of Israel's exchange of 1,027 terrorist prisoners for the life of one kidnapped Israeli soldier, Gilad Shalit, or when terrorists slaughtered the Fogel family or the three Israel teenagers.[752] They maintained their silence throughout the firing of thousands of rockets into Israel from Gaza, never demanding balance with equal rocket fire from Israel to Gaza.

To define this further, Israel follows the rules of war and targets military combatants (after warning Palestinian citizens to escape the forthcoming retaliation), whereas Hamas intentionally targets civilians, deliberately focusing on children, thereby breaking two rules of war — killing their own and Israel's children. The media grumble that there weren't enough Jewish children killed to match the number of Muslim children, and they want to blame only Israel for the death of Muslim children even when Hamas is entirely responsible.[753] All the wars began with Muslim attacks and, by international law, Israel has every right to defend herself — her boundaries and her citizens.

The media offer little coverage when the Islamic culture encourages children to detonate themselves among Israelis,[754] and when parents celebrate the occasions with candy, enjoying Hamas's gifts, and name town squares after their expendable offspring. And although sharia law denounces music and dance, it appears to be acceptable to revel in the streets for their martyred sons and daughters.

The antagonistic Guardian and similar news sources raise their voices only for the number of Palestinian children killed, although the BBC[755] has been awakened to new evidence that numbers received from Gaza are quite skewed. Israel provides shelters for their children; Gazans provide shelter for their rockets and endanger children for an increased body count for public sympathy. And while Israel›s hypocritical enemies, including Hillary Clinton and Nancy Pelosi, call Hamas a humanitarian organization, the West continues its funding for inhumane reasons — such as for the extensive system of tunnels dug for access to Israeli children›s schools and kibbutzim for an impending hands-on carnage.

Land acquisition is a major priority for the Islamic agenda, and the Koran allows deception, lies, and human sacrifice for the cause.[756] Islam also relies on the humanity and basic decency of Judeo-Christian people and nations to disbelieve what we find revolting. Jihad exists in many ways, from Israel to Africa, Scandinavia, Spain, Germany, China, America and England. Few journalists are fit to report accurately or willing to accept the truth for themselves. None of these host countries, including Israel, is an "occupier," but each is an invaded land, and we should all be defending our homeland NOW, or be prepared to relinquish our identity and culture to Islamic oppression.

As in the greater Middle East, where previous peoples have been annihilated or Islamized, they could not adequately defend themselves and were conquered by Islam. Israel can, will, and has every right to do so under international law.

Jihad training begins with treating children as chattel and indoctrinating them at an early age to hate the *kaffir* (the "rejecter" of Allah). Pedophilia,[757] demoralizing and frightening to the children, is legalized, and "thighing" infants to raping young children will continue in the Muslim world as long as "Allah" encourages men to be owners instead of husbands and fathers. Sodomizing a baby is *halal* (permitted under sharia).

Pre-adolescent marriage is codified in Koran 65:4, and women are held hostage under law, subject to severe punishment, and it is under these circumstances that children are raised to be fearful and subservient to their master. Polygamy also affects children, immersing them in a self-pitying, resentful, victim mentality. If the reader would like to delve further into this depraved culture, please read Nonie Darwish's Cruel and Usual Punishment.[758]

The primarily unschooled, illiterate majority, who foresee no self-fulfillment or escape, become hair-trigger-angry young men who hate their lot in life, are brainwashed and compelled to do as bidden, and prepared to die for the cause. In so doing, they see a way out — an escape to tranquility and the promise of sexual pleasures in Paradise.

These are but a few of the reasons that create an unfeeling underclass of warriors who have no sympathy for children, but will use them for the common purpose.. Keeping children near explosives[759] and bombs will ultimately lead to an increased body count, just as using child labor for tunnel excavation resulted in the loss of more than 130. Not only are women and children placed on rooftops of targeted buildings (those from which rockets are fired into Israel) and used as human shields, but a recent video showed young children crying while hanging [760] from a targeted building's fence. And if these children do survive their childhood, they will become the next generation of damaged, merciless robotic killers who are inured to pain and bloodshed.

This is a horrific example of child abuse to which the media turn a blind eye, and the U.N. fails to address. Rather, the immoral go out of their way to blame the IDF for harming women and children who are forced into such circumstances by their families. The media fail us. Journalists like Milne, whether cowardly or deceptive, would become an acquiescent, obedient dhimmi, a "useful idiot" that represents the Islamic-fascist mentality, willing to accept caliphate domination in the interest of hate or "peace."

A recently discovered Hamas manual verifies its method of urban warfare. "Introduction to the City War" extols the benefits of civilian deaths and admits that Israel tries to avoid them. This is not a Hamas war against "occupiers," but an Islamic war to annihilate the entire state of Israel, against which Israel must continue to defend until there is unconditional surrender. It is also a reminder that this is WAR — a global war — against all who will not accept Islamic sharia. And, if the media continue its stance against Israel, and continue to look away from Islam's slaughter of Christians, they may well be designing a future for themselves under the very cruel and severe Sword of Allah, from which no conquered nation has ever recovered.

MEN OF IDEALS

A heartless political murder is used for theater and to slowly Islamize the American psyche.

> *"You Jews are always complaining of your own suffering, but you get fat off the poor, cheat the simple, exploit the virgin, pollute where you've exploited – America is one Big Jew! We are soldiers fighting a war. We are not criminals and we are not vandals but men of ideals."*

Such are the lines spoken by a Muslim-Palestinian terrorist in *The Death of Klinghoffer,* an American opera based on the 1985 hijacking of the passenger liner, Achille Lauro,[761] by the Palestine Liberation Front, and their murder of a wheelchair-bound, stroke victim — the Jewish-American passenger Leon Klinghoffer, on holiday with his wife and daughters. However, the words came from the mind of librettist Alice Goodman, an anti-Semitic, Jewish apostate-turned-Anglican priest, who found an "artistic" channel for her own animus, hatreds and biases.

Commissioned by five American and European opera companies and the Brooklyn Academy of Music, the composers have turned a heartbreaking event into musical entertainment. The story is of a malevolent crime of Islamic jihadi (a terrorist), presented with consideration for the villains and indifference to the innocent victim. There is something deeply perverse — nay, depraved — in producing this for showbiz, as I see our once-great civilization sinking into the depths of a fascistic Islamic evil.

It is said that there can only be peace when the Muslims stop revering death the way Jews revere life. Islam's militaristic, expansionist, religious, oppressive ideology revolves around subjugation, mutilation, and death — all that is antithetical to our Western civilization. As a nation, we debate about length of prison terms, the death penalty, humaneness for animals; yet there are some who will create, perform, and view a callous, political murder as "theater," as well as provide a venue for slowly Islamizing the American psyche.

Surely, the Muslim Brotherhood would agree with Goodman, composer John Adams, theater director Peter Sellars, and general manager Peter Gelb, that this jihadist show be produced despite protests. They prefer that we Americans remain silent about the Holocaust; Mohammed's slaughter of Jews in Mecca and Medina; Islamic attacks on Christians in Africa, Indonesia and Europe; Spain's "Golden Era" of humiliation and punishment; to the constant attacks and massacres of Jews long before the Jewish state became an alibi. We must remain silent to protect the guilty as they continue to terrorize, spill blood and display severed heads[762] — and whitewash their psychoses.

Have the Jews always complained of their suffering? They have done more than just complain! They endured and remembered, created monuments and museums, but sought no revenge. They used their energy to build a nation out of a desert and malarial swamps, to a position of leadership in technological advancements in science, medicine, publishing, music and art, and more, in 66 brief years — the same number of years it took the Palestinians to create a culture of hate and death, where they abuse their children who will, in turn, abuse others.

When the Palestinians complain to the United Nations of a fictitious apartheid and a fabricated disproportionate war, they reap millions of dollars in benefits — more than enough to sustain their victimhood status, construct terror tunnels and amass weaponry for more barbarian warfare.

The opera takes the position of the Palestinians against Israel, but the rhetoric quickly turns to hate of all Jews — and Americans. Do the Jews get fat off the poor and cheat the simple? As the labor of Americans — and Jews, specifically — improve their country and raise the standard of living for all citizens, they are among the most generous in the world (tzedakah)[763] — their names noted for endowments to science, medicine and the arts. The Jewish two percent of the American population is responsible for 30 percent of America's most generous donors! Israelis and Americans are among the first responders to disasters around the world, and Israel's hospitals are renowned for their advanced medical treatment of all, including Muslims.

On the other hand, Islam's Five Pillars of Faith[764] include alms-giving *(zakat),* the obligatory charity based on accumulated wealth, which is meant to ease the economic hardship for other Muslims within the community and to eliminate inequality for followers of Islam *only. "It is not permissible to give Zakat to a non-Muslim " (Umdat al-Salik, h8.24);* neither do they provide help to other countries. *Zakat* must be given to Jihad.

Goodman's accusation of "exploit the virgin" is not merely a vicious lie, but pure projectionism, as no children suffer as much as those under Islam. Despite their perpetual state of threats of war — or perhaps because of it — Israelis are among the happiest nations in the world. They work to improve their own lives, and the government provides superior defense, protection and shelters for their citizenry. Additionally, ten years ago, Israel began integrating disabled youth[765] into the Israel Defense Forces, allowing these children to overcome their limitations and help prepare them for independent life in Israeli society, the community and the workforce —while they and their parents reap the rewards of joy and pride in accomplishment.

By contrast, under Islam, young girls undergo female genital mutilation[766] (an unsafe surgical procedure without anesthesia). In their perpetual wars, Islamic combatants use children as human shields to increase their death toll to gain sympathy from the United Nations. Child labor was used to construct the underground terrorist tunnels, which also increased the death toll, and children are taught at a very young age to behead a *kafir* (infidel).[767] Further, throughout the Islamic world, since the days of Mohammed, they continue the practice of kidnapping girls and boys and raping and selling them into sexual slavery. Daughters may suffer honor killings by their own parents or be given in servile marriages. All children, and particularly the vulnerable disabled, are intimidated into suicide bombings. Because of Islam's practice of consanguineous marriage, there are many such disabled children and the parents are rewarded with $2,500 for each martyr.[768]

Finally, the operatic rant claims the terrorists to be neither criminals nor vandals, but men of "ideals." Although undefined, the ideals are a worldwide caliphate, a "one-world order," where the same rules of sharia apply to all. Therefore, Judaism, Christianity, Buddhism, Hinduism, and all other religions must be obliterated, and their adherents converted to Islam or killed. Once converted, women are relegated to a status inferior to men or be beaten or killed. If a child "dishonors" a parent, the child may be killed. If a Muslim converts out of Islam, the apostate must be killed. If a male or female is accused of adultery, he may be killed and she stoned to death. Antisemitism is inherent in sharia, a practice based on Mohammed's genocidal behavior when he eradicated the entire Jewish population of the Arabian Peninsula. Jihad is warfare to spread Islam — or kill those who will not submit to the "religion of peace."

"We are soldiers fighting a war," says Goodman (a misaptonym, at best) through the assassin. She gets it. She understands that these words and the entire opera may incite riots in the streets to burn synagogues or attack and kill Jews. It is not her concern that this "art form" might encourage the Muslim Student Associations to increase their attacks on Jewish students on campuses. Her use of inflammatory words of "suffering," "cheating," and "exploitation" have already permeated the student body and may now be used to incite. She, Adams, Sellars, and Gelb, agree on the purpose. Immersed in their hostility toward religion, Americanism, and our Constitution, they have found a way to exalt in our destruction.

Heaven help us.

NO, NO, NORAH

Norah O'Donnell broadcasts disinformation about Israel to support the false Palestinian narrative.

Norah O'Donnell is called an "anchorwoman," defined as "a television reporter who coordinates a broadcast to which several correspondents contribute." However, would she not vet the material before airing erroneous contributions, or is there intentional duplicity?

O'Donnell reported the brutal attack by two Palestinian boys in a Jerusalem synagogue, killing four rabbis and injuring seven. In fact, it was a massacre, with blood everywhere, including on the Torah — but she called the synagogue a "contested religious site."[769] Contested? Neither the Har Nof synagogue nor the Har Nof neighborhood of Jerusalem is contested. Jerusalem is the eternal capital of the Jewish people, has been the capital of the Jewish people through most of history, and was declared the capital when Israel became a state; therefore, the neighborhood and the synagogue are indisputably legal. If it is contested, it is only a war tactic by jihadis, who will use any method to garner supporters when they fear the possibility of loss by modern warfare.

Does O'Donnell also contest the Christian churches or Bahi'a, Buddhist, or Hindu temples in Israel? Does she contest the Al Aqsa mosque, over which dominion was ceded by Israeli General Moshe Dayan, whether out of generosity or naïveté and his hope for peace with barbarians. How could he have known that the courtyard would someday be a soccer field for boys who use severed heads for sport? Perhaps he should have been more aware of Islam's bloody 1400-year history![770]

Well, the Al Aqsa mosque *should* be contested, because it sits on the Temple Mount, the holiest site in Judaism, where King Solomon built the First Temple in Jerusalem as a monument to God and a permanent home for the Inner Sanctuary, which contained the

Ark of the Covenant that held the two stone tablets given Moses at Mt. Horeb. The ground beneath the Temple Mount to this day offers up artifacts[771] that verify the existence of the Jewish people who worshipped in that Temple; the coins of the monetary system used by the Jews before the Christian Era, pottery, stones with inscriptions, an arch, a colonnade, a grand stairway, Solomon's Stables, thousands of mikvehs (ceremonial baths), and the continuation of the Western Wall now leading to the city walls and the Lion's Gate. It should also be contested because the imams have the audacity to preach hate and death to all the Jews from the mosque that sits on Jewish land!

EN GARDE!

The Guardian, known for nonsensical, insulting and destructive propaganda that appeal to the ignorant, blames Israel for abusive Palestinian husbands.

What The Guardian does for its UK reading public, the Bill and Melinda Gates Foundation does for American students, and that is to provide a wealth of disinformation for a cause.[772] In its section, writer Liz Ford wrote of the role of girls and women under Islam, specifically Palestinians, and the violence to which they are subjected in their society.

Because her itemization was inaccurate and lacking in references, I can provide some specifics about their driving force:

Koran 4:34 Allah has made men superior to women and, therefore, women must be obedient or be admonished and beaten.

M10-12 If the wife is rebellious, the man may warn her, follow with hitting, and beating but not breaking her bones or damaging her face. He may even imprison her in a room and withhold food and clothing.

M10:4 A man may forbid his wife to leave the home.

022:1 Women may never become judges (they are not equal)

L10:3 A woman's value is half that of a man, because her "mind is deficient." A woman should receive half the money of a man in an indemnity case, because women lack in intelligence and religion.

2:282 Her testimony is worth half the man's.

Bukhari 7,722,229 Deals with female genital mutilation and is compulsory. The term "circumcision" deceptively applies to both men and women, but what they do to women is indeed severe mutilation.

012.6 Extra-marital relations are forbidden, and the penalty for women is stoning to death; it is also recommended in "honor" killings. Men are held blameless.

Bukhari 7,62.18 It is lawful to take a child bride. Mohammed was 51 when he proposed to six-year-old Aisha. Recently it was announced that a man may marry an infant who is still being breastfed.

The Palestinian National Authority Ministry of Women's Affairs (MoWA) is acknowledging its gender issues in order to work toward developing a Palestinian state. According to a report published by the Palestinian Authority[773] in 2011, culture and tradition were often the main justifications for violence against women in "Palestine." Although they attempt to lay blame on Israel's "occupation," even where Israel has left the territories with the expectation of peace and cessation of attacks, each of the reasons for humiliation and cruelty towards women is included in the Koran, some of which are noted above.

Despite the report's admission that specified Islamic culture and tradition as the cause of abuse toward women, the Guardian's writer, Ford, has chosen to blame Israel — the only country in the Middle East where *all* its citizens live in freedom and with equal rights. She has also called Israel an "occupier," when, in fact, the territory is "disputed." The territory has been Jewish Judea and Samaria for thousands of years, which Jordan annexed for a mere nineteen years (1948–1967) after the aggressive Arab war against the new Jewish State. Thus, Ford's information was incorrect, misleading and inflammatory. The mistreatment of women by Arabs and Muslims began at least fourteen centuries earlier.[774] Note, too, that if we delve into the times of Jews in restricted areas (ghettos), in the Middle East, Spain, Italy and Eastern Europe, a loving Jewish family life is what kept them stronger under duress.

Another study in the same report, conducted by UN Women in 2009, blamed the men's violence against women on the stress they felt after Israel's military strikes on Gaza in December 2008. With that reasoning, Jewish men who suffered post-traumatic stress syndrome from the preponderance of Palestinian rocket fire on Israel or sudden attacks on the street should have been equally violent, but there are no reports of comparable familial abuse in Israel.

Through World Wars I and II, we heard of no abuse between husbands and wives who were fleeing for their lives from the impending horrors. If anything, families were protective and more caring of each other. And, despite the constant conditions of war from neighboring Islamic states, Israelis were rated among the happiest people in the world — not stressed from spousal abuse. In fact, it is highly unlikely that Israel's medical, technological, and other creative innovations and advancements could have been made by abused, unhappy, depressed individuals.[775]

Are we to believe that Palestinian men have no self-control following military strikes on Gaza? By now, we have learned that Palestinian men have no self-control, period. In several previous articles, I reported how the children are taught to hate and abuse animals, practice with weapons and hope to be *shaheeds* (martyrs), continue their training to behead live animals and captured humans, and increase their propensity for violence with staged "days of rage." They cover their faces uniformly, hiding human expression, thereby hindering camaraderie, bonding, and sensitivity to others. They celebrate death with sweets distributed when a son is killed while murdering Jews. Men gather in plazas to participate and share in the stoning to death of someone›s wife. They have been robbed of all kindness and there is nothing left for even their own family members. Clearly, Islamic sharia law, destroying freedoms and the sanctioning of hate, victimization, abuse, and killing, leads to dehumanization, pain, contempt, and despair.

Another Guardian writer, Angela Robson, blamed the blockade for her husband's job loss and consequential beastly behavior. Ohio was fifth in the U.S. for job losses (more than 303,000) attributed to the non-oil trade deficit in 2007. Michigan lost 319,200 jobs, 7.5 percent of total employment lost. California ranked first in terms of actual job losses, 696,000. The Economic Policy Institute reported four million jobs lost nationally in the U.S. in 2007, 70 percent of the displaced jobs in the manufacturing sector. America had no comparable increase in spousal abuse.

The Guardian has been repeatedly responsible for news reports that are irrational, insulting and destructive, propaganda that appeals to the ignorant. It makes one wonder how they can benefit from lying about a democracy while supporting a tyrannical regime. Is the Guardian welcoming the Islamic takeover in the UK? Does it welcome an ever-growing welfare role of immigrants who will never assimilate, but who will amplify violence on the streets of England's fair cities, and ultimately impose sharia laws on the land? The average citizen is alleged to be apolitical and unaffected. It makes one wonder just how many people in Merrie Olde England have lost sight of any lessons from WW II and are choosing to slumber again.

James Madison, of English descent, wisely said, "The advancement and diffusion of knowledge is the only guardian of true liberty."

BIAS AT THE BBC

Tim Willcox displays an almost unparalleled apathy and mercilessness in his biased reporting.

During an interview of a Jewish woman at the unity march in Paris, BBC Reporter Tim Willcox[776] had the temerity to admonish her, saying, "Many critics of Israel's policy would suggest that the Palestinians suffer hugely at Jewish hands as well." This was a woman who herself might have been murdered in that very supermarket earlier that day. Clearly, Willcox lacks sensitivity and benevolence, and could never have visited Israel. He may well have attended the march not as a reporter of events, but as one whose ideology was to challenge its purpose where Jews were concerned.

The march was called and attended by more than 40 world leaders because Muslim terrorists killed 17 people — 13 for their occupation (publish a satirical newspaper) and four for their religion (Jewish). Willcox attempted to justify the murder of the latter. His later retraction of the comment and explanation evidenced no understanding of the Middle East and Islam's 1400-year history of carnage in the name of their god, conducted with the intent to establish a worldwide Caliphate ruled by sharia law. The Jews have always stood against tyranny and inequality, from the Biblical days of the Pharoah to the present. Where Israeli law specifies liberty and equality for all, Islamic law specifies subjugation and inequality for all. Willcox, who has drifted into bigotry[777] before, doesn't get it, or doesn't care to.

Even now, when Africa is afire with burning churches and villages and the streets are strewn with the bodies of thousands of dead Christians, Willcox cannot focus on the offenders. European cities are being flooded with armed forces in search of jihadi cells that are priming to kill, but Willcox's only conclusion is that Jews are the cause. Apparently, if not for the Jews who live quietly from day to day, and work and contribute to their country's welfare, Europe would be safer. Similarly, if not for Israel, where Jews have become among the most innovative on the planet to create new products and discover cures for mankind's diseases, the Middle East would be calmer. Indeed, if not for the Jews who are morally and legally entitled to their one one-thousandth of the magnitude of land controlled by Islam, there would be Utopia on earth. And by the same perverse logic, if not for the Jews, Islam would be a religion of peace ... Well, except that then, less distracted, the Muslims could turn their full demonic attention on the rest of the 'infidels' of the world; we already know that Jews are the canary in the coal mine.

It appears doubtful that Willcox is aware that Muslims are responsible for the death of 890 million over fourteen centuries, the number increasing daily. One arm of Islam alone, Boko Haram,[778] only recently razed the village of Baga, Nigeria, slaughtering 2,000 people. They massacred more than 10,000 people in 2014, displaced about a million within Nigeria, while hundreds of thousands fled to neighboring countries, Chad and Camaroon. This is Islam, and this is the same Islam that wages war against Israel and preys upon the West.

The problem lies not with the Jews but with a culture that seeks to dominate and impose sharia law in every nation in the world. It lies with the countries, such as France, England, Germany, and Sweden, that made multiculturalism their religion and nationality — whose political leaders welcomed migrants who have no intention of embracing the new land, assimilating, learning the new language and customs, or qualify for citizenship.

Rather, they came to replace the new country's heritage and culture with their own, through the classroom and textbooks, laws, and demands on the lives of the native population.

The problem also lies with French President Francois Hollande who hosted an anti-terrorism march while inviting known terrorist *par excellence,* Mahmoud Abbas,[779] whose credentials include bankrolling the infamous Munich Massacre, instigating Palestinian terrorism and martyrdom, creating the custom of celebrating Jewish deaths by providing new homes for the martyr's parents and distributing sweets to the townsfolk. In fact, only one day after Abbas participated in the anti-terror march in Paris, his Fatah party memorialized one of the worst Palestinian terror attacks in Israel's history, the 1978 Coastal Road Massacre,[780] when terrorists attacked a bus, brutally murdering 37 Israeli citizens and wounding more than 70.

To Willcox, these crimes are defensible because he mistakenly believes in an invented people (the Palestinians that never existed before 1967) that decreed land for themselves, and it suits his predisposition to recognize the known extremists rather than what he would term, under any circumstances, the Jewish Lobby. His position clearly is to damn all the Jews for the acts of the Israeli government under circumstances that he cannot or will not understand.

It has been suggested that the BBC adopt a definition of anti-Semitism into its editorial guidelines, so that their journalists may grasp that their insensitive, unsympathetic statements and reporting may be very destructive and may incite more readers to join the jihadi mentality. The time has come for the BBC and its staff to be held accountable for their biased reporting that is strengthening the growing onslaught of Islam against the Jews. They also need to understand that once the Jews are silenced, full attention will then be turned upon the Christians, Hindus, Buddhists and, oh yes, upon the free Western Press.

What then, Tim Willcox? What then?

BBC, A MISSION ASTRAY

Something is seriously wrong when England, her people befogged by media information, lionizes her enemy and boycotts her ally.

The indictments one could level against the BBC are too numerous to mention and their range too extensive to fathom. As new stories air on the BBC, the narratives become more twisted to acquit the Palestinians and Islamists of every wrongdoing and, instead, reproach Israelis and Jews. A brew of false narratives repeated, proven facts selectively omitted, acts by Palestinians blamed on Israelis, and the viewing public receives a tale that is forever embedded in their memory, that Israel is guilty — of aggression, apartheid, land acquisition, killing innocents, confining refugees, murder,

224 I TABITHA KOROL

massacres, building walls, withholding food and water, intensive checkpoints, and the ever popular "Palestinians have been victimized since time began." Palestinian Arab[781] became a political movement after they lost the 1967 Six-Day War, and needed an identification that would resonate with the international community.

Regarding the selective omission or rearrangement of facts just hours after Palestinians attacked Eilat, Israel,[782] in August, 2011, leaving eight dead and many wounded, the BBC announced, "Israel pounds Gaza after deadly attacks near Eilat." The Palestinians' 100-plus rockets fired into Israel were left unmentioned as were the mayhem, deaths and injuries that Israeli citizens suffered, but the retaliation — because Israel had to stop the assault to protect her citizens — was what the BBC labeled "aggressive action."

Misinformation abounds in programs hosted by unethical journalists Christiane Amanpour and Jane Corbin. The latter called Israel "the most racist state in the world," this nation that is home to innumerable races and religions. Israel saved and welcomed 14,324 Ethiopian Jews[783] with their descendants, and Israeli Arab households flourished by 146 percent between 1967 and 1995. By contrast, during Islam's brief rule over Jerusalem, Caliph Omar limited the number of Jews to 70 families, and Islam continues to wage jihad attacks[784] against five religions in 38 countries.

Corbin also called the Palestinians' illegally erected homes "the battlefield," never clarifying that the conflict was over their violated building codes and public services, and the archaeological, architectural, and historical heritage laws that must apply to all citizens. When the program is over, the charges made, it becomes too late to reeducate the infected mindset.

The BBC's production, "The Story of the Jews,"[785] narrated by historian Simon Schama, contained a duplicitous explanation of Jews and their homeland. (The commentary by viewers on the site is a pathetic response to the propaganda.) Schama›s statement, "Palestinian towns and villages became part of Israel," was deceptive. 1) Britain and the League of Nations created the Palestine Mandate as a Jewish National Home because of Jewish achievements before WW I. 2) Zionists continued purchasing and restoring wasteland, developing industry, power plants, urban life and social institutions. 3) About 100,000 Arab immigrants and 363,000 Jews immigrated to Israel between 1922 and 1946 alone.

Simon Schama's surname strongly suggests Hebrew origin, a version of "Shema," a liturgical prayer, prominent in Jewish history and tradition. It is repeated during morning and evening prayers as a Jewish confession of faith. The work of this historian is clearly a discredit, even an insult, to his heritage.

Israel accepted the Mandated land and was granted statehood in 1948; the Arabs refused their (larger) partition and began an aggressive war against the new State. Arab generals encouraged Arabs to stay clear of their advancing armies, promising return after victory, thus causing their own "displacement." Arabs (~160,000) who chose to stay in Israel and accept Israeli nationality are now fully participating citizens, today numbering about 20 percent of Israel's population.

More than 10,000 Jews who became refugees from the Palestine Mandate where Arab armies prevailed and 850,000 Jews fleeing persecution from Arab lands[786] all became Israeli citizens. The Palestinian Arabs (numbering 472,000, according to UN accounts) were not "driven out" but commanded to leave by Arab generals with a promise of return after victory. When the Arabs lost the war, the refugees were refused entry to Arab countries, and abandoned in refugee camps as pawns in a psychological battle against Israel. Schama's narrative provides an imbalanced view of facts, ultimately painting Israel with the Arab palette.

"The [refugee] problem was a direct consequence of the war that the Palestinians – and . . . surrounding Arab states — had launched." — Israeli historian, Benny Morris.

Other reprehensible anti-Semitic broadcasts abound when BBC interviewers host fanatical anti-Semites, Stephen M. Walt and John J. Mearsheimer, and dedicated anti-Zionist, Norman Finkelstein. They slant the news coverage with the canards of "Israel Lobby" and "Jewish Lobby," but never the Arab Lobby[787] that has historically consisted of the oil industry, Christian groups and missionaries hostile to Israel, European and current or former US diplomats, Arabists who have long influenced our State Department, paid media spokesmen, academics who hold chairs endowed by Arab money, "human rights" organizations, assorted UN agencies, and US›s 80-year "friend," Saudi Arabia.

Most recently, Islamic apologists, Tim Willcox and Jeremy Vine, on separate occasions, attempted to minimize the jihadist attack on Jewish citizens in a Paris supermarket. Vine interviewed the Muslim Public Affairs Committee,[788] the "UK's leading Muslim civil liberties group, which admits to empowering Muslims to focus on *non-violent Jihad* and political activism." The group rejects responsibility for attacks against the Jews, but blames the government's foreign policy for Islamic terrorism. The members self-identify as *stealth jihadis* — meaning Muslim jihadis who wage a non-violent war against the West.

English historian David Cesarani, is Jewish and specializes in Jewish history. Rather than denounce the Islamic scourge that threatens the lives of Jews and all English citizens, he accuses British Jews of disloyalty for leaving England in fear — an unlikely comment from a student of the Holocaust who knows the fate of Jewish victims who did not leave Europe soon enough.

Although the Jews fought on the side of England during WW II, and the Arabs on the side of Nazi Germany, the BBC continues to assail its friends, Israel and Jews, at every turn, and self-censors its reports about its foes, Islamic jihadis. The future is clear: if the media continue to betray themselves and the country by painting the Jews as evil and the Islamists as victims, the West will fall to terrorism, and be overwhelmed by all the brutal rapes, riots, car burnings, broken windows, stabbings and beheadings we see worldwide. Unless honesty prevails in the media, we will descend into the abyss of violence such as Africans are suffering now under the sword of Islam.

Spanish writer Sebastian Vilar Rodrigez authored "European Life Died in Auschwitz." A section is appropriate here:

"We killed six million Jews and replaced them with 20 million Muslims. In Auschwitz we burned a culture, thought, creativity, talent. We destroyed the chosen people, truly chosen, because they produced great and wonderful people who changed the world. The contribution of this people is felt in all areas of life: science, art, international trade, and above all, as the conscience of the world ... And under the pretense of tolerance, and because we wanted to prove to ourselves that we were cured of the disease of racism, we opened our gates to 20 million Muslims, who brought us stupidity and ignorance, religious extremism and lack of tolerance, crime and poverty, due to an unwillingness to work and support their families with pride. They have blown up our trains and turned our beautiful Spanish cities into the third world, drowning in filth and crime. Shut up in the apartments they receive free from the government, they plan the murder and destruction of their naive hosts."

Danny Cohen, described as "the Boy Wonder of British television," now has what might be his only chance to effect a change at the BBC. Once Head of Documentaries, Head of Factual Entertainment, Controller, and other formidable titles, he became Director of BBC Television in May 2013. In a recent interview, he admitted to feeling the sting of anti-Semitism more this past year than ever before. Has he been so busy or dozing through their own programs?

In its mission statement, the BBC pledges to promote its public purposes, provide programs and services that inform and educate, and be impartial and honest, in keeping with The Royal Charter and Agreement. The BBC is endangering the lives of the people. Perhaps Cohen and others might yet attempt to reverse its current policy of destruction, not just to Jews, but to all the citizens, and regain its original purpose.

There is something seriously wrong when England, her people befogged and deceived by media information, lionizes her enemy and boycotts her ally. Israel will survive, but not the country that has forsaken honesty.

DISSOCIATED PRESS

Associated Press is known for sloppy, dishonest, biased and unreliable reporting on the Middle East.

Associated Press (AP), one of the largest and most trusted sources of independent newsgathering, reported "Israeli house strikes killed mostly civilians." It reported 247 airstrikes (bombings) in Gaza during the summer of 2014, killing 840. Of that number, 508 (60%) were civilians, 96 (11%) were terrorists, and 240 (29%) remained uncharacterized. The failure to seek identification of the "uncharacterized" reveals a scheme to reengineer the outcome, and a flawed count means a flawed conclusion.

AP professes a commitment to the highest standards of objective, accurate journalism over the past 165 years. It employs the latest technology to collect and distribute news and photos, with a 24-hour update process, and has one of the largest collections of historical and contemporary imagery. Headquartered in New York, it operates in more than 180 locations worldwide, including every US statehouse, and has won 51 Pulitzer Prizes since the Prize's establishment in 1917.

Regrettably, the wire services, which include AP, Reuters, and similar sources of news for broadcast, print media, and on-line news, are responsible for the blatant lies peddled and truths compromised when the original story opposes the Arab Muslim narratives. A recent example was an international wire service report that accused Israel of releasing water to deliberately flood the Gaza Valley, destroying houses and causing hundreds of Gazans to flee. When caught in this lie, *Daily Mail*[789] apologized and clarified that there are no dams in southern Israel, that the flooding was caused by unusually heavy rain and drainage issues. Al Jazeera retracted its statements and the photos of rushing waters. Similarly, *Reuters* had been found guilty of switching photos or cropping photo edges, such as when they excluded weapons held by activists aboard the Mavi Marmara[790] during the Gaza flotilla raid. This is serious treachery.

We have now learned that the 240 "uncharacterized" males were indeed terrorists (ages 16-59), changing the total from 96 to 336 terrorists (40%), not an unusual ratio of women and children to terrorists, as these poor victims are customarily used as human shields, whether alongside the rocket sites or within the buildings. Hamas often secretes rockets and explosives in residential homes, which certainly contributes to the civilian casualty count. AP never reports Israel's warnings[791] to civilians to evacuate residential areas, never cites Israel's casualties, and never reveals that the strikes are always retaliatory for wars begun by the Arabs.

AP has repeatedly sought to discredit Israel by accusing her armed forces of conducting disproportional warfare against Palestinians, when no war or sport has ever been fought for an equal outcome. From 2001 to July 2014, Palestinians have conducted a war of terror against Israel, resulting in psychological trauma (PTSD) to more than 50 percent of the Israeli children and depression and miscarriages to adults, and using more sophisticated rockets (some containing white phosphorous[792]) to reach larger cities. AP did not propose that Israel conduct a comparable rocket attack into Gaza for the sake of proportionality, or suggest Israel bomb Palestinian school buses, or advocate that Israel dig an equivalent number of terror tunnels leading to Palestinian children's schools and dormitories when Hamas's were discovered.

In an attempt to further paint Israel as the aggressor, AP incorporates "evidence" to accuse Israel of intentionally targeting civilians. Hence, it presented the fatality figures of 844 against the backdrop of 247 air strikes, an equation of 3.4 people per bombing when, in fact, Israel made 20,000 air strikes, and achieved a .04 fatality figure per bombing. These percentages verify that AP's reporters script deceptive, damaging information and that Israel does its utmost to *avoid* civilian casualties.[793] Israel's record is in fact, unequalled.

AP also failed to provide comparative analyses, such as how these numbers match up to other wars and air strikes conducted in urban areas. Withheld information is as dishonest and harmful as erroneous information. Investigative journalist Richard Behar's studies of conflicts since World War II show that the norm of fatalities is 85 to 90 percent civilian. We might well be reminded of Germans' killing 28,000 civilians in the London Blitz; the Allies' killing 25,000 civilians when they bombed Dresden and destroyed the Nazi industrial center; our killing 130,000 civilians with our nuclear bombs on Hiroshima and Nagasaki in 1945, which brought about Japan's unconditional surrender and peace.

The United Nations' figures cited at least 1,483 Gazan Palestinian civilians killed, with an overall death toll of 2,205, the balance being militants, its informational source the Hamas-controlled Gazan Health Ministry. It is known that AP did have access to figures from a trustworthy, private research institute in Israel, Meir Amit Intelligence and Information Center, but chose not to avail itself of them — although they do sort through their information if they can contribute to a war crimes accusation against Israel.

Oddly, throughout the world, Imams spew hate and incite to kill from their mosque podia. Muslims murder Jews and Christians because of their religion or, as with *Charlie Hebdo,* because of cartoons against their prophet. Muslims (Hamas) fire deadly rockets for (Israeli) territory. Muslims (ISIS) chop off people's heads and burn others alive, and just kidnapped 90 Christians. Muslims (Boko Haram) young girls for sexual slavery and buried some alive. Muslims (Chechens) beheaded Russian soldiers and attacked, kidnapped and killed children and school staff. Muslims appear to have reached the percentage at which they are now capable of conquering the Nordic countries, and the natives are committing cultural suicide without a fight. We know of this through AP, yet AP continues its deception as well as its unparalleled accusations not against Muslims, but against Israel primarily.

Not only has Associated Press[794] become known for its sloppy, dishonest and unreliable reporting, but it has also been accused of biased reporting on the Middle East by its own journalists.[795] Indictments included storylines showing Arabs and Palestinians to be entirely blameless and Israel fully culpable; refusing to print a 2008 Israeli peace proposal when it would have verified Israel's desire for peace; and killing a story that would have shown Israel appropriately.

It is time these wire services were rewired to overhaul their failed policies, and return to responsible, honest journalism.

MUSLIMS ARE NOT JEWS
Kristof presents Jewish Holocaust victims' flight from imminent extermination as equal to Islamic hijrah for colonization and conquest.

When Nicholas Kristof, a writer for the *New York Times,* wrote Anne Frank today is a Syrian girl,[796] he was publicizing his own distorted view that all immigrants are equal, period. He compared the dilemma of the Jewish Holocaust victims' flight from imminent torture and extermination by the Nazis and collaborating European regimes with the experience and intent of the Syrian migrants. By failing to conscientiously compare the people, their circumstances, and the ultimate purpose of their migration, he failed as a journalist and went headlong into moral equivalence. Kristof is presenting the migratory Muslims in the role of hunted Jews. Claiming two situations equal on the basis of superficialities is due to either lazy thinking or outright deceit.

Beginning with the discovery of a World War II letter penned by Otto Frank (father of Anne Frank), who sought a visa out of Amsterdam to any country that offered safety for himself and his family, Kristof pointed out the West's indifference to Jewish refugees at that time. Far from being an awakening of sympathy, however, he was preparing his readers to accept a comparative analysis between the reluctant, meager acceptance of the Jews in their desperate flight from certain annihilation and the extravagant welcoming of Islamic migrants who bring with them an ideology calamitous to democracy.

The records show that of the Jews who fled Europe during the Holocaust, America accepted only 95.000 Jews in 1939,[797] before the doors closed and Jews were banned from leaving Germany (October 1941). To prepare us for the disparity of Syrian numbers, Kristof reminds us that the American government resisted Jewish entry because of anti-Semitism and fears of Communism and Nazism. He failed to mention the malicious, devious journalistic practices of his own employer, the *New York Times,* that calculatedly toned down the frantic plight of the Jews and Hitler's "final solution to the Jewish question." With malevolent intent, the Times omitted crucial information and limited such articles to the back pages (a practice exposed by journalist Laurel Leff in Buried in the Times, 2005),[798] keeping the public in the dark about the Jews' desperation and the horrors that awaited them.

By contrast, the US received some 757,626 Arabs between 1967 and 2003, who number more than one million today. Seeking a partisan advantage, Homeland Security accepted an additional 10,000 Syrian refugees ahead of Obama's schedule, and wrongly granted citizenship to another ineligible 850 migrants.[799] Further, Hillary Clinton aired her determination to bring in as many as 500 times that number (5 million). While it is true that there are wars raging in the Middle East and the masses are endangered, Obama continues to favor the Sunni perpetrators and virtually ignores the Christians. Of the 2,300 refugees[800] accepted in June, 2016 alone, more than 99 percent were Sunni while only eight identified as Christians. In August 2016, 150,000 Iraqi Christians were driven from their ancestral homes into Kurdistan, although primarily Christians and minorities are the ones who suffer most in Syria.

Not to the Christians is our administration's generous hand extended, but to the indoctrinated youth, the jihadis, who are calling for our blood while our Politically Correct provide them with hypothetical grievances. This is hijrah,[801] the journey of the vanguards that are colonizing America by the neighborhoods, the majority of whom have no intention of assimilating and openly declare that they will never accept American law over sharia. Yet Kristof would have us believe that there is nothing to distinguish the Jewish refugees of an earlier generation with the assorted Muslim refugees of today.

If he were seriously pursuing a comparison between European Jewry and Syrian Islamists because he was inspired by their superficial similarity of refugee status, then he should compare their countries, values, belief systems, industry, progress, and humanitarianism (or lack thereof). I shall attempt to finish his work.

A mere 68 years ago, the Jews began their labor of love, the long-awaited re-creation of the State of Israel. On what had become neglected desert and swampland, persecuted refugees from every part of the globe joined their brethren to restore, redevelop, rebuild and defend their ancestral land from neighboring marauders who refused to join the modern world. The Israelis built one of the most vibrant, diverse, inspiring nations the world had ever seen — culturally, economically and in terms of human dignity and equality before the law. Their innovations in science, medicine, academia, and in humanitarianism have been exceptional and praiseworthy, and they eagerly offer their expertise and hands-on assistance to non-Jewish countries in despair after earthquakes, tsunamis, drought, and war. Israel's technological advancements are extended to all to improve quality of life on earth, regardless of religion, race or gender.

Jewish law is based on love and kindness. The Golden Rule, "Don't do to others what you would not want done to you," comes from the Talmud. The 613 Commandments provide guidelines on loving Jews and the stranger; to give charity (*tzedakah*) to the poor and needy (charity equates to justice); not to wrong anyone in speech or business; never to pervert the law with deception; and to include the worker and the animal when honoring the Sabbath. The Israeli system of government is based on parliamentary democracy. The Basic Law of Israel exists to ensure the preservation and protection of life, body, dignity, property, and personal liberty for all, and all governmental authorities are bound to respect those rights.[802] The young Israel is a dignified modern State that stands on par with any western democracy that has been centuries in the making.

By contrast, the ideology of Islamic law, sharia, held sacred and inviolable by the majority of these new migrants, is rooted in intolerance and hatred, with decrees that undermine the individual's dignity and freedoms. The Koran espouses hate of others,[803] brutality, and methods of killing non-Muslims, including cruel beheadings and chopping off limbs. Theft is punishable by amputation; criticizing the Quran, Mohammed or Allah is punishable by death; apostasy is punishable by death; a non-Muslim man who marries a Muslim woman is punishable by death; and Muslims must lie to advance Islam. According to Islamic law, charity (*zadak*)[804] must be directed to their own faith; 99 percent of their assistance is so targeted. Animals sacrificed[805] for the holy season of Eid may be brutally tortured until dead and their blood runs like rivers.

Muslim women[806] are particularly singled out for barbaric FGM (female genital mutilation) and for marriage as an infant with consummation at age nine. She may be beaten for insubordination and lose her children when divorced. She needs the testimony of four male witnesses to prove rape, but she may not testify in her own behalf; her testimony in property cases carries half the weight of a man's. She may inherit only half of what a male inherits. She may not drive a car, attend school, or speak to a man who is not her relative. When her sexual purity is suspect, the young woman may be tortured and murdered. Children may be trained for suicidal jihad missions and used for human shields and adult sexual satisfaction

To their lasting shame, Islamic countries continue unabated their fourteen centuries of enslavement, severe rule, and wars of conquest by migration and terror, rioting and rape. Islamic fundamentalism keeps their people in fear, poverty, hopelessness and resentment of the West's modernity and higher standard of living, and the terror is seen in Israel, Europe and the Americas. Recently classified an Ameriphobe,[807] Hillary endorses the increased immigration with preference given to Muslims. Dr. Juhdi Jasser, however, has just warned that flooding America with unvetted migrants and promoting the erroneous description about petty criminal Michael Brown and Ferguson, Missouri (Black Lives Matter), and others, are intended to unravel our national identity.[808]

The purpose of hijrah is to build a worldwide Islamic caliphate and to blame and destroy Western powers for Islamic bloodshed. Barack Obama, Hillary Clinton and their devotees are dedicated to changing America, turning our country into one great, lawless "sanctuary city." On September 29, 2016, FBI director James Comey predicted a terrorist diaspora[809] on American soil within two to five years.

Nicholas Kristof's attempt to draw an equivalence between Jewish refugees and the current influx is either hopelessly inadequate judgment or something more troubling that emanates from his and his paper's complicity with the Left's assault on America. It would not be surprising if, in the writer's next article, he would draw comparisons between the Fuhrer and Groucho Marx because, after all, both had moustaches.

THE TIMES THAT TRY MEN'S SOULS

The New York Times issued a rededication to fairness, truth, and scrutiny that it couldn't keep.

Arthur O. Sulzberger, Jr., publisher of *The New York Times*, and Dean Baquet, executive editor, issued their reflection to their readers. After reviewing it several times, I realized that the election of Donald J. Trump to the highest office in our country did much more than anyone could have anticipated. Not only did Trump fight the establishment, press and academia, and motivate American citizens to awaken from an eight-year period of fear and despair to demand a reversal of Obama's executive orders, but he inspired the Times' principals to make an unprecedented outreach to the public with a kind of desultory apology. They professed a purpose of rededication "to report to America and the world honestly, without fear or favor, striving always to understand and reflect all political perspectives and life experiences in the stories … impartially and unflinchingly."

Although it was their use of biased analyses and writing assumptions over accuracies that diminished their readership, it is evident that they miss the point when they attempt to reassure their depleted readership that they can "rely on *The New York Times* to bring the same fairness, the same level of scrutiny, the same independence to our coverage." It is precisely that same coverage and same corruption that the American public will no longer tolerate.

Is it possible for a publisher and executive director to plan for a future without defining and owning up to the past? Will they re-educate the same staff writers who pandered to the establishment, the leftists and the globalists; the Soros- and Islamic-supported hate-mongers of (BLM) Black Lives Matter, J-Street, (SJP) Students for Justice in Palestine and the (MSA) Muslim Student Association; the anti-Semitic revisionists; the corrupt elitists and academicians who delight in seeing their skewed views validated; the youths, immersed in socialism, who have been taught not how to think, but what to feel; and the populace that could not discern fact from propaganda?

Upon what standard lies were the *Times* readers nourished? When the *Times* repeatedly accused Israel of planning new "developments" northeast of Jerusalem that would allegedly split Judea-Samaria (West Bank), despite the map that was produced to prove the impossibility of their claim, a correction was never issued. When *they* claimed that singer-songwriter Eric Burdon was boycotting Israel, it was another falsehood not rescinded. When an article blamed Ariel Sharon's entry into the Al Aqsa mosque in Jerusalem in 2000 for triggering the second intifada, the truth was that Sharon never entered the mosque and the second intifada was verified to have been premeditated. When the *Times* repeatedly asserts that Gaza is occupied by Israel, but Israelis left in

2005 and Hamas is the sole occupier. When John Kerry spoke about brokering peace between Israel and Palestinians, and the *New York Times* amended it with a Palestinian narrative. Israel is routinely portrayed by *The Times* as being the obstacle to peace, while the Palestinians have consistently rejected all Israeli positions.[810]

The *Times* overlooks Israel›s archaeological and historic ties to the country, her amazing technological and medical achievements, and her first-responder activities to America's Boston Marathon, California droughts, and countries hit by natural disasters. The infamous slaughter of the Fogel family never made first page, and Israelis beaten or knifed are often disregarded. Further, the *Times* omits stories of Palestinian children practicing jihad and beheadings or declarations that they intend to harvest Jewish skulls. The reporters restructured stories of Boko Haram's terrorizing and systematically kidnapping, converting and killing Christian female students in Nigeria, or burning students to death, and butchering entire villages while intoning *Allahu Akbar, Allah is the greatest.*

Following the UNHRC, United Nations Human Rights Council's resolution to blacklist Israeli companies that operate or trade with Israel beyond the 1949 Armistice Lines (Obama's arbitrary division), a bipartisan legislation, titled Protecting Israel Against Economic Discrimination Act[811] was introduced to combat the Boycott, Divestment and Sanctions (BDS) movement against Israel. It would also now include international organizations that strive to economically isolate Israel.

Another major assault on Israel is UNESCO's denial[812] of the 3,700-year Jewish connection to the Land of Israel — the 400-year monarchy and the constant link of Jews to their land, verified by archaeological discoveries. Legitimate critics accept Israel's right to exist; anti-Semites do not, and the *Times* has opted to join the United Nations in this civilizational jihad by querying the strong biblical and historical basis for the Jewish claim to divinely promised land. Although Palestinians claim Jerusalem's holiness, it is not mentioned in their Koran and, despite oil money, they allowed it to turn to squalor — without running water, electricity, or plumbing. Youths have been videotaped playing soccer with real severed heads on this "third holy site of Islam."

Another offensive is the latest Palestinian claim to the Dead Sea Scrolls. Unable to conquer Israel by warfare, they use the UN[813] and media, including a cooperative *New York Times*. Jane Cahill, archaeologist and practicing attorney, in her Times article "Historical Certainty Proves Elusive at Jerusalem's Holiest Place," claimed that standard proof is not beyond a reasonable doubt. Predictably, we see the *Times'* blend of witlessness and malevolence. Reporter Rick Gladstone also contested whether the Jewish Temples were precisely on that spot or a small distance away, suggesting Zionist aggression. History proves that Islam builds atop other religions' holy sites[814] and that the Dome of the Rock, never mentioned in the Koran, was constructed precisely over the Temple because they acknowledged its sanctity to the Jews.

CAMERA's (Committee for Accuracy in Middle East Reporting in America) six-month study found *The New York Times* replete with skewed headlines and misleading photos, supporting a double standard that de-emphasizes Palestinian attacks and avoids revealing Israeli fatalities. When reporting of Israeli retaliatory strikes against Palestinians for Israeli casualties, the *Times* will often use a photo of a grieving Arab mother.

Ira Stoll wrote of several issues covered by the *Times*, from which I chose the following to illustrate the nature of their leanings. In 2016, the paper›s art section featured an exhibit, "The First Jewish Americans: Freedom and Culture in the New World," at the New York Historical Society (in New York for New York readers), in 1,100 words with three photographs. It should be noted that the exhibit included paintings, one of them of Commodore Uriah P. Levy, War of 1812 naval hero and philanthropist who was instrumental in abolishing flogging. Other items were threadbare memoirs and prayer books that withstood the centuries, a charred Torah scroll, a pair of exquisite silver-belled ornaments crafted for a Torah scroll by venerated silversmith Myer Myers, an ancient illustrated marriage contract, and thank you letters from Jewish congregations to George Washington for being so welcoming. Despite the beauty and solemnity of the exhibit that validates a culture that contributed to every component of American history, the New York Historical Society's president, Louise Mirrer, provided a demeaning quote, in which she joins *The New York Times* in the blame-the-victim mentality: "In the exhibit, we see the kind of religious fervor that promotes a kind of violence against certain groups."

Now compare this to another *Times* exhibit, "The Art of the Qur›an: Treasures from the Museum of Turkish and Islamic Arts," not held in New York (home of the readers) but at the Sackler Gallery, Washington, DC. This rated a review on the front cover of its weekend arts sections, warranting 1,700 words, seven photographs, and about three times the column space. Instead of a demeaning quote there was exaltation, "It's a glorious show... art of a beauty that takes us straight to heaven. And it reminds us of how much we don't know — but, given a chance like this, will love to learn — about a religion and a culture lived by, and treasured by, a quarter of the world's population ... everything seems to glow and float, gravity-free ... miraculously beautiful things."

How will the "new" *New York Times* re-educate its readers about the ties between the holy site of the Temple Mount and Jewish history, and retract and revise its previous delegitimization and denial of the Jewish people›s right to their Jewish homeland? A friend to fascism, with decades of unprofessionalism dating back to the Holocaust, the *Times* has ignored all pertinent evidence that does not support the Muslim narrative, thereby denying the Jewish State and the right of Jews to live anywhere in their country. How will the *Times* present the Palestinians as they now challenge the 99-year Balfour Declaration that paved the way for Jewish and Arab states in Palestine, as held by the

United Nations› majority vote? How will the Times handle the recent Muslim ultimatum to either build mosques in Italy or surrender[815] the Vatican? How will it present Hamas-CAIR's[816] threat to overthrow the U.S. government?

On the home front, when separate swim times were established to accommodate Muslims in Toronto, the *Times* praised it as a "model of inclusion," but when a Brooklyn pool did the same to accommodate Orthodox Jewish women, the *Times* denounced the practice. The paper also denounced the use of chickens in a Jewish ritual but reported impartially about a Senegalese ritual involving caged birds. Such disparate evaluations are typical of the *Times* and if they continue to treat their readers to "the same fairness, the same level of scrutiny, the same independence to our coverage," then we can predict a vanishing readership.

With the election of President-elect Donald J. Trump, and heightened tensions, *The New York Times* ran AP (Associated Press) information with the fear-provoking headline, "Hate Crimes against Muslims up by 67 percent in 2015." Not only does this fault Mr. Trump, but in a nation of more than 300 million Americans, of which 2.57 million are Muslim, only 257 crimes against Muslims were reported, and not all violent. Such reporting supports the narrative that America is a racist country — the accusation of racism is a form of jihad to depict Muslims as victims and to reinforce Islamophobia against our freedoms of speech and the press. Omitted were the FBI statistics of 664 hate crimes against Jews, an increase of nine percent, and the dozens of false accusations against Trump supporters.

Will the *New York Times,* AP, and other news sources rethink their purpose and values, or join the dustbin of history?

More than 70 percent of the American people expressed their distrust of the media during the 2016 election period; it appears that the proverbial cat is out of the bag. President Obama has had his personal records permanently sealed from public scrutiny and, by contrast, President-elect Trump has been in the public eye all his adult life and recently hosted a show of his life on Fox Cable News, yet Sulzberger and Baquet called Trump an enigmatic figure. We naturally conclude that the promises issued by the *New York Times* will not be worthy of the paper on which they were printed and signed, and that the operative word will be the thrice-repeated "same."

ISRAEL IN DISPUTE

The New York Times is quick to disparage Israel's rights with deceptive terminology, but sometimes, regardless of the issue's importance, the staff pretends it never happened.

The New York Times is among the most sorely biased mainstream media outlets for its pro-Palestinian and anti-Israel reportage, and the editors and writers ignore the watchdogs, refusing to be held accountable.

Committee for Accuracy in Middle East Reporting in America (CAMERA) and StandWithUs (SWU) are two of numerous groups that have frequently called the paper out for its particularly jaundiced language to describe Israel-Palestinian issues. Of all the disputed territories worldwide, only Israel's[817] have consistently been mischaracterized as "occupied," and only Israel's new home construction mischaracterized as "settlements," Islamic terrorism is given legitimacy with the term of "uprisings," with Israel's self-defense publicized as "massacres." The Times also amplifies a body count (which includes martyred Palestinian children) designed to show Islamic "victimhood," but underreported the massacre of the Fogel family.

The egregious deeds of false news, alternative or selected facts, are inexcusable pro-Islamic propaganda, but The Times prefers totalitarian ideologies and the destruction of fundamental rights. The reporters subvert history, morality, and democracy and facilitate Islam's civilizational jihad, a narrative to educate the masses.

The ideology of Islam has been territorial since its bloody conquest of Medina in the 7th century, through fourteen centuries and thousands of miles of what we now accept as the Islamic world, including Algeria, Egypt, Iraq, Iran, Libya, Morocco, Syria, Tunisia, and parts of India and China. They sacked the Romans and the Vatican in 846 (returning to Italy with a vengeance) and Christendom›s Constantinople in 1453. They went as far as Iceland, and plundered America in the 1800s, when they captured citizens and sailors and sold them into slavery in Algiers. They proceeded into Albania, Armenia, Austria, Belarus, Bulgaria, Bosnia-Herzegovina, Crete, Cyprus, France, Georgia, Greece, Hungary, Italy, Lithuania, Macedonia, Moldova, Montenegro, Poland, Portugal, Romania, Russia, Sardinia, Serbia, Sicily, Slovakia, Switzerland, and Ukraine, and they are in the US, changing our school system, laws, and government, yet Islam is painted as a genuine religion and its adherents as victims in an intolerant world.

But always the battle is fiercest over Israel. Where Muslims cannot migrate, flood the land, infiltrate the infidels and impose Islamic rules for Western accommodation, they create a false narrative of previous existence and ownership in Israel, with accusations that Jewish population growth is overtaking "Palestinian land." The Jewish population of the West Bank, historically and biblically called Judea and Samaria, has been part of the landscape for centuries. Despite Arab revisionism and the New York Times' insistence, the homes are not settlements and the territory is neither "occupied" nor Palestinian.

In 1994, Madeleine Albright, then-Ambassador to the UN, said: "We simply do not support the description of the territories occupied by Israel in the 1967 war as 'occupied Palestinian territory.' In the view of my government, this language could be taken to indicate sovereignty; a matter which both Israel and the PLO have agreed must be decided in negotiations on the final status of the territories. The land is 'disputed.' The mischievous and inaccurate term 'occupied territories' should never be parroted by a journalist trained to value truth above all."

In 2013, Alan Baker, ambassador to Canada and expert in international law, penned *Ten Basic Points: Israel's Right to Judea and Samaria*.[818] He explained that the legality of the Judean and Samarian communities, stemming from the historic, indigenous and legal rights of the Jewish people to settle in the area, were granted pursuant to valid and binding international legal instruments accepted by the international community — and they remain undeniable and unquestionable. The Palestinian leadership, in the still valid 1995 Interim Agreement (Oslo 2), agreed to and accepted Israel's continued presence pending the outcome of the permanent status negotiations, without restrictions of planning, zoning, home construction or communities. Israel's presence in the area is not illegal. This expert in international law affirmed that the "oft-used term in the UN resolutions 'occupied Palestinian territories' has no legal basis or validity whatsoever." The Palestinian leadership was to settle all outstanding issues (borders, settlements, security, Jerusalem and refugees) by negotiation only; their calls for preconditions or settlement freezes are in violation of the agreements.

When Israel took control of the area in 1967, as a result of its defensive war against the attacking Arabs countries, the Kingdom of Jordan did not have prior legal sovereignty and has since officially renounced such rights. When Israel became the administering power, she chose to implement the humanitarian provisions of the Geneva Convention to ensure basic day-to-day rights of the local populace as well as to protect her own forces. There are no special laws that apply to Israelis' choosing to reside in Judea and Samaria; therefore, 'settlement' activity does not violate international law. No legal instrument has ever determined that the Palestinians had or have sovereignty over them. Judea and Samaria remain in dispute between Israel and the Palestinians, subject only to the outcome of permanent status negotiations between the two parties.

These "settlements," incidentally, are not rag-tag collections of log cabins, but fully functioning communities with public services, such as transport, schools, shops, and libraries.

Any Palestinian attempt to unilaterally change the status of the territory would violate Palestinian commitments set out in the Oslo Accords and prejudice the integrity and continued validity of the various agreements with Israel, thereby opening up possible unilateral action by Israel.

After the election of President Donald Trump, the publisher and executive editor of the *Times* attempted an unprecedented outreach to their diminishing readership, professing a rededication to honest reporting. Disappointingly, they followed with a promise for the same fairness, same level of scrutiny, and the same corruption of facts; and they continue to summarily award the land to Palestinians. Despite the verification, The *New York Times* recently informed CAMERA that their reporters do not like and will not use the term "disputed."

Now, the Palestinians are exploring new tactics to delegitimize Israel. They brought suit in France against two French companies that were building a light rail system in Israel, but their efforts were to seriously backfire.

The bid took place in the 1990s, the rail was completed in 2011, and the system crossed Jerusalem to the east side into "occupied territories." Following the completion, the PLO filed a complaint that the tram construction was illegal since the UN, EU and many NGOs and governments consider Israel to be illegally occupying Palestinian territories. The lawsuit was built upon a lie and serves as a perfect example of the power of words to falsify reality.

International legislation had to (1) establish whether the light rail construction was legal, (2) seek texts of international law, and (3) examine international treaties, in order to establish the respective rights of Palestinians and Israelis. This was the first time that an independent, non-Israeli court would examine the legal status of the West Bank (Judea and Samaria). Although this would not affect international law, it would clarify the legal reality.

The Versailles Court of Appeal considered all arguments on both sides and concluded that propaganda (such as the PLO's assessment) is not international law, that humanitarian law (conjured by the Palestinians) was not violated, and that the Palestinians have no rights in the international legal sense to the region, unlike Israel, which is legitimately entitled to occupy all the land beyond the '67 line. Inasmuch as Israel has real rights to the territories, its decision to build a light rail or anything else in that area is legal, and the judges rejected all arguments presented by the Palestinians. The Court of Appeals sentenced the PLO (and Association France Palestine Solidarité AFPS (co-appellant) to pay 30,000 euros ($32,000) to each of the two construction companies.

In an historical trial carefully *forgotten* by the media, the 3rd Chamber of the Court of Appeal of Versailles declared that Israel is the legal occupant of the West Bank.[819] Not surprisingly, *The New York Times* did not report this story on their *respected* pages.

ASYLUM!

While European countries are experiencing open borders and rampant crime, this American Muslim welcomes the same circumstances for his new home.

Adam Ghahramani, a digital product and marketing director in New York, is an Iranian-American who penned his concerns on VentureBeat, that President Trump will prevent all Muslims from seeking asylum in these United States. He maintains that Iranians have the talent and potential to become successful, productive, good citizens, and he joined mainstream media, sundry entertainers and city officials in expressing his unfounded fears of this new administration.

An asylum of sorts may indeed be needed by the rioters who appear to be in perpetual meltdown. They articulate their doubts even when President Trump clearly iterated that he is following through on his campaign promise of security for all citizens — Christian, Jewish, and Muslim alike. In fact, based on reports by the Director of National

Intelligence, the Secretary of State, and the Secretary of Homeland Security (DHS) for the previous administration, Iran, Syria, Iraq, Libya, Yemen, Sudan and Somalia were identified by President Obama as the source of increasing terrorism. This is clearly a terror-prone region, home to only eight percent of Muslims worldwide. Since January 2009, we have had 32 terrorist attacks, with 83 fatalities and 402 injuries in the US, attributed by President Obama to these seven countries.

Iran: The US government classified the Islamic Republic of Iran as the "most active state sponsor of terrorism since 1948, both by direct attacks and by proxy through providing weapons, funds, training, and sanctuary to Hezbollah, Hamas, the Taliban, and militias in Iraq." The year 2012 showed a marked resurgence of state-sponsored terrorism not seen since the 1990s.

Syria: Classified the world's worst state sponsor for terrorism since 1979, Syria also gives asylum to Hamas, Palestinian Islamic Jihad, Popular Front for the Liberation of Palestine-General Command, and arms Hezbollah forces in Lebanon with SCUD missiles. Syria was responsible for movement of foreign Al Qaeda affiliates into Iraq.

Iraq: Provides safe haven, training, financial support to terrorist groups, and support to some Islamist Palestinian groups. Iraq played a role in the 1985 Achille Lauro cruise ship hijacking, the 1993 World Trade Center bombing, and provided financial support for Hamas, Islamic Jihad, Palestine Liberation front, Arab Liberation Front; and finances families of Palestinian suicide bombers.

Libya: Our State Department warns US citizens against all travel to Libya; our embassy in Tripoli is closed and extremist groups continue to plan terrorist attacks against US interests in Libya and the Middle East. Violent activity against civilian commercial interests, US officials and citizens remains high.

Yemen: US government describes Yemen as an "important partner in the global war on terrorism." A Yemini Al Qaeda masterminded the USS Cole bombing (2000); Al Qaeda militants have threatened the Jewish community (2007) and attacked the US Embassy (2008); bomb devices have been found on aircraft (2010), and deadly terrorist strikes are a continuous threat since 2001.

Sudan: Designated a "State Sponsor of Terrorism" in 1993, the Sudanese government continues to harbor international terrorist groups. President Bill Clinton prohibited transactions with Sudan; US bombed Sudanese Al-Qaeda network; Sudan maintains direct relations with Iranian Hamas, Palestinian Islamic Jihad, and Popular Resistance Committee. Sudan is key transit route of weapons to Gaza.

Somalia: Radical Islamist terrorist group al-Shabab targets to recruit Minneapolis Somali-American refugees to become jihadis, with the intent of imposing strict sharia law on Somalia and to attack the United States.

That we cannot vet all refugees for ties to terror has been confirmed by FBI Director James Comey, National Intelligence Director James Clapper, former

Rep. Mike Rogers (Mich), and Hillary Clinton. With such verification, it is no surprise that President Trump, a man of his word, would issue a travel ban on those countries (only) so that the DHS might establish a comprehensive vetting process. He had promised to institute a policy designed to protect our sovereignty and citizens once he took office, and within days of his inauguration, he began to fulfill his promise by taking the steps needed to defend our values.

It would be irresponsible to continue accepting untold unidentified migrants, of which any number could bring with them the instability and hostility that permeates their homelands, endangers our women and children for the dishonest cause of multiculturalism that has befallen Sweden and Germany. Unvetted immigration has turned Sweden into the Rape Capital of the West and Germany appears to be competing for the title.

But while some of our population has been provoked to deep anxiety about this brief and insignificant hiatus, we can't help but wonder at the absence of outrage when Christians are raped and murdered by Muslims or when the entire Muslim world enacts a travel ban against travelers' bearing passports with Israeli connections that has thus far lasted for seven decades.

Still, Mr. Ghahramani warned that America would experience a dearth of talented, industrious workers from the Middle East, exampling successful children of those refugees — Steve Jobs (Apple), Pierre Omidyar (eBay), Omid Kordestani (Google), Salar Kamangar (YouTube), Arash Ferdowsi (Dropbox), Kordestani and Ali Rowghani (Twitter), Bob Miner (Oracle), Shahram Dabiri (World of Warcraft) and Sean Rad (Tinder). Yet the ban has nothing to do with a success potential.

Learning why people emigrate from the Middle East to the West will shed much-needed light on the subject because people do not migrate when life is good. These families left an oppressive existence in a tyrannical Islamic regime, an all-encompassing social, political and legal system that breeds hate against Jews, Christians, and all non-Islamic civilization — and even among themselves. Such theocratic governments confine their people into a narrow uniformity. Medieval suspicion is instilled toward the modern world, stifling creativity in the arts and sciences. Five-times-daily rituals of prescribed prayer further drain the vitality of creative energy.

"The influence of the religion paralyzes the social development of those who follow it." "No stronger retrograde force (than Islam) exists in the world." — Winston Churchill.

This enervating process is the daily background to the practice of FGM (female genital mutilation), honor killing of daughters, parents sending off their children wrapped in explosives, and husbands taking several wives and stoning to death the unwanted. The frustrated human spirit protests in hatred and savagery. From the earliest age, they are taught and urged to stab, kill, rape, humiliate, stone, and drive vehicles into crowds of Jews and Christians, and homosexuality and apostasy are punishable by death.

The peoples of the current Islamic territories were once Zoroastrian, Christian, Pharoahan, Berber/Imazighen, Jewish, Baha'i, etc., until the Arabs swept out of the Arabian Peninsula in all directions, conquering and confining their victims to the life-denying cult known as Islam. It is they who now seek American freedoms, longing for the light, as does all life, and that is why we must remain vigilant. But a significant percentage wants to enslave us under the same mortifying system that they had and to fulfill their ingrained obligation of hijra — conquest by numbers and the gradual imposition of sharia law in schools and workplaces across America. Their national goal is Islamic world domination.[820]

How devastating if our founding fathers had escaped their authoritarian monarchy to establish a freer government, only to find themselves in another repressive dictatorship. How cruel and ironic if our ancestors had fled from Europe's socialism, Marxism, and communism only to find themselves overcome by domination under the same doctrines. Our society is not only a haven for the talented and creative, but it is also a seedbed that we have the duty to preserve.

Should we allow the new jihadis or enemy from within to turn this Constitutional Republic into an Islamic theocracy, a caliphate, with all the intolerable restrictions of sharia law that the new Americans thought they left behind?

We must not fail our citizens through negligence or a misplaced sense of compassion and think that we should accept all who alight on our shores. Egyptian-American author Nonie Darwish[821] reminds us that some of the unhappy populations must stay behind and work to reform Islam and restore the Middle East. Here, we must vet all entrants to ensure their embrace of our values and that they will become productive members of our society — because those who will not will continue to teach their children their own tenets of obsessive hate, and we have enough troubles already.

The purpose of the Islamic ideology is to rule the world — and to destroy Israel, a stubborn bastion of freedom. Failure to perform jihad will lead to "spiritual death." The Muslim Brotherhood, Islamic Society of North America, Organization of Islamic Cooperation, the Muslim Student Association, ISIS, Hamas, Hezbollah and other affiliates are bound to insinuate into our society, and slowly implement sharia changes into every facet of our lives. We already have a sharia-compliant Muslim population of 3.3 million in more than 300 American cities and towns.[822]

Only extraordinary measures will save the West from the extraordinary threat to her survival.

242 | TABITHA KOROL

CONCLUSION
Islam's Stark Reality

With the end of the eight Obama years came the hope that we might quickly overcome and repair the damage done to America. Instead, we are being subjected to an intensifying twofold attack. If there is a design, as many suspect, then these twin jaws are evidently engineered to crush the substance of our culture.

While Islam slowly operates to grind down our current generation by intimidation and indoctrination, in academia, the media, and religious institutions, the Left has grown obsessed with destroying our core institutions; demolishing our historic monuments; erasing our common sense and freedoms; redefining the family unit, the sexes, our laws and policies; dismembering our language, and dividing our citizens into separate antagonistic camps. The danger of multiculturalism is that it intimidates the generous heart to suspend all intelligent discernment. Islamophobia curbs our inalienable rights and makes us submissive; and, as Aristotle warned, *"the worst form of inequality is to try to make unequal things equal."* We are in danger of losing the best of what we have achieved.

As I was bringing this book to a close, I became aware of an intrinsic component of destruction within Islam that I had somehow not acknowledged. Islam appears to have been precisely invented as the antithesis of Judaism and Christianity — not just as Mohammed's vengeance for failing to convert all the infidels, but the theme for centuries to come. Whereas our religions provide our people with an answer to the mystery of creation and laws for morality, harmony, and justice, Islam provides religious, cultural, political and military laws that lead to physical and psychological pain to its every follower and danger to the infidel, and for one very specific purpose.

It all came together when I responded to a report by the UN Human Rights Rapporteur on Violence against Women, Dubravka Simonovic, who iterated the Islamic narrative of victimization and blame — that Palestinian men's increased abuse of their wives is due to Israel's retaliation to jihad attacks. Given that premise, Israeli men should be increasingly abusive to their wives due to the Palestinians' intensified rocket and street attacks. Yet that is not the case. If anything, Jewish families were shown to be more caring and protective during times of stress, through the Inquisition, the incessant pogroms, two world wars with the Holocaust, and the constant attacks by neighboring Arabs. Israel is ranked among the happiest countries in the world, whose people could not have made extraordinary medical, technological and other creative advancements if they were abused, unhappy and depressed. Simonovic's accusation is fallacious, her conclusion malicious. Islamic violence is embedded in Islam and nurtured in the home.

Family life is a microcosm of the surrounding culture. Inside and outside the Islamic home, there is oppression, subordination, envy, animosity, shame, enslavement, and emotional and physical pain for any deviation. The Koran is filled with directives for disrespecting and harming women and it encourages men to take up to four wives and sexual slaves, resulting in the women's insecurity, anxiety, competition, jealousy, disrespect, and no female friendships. A rebellious wife may be beaten by her husband or confined under house arrest without food or clothing. She may be divorced as easily as the husband's thrice-uttered declaration, and left penniless, without her children or recourse in a court of law. The children also suffer in this exceptionally discordant environment.

Muslim women are among the poorest, most oppressed, and least educated in the world, caged by their cumbrous shrouds in the insufferable desert heat, by their chauvinist husbands and misogynist sharia laws. Girls may be subjected to painful female genital mutilation by age seven, without anesthesia or bona fide medical treatment, followed by interference with normal female bodily functions, infections, psychological impairment from their parents' betrayal, and possible exsanguination and death. They may be given in marriage at any age to a man of any age, and face another agonizing surgery of reversal. If raped, she may be accused of adultery and suffer whippings or be stoned to death.

Entirely covered, women may not socialize with men. The burqa becomes a symbol of humiliation, servitude and protection from men who know no restraint. Morally, she is deprived of freedom and individuality; physically, of sunlight and Vitamin D, so she is more likely to develop osteoporosis and experience pelvic fracture during childbirth — and have children who may develop seizures. Music is banned; art is restricted to geometric patterns and calligraphy; creativity and imagination are stifled. Birthday celebrations are forbidden, and marriage is a matter of the man's signature on paper. Joy and the wonder of life have been excised from every facet of the culture.

Sexual attraction, considered normal in the West but shameful in Islam, is daubed with an unhealthy negativity, yielding fear and hostility. Deprived of interaction typical to western youth, Arab men must indulge in homosexuality with boys or humiliated, emasculated men. The intense sexual repression and misogyny turn youths into raging assassins and rapists of non-Muslim, non-mutilated women. Again, frustration and distress are imposed unswervingly.

It has been medically proven that their five-times-daily prayers, each requiring 34 head-to-prayer-mat contacts, often resulting in a serious contusion, named a zebibah, can cause Traumatic Brain injury (TBI) — mental disorders, depression, aggression, and cognitive impairment to feed the war and cult mentality. This society produces nothing but harm.

The Muslim family is a breeding ground for deviant behavior, its dynamics providing constant stress and rage that also extend to sadistic torture of animals brought to slaughter for holidays. Some Muslim societies encourage consanguineous marriages, producing sick, dysfunctional children, suitable for aggression, suicidal murder and martyrdom.

Small children are taught to carry on Mohammed's hate for Jews and Christians, to handle knives and swords and practice beheading on small animals. Children may be used as human shields to increase the death toll of Israel's reprisals and evoke pity from the West, and for the dangerous construction of terror tunnels. The cultural disrespect and irreverence for all life are both cause and consequence for all Palestinian and Islamic fury and aggression.

For fourteen centuries, Mohammed's examples of captivity, looting, decapitation and conquest have been the paradigm for his followers. The masses are kept focused on their own anxieties and wretchedness and the state's passion for a caliphate. Illiteracy is maintained, love is prevented and replaced by anxiety, anger, blame and shame. Their methods of radicalization and conversion attract foreign fighters from the West, and the price paid for the unending misery and bloodshed has been their humanity. And the ultimate purpose? To feed the war machine. To wage jihad against the world until there is nothing left of us.

INDEX

PART ONE: ISLAM

12 1400 Years of Suspicion
60 A la Fiorina
15 Bedouin Brouhaha Baseless
22 Beware of CAIR
46 CAIR Visits Franciscan Sisters
73 Chelm
56 Destroy the History, Dread the Future
78 Engraved in Stone
81 Female Jihadi, The
44 From Hijab to Jihad
24 Goodbye, Columbus
29 Hunter is the Prey
65 Iceland's Meltdown
48 Jews Don't Behave Like Muslims
58 Jihadis of Tomorrow
16 Lawfare – Legal Warfare
11 Many Faces of Grand Jihad, The
64 Mosquitoes in the Mosque
75 Musings of a Muslim Father
19 Myth-illogical Apartheid
34 Not the Same God
53 Pack of Wolves
41 Quest for Commonality, A
31 Sins Cast Long Shadows
36 !Smitciv
68 Takk Fyrir
50 Training for Treachery
70 Very Syrious Matter, A
26 Violence of the Lambs
39 Wooing Wyoming

PART TWO: ACADEMIA

127 Art of War, The
113 ASA, Anti-Semitic Association
108 ASA: Academics Surrender to Allah
94 BDS – A case of Myth-taken Identity
89 BDS – Bigoted, Deceptive, Shameless
91 BDS, Agents of Destruction
102 Broken College, Office of Submissions
106 Cary's Canards
132 Changing Minds
158 Choice of One, A
111 Communizing Common Core
122 Dawa at Chautauqua
153 Education in Corruption, An
160 Good Morning, Little Comrades
85 Harvard, the Higher Madrassa
84 Jihad at Kent State
138 Joy of Witlessness
135 Mobocracy in Academia
120 Moderate Vanguard, The
131 Morality at Missouri U
104 Oberlin's Onus
141 Of Villainy in Vassar
145 Offense by Design
148 Offense by Design, 2
124 Precarity
115 Purging Israel for Profit
97 Textbook Taqiyyah
87 UP on the Decline
118 Veiled Pursuit

PART THREE: MEDIA

179   60 Minutes of Mendacity

172   A Twist of Hate

238   Asylum!

223   BBC, A Mission Astray

221   Bias at the BBC

209   Board Gets Nailed, The

242   Conclusion – Islam's Glaring Reality

226   Dissociated Press

219   En Garde!

165   Foul Play

212   Guardian with Guile

174   HARDtalk, Hard to Swallow

194   Honor for Dishonor

235   Israel in Dispute

196   L'Americaine

177   Lourdes of the Lies

215   Men of Ideals

207   Metropalistan Opera, The

229   Muslims Are Not Jews

218   No, No, Norah

168   NPR, Notorious for Palestinian Revisionism

200   Nuremberg Revisited

184   Oren on Honesty

181   Palestine Khouri Doesn't Know, The

191   Polluted Waters

198   Probing the Propaganda

170   Restricted Vision

232   Times That Try Men's Souls, The

186   Times Un-Square

188   Two-Time Oscar Winner Two-Times

164   Value of One, The

205   We Have MET the Enemy

Endnotes

PART ONE: ISLAM
The Many Faces of Grand Jihad

1   Ethiopian Monitor, Why Islam is not a Religion, http://ethiomonitor.blogspot.com/2011/06/nigeria-Muslim-hordes-mass-slaughter.html

2   Jerusalem Center for Public Affairs, http://www.jcpa.org/jl/vp483.htm

3   Beliefnet, *Buddhism*, http://www.beliefnet.com/faiths/buddhism/2001/03/taliban-destroy-more-pre-islamic-religious-artifacts.aspx

4   Jerusalem Center for Public Affairs; Ami-El, Mark, *The Destruction of the Temple Mount Antiquities*; http://www.jcpa.org/jl/vp483.htm

5   *Truth and Grace, A Christian Review of Bad Religions and Beliefs*; http://truthandgrace.com/Muslimslavery.htm

6   The Religion of Peace, What makes Islam so different; http://www.thereligionofpeace.com/pages/quran/slavery.aspx

7   The Religion of Peace – Islam: The politically Incorrect Truth; http://www.thereligionofpeace.com/

8   Muslim extremists call for Jihad in the England (Great Britain); https://www.youtube.com/watch?v=31NHNhTrDMc

9   ynet World News, Sweden threatened with jihad; http://www.ynetnews.com/articles/0,7340,L-3135697,00.html

10 Investigative Report, violent jihad in the Netherlands; http://www.investigativeproject.org/documents/testimony/50.pdf

11 Pipes, Daniel, Middle East Forum, The 751 No-Go Zones of France; http://www.danielpipes.org/blog/2006/11/the-751-no-go-zones-of-france

12 Triumphal rabat mosque: http://photobucket.com/images/Mosque%20Dome,%20Rabat,%20Morocco

13 Amazon: Offensive and Defensive Lawfare: Fighting Civilization Jihad in America's Courts; https://www.amazon.com/Offensive-Defensive-Lawfare-Fighting-Civilization-ebook/dp/B016Z3EWGI

14 Jihad watch, Robert Spencer: https://www.jihadwatch.org/2008/05/us-public-school-history-books-whitewashing-and-promoting-islam

15 Gerstenfeld, Dr. Manfred, Jerusalem Center for Public Affairs, Academics against Israel and the Jews; http://jcpa.org/article/academics-against-israel-and-the-jews-2/

16 Pipes, Daniel, and Chadha, Sharon, Middle East Forum; CAIR: Islamists Fooling the Establishment; http://www.meforum.org/916/cair-islamists-fooling-the-establishment

17   FactCheck.org; http://www.factcheck.org/2010/11/Muslims-appointed-to-homeland-security/

18   Dershowitz, Alan, Harvard Public Law Working paper No. 10-26; https://www.gatestoneinstitute.org/1030/the-case-against-the-goldstone-report-a-study-in-evidentiary-bias

19   Keinon, Herb, The Jerusalem Post; http://www.jpost.com/International/Israel-urges-West-against-flotillas

20   Hoft, Jim; Gateway Pundit; http://www.thegatewaypundit.com/2011/09/obama-administration-warns-against-even-symbolically-recognizing-jerusalem-as-capital-of-israel/

1400 Years of Suspicion

21   Islam has massacred over 669+ million non-Muslims since 622AD, Israel Islam & EndTimes; https://www.israelislamandendtimes.com/muslims-massacred-669-million-non-muslims-since-622ad/

22   Dr. Moorthy Muthuswamy, Quotes from and about Islam, *Truth Beknown;* ww.truthbeknown.com/islamquotes.htm

23   LetUsReason Ministries; http://www.letusreason.org/islam12.htm

24   Daily Mail Reporter, Daily Mail.com; http://www.dailymail.co.uk/news/article-2055047/Muslim-students-accuse-Catholic-University-violating-human-rights-Washington-DC.html?ito=feeds-newsxml

25   ACT Mission Viejo; http://www.actforamerica92691.org/resources/ISLAM_In_America$27s_Classrooms_ver_1.54b.pdf

26   Wikipedia, Permanent Residence (United States); https://en.wikipedia.org/wiki/Permanent_residence_(United_States)

27   Teach, William, Right Wing News, Imam Rauf: "We Gotta Build the Mosque at Ground Zero…" http://rightwingnews.com/rop/imam-rauf-we-gotta-build-the-mosque-at-ground-zero-otherwise-islamists-will-get-violent/

28   Geoff Stamp, Christianity Today, Christian Villages Burn Again in Central Indonesia; http://www.christianitytoday.com/ct/2002/augustweb-only/8-19-23.0.html2787298/posts

29   Yaar, Chana, Arutz Sheva, Attackers Carve Jewish Star into Back of Irqi Poet in St. Louis; http://www.freerepublic.com/focus/f-news/

30   The Daily Caller, 20-21-2011; Obama administration pulls references to Islam from terror training materials, official says; https://www.yahoo.com/news/obama-administration-pulls-references-islam-terror-training-materials-044605689.html?ref=gs

31   Wikipedia, Lawfare; https://en.wikipedia.org/wiki/Lawfare

32   Ron Kampeas, J Street owns up to Soros funding, 09.26.10; http://www.jta.org/2010/09/26/news-opinion/united-states/j-street-owns-up-to-soros-funding

Baseless Bedouin Brouhaha

33   Center for Sinai; http://www.centre4sinai.com.eg/tent.htm

34   Bare Naked Islam, Why do Palestinians get more financial aid per capita than any other country on earth?, 07.21.11; http://www.barenakedislam.com/2011/07/21/why-do-palestinians-get-more-financial-aid-per-capita-than-any-other-country-on-earth/

Myth-illogical Apartheid

35   Wikipedia, List of cities with defensive walls: https://en.wikipedia.org/wiki/List_of_cities_with_defensive_walls

Beware of CAIR

36   Middle East Forum, Spring 2006, Vol. 13:No.2; http://www.meforum.org/916/cair-islamists-fooling-the-establishment

37   IPT:The Investigative Project on Terrorism, 3.12.10; http://www.investigativeproject.org/1854/doj-cairs-unindicted-co-conspirator-status-legit

38   WND Frontpage, 11.23.10, Federal Judge confirms CAIR is Hamas; http://www.wnd.com/2010/11/232181/watch.org/article/id/12297

39   Ben Barrack, 5.8.12. Shoebat.com, Awareness and Action. http://shoebat.com/2012/05/08/report-university-of-central-arkansas-jumps-head-first-into-the-dhimmi-pool/

40   Antelique Chrisafis, 9.29.11; https://www.theguardian.com/world/2011/sep/19/battle-for-the-burqa

41   Marc Sheppard, Americanthinker, Free Republic, How do you Solve a Problem like Sharia?, http://www.freerepublic.com/focus/f-news/1702092/posts

42   Bar Ye'or, Dhimmitude: History: Dhimmitude, http://www.dhimmitude.org/d_history_dhimmitude.html

Goodbye, Columbus

43   Political Islam, Sharlia Law for Non-Muslims Chapter 5, The Kafir; https://www.politicalislam.com/sharia-law-for-non-Muslims-chapter-5-the-kafir/

44   PMW Palestinian Media Watch, http://palwatch.org/main.aspx?fi=479

45   http://media.radicalislam.org/misc/pdf/Muslim+Brotherhood+General+Strategic+Goal+f or+North+America.pdf

46   Wikipedia, Buddhas of Bamiyan; *https://en.wikipedia.org/wiki*Buddhas_of_Bamiyan#Attacks_on_the_Buddha.27s_statue

47   Encyclopaedia Britannica, Taliban; https://www.britannica.com/topic/Taliban

48   History, Jan 02, This day in History, 1492 Reconquest of Spain; http://www.history.com/this-day-in-history/reconquest-of-spain

49   Sheikyermami, Winds of Jihad, 4.1.10, Mohammedan "Tourists" Storm Cordoba, http://
     sheikyermami.com/2010/04/mohammedan-tourists-storm-cordoba-cathedral-2-security-
     guards-seriously-injured/

50   Mark Rose, Archaeology; abstracts; http://www.jewishvirtuallibrary.org/jsource/Judaism/
     joetomb.html

51   WikiIslam, Worship Places Converted or Destroyed by Muslims; http://wikiislam.net/
     wiki/Worship_Places_Converted_or_Destroyed_by_Muslims#cite_ note-5

52   Laurie Goodstein, The New York Times, 8.7.10, Across nation, Mosque Projects Meet Opposition;
     http://www.nytimes.com/2010/08/08/us/08mosque.html?pagewanted=all&_r=1http://www.
     clarionproject.org/analysis/four-islamists-gov-christies-Muslim-outreach-committee#

53   Ryan Mauro, Discover the Networks, 11.15.10, Four Islamists on Gov. Christie's
     Muslim Outreach Committee; *http://www.discoverthenetworks.org/printgroupProfile.
     asp?grpid=6380*

54   Discover the Network, Org., Islamic Circle of North America (ICNA); *http://www.
     discoverthenetworks.org/printgroupProfile.asp?grpid=6380*

55   The Clarion Project, the Muslim Brotherhood's Strategic Plan for America – Court Document;
     http://www.clarionproject.org/Muslim_Brotherhood_Explanatory_Memorandum

56   Neil Munro, White House Correspondent, The Daily Caller, 01.04.13; http://dailycaller.
     com/2013/01/04/cair-chief-claims-Muslims-discovered-america-first/

57   Memri-TV YouTube, 1/04/13; Muslims Discovered America according to CAIR; http://
     www.youtube.com/watch?v=FYN6OkmlUYw,

Violence of the Lambs

58   Waseem@umdbk.com, The Diamondback, 2.26.14, *http://www.diamondbackonline.com/
     news/national/article_d527867e-8094-11e2-a457-001a4bcf6878.html*

59   https://en.wikipedia.org/wiki/Homonationalism andWikipedia.org, Pinkwashing; https://
     en.wikipedia.org/wiki/Pinkwashing and homonationalism

60   Wikipedia, LBGT rights in Iran, *https://en.wikipedia.org/wiki/LGBT_rights_in_Iran*

61   Alalam, 2.22.15; Daesh 'Burned alive 43 People in Anbar Cages'; *http://en.alalam.ir/
     news/1678760*

62   World Health Organization, May 16, 2016; New Who guidelines to improve care for
     millions living with female genital mutilation; http://www.who.int/topics/female_genital_
     mutilation/en/

63   Wikipedia, Untermensch; https://en.wikipedia.org/wiki/Untermensch

64   Joel Brinkley, SFgate, August 29, 2010; Afghanistan's dirty little secret; http://www.
     sfgate.com/opinion/brinkley/article/Afghanistan-s-dirty-little-secret-3176762.php

65   Jamie Glazov, Front Page Magazine, Boys of the Taliban, 01.01.07; http://archive.
     frontpagemag.com/readArticle.aspx?ARTID=852

66 Dr. Sanity, 2.15.08, Islam's Vicious Misogyny; http://drsanity.blogspot.com/2008/02/islams-vicious-misogyny.html

67 Wikipedia, Hitler's Willing Executioners; https://en.wikipedia.org/wiki/Hitler%27s_Willing_Executioners

68 Yair Altman, 13.03.11, Itamar massacre,Fogel family butchered while sleeping; ynet news.com,http://www.ynetnews.com/articles/0,7340,L-4041237,00.html

69 Jewish Virtual Library, The Holocaust: Glossary of Terms, Places, Personalities; http://www.jewishvirtuallibrary.org/jsource/Holocaust/wiesenthal_glossary.html

Hunter is the Prey

70 The Florida Senate, CS/CS/SB 58: Application of Foreign Law I Certain Cases; http://www.flsenate.gov/Session/Bill/2013/0058

71 TheReligionofPeace, 5.10.12, What makes Islam so different?; http://www.thereligionofpeace.com/

72 Silas, Slavery in Islam; http://www.answering-islam.org/Silas/slavery.htm

73 US Department of State, 8/5/05, The Facts about Children Trafficked for Use as Camel Jockeys; http://tribune.com.pk/story/545794/camel-jockeys-popular-arab-sport-costs-pakistani-children-their-sanity/ and https://2001-2009.state.gov/g/tip/rls/fs/2005/50940.htm

74 Memri-TV, 5.10.12, Necrophilia; https://www.youtube.com/watch?v=u7z5M4QTINY

75 Shoebatlcom, 3.07.13, The Promotion of Huma Sacrifice and Cannibalism in Egypt; http://shoebat.com/2013/03/07/the-promotion-of-human-sacrifice-and-cannibalism-in-egypt/

76 Kevin A Lehmann, Tea Party Tribune, 9.27.12, How Islam and Sharia Violates the US Constitution and Declaration of Independence; http://www.teapartytribune.com/2012/09/27/how-islam-and-sharia-violates-the-us-constitution-and-declaration-of-independence

Sins Cast Long Shadows

77 Yahoo! Answers: Koran 2:216; Koran 4:89, Koran 9:36

78 CNP Webmaster, CN Publications, Reporting on the Middle East, Science, and Education, 08/20/12; http://cnpublications.net/2012/08/20/israel-is-a-leader-in-international-humanitarian-aid/

79 Israel behind the headlines, Christians United for Israel, http://makeadifference.cufi.org/israel-trained-medical-team-responded-to-boston-attack/

80 The Times of Israel, Hamas said urging Palestinians to carry out suicide bombings, 10-19-15; http://www.timesofisrael.com/hamas-said-urging-palestinians-to-carry-out-suicide-bombings/, 05.26.11.

81 LiveLeak, Oslo, Norway – all Sexual Assaults Involving Rape in Past 5 Years Committed by Muslims; http://fjordman.blogspot.com/2005/02/Muslim-rape-epidemic-in-sweden-and.html

82 Breitbart News, Religious war: African Muslims burn Christian Churches to Ground, 1/17/15; The New York Times, Africa, Churches Burn in Niger as Muslim Rally is Banned, 01.17.15; VOA, Ethiopia Charges 130 in Church Burning Incidents, 03/07/11;

CBN News, Muslims burn 69 churches; Christians Forgive; *http://us.yhs4.search. yahoo.com/yhs/search;_ylt=A0oG7ob1YHBRjxUA3M5XNyoA*p=africa%20%2B%20 burning%20churches%20_%20Muslims&fr2=sbtop&hspart=Babylon&hsimp=yhs-002&type=br101dm25&type_param=br101dm25

83 Issa Sikita da Silva, Inter Press Service, Little Hope for the Children Abducted in Mali's War, 03.22.13; http://www.ipsnews.net/2013/03/little-hope-for-the-children-abducted-in-malis-war/

84 Sebastian Vilar Rodriguez, Bare Naked Islam, All European Life Died in Auschwitz; http://www.barenakedislam.com/2013/04/17/new-jewish-exodus-from-france-the-result-of-Muslim-hatred-for-and-violence-against-jews-there/

85 Carol Kuruvilla, New York Daily News, Musli Patrol enforcing Sharia in E. London; *http://www.nydailynews.com/news/world/Muslim-patrol-enforcing-sharia-e-london-article-1.1253893*

86 ADL Anti-Defamation League, Major Terrorist Attacks in Israel,*://archive.adl.org/israel/ israel_attacks.html # .VYW-QzWUk*

87 Bill Warner, Political Islam, Tears of Jihad, 03.-3.08; http://dev-political-islam. pantheonsite.io/tears-of-jihad/

88 C. Read, Ab,We need more islamophobia – not less. Islam is a death cult, not a religion, 12/02/10; we-need-more-islamophobia-not-less-islam-is-a-death-cult-not-a-religion-3773099

89 Aaron Klein, WND, Muslims: Jesus was 1st 'Palestinian Martyr', 12,24,10; http://www. wnd.com/2010/12/243545/

Not The Same God

90 Soeren Kern, Gatestone Institute, 05.31.13; https://www.gatestoneinstitute.org/3735/ britain-islamic-future

91 One Law for All, Sharia Law in Britain, 6.17.10; http://www.onelawforall.org.uk/new-report-sharia-law-in-britain-a-threat-to-one-law-for-all-and-equal-rights/

92 Bruce Bawer, The Daily Caller, 10/16/11; http://dailycaller.com/2011/10/16/how-Muslim-immigration-has-transformed-european-politics/

93 Geoff Pingree, The Christian Science Monitor, In Spain, dismay at Muslim converts holding sway; http://www.csmonitor.com/2006/1107/p04s01-woeu.html\

94 Raymond Ibrahim, Middle East Forum, Obama's Proxy War on Mideast Christians, 06/27/13; http://www.meforum.org/3546/obama-proxy-war-christians

95 Bryan Preston, PJ Media, Catholic Archbishop Dolan Tells Muslims 'You Love God, we Love God and he is the same God'; https://pjmedia.com/blog/catholic-archbishop-dolan-tells-Muslims-you-love-god-we-love-god-and-he-is-the-same-god

96 Lori Lowenthal Marcus, The Jewish Express, Catholic priest murdered by Al Qaeda affiliated Syrian rebels, 07/03/13; http://www.jewishpress.com/uncategorized/catholic-priest-murdered-by-syrian-rebels-perhaps-beheaded/2013/07/03/

97 Pamela Geller, Albanian jihadists attack children's buses in Kosovo, 07.03.13; http://pamelageller.com/2013/07/albanian-jihadists-attack-on-childrens-buses-in-kosovo.html/

98 Pamela Geller, Jewish School Bus Hit by Islamic Rockets from Gaza, 04.07.11; http://pamelageller.com/2011/04/jewish-school-bus-hit-by-islamic-rockets-from-gaza.html/

99 Robert Spencer, Stealth Jihad, P. 15/*https://books.google.com/books* id=3eLfhvNQBkg C&pg=PA15&lpg= PA15&dq=Islam%E2%80%99s+double+identity+takes+the+form+o f+groups+that+appear+outwardly+to+be+moderate ...

! Smitciv

100 Editors, *Jizya*, Encyclopaedia Britannica; https://www.britannica.com/topic/jizya

Wooing Wyoming

101 Jaweed Kaleem, The Huffington Post, Islam in America: Mosques see Dramatic Increase in Just Over a Decade, According to Muslim Survey, 2.29.12; http://www.huffingtonpost.com/2012/02/29/mosques-in-united-states-study_n_1307851.html

102 Baron Bodissey, Gates of Vienna, Targeting the Disabled in Hamburg, 9.29.09; *http://gatesofvienna.blogspot.com/2009/09/targeting-disabled-in-hamburg.htm*

103 Religion of Peace, What makes Islam so different?; http://thereligionofpeace.com/

104 Texas95, The Oil for Your Lamp, Islam Assimilation or Conq2uest? Britain's lessons. 01.28.16; https://theoyl.com/2016/01/28/islam-assimilation-or-conquest-britains-lessons/

105 Dale Hurd, CBN News, Native French under Attack in Muslim Areas, 09.08.14; http://www1.cbn.com/cbnnews/world/2014/April/Native-French-under-Attack-in-Muslim-Areas

106 Soeren Kern, Gatestone Institute, Belgium Will Become an Islamic State, 11.09.12; https://www.gatestoneinstitute.org/3442/belgium-islamic-state

107 Admin, Word Press, the Muslim issue, 10.08.12; https://theMuslimissue.wordpress.com/2012/10/08/Muslim-population-in-sweden-and-denmark-doubled-in-14-years/

108 Dale Hurd, CBN News, Norwegian Muslims Call for Beheadings and a Muslim State, 08.23.12; https://theMuslimissue.wordpress.com/2012/10/08/Muslim-population-in-sweden-and-denmark-doubled-in-14-years/

109 Laura J. Alcorn, America Conservative 2 Conservative, 01.17.14; http://americac2c.com/forum/topics/rape-jihad-europe-s-Muslims-name-their-rape-gangs-take-your-turn-?xg_source=msg_mes_network

110 Pamela Geller, Geller Report, Muslims demand breakaway Islamic nation in Norway or another 9/11 threatened, 08.19.14; http://pamelageller.com/2014/08/Muslims-demand-breakaway-islamic-nation-norway-another-911-threatened.html/

111 Dale Hurd, CBN News, Under Siege? Spain Resists Islamic 'Invasion,' 02.12.12; http://www.cbn.com/cbnnews/world/2012/february/under-siege-spain-resists-islamic-invasion-/?mobile=false

112 aaiil.org, Chapter 4: Al-Nisa'-The Women: http://www.aaiil.org/text/hq/trans/ch4.shtml

113 Robert S. Leiken, Council on Foreign Relations, Europe's Angry Muslims, 07/08.2005; ://www.cfr.org/religion/europes-angry-Muslims/p8218

114 Laura J. Alcorn, America Conservative 2 Conservative, What Happens When Muslims Re-populate Your Country, 01.16.14; ://americac2c.com/forum/topics/what-happens-when-Muslims-re-populate-your-country?xgsource=msg_mes_network

A Quest for Commonality

115 Part 1 – Torah, Chapter Three, Exodus; Deliverance and Covenant http://barrybandstra.com/rtot4/rtot4-06-ch3.html

116 Jewish Virtual Library, Israel: Origins of the name "Palestine," 2016; http://www.jewishvirtuallibrary.org/jsource/History/palname.html

117 The Counter Jihad Report, 08.15.16, Muslims Paying Zakat are Funding Terror, https://counterjihadreport.com/category/zakat/

118 Acharya S.D.M. Murdock, *Freethought Nation*, What does the Koran say about nonbelievers? 09.06.13; http://freethoughtnation.com/what-does-the-koran-say-about-nonbelievers/

From Hijab to Jihad

119 Adriana Stuut, Digital Journal, 05.08.09, Women could endanger their health by wearing burqas; http://www.digitaljournal.com/article/272307http://www.digitaljournal.com/article/272307

120 Media centre, Female genital mutilation, *World Health Organization*, 02.2017; http://www.who.int/mediacentre/factsheets/fs241/en/

CAIR Visits Franciscan Sisters

121 Wikipedia, Islamophobia, https://en.wikipedia.org/wiki/Islamophobia

122 Investigative Project, Attachment A., List of Unindicted Co-conspirators and/or Joint Venturers; http://www.investigativeproject.org/documents/case_docs/423.pdf

123 Ted, Shoebat.com, 03.06.14, Muslims Kill an Entire Christian Family and Burn Down 20 Christian Homes; https://shoebat.com/2014/03/06/Muslims-kill-entire-christian-family-burn-200-christian-homes-2/

124 Dr. Sami Alrabaa, Islam in its own words, Minarets are Symbols of Bigotry, 10.05.13; http://islaminitsownwords.blogspot.com/2013/10/minarets-are-symbols-of-bigotry.html

125 The Religion of Peace; http://www.thereligionofpeace.com/index.aspx

126 Reliance of the Traveller, The Objectives of Jihad, o9.8; page 602.

127 Adam Lebor, Newsweek, Exodus, Why Europe's Jews are Fleeing once Again, 7.29.14; http://www.newsweek.com/2014/08/08/exodus-why-europes-jews-are-fleeing-once-again-261854.html

128 Bob Unruh, WND, Coming Soon: America's Own Islamic 'No-go' Zones," 07.23.13; http://www.wnd.com/2013/07/coming-soon-americas-own-islamic-no-go-zones/

129   Honor Diaries: The Film, http://www.honordiaries.com/

130   Memri-TV, //www.memritv.org/

131   Noni Darwish, Cruel and Usual Punishment; https://www.amazon.com/Cruel-Usual-Punishment-Nonie-Darwish/dp/159555209X

132   Brigitte Gabriel, Because They Hate; *https://www.amazon.com/s?ie=UTF8&field-author=Brigitte%20Gabriel&page=1&rh=n%3A283155%2Cp_27%3ABrigitte%20Gabriel*

133   Ayaan Hirsi Ali, Infidel; https://www.amazon.com/Infidel-Ayaan-Hirsi-Ali/dp/07432896 92

134   Answering Islam, 164 Jihad Verses in the Koran; http://www.answering-islam.org/Quran/Themes/jihad_passages.html

135   The Religion of Peace, What Does Islam Teach About Violence; *http://www.thereligionofpeace.com/pages/quran/violence.aspx*

136   Brigitte Gabriel, Because They Hate; https://www.amazon.com/Because-They-Hate-Survivor-Islamic/dp/0312358385

137   Roger Kimball, PJ Media, 04.28.08, Civilizational Suicide: the 12-stop program; https://pjmedia.com/rogerkimball/2008/04/28/civilization_suicide_the_12ste/

Jews Don't Behave Like Muslims

138   Lorna Salzman, July 2014, New English Review; http://www.newenglishreview.org/Lorna_Salzman/Jews_Behaving_Like_Muslims/

139   Gaza Strip, Wikipedia; https://en.wikipedia.org/wiki/Gaza_Strip

140   Second Intifada, Wikipedia; https://en.wikipedia.org/wiki/Second_Intifada Second Intifada, Wikipedia; https://en.wikipedia.org/wiki/Second_Intifada

141   Judy Lash Balint, ISJ Chutzpa, International Solidary Movement; http://www.israelnewsagency.com/internationalsolidaritymovement.html

142   Human shield, Wikipedia; https://en.wikipedia.org/wiki/Human_shield

143   Gaza War: Wikis, Encyclopedia, the full wiki; http://www.nytimes.com/2009/01/11/world/middleeast/11hamas.html?_r=2

144   Ari Lieberman, The Rachel Corrie the New York Times doesn't want you to see, 03.19.13; http://www.frontpagemag.com/fpm/182187/rachel-corrie-new-york-times-doesnt-want-you-see-ari-lieberman

145   Gil Ronen, Left Silences Victims, 09.21.10; http://www.israelnationalnews.com/News/News.aspx/139738#.TkASaIKwVgQ

146   Dales Amos, Haaretz, http://daledamos.blogspot.com/2010/07/humanitarian-activists-trying-to-bury.html

147   Wikipedia, Category: Jewish opera singers; https://en.wikipedia.org/wiki/Category:Jewish_opera_singers

148   Tzedakah, Wikipedia; https://en.wikipedia.org/wiki/Tzedakah

Training for Treachery

149   Gordon Rayner and Steven Swinford, 05.22.13; Woolwich attack: terrorist proclaimed 'an eye for an eye' after attack; *http://www.telegraph.co.uk/news/uknews/terrorism-in-the-uk/10073910/Woolwich-attack-terrorist-proclaimed-an-eye-for-an-eye-after-attack.html*

150   Life Leak, Woman Beheaded in Back Garden; *http://romancatholicimperialist.blogspot.com/2014/09/Muslim-sodomized-dog-then-beheads-woman.html#!/2014/09/Muslim-sodomized-dog-then-beheads-woman.html*

151   The Patriot, London: Police smash suspected Islamic terror attack plot after 4 Muslims were captured by armed officers, 10.14.13; boltonbnp.blogspot.com/2013/London-police-smash-suspected-islamic-terror-attack-plot-after-4-Muslims-were-captured-by-armed-office

152   Watchman Watch, TheSeason.Org, Watchman Watch – Daily News, 700 beheaded, crucified and shot after revolt against militants; http://theseason.yuku.com/topic/29780/700-beheaded-crucified-shot-revolt-militants#.WA1hoeQzWUk

153   USA Today, Canada: convert to radical islam ran down soldiers, 10.21.14; http://www.usatoday.com/story/news/world/2014/10/21/driver-hits-canadian-soldiers/17649449/

154   Before It's News, Jewish terrorism and genocide—a partial listing, 02.13.16; http://beforeitsnews.com/israel/2016/02/jewish-terrorism-and-genocide-a-partial-listing-2459296.html

155   Shimon Prokupecz and Greg Botelho, CNN, Man attacks New York police officers with a hatchet, 10.24.14; *http://www.cnn.com/2014/10/23/us/new-york-police-attacked/index.html*

156   What makes Islam so different?; *http://www.thereligionofpeace.com/index.aspx*

157   Wikipedia, Walid Shoebat; *https://en.wikipedia.org/wiki/Walid_Shoebat*

158   Amazon, Why I Left Jihad: The Root of Terrorism and the Return of Radical Islam; https://www.amazon.com/Why-Left-Jihad-Terrorism-Radical/dp/0977102114

159   Fox News U.S., Oklahoma beheading: FBI probing suspect's recent conversion to Islam, 09/27/14; http://www.foxnews.com/us/2014/09/27/woman-beheaded-at-oklahoma-food-distribution-center-police-say.html

160   The Counter Jihad Report, Ryan Mauro and Michael Cutler vs. CAIR on Newsmax TV: Terror Camps in USA, 02/27/16; https://counterjihadreport.com/tag/terror-training-camps-in-us-2/

161   Military.com, Terrorist Training Camps in the US, 02.18.09; http://www.military.com/video/operations-and-strategy/domestic-terrorism/terrorist-training-camps-in-the-us/660940716001

162   Wikipedia, Beltway sniper attacks; https://en.wikipedia.org/wiki/Beltway_sniper_attacks

Pack of Wolves

163   Steven Emerson, IPT News, The Terrorist Attack in Australia: Coming to a Theater Near You, 12.15.14; http://www.investigativeproject.org/4703/the-terrorist-attack-in-australia-coming-to

164   Wikipedia, 7 July 2005 London bombings; https://en.wikipedia.org/wiki/7_July_2005_ London_bombings

165   Isabel Kershner, The Sydney Morning Herald, Jerusalem: Four rabbis killed in attack on synagogue, 11/198/14; http://www.smh.com.au/world/jerusalem-four-rabbis-killed-in-attack-on-synagogue-20141118-11p8fd.html

166   Ted Shoebat, Muslims Behead Hundreds of People, and Feed Their Corpses to Dogs, Shoebat.com Awareness and Action, 03/29/14; http://shoebat.com/2014/03/29/muslims-behead-hundreds-people-feed-corpses-dogs/

167   Bare Naked Islam, Zansibar: Muslim savages throw acid in the faces of two British Jewish teenagers,   08.09.13;   http://www.barenakedislam.com/2013/08/09/zanzibar-Muslim-savages-throw-acid-in-the-faces-of-two-british-jewish-teenagers/

168   Jim Hoft, Gateway Pundit, Muslikm Mob in France Beats Jewish Youths with Hammers and Iron Bars on Sabbath, 06.03.12; http://www.thegatewaypundit.com/2012/06/Muslim-mob-in-france-beats-jewish-youths-with-hammers-and-iron-bars-on-sabbath/

169   Joshua Keating, Slate, Why Terrorists Use Vehicles as Weapons, 11/05/14; http://www.slate.com/blogs/the_world_/2014/11/05/car_attack_in_jerusalem_why_are_terrorists_ramming_vehicles_into_crowds.html

170   Aminu Abukabar and Josh Levs, CNN, Boko Haram leader says of Kidnapped Nigerian girls, 05.06.14; http://www.cnn.com/2014/05/05/world/africa/nigeria-abducted-girls/index.html

171   Fjordman, Muslim Rape Epidemic in Sweden and Norway – Authorities Look the Other Way, 02.20.05; http://fjordman.blogspot.com/2005/02/Muslim-rape-epidemic-in-sweden-and.html

172   Bare Naked Islam, Sharia in Action: Latest stoning to death of a Muslim woman, 05.20.13; http://www.barenakedislam.com/2013/05/20/sharia-in-action-latest-stoning-to-death-of-a-Muslim-woman/

173   My Greek Spirit, Father beheads his own daughter, 06/19/12; https://en.wikipedia.org/wiki/List_of_designated_terrorist_groups

174   Wikipedia, List of designated terrorist groups; https://en.wikipedia.org/wiki/List_of_designated_terrorist_groups

175   Ted, Shoebat.com, Muslims behead Hundreds of People, and feed their corpses to dogs, 03.29.14, http://shoebat.com/2014/03/29/Muslims-behead-hundreds-people-feed-corpses-dogs/

176   YouTube, Palestinian Children Taught to Hate, 09..13.09; https://www.youtube.com/watch?v=etDb5tXPawc

177   ASKDrBrown, YouTube, 90 Seconds of Truth about Hamas, 08.17.14; https://www.youtube.com/watch?v=yOEHvi7qGsk

178   Theodore Shoebat, Shoebat.com, Muslims Use Dolls to Train Their Kids hot to Behead Infidels…, 08/24/14; http://shoebat.com/2014/08/24/Muslims-use-dolls-train-kids-behead-infidels-say-teach-children-cut-necks-tomorrow-will-rotten-heads/

179   Bare Naked Islam, Australia: Beheading 101 lessons for very young Muslim children, 04.26.15; http://www.barenakedislam.com/2015/04/26/australia-beheading-101-lessons-for-very-young-Muslim-children/

180   Midnight Watcher's Blogspot, That's My Boy"— Proud Muslim Father from Australia posts photo of 7-year-old boy Holding Beheaded Enemy, 08/11/14; https://midnightwatcher.wordpress.com/2014/08/11/thats-my-boy-proud-Muslim-father-from-australia-posts-photo-of-7-year-old-son-holding-beheaded-enemy/

181   Theodore Shoebat, Shoebat.com, Muslims Play Soccer with the Heads of Their Victims, 12.29.13; http://shoebat.com/2013/12/29/Muslims-play-soccer-heads-victims/

182   Year in Egypt, Eid Al-Adha, 11/24/16; http://mikemcmullen.org/?p=338

183   Daniel Greenfield, Frontpage mag Eid Halal Slaughter in Gaza: "Worst Animal Cruelty in History", 12.13.13; http://www.frontpagemag.com/point/213165/eid-halal-slaughter-gaza-worst-animal-cruelty-daniel-greenfield

184   Kathryn Hill, Kitchn, Good Question: What is Halal Meat?, 08/28/08; http://www.thekitchn.com/good-question-what-is-halal-me-60979

185   Amazon, What the modern Martyr Should Know; http://source.southuniversity.edu/examining-the-mob-mentality-31395.aspx

Destroy the History, Dread the Future

186   JewsNews, Why Did Kidnapping Girls, but Not Burning Boys Alive, Wake Media up to Boko Haram:, 05.15.14; http://www.jewsnews.co.il/2014/05/15/why-did-kidnapping-girls-but-not-burning-boys-alive-wake-media-up-to-boko-haram.html

187   Wikipedia, Battle of Vienna; https://en.wikipedia.org/wiki/Battle_of_Vienna

188   1001 Inventions, Discover a Golden Age; www.1001inventions.com

189   Aaron Klein, WND, Christmas Surprise: Jesus Declared a Palestinian, 12.28.14; http://www.wnd.com/2014/12/christmas-declared-a-palestinian-holiday/

190   Itamar Marcus and Nan Jacques Zilberdik, PMW, Moses was a Muslim who led Muslims in Exodus from Egypt, says PA university lecturer on PA TV, 04.2.12; http://www.palwatch.org/main.aspx?fi=157&doc_id=6716

191   WND, You Didn't Know? Einstein was Muslim; http://www.wnd.com/2014/03/you-didnt-know-einstein-was-Muslim/

192   Ishaan Tharoor, Washington Post, Muslims discovered America before Columbus, claims Turkey's Erdogan, 11.15.14; https://www.washingtonpost.com/news/worldviews/wp/2014/11/15/Muslims-discovered-america-before-columbus-claims-turkeys-erdogan/

193   Rachna Uppal, Arabian Business.com, Dubai World's Istithmar CEO Resigns, 01.20.10; http://www.arabianbusiness.com/dubai-world-s-istithmar-ceo-resigns-9497.html#.VQTHOGd0yUk

194   RadioFreeEurope RadioLiberty, Tajik IS Militant in Syria: 'We'll Convert Native Americans to Islam and Built Them Mosques'; http://www.rferl.org/a/tajikistan-islamic-state-fighters-recruiting-sharia-syria/26821694.html

Jihadis of Tomorrow

195 Tawfik Hamid.com; www.tawfikhamid.com

A la Fiorina

196 Tim Brown, Freedom Outpost, Carly Fiorina: Islamic Civilization was "Greatest in the World" 06.15.15; http://freedomoutpost.com/carly-fiorina-islamic-civilization-was-greatest-in-the-world/

197 Editors of Encyclopedia Britannica, Jizya Islamic tax, 07.11.07; https://www.britannica.com/topic/jizya

198 Wikipedia, Islamic architecture; https://en.wikipedia.org/wiki/Islamic_architecture

199 Wikipedia, Hindu-Arabic numeral system; *https://en.wikipedia.org/wiki* Hindu%E2%80%93Arabic_numeral_ system

200 Wikipedia, Fibonacci number; https://en.wikipedia.org/wiki/Fibonacci_number

201 Matt Peckham, TIME, Who Really Invented the Computer? 11.10,11; http://techland.time.com/2011/11/10/who-really-invented-the-computer/

202 Stanford Encyclopedia of Philosophy, Alan Turing, 06.03.02/09.30.13; http://plato.stanford.edu/entries/turing/

203 Cryptography: The Ancient Art of Secret Messages; http://www.pawlan.com/monica/articles/crypto/

204 A. Loewenthal Kaufmann Kohler, Jewish Encyclopedia, Avicenna (Abu Ali Abn Abdallah Ibn Sina); http://www.jewishencyclopedia.com/articles/2168-avicenna-abu-ali-ibn-abdallah-ibn-sina

205 Neil MacGregor, BBC Radio, A History of the World in 100 Objects Omnibus; http://www.bbc.co.uk/programmes/b00st9z8

206 Jews and Navigation, Jewish Maritime Historical Society, 10.27.09; http://jewishmaritime.blogspot.com/2009/10/jews-and-navigation.html

207 Wikipedia, Abraham Zacuto; https://en.wikipedia.org/wiki/Abraham_Zacuto

208 Calbuzz, Hurricane Carly Fiorina, HP & the Iran Connection, 09/21/09; http://www.calbuzz.com/2009/09/hurricane-carly-fiorina-hp-the-iran-connection/

209 LiveLeak, Muslims are the world's poorest, weakest and illiterate, 05-29-13; http://www.liveleak.com/view?i=d07_1369844469

210 SimpletoRemember.com, Judaism Online, Jewish Nobel Prize Winners; http://www.simpletoremember.com/articles/a/jewish-nobel-prize-winners/

Mosquitoes in the Mosque

211 Daniel Pipes, Middle East Forum, Muslims killed 600 Million Hindus, 05.18.10; http://www.danielpipes.org/comments/172982

Iceland's Meltdown

212   United with Israel, Eretz Israel: The Indigenous Home of the Jewish People, 04.23.13; *https://unitedwith* israel.org/eretz-israel-the-indigenous-home-of-the-jewish-people/

213   Wikipedia, List of Walls; https://en.wikipedia.org/wiki/List_of_walls

214   Mitchell Bard, Jewish Virtual Library, Myths & Facts, Chapter 19: The Peace process; http://www.jewishvirtuallibrary.org/jsource/myths3/MFpeace.html

215   Wikipedia, Barbary Pirates; https://en.wikipedia.org/wiki/Barbary_pirates

216   Richard C. Csaplar, Jr., CBN News, Jihad Watch, 1,400 Years of Islamic Aggression: An Analysis; https://www.jihadwatch.org/2004/10/1400-years-of-islamic-aggression-an-analysis

217   Nick Meo, The Telepgraph, Jews leave Swedish city after sharp rise in anti-Semitic hate crimes; http://www.telegraph.co.uk/news/worldnews/europe/sweden/7278532/Jews-leave-Swedish-city-after-sharp-rise-in-anti-Semitic-hate-crimes.html

218   Louise Osborne, The Guardian, Why Germany is ow Europe's Biggest brothel, 06.12.13; *https://www.the*guardian.com/world/shortcuts/2013/jun/12/germany-now-europes-biggest-brothel

219   StandWithUs, Hamas: By the Numbers; http://www.standwithus.com/video/?tags=BDS

220   Israel Ministry of Foreign Affairs, Behind the headlines: Hamas' terror tunnels, 07.22.14; http://mfa.gov.il/MFA/ForeignPolicy/Issues/Pages/Hamas-terror-tunnels.aspx

221   Myer Freimann, Tablet, Hamas killed 160 Palestinian children to build tunnels, 0.25.14; *http://www.tabletmag*.com/scroll/180400/hamas-killed-160-palestinian-children-to-build-terror-tunnels

222   Wikipedia, Palestinian rocket attacks on Israel; *https://en.wikipedia.org/wiki/Palestinian_rocket_attacks_on_* Israel

223   Wikipedia, Kenneth Meshoe, Israel; https://en.wikipedia.org/wiki/Kenneth_Meshoe

224   Bare Naked Islam, Update on the Muslim savages rioting in Sweden, 05.21.13; http://www.barenakedislam.com/2013/05/21/update-on-the-Muslim-savages-rioting-in-sweden/

225   Soeren Kern, Gatestone Institute, Iceland to Get its First Mosque, 09.27.13; https://www.gatestoneinstitute.org/3994/iceland-mosque

226   Lizzie Dearden, Independent, More than 11,000 Icelanders offer to house Syrian refugees to help European crisis; http://www.independent.co.uk/news/world/europe/more-than-11000-icelanders-offer-to-house-syrian-refugees-to-help-european-crisis-10480505.html

227   Carol Brown, American Thinker, The Muslim population of America is expanding at warp speed, 01.21.15; *http://www.americanthinker.com/articles/2015/01/the_Muslim_population_of_america_is_expanding_at_warp_* speed.html#ixzz3m3ZUHcM3

Takk Fyrir

228   Wikipedia, List of mosques in the United States; *https://en.wikipedia.org/wiki/List_of_mosques_in_the_United_*States

229 A Crash Course in Middle East History, Nationhood and Jerusalem; *http://www. christadelphians.com/crash_* course_in_middle_east_history.htm

230 Mitchell Bard, Jewish Virtual Library, Myths & Facts, Chapter 15: Jerusalem; *http://www. jewishvirtuallibrary.org* /jsource/myths3/MFjerusalem.html

231 Maurice Ostroff, The San Remo Conference in Context; http://www.maurice-ostroff.org/ the-san-remo-confeerence-in-context/

232 Target of Opportunity.com, The Truth about the Palestinian People; http://www. targetofopportunity.com/palestinian_truth.htm

233 Wikipedia, The River War; *https://en.wikipedia.org/wiki/The_River_War*

A Very Syrious Matter

234 Nicole Duran, Washington Examiner, Obama announces 85,000 more refugee slots in 2016, 9.29.15; http://www.washingtonexaminer.com/obama-announces-85000-more-refugee-slots-in-2016/article/2573065

235 JTF News, DHS Confesses: No information or databases exists to screen Syrian "refugees" for Muslim terrorism, 20/07/15; http://jtf.org/dhs-confesses-no-information-or-databases-exists-to-screen-syrian-refugees-for-Muslim-terrorism/

236 Hannah Roberts, Daily Mail, ISIS threatens to send 500,000 migrants to Europe as a psychological weapon ..., 02.18.15; http://www.dailymail.co.uk/news/article-2958517/The-Mediterranean-sea-chaos-Gaddafi-s-chilling-prophecy-interview-ISIS-threatens-send-500-000-migrants-Europe-psychological-weapon-bombed.html

237 Serge Trifkovic, The Sword of the Prophet, 02.19.07; https://www.amazon.com/The-Sword-Prophet-History-Theology/dp/1928653111

238 Fjordman, Immigrant Rape Wave in Sweden, 12.12.05; http://fjordman.blogspot.com/2005/12/immigrant-rape-wave-in-sweden.html

239 Raheem Kassam, Analysis: BBC Pictures show 53% migrant kids, just 36% men – Hugely out of step with official stats, 09.21.15; http://www.breitbart.com/london/2015/09/21/analysis-bbc-pictures-show-53-migrant-kids-just-36-men-out-of-step-with-reality/

240 Harriet Sherwood, theGuardian, Take in Syrian refugees, aid agencies tell rich countries, 12.07.14; https://www.theguardian.com/world/2014/dec/08/take-in-syrian-refugees-rich-countries

241 IWB-Investment Watchdog Blog, These 11 States now have More People on Welfare than they do Employed!, 03.04.13; http://investmentwatchblog.com/these-11-states-now-have-more-people-on-welfare-than-they-do-employed/

242 Wikipedia, Kaffir (racial term); https://en.wikipedia.org/wiki/Kaffir_%28racial_term%29

243 The Judicial Watch Blog, Obama Task Force to Strengthen Immigrant Integration Infrastructure," 04.21.15; https://www.judicialwatch.org/blog/2015/04/obama-task-force-to-strengthen-immigrant-integration-infrastructure-2/

244 Matthias Soboolewski, Reuters World News, Ballooning refugee costs threaten Germany's cherished budget goals, 09.17.15; http://www.reuters.com/article/us-europe-migrants-germany-budget-idUSKCN0RH22320150917

245 Mike T., The Muslim Observer, An Inspiring Tale: Fatima Noor, 11.04.16; http://Muslimobserver.com/presidential-appointment-fatima-noor/

246 NumbersUSA, Educating Americans on the need for policies of controlled immigration for the nation al interest; https://www.numbersusa.com/

247 News TV Premier, Refugees 'threaten Europe's Christian identity': Orban, 09.03.15; *http://www.channelnews* asia.com/news/world/refugees-threaten-europe/2099246.html

248 Ann Corcoran, Refugee Resettlement Watch, 97% of Syrian refugees admitted to US in 2015 are Muslims, 09.03.15; https://refugeeresettlementwatch.wordpress.com/2015/09/03/97-of-syrian-refugees-admitted-to-us-in-2015-are-Muslims/

249 Julia Hahn, Breitbart News, Federal Data: U.S. Annually Admits quarter of a million Muslim migrants, 09.14.15; http://www.breitbart.com/big-government/2015/09/14/federal-data-u-s-annually-admits-quarter-of-a-million-Muslim-migrants/

Chelm

250 Holocaust Education & Archive Research Team, The Jews of Chelm & Escape from Borek Forest, http://www.holocaustresearchproject.org/revolt/chelmborek.html

251 Jewish English Lexicon, Chacham; http://www.jewish-languages.org/jewish-english-lexicon/words/1375

252 Ross Clark, Questions Al Gore on climate change and he'll call you a denier, The Spectator, 08.19.17; https://www.spectator.co.uk/2017/08/question-al-gore-on-climate-change-and-hell-call-you-a-denier/

253 James Zumwalt, The Daily Caller, Sweden Opened its Doors to Muslim Immigration, today it's the Rape Capital of the West. Japan Didn't, 10.23,15; http://dailycaller.com/2015/10/23/sweden-opened-its-doors-to-Muslim-immigration-today-its-the-rape-capital-of-the-west-japan-didnt/#ixzz3sM0zXEHt

254 Dumbocrat Quotes.com, John Kerry Quotes, 02.16.14; *http://www.dumbocratquotes.com/viewbyperson.php?personid=11*

255 Steven Crowder, Western Journalism, New Poll: Majority of American Muslims want Sharia, Shocking Numbers on Jihad, 06.24.15; http://www.westernjournalism.com/new-poll-majority-of-american-Muslims-want-sharia-shocking-numbers-on-jihad/

256 Andrew Napolitano, WND, Obama's Rejection of the Rule of Law, 07.10.13; http://www.wnd.com/2013/07/obamas-rejection-of-the-rule-of-law/

Musings of a Muslim Father

257 Wajahat Ali, Sunday Review, Raising American Muslim Kids in the Age of Trump, 08.06.16; http://www.nytimes.com/2016/08/07/opinion/sunday/raising-american-Muslim-kids-in-the-age-of-trump.html?_r=2

258 Ali Vitali, NBC News, Donald Trump Shifts on Muslim Ban, Calls for 'Extreme Vetting,' http://www.nbcnews.com/politics/2016-election/donald-trump-shifts-Muslim-ban-calls-extreme-vetting-n611276

259 Ashley Edwardson, Allen B. West, Shocking: Sweden is now the RAPE capital of the West. Here's why, 10,20,15; http://www.allenbwest.com/ashleyedwardson/mainstream-media-wont-tell-you-why-sweden-is-now-rape-capital-of-the-west

260 Ruth Alexander, BBC News, Sweden's rape rate under the spotlight, 09.15,12; http://www.bbc.com/news/magazine-19592372

261 Rick Noack, The Washington Post, leaked document says 2,000 men allegedly assaulted 1,200 German women on New Year's Eve, 07.11.16; https://www.washingtonpost.com/news/worldviews/wp/2016/07/10/leaked-document-says-2000-men-allegedly-assaulted-1200-german-women-on-new-years-eve/

262 Confessions of a Closet Republican, The Ugliest Islamic Face Feil of All-The Burghu, 11.15.13; http://republicaninhearts.blogspot.com/2013/11/the-ugliest-islamic-face-veil-of-all.html

263 Sam Solomon and E. Al Maqdisi, Amazon, Modern Day Trojan Horse: Al-Hijra, the Islamic Doctrine of Immigration, Accepting Freedom or Imposing Islam?

264 Paul Sperry, Breitbart, Khizr Khan Believes the Constitution 'Must Always be Subordinated to the Sharia', 08.02.16; http://www.breitbart.com/national-security/2016/08/02/khizr-khan-constitution-sharia/

265 US immigration legislation online, 1952 Immigration and Nationality Act, a.k.a. the McCarran-Walter Act; http://library.uwb.edu/static/USimmigration/1952_immigration_and_nationality_act.html

Engraved in Stone

266 Sierra Rayne, American Thinker, Polls show high levels of support for sharia law and violence among American Muslims, 06.25.15; *gttp://www.americanthinker.com/blog/2015/06/poll_shows_high_levels_of_support_for_shariah_law_and_violence_among_american_Muslims.html#ixzz4Jye39t2x*

The Female Jihadi

267 D.C. McAllister, Islamism Is The World's War on Women, World Affairs, *The Federalist,* 04.21.16; http://thefederalist.com/2016/04/21/islamism-is-the-worlds-war-on-women/

268 Lewis Loflin, Honor Killings of girls-women in Islam; http://sullivan-county.com/w/cul_death.htm

269 Heidi Mirza and Meetoo V., Gendered surveillance and the social construction young Muslim Women in schools, Chapter 8, 2013; https://www.academia.edu/4309255/Gendered_surveillance_and_the_social_construction_young_Muslim_Women_in_schools

270 Quran, A Woman's Worth, What Makes Islam so Different?, *The Religion of Peace;* https://thereligionofpeace.com/pages/quran/women-worth-less.aspx

271 Sharia Law, *BillionBibles.Org,* 2018; http://www.billionbibles.org/sharia/sharia-law.html

272 Raymond Ibrahim, Muslim Prayers of hate, 11.07.11; http://raymondibrahim.com/2011/11/07/muslim-prayers-of-hate/

273 Media Centre, Female genital mutilation, *World Health Organization,* 01/2018; http://www.who.int/mediacentre/factsheets/fs241/en/

274 Tabitha Korol, Sacrificing the children, *RenewAmerica,* 08.30.17; http://www.renewamerica.com/columns/korol/170830

275 Quran Teachers, *Faith, Freedom International;* http://faithfreedom.org/Articles/quran_teaches.htm

276 Amy Moreno, Breaking: Women's March Organizer Linda Sarsour to Speak at Event with Convicted Terrorist, *Truth Feed,* 02.10.17; http://truthfeed.com/breaking-womens-march-organizer-linda-sarsour-to-speak-at-event-with-convicted-terrorist/51305/

277 Barry Shaw, Linda Sarsour calls American Muslims not to assimilate and for jihad, *Canada Free Press,* 07.08.17; http://canadafreepress.com/article/linda-sarsour-calls-american-muslims-not-to-assimilate-and-for-jihad

278 Arutz Sheva Staff and JTA, Watch: Protest against Sarsour commencement speech, *Arutz Sheva,* 05.26.17; http://www.israelnationalnews.com/News/News.aspx/230230

279 WITW Staff, Ayaan Hirsi Ali says controversial Women's March organizer is a 'fake feminist,' Fighting Words, *Women in the World, 02.02.17;* https://womenintheworld.com/2017/02/02/ayaan-hirsi-ali-says-controversial-womens-march-organizer-is-a-fake-feminist/?refresh

PART TWO: ON ACADEMIA
Jihad at Kent State

280 *The Huntington Post,* Julio Pino, Kent State Professor, Yells 'Death to Israel' During Lecture by Israeli Diplomat, 1/31/11; http://www.huffingtonpost.com/2011/10/31/julio-pino-kent-state-pro_n_1067366.html

Harvard, the Higher Madrassa

281 Judith Anne, *The American Thinker,* the Anti-Semitism of the Presbyterian Church, USA, 4.14.10; http://www.freerepublic.com/focus/f-religion/2492874/posts

282 *Human Events,* Top 10 Reasons George Soros is Dangerous, 04.02.11; http://humanevents.com/2011/04/02/top-10-reasons-george-soros-is-dangerous/

283 Algemeiner Staff, *the Algemeiner,* Report: Anti-Israel Agenda at Harvard Middle East Center, 12.21.11; https://www.algemeiner.com/2011/12/21/report-anti-israel-agenda-at-harvard-middle-east-center/

284 Ibid.

Up on the Decline

285 Lee Kaplan, *FrontPageMag.com,* The Saudi Fifth Column On Our Nation's Campuses, 04.05.04; http://archive.frontpagemag.com/readArticle.aspx?ARTID=13551

286 UK: Muslims, We Will not Assimilate, 01.23.09; Islam in Action; http://islaminaction08.blogspot.com/2009/01/ukMuslims-we-will-not-assimilate.html

287 Now The End Begins, The Muslim Plan for World Dominance; http://nowtheendbegins.com/pages/iran/Muslims_plan_for_world_dominance.htm

288   Uzi Silber, *Haaretz*, The Jew Flu: The Strange Illness of Jewish anti-Semitism, 01.01.09; http://www.haaretz.com/jewish/news/the-jew-flu-the-strange-illness-of-jewish-anti-semitism-1.267172

289   Muslim-on-Muslim inhumane treatment, removed from Internet.

290   Ruth King, *Ruthfully Yours*, Shining a Light on Sharia Creep in Oklahoma, 11.11.10; http://www.ruthfullyyours.com/2010/11/11/shining-a-light-on-sharia-creep-in-oklahoma/

291   *Wikipedia*, Merneptah Stele; https://en.wikipedia.org/wiki/Merneptah_Stele

UP on the Decline

292   *The History Place*, World War II in Europe; http://www.historyplace.com/worldwar2/timeline/boycott.htm

293   *Wikipedia*, Boycotts of Israel; https://en.wikipedia.org/wiki/Boycotts_of_Israel#Arab_League_boycott

294   Raphael Katz, *NGO Monitor*, Durban Conference 2001; http://www.rkatz.com/webdesign/ngomonitor/issues/durban.htm

295   *Wikipedia*, Green Line (Israel); https://en.wikipedia.org/wiki/Green_Line_(Israel)

296   European Parliament Working Group on Antisemitism; http://www.antisem.eu/projects/eumc-working-definition-of-antisemitism/

297   Marcus Dysch and Simon Rocker, *The Jewish Chronicle Online,* Fury as Methodists vote to boycott Israel, 07.01.10; http://www.thejc.com/news/uk-news/33594/fury-methodists-vote-boycott-israel

298   Stephanie Westbrook, *CounterCurrents.Org,* The Italian Movement for Boycott, Divestment and Sanctions against Israel Gains Strength, 02.02.12; http://www.countercurrents.org/westbrook020212.htm

BDS — Agents of Destruction

299   BDS movement, Palestinian Civil Society Call for BDS, 07.09.05; https://bdsmovement.net/call#top

300   Hasan Abu Latifa, *Badil Resource Center;* http://www.badil.org/en/?catid=0&id=105

301   *Clarion Project,* The Third Jihad – Radical Islam's Vision for America, 11.21.12; https://www.youtube.com/watch?v=4XUub1no1qw

302   *Wikipedia,* One-state solution; https://en.wikipedia.org/wiki/One-state_solution

303   *The Huffington Post,* Ahmed Moor; http://www.huffingtonpost.com/author/ahmed-moor

304   *The Lawfare Project;* http://thelawfareproject.org/

305   Helena Cobban, *The Nation;* https://www.thenation.com/authors/helena-cobban/

306   *Daniel Pipes,* The Palestinian Liberation Organization: People, Power and Politics; 03/25/84; http://www.danielpipes.org/16/the-palestinian-liberation-organisation-people-power

307 David Bernstein, *The Washington Post*, Mondoweiss is a hate site, 05.04.15; https://www.washingtonpost.com/news/volokh-conspiracy/wp/2015/05/04/mondoweiss-is-a-hate-site/?utm_term=.5933cd93d9d6

308 *ADL*, Sabeel Ecumenical Liberation Theology Center: An ADL Backgrounder, 04/18/08; http://archive.adl.org/main_interfaith/sabeel_backgrounder.html#.WEMi1FxSKaI

309 *ADL*, Backgrounder: The Council for the national Interest (CNI), 04.30.08; http://archive.adl.org/main_anti_israel/cni.html#.WEMjGFxSKaI

310 *ADL*, Jewish Voice for Peace, 09.27.10; http://www.adl.org/israel-international/anti-israel-activity/c/backgrounder-jewish-voice.html

311 American Jews for a Just Peace, Jewish People Supporting BDS, 08.03.11; https://craignielsen.wordpress.com/tag/american-jews-for-a-just-peace/

312 Abraham Greenhouse, *The Electronic Intifada*, Activism and BDS Beat, 01.04.12; https://electronicintifada.net/blogs/abraham-greenhouse/its-never-too-late-boycott-israel-proper-disposal-already-purchased-goods

313 Kate Evans-Taylor, *Hagmann's Northeast Intelligence Network*, A covert look at Dalit Baum New Israel Fund, 04.01.10; http://www.homelandsecurityus.com/archives/3660

314 Ilan Pappe, *The Middle East Quarterly*, The Ethnic Cleansing of Palestine, 2006; http://www.meforum.org/1886/the-ethnic-cleansing-of-palestine

BDS — A Case of Myth-Taken Identity

315 *Midnight Watcher's Blogspot*, Education in America: Textbooks are Being Systematically Rewritten to Include Lies, Half-Truths, and Misleading Narratives to Promote Islamist Agenda, 04.23.12; https://midnightwatcher.wordpress.com/2012/04/23/education-in-america-textbooks-are-being-systematically-rewritten-to-include-lies-half-truths-and-misleading-narratives-to-promote-islamist-agenda/

316 Bat Ye'or, *The Middle East Quarterly*, Delegitimizing the Jewish State, Winter 2011; http://www.meforum.org/2813/delegitimizing-the-jewish-state

317 *WikiIslam*, Worship Places Converted or Destroyed by Muslims; http://wikiislam.net/wiki/Worship_Places_Converted_or_Destroyed_by_Muslims

318 *Wikipedia*, Persecution of Zoroastrians; https://en.wikipedia.org/wiki/Persecution_of_Zoroastrians

319 Murad Makhmudov and Lee jay Walker, *Modern Tokyo Times*, Islamic Terrorism and Religious Persecution, Afghanistan: a nation where converts to Buddhism and Christianity face death, 11.18.11; https://islamicpersecution.wordpress.com/category/persecution-of-buddhists/

320 Anwar Shaikh, *Hindu Writers Forum*, Why did the Muslims destroy Hindu temples, Nov., 2001; https://www.scribd.com/doc/16988267/Why-Muslims-Destroy-Hindu-Temples

321 Raymond Ibrahim, *Front Page Mag*, Why Egypt's Muslims Resent Coptic Christians, 10.11.16; http://www.frontpagemag.com/fpm/64435/why-egypts-Muslims-resent-coptic-christians-raymond-ibrahim

322 *The Religion of Peace*, Islamic Terror on Christians, List of Islamic Terror Attacks; http://www.thereligionofpeace.com/attacks/christian-attacks.aspx

323 Ibrahim N. Omer, *Ancient Sudan-Kush,* Investigating the Origin of the Ancient Jewish Community at Elephantine: A Review; http://www.ancientsudan.org/articles_jewish_elephantine.html

324 *United with Israel,* The Jewish Connection to Israel Throughout History; https://unitedwithisrael.org/the-jewish-connection-to-israel-throughout-history/

325 *Jewish Virtual Library,* Judaism: The Written Law – Torah; http://www.jewishvirtuallibrary.org/jsource/Judaism/The_Written_Law.html

326 *The Life and Teachings of Jesus,* VI Ordination of the Twelve; http://www.lifeandteachingsofjesus.org/son-man/22-the-sermon-on-the-mount/

327 Judea and Samaria; http://www.palestinefacts.org/pf_early_palestine_judea_samaria.php

328 *In the name of Allah.org,* Ilya/Jerusalem; http://www.inthenameofallah.org/Ilya%20Or%20Jerusalem.html

329 The Temple Mount in Jerusalem, History of Jerusalem and the Temple mount; http://www.templemount.org/

330 *Jewish Virtual Library,* Israel: Origins of the Name "Palestine"; http://www.jewishvirtuallibrary.org/jsource/History/palname.html

331 *Myths, Hypotheses and Facts;* The True Identity of the So-called Palestinians; http://www.imninalu.net/myths-pals.htm

332 *Bible History Online,* The Israel Stela (Merneptah Stele); http://www.bible-history.com/archaeology/egypt/2-israel-stela-bb.html

333 Shaykh Prof. Abdul Hadi Palazzi, *The Kur'an and the Land of Israel,* What the Qur'an Really Says; http://www.templemount.org/quranland.htm

334 *Australia/Israel & Jewish Affairs Council,* Temple Denial, 09.02.11; http://www.aijac.org.au/news/article/temple-denial

335 Point of No Return: Jewish Refugees from Arab Countries, Ezekiel's shrine has suffered 'irreversible damage,' 01/23/10; http://jewishrefugees.blogspot.com/2010/01/ezekiels-shrine-has-suffered.html

336 Jonathan Mark, *The Jewish Week,* Media Watch: Rachel's Tomb is now a Mosque – Who Cares?, 11.22.10; http://www.thejewishweek.com/news/new_york/media_watch_rachels_tomb_now_mosque_who_cares

337 Jonathan S. Tobin, *Commentary,* Murder at Tomb Illustrates the Future of Jewish Holy Sites in a Palestinian State, 04.24.11; https://www.commentarymagazine.com/culture-civilization/religion/judaism/murder-at-tomb-illustrates-the-future-of-jewish-holy-sites-in-a-palestinian-state/

338 *CenturyOneBookstore,* Dead Sea Scrolls; http://www.centuryone.com/25dssfacts.html

339 Ellen Levy-Coffman, A Mosaic of People: The Jewish Story and a Reassessment of the DNA Evidence, 02.25.05; http://www.jogg.info/pages/11/coffman.htm

Textbook Taqiyyah

340 *ACT! for America*, Education or Indoctrination; http://www.act5280.org/PDF/Textbook_ Analysis_Summary.pdf

341 Perry Chiaramonte, *Fox News U.S.*, Tampa parents rip school for letting controversial Muslim group to students, 02.15.12; http://www.foxnews.com/us/2012/02/15/uproar-among-parents-after-cair-visits-to-public-schools.html

342 David Gavron, *Jewish Virtual Library*, History of Jerusalem: Myth and Reality of King David's Jerusalem; http://www.jewishvirtuallibrary.org/jsource/History/davidjer.html

343 *The Religion of Peace*, Myths of Islam: Islam is a Religion of peace; http://www.thereligionofpeace.com/pages/myths/peace.aspx

344 *The Religion of Peace*, Myths of Islam: Jihad Means 'Inner Struggle'; http://www.thereligionofpeace.com/pages/myths/jihad.aspx

345 Islam and Europe Timeline (355-1291 AD), The Latin Library; http://www.thelatinlibrary.com/imperialism/notes/islamchron.html

346 Ishaan Tharoor, *TIME*, Timbuktu's Destruction: Why Islamists are Wrecking Mali's Cultural Heritage, 07.02.12; http://world.time.com/2012/07/02/timbuktus-destruction-why-islamists-are-wrecking-malis-cultural-heritage/

347 Mark Evi-El, *Jerusalem Center for Public Affairs*, The Destruction of the Temple Mount Antiquities, 08.01.02; *http://jcpa.org/jl/vp483.htm*

348 What Does Islam Teach About A Woman's Worth, Quran (4:11), (2:282), (2:228), 5;6), 24:31), (4:3), (53:27), (4:24), (33:50), the Religion of Peace; https://www.thereligionofpeace.com/pages/quran/women-worth-less.aspx

349 *The Religion of Peace*, Myths of Islam: Islam Respects Women as Equals: http://www.thereligionofpeace.com/pages/myths/women.aspx

350 Robert Spencer, *Jihad Watch*, The Islamic slave trade, 10.2-.09; https://www.jihadwatch.org/2009/10/the-islamic-arab-slave-trade

351 *Wikipedia*, British Mandate for Palestine (legal instrument); *https://en.wikipedia.org/wiki/British_Mandate_for_* Palestine_(legal_instrument)

352 Sabrina Ford, *New York Post*, Arabic mandatory at city public school, 05.24.12; http://nypost.com/2012/05/24/arabic-mandatory-at-city-public-school/

353 Larissa Scott, *American Thinker*, Stealth Islamic Propaganda Shown to Six Million American Students, 25.12; *http://www.americanthinker.com/articles/2012/05/stealth_ islamic_propaganda_shown_to_six_million_american_* students.html

354 *Florida Family Association*, Channel One network broadcasts version of All American Muslim...; http://floridafamily.org/full_article.php?article_no=157

355 *CBSN 60 Minutes*, US Charter Schools Ties to Powerful Turkish Imam, 05.13.12; http://www.cbsnews.com/news/us-charter-schools-tied-to-powerful-turkish-imam/

356 Aaron Klein, *WND*, Christmas surprise: Jesus declared a Palestinian, 12.29.14; https://en.wikipedia.org/wiki/British_Mandate_for_Palestine_(legal_instrument)

Broken College, Office of Submissions

357 Alan Dershowitz, *Daily News*, Brooklyn College's anti-Israel hatefest, 1.30.13; http://www.nydailynews.com/opinion/brooklyn-college-anti-israel-hatefest-article-1.1250553

358 *Brooklyn College*, Mission Statement; http://brooklyn.cuny.edu/web/academics/centers/italian/mission.php

359 *Citizen Warrior*, What Non-Muslims can do about Islam; http://www.citizenwarrior.com/2008/09/what-can-civilian-really-do.html

360 Josh Keller, *The Chronicle of Higher Education*, California Jury Convicts 10 Muslim Students of Interrupting Campus Speech, 09.23.11; http://www.chronicle.com/article/California-Jury-Convicts-10/129159/

361 Erick Stakelbeck, *CBN News*, Inside the Muslim Brotherhood in the West, 08.08.12; http://www.cbn.com/cbnnews/world/2012/august/inside-the-Muslim-brotherhood-in-the-west/?mobile=false

362 Michael S. James and Lara Setrakian, *ABC News*, 'Ground Zero Mosque' Imam says Project must go forward in the Internet of National Security, 09.09.2010; http://abcnews.go.com/US/ground-mosque-imam-project-ahead-interest-national-security/story?id=11589316

363 *Stand With Us*, The BDS Movement; https://www.swuconnect.com/insys/npoflow.v.2/_assets/pdfs/fact_sheets/BDS%20factsheet.pdf

364 *Wikipedia*, Boycott, Divestment and Sanctions; https://en.wikipedia.org/wiki/Boy

Oberlin's Onus

365 Rebecca Gould, *The Montreal Review*, From Hijrah to Khilafah, May 2015; http://www.themontrealreview.com/2009/Hijra-before-ISIS.php

366 Pierre Tristam, *About news*, What is the PLO – The Palestine Liberation Organization? *http://middle* east.about .com/od/israelandpalestine/f/me080519a.htm

367 Ron Gluckman/Dubai,UAE, Death in Dubai; http://www.gluckman.com/camelracing.html

368 Rush Limbaugh, Egypt's Muslim Brotherhood passes law allowing husbands to have sex with dead wives up to six hours after death, *The Rush Limbaugh Show*, 04.27.12; https://www.rushlimbaugh.com/daily/2012/04/27/egypt_s_Muslim_brotherhood_passes_law_allowing_husbands_to_have_sex_with_dead_wives_up_to_six_hours_after_death/

369 Wikipedia, *Untermensch*; https://en.wikipedia.org/wiki/Untermensch

Cary's Canard

370 Editors, *Encyclopaedia Britannica*, Philistine, 11.20.15; https://www.britannica.com/topic/Philistine-people

371 *Wikipedia*, Genetic genealogy; https://en.wikipedia.org/wiki/Genetic_genealogy

372 *Japan Air Raids.org.*; http://www.japanairraids.org/

373   *Wikipedia*, Promised Land; https://en.wikipedia.org/wiki/Promised_Land

ASA: Academics Surrender to Allah

374   JNS.org, *the Algemeiner*, Israeli Universities Rank Among World's Top 100, 03.22.16; https://www.algemeiner.com/2016/03/22/israeli-universities-rank-among-worlds-top-100/

375   Michael Eisenstadt and David Pollock, *The Washington Institute*, Friends with Benefits: Why the US-Israeli Alliance is Good for America, 11-07-12; http://www.washingtoninstitute.org/policy-analysis/view/friends-with-benefits-why-the-u.s.-israeli-alliance-is-good-for-america

376   *Bnai Zion Foundation*, http://www.bnaizion.org/mission.php

377   Dr. David Stone, *University of Glasgow*, fathom journal.org; http://fathomjournal.org/wp-content/uploads/2014/12/Has-Israel-damaged-Palestinian-health.pdf

378   *Wikipedia*, Arab citizens of Israel; https://en.wikipedia.org/wiki/Arab_citizens_of_Israel

379   Human Trafficking & Modern-day Slavery; http://www.gvnet.com/humantrafficking/UnitedArabEmirates.htm

380   *Jewish Virtual Library*, Ancient Jewish History: Jews of the Middle East and North Africa; http://www.jewishvirtuallibrary.org/jsource/Judaism/mejews.html

381   Glynis Cousin and Robert Fine, *Core*, A common cause: reconnecting the study of racism and antisemitism.

382   A List of the 613 Mitzvot, *Judaism 101;* http://www.jewfaq.org/613.htm

383   *Wikipedia*, Hindy-Arabic Numeral System; *https://en.wikipedia.org/wiki*Hindu%E2%80%93Arabic_numeral_ system

Communizing Common Core

384   Lynette Khalfani-Cox, What is the American Recovery and Reinvestment Act?, 01-13-12; *http://askthemoney* coach.com/2012/01/american-recovery-reinvestment-act/

385   Dr. Sandra Stotsky, *Pioneer Institute*, 04-09-13; http://pioneerinstitute.org/videos/sandra-stotsky-discusses-common-core/

386   Dr. Susan Berry, *Breitbart*, Common Core Blockbuster: Mathematician Dr. Jim Milgram warns...   09-01-14;   http://www.breitbart.com/big-government/2014/09/01/common-core-blockbuster-mathematician-dr-jim-milgram-warns-common-core-will-destroy-america-s-standing-in-technology/

387   *zoominfo*, Dr. Jonathan Goodman, Courant Institute of Mathematical Sciences; http://www.zoominfo.com/p/Jonathan-Goodman/1726334

ASA, Anti-Semitic Association

388   *Wikipedia*, List of Israeli inventions and discoveries; *https://en.wikipedia.org/wiki/List_of_Israeli_inventions_* and_discoveries

389   Raymond Ibrihim, *The Christian Post*, 12.08.14; http://www.christianpost.com/news/

islam-built-on-the-blood-of-christian-martyrs-130877/

390 Rev. Father Raphael Moore, In Memory of the 50 million Victims of the Orthodox Christian Holocaust, 10.99; http://www.serfes.org/orthodox/memoryof.htm

391 Koenraad Elst, Negationism in India, *Amazon;* https://www.amazon.com/Negationism-India-Concealing-Record-Islam/dp/8185990956/ref=sr_1_1?s=books&ie=UTF8&qid=1 415843766&sr=1-1&keywords= Negationism+in+India

392 Shrinandan Vyas, Hindu Kush means Hindu Slaughter; http://www.hindunet.org/hindu_history/modern/hindu_kush.html

393 Transculutral Buddhism, Islam will Dominate – the Islamic Threat to Buddhism, 12.31.09; http://seanrobsville.blogspot.com/2009/12/what-buddhists-and-pagans-need-to-know.html

394 *Bill Warner,* Why We Are Afraid, a 1400 Year Secret, 09.31.12; *https://www.youtube.com/watch?v=t_Qpy0mXg* 8Y

395 *Ben Shapiro:* The Myth of the Tiny Radical Muslim Minority, 10.15.14; https://www.youtube.com/watch?v=g7TAAw3oQvg

396 *Jewish Virtual Library,* Munich Olympic Massacre: Background & Overview, 09.05.72; *http://www.jewish* virtuallibrary.org/jsource/Terrorism/munich.html

397 Yair Altman, *ynet,* Itamar massacre; Fogel family butchered while sleeping;, 03.13.27; http://www.ynetnews.com/articles/0,7340,L-4041237,00.html

398 Moshe Phillips and Benyamin Korn, *the Algemeiner,* Conclusive proof that Hamas uses Palestinians as Human Shields, 08.07.14; http://www.algemeiner.com/2014/08/07/conclusive-proof-that-hamas-uses-palestinians-as-human-shields/

399 Moshe Phillips and Benyamin Korn, *the Algemeiner,* Surprise! Peaceful Palestinian Leaders Tolerate Terror Buildup, 06.26.14; http://www.algemeiner.com/2014/06/26/surprise-peaceful-palestinian-leaders-support-terrorism/

400 oav Zitun, VIDEO: Terrorists fire rockets from Gaza hospital, *Ynetews.com,* 07.23.14; http://www.ynetnews.com/articles/0,7340,L-4548760,00.html

Purging Israel for Profit

401 Diana Muir Appelbaum, *Academia, Inc.,* Islamic Supersessionism in the Ottoman and Turkish States; http://www.academia.edu/3887509/Islamic_Supersessionism_in_the_Ottoman_and_Turkish_States

402 Ari Soffer, *Arutz Sheva,* Abbas's Fatah Celebrates 50 Years – with 'Jewish Skulls' 02.02.15, http://www.israelnationalnews.com/News/News.aspx/189387

403 Nonie Darwish, *Amazon,* Cruel and Usual Punishment; https://www.amazon.com/Cruel-Usual-Punishment-Nonie-Darwish/dp/159555209X

404 1001 Inventions; http://www.1001inventions.com/

405 *Zionism and the State of Israel,* Mark Twain and the Holy Land; https://zionismandisrael.wordpress.com/2008/08/28/mark-twain-in-the-holy-land/

406   Tamara Christine Van Hooser, *eHow,* How Did the Bible Influence the US Constitution?; http://www.ehow.com/info_11384841_did-bible-influence-us-constitution.html

407   A. Ahmed, *Daniel Pipes Middle East Forum,* To Asim; Muslims killed 80 million Hindus in 500 years, 12.15.05; http://www.danielpipes.org/comments/30022

408   Eternal Source, Islam has massacred over 669+ million non-Muslims since 622AD, Israel, Islam & Endtimes, 03.08.16; *IsraeliIslamandendtimes.com,* 03.08.16.

Veiled Pursuit

409   Amazon, *Cruel and Unusual Punishment;* https://www.amazon.com/Cruel-Usual-Punishment-Nonie-Darwish/dp/159555209X

410   Adriana Stuut, *Digital Journal,* Women could endanger their health by wearing burqas, 05.08.09; http://www.digitaljournal.com/article/272307

411   Art Moore, WND, *Should Muslim Quran be USA's Top Authority?,* 05.10.03; http://www.wnd.com/2003/05/18561/

412   Ryan Mauro, *The Clarion Project,* Council on American Islamic Relations (CAIR) — Nat'l Headquarters—1/17/13; http://www.clarionproject.org/analysis/council-islamic-relations-cair

The Moderate Vanguard

413   Nick Dorman, *Mirror,* Islamic State fanatics kidnap more than 3,000 women and girls in 2-week rampage, 08.16.14; http://www.mirror.co.uk/news/world-news/islamic-state-fanatics-kidnap-more-4062810

414   Avi Asher-Schapiro, *National Geographic News,* Who are the Yazidis, the Ancient, Persecuted Religious Minority Struggling to Survive in Iraq, 08.11.14; http://news.nationalgeographic.com/news/2014/08/140809-iraq-yazidis-minority-isil-religion-history/

415   Shoebat Foundation, *Shoebat.com,* ISIS is Now Selling Thousands of Underaged Sex Slaves in The Nude, 12/22/14; http://shoebat.com/2014/12/22/isis-now-selling-thousands-underaged-sex-slaves-nude-watch-rare-video-sex-slavery-market/

416   *Forty eight hours,* Tragedy in Beslan, 09.01.04; http://www.cbsnews.com/pictures/tragedy-in-beslan-2/

417   Daniel Greenfield, *Frontpage Mag,* 1 in 4 Swedish Women Will Be Raped as Sexual Assaults Increase 500%, 01/29/13; http://www.frontpagemag.com/point/175434/1-4-swedish-women-will-be-raped-sexual-assaults-daniel-greenfield

418   Ben Shapiro, *YouTube,* The Myth of the Tiny Radical Muslim Minority, 10.15.14; *https://www.youtube.com/watch?v=g7TAAw3oQvg*

419   Robert Spencer, *Jihad Watch,* Sharia Courts in … Texas!, 02.08.08; https://www.jihadwatch.org/2008/02/sharia-courts-intexas

420   Bare Naked Islam, *Massachusetts: Parents in Revere outraged that students are being taught about Islam in publish schools,* 10.23.14; http://www.barenakedislam.com/2014/10/23/massachusetts-parents-in-revere-outraged-that-students-are-being-taught-about-islam-in-public-schools/

421 Megyn Kelly, *Clarion Project.org*, Florida Parents confront school board over Islam bias in textbook; http://www.clarionproject.org/videos/florida-parents-confront-school-board-over-islam-bias-texbook

422 Jason Howerton, *the blaze*, Dad saw text on Son's phone reminding him to complete Islam assignment, 02.10.15; http://www.clarionproject.org/videos/florida-parents-confront-school-board-over-islam-bias-textbook

423 Quora, *Why do Muslims slaughter the animal in a ruthless manner by torturing it and slowly and painfully killing it?;* https://www.quora.com/Why-do-Muslims-slaughter-the-animal-in-a-ruthless-manner-by-torturing-it-and-slowly-and-painfully-killing-it

Dawa at Chautauqua

424 The US Economy is in BIG Trouble, *Rense.com;* http://rense.com/general27/useco.htm

425 CMS news, *CMS.gov, Centers for Medicate & Medicade Services;* https://www.cms.gov/

426 Tracy Connor and Jim Miklaszewski, Pentagon Set to Slash Military to Pre-World War II Levels, *NBC News;* 02.24.14; http://www.nbcnews.com/storyline/military-spending-cuts/pentagon-set-slash-military-pre-world-war-ii-levels-n37086

427 Tabitha Korol, Mosquitoes in the Mosques, *Canada Free Press*, 07.29.15; http://canadafreepress.com/article/mosquitoes-in-the-mosques

428 Chuck Goudie, ISIS Present in All 50 States, FBI Director Says, *ABC Eyewitness News*, 02.25.15; http://abc7chicago.com/news/isis-present-in-all-50-states-fbi-director-says/534732/

429 Robert Spencer, *Jihad Watch*, Duke tabs Omid Safi, dishonest supporter of jihad against Israel, to head Islamic Studies Center, 09.03.14; https://www.jihadwatch.org/2014/09/duke-tabs-dishonest-supporter-of-jihad-against-israel-to-head-islamic-studies-center

430 Frimet and Arnold Roth, *The Jewish Press*, Lumping Deir Yassin and the Holocaust Together, 04.14.13; http://www.jewishpress.com/blogs/this-ongoing-war/lumping-deir-yassin-and-the-holocaust-together/2013/04/15/

Precarity

431 Clarence H. Wagner, Jr., Significant Facts about Israel's History, *Focus on Jerusalem*, February, 2005; http://www.focusonjerusalem.com/significantfacts.htm

432 Susan Brinkmann OCDS, Study: 81% of *American Mosques Promote Violence, Women of Grace*, 06.14.11; http://www.womenofgrace.com/blog/?p=8333

433 Michael C Duke, Jerusalem: Our redeemable right: Jews hold legal sovereignty over Israel's entire capital city, *Think-Israel;* http://www.think-israel.org/duke.gauthierjerusalem.html

434 Jerusalem 3000 years after David (part 1), https://www.youtube.com/watch?v=bnRXU_tTVFM

435 Jewish Defense League UK, Get it right, It's ISRAEL, not Palestine," 03.17.12; http://www.jdl-uk.org/2012/03/get-it-right-its-israel-not-palestine.html

436 Uriel Heilman, *B'nai B'rith Magazine*, Winter 2011; http://urielheilman.com/010-israels-first-responders.html

437 Michael Eisenstadt and David Pollock, *The Washington Institute*, Friends with Benefits: Why the US-Israeli Alliance is Good for America, 11.07.12; http://www.washingtoninstitute.org/policy-analysis/view/friends-with-benefits-why-the-u.s.-israeli-alliance-is-good-for-america

438 *British-Israel Chamber of Commerce North West;* http://biccnw.org.uk/

439 Yoram Ettinger, *The Ettinger Report,* Israel – a global leader in bio-tech and defense products; 06.14.13; http://www.theettingerreport.com/Overseas-Investments/Israel-%E2%80%93-a-global-leader-in-bio-tech-and-defense-p.aspx

440 Karin Kloosterman, *Israel 21c,* Israelis imagine a better future for Sudan's girls, 03.13.12; http://www.israel21c.org/israelis-imagine-a-better-future-for-sudans-girls/

441 Islam in Somalia: Warning! Hands and feet cut off for petty theft, 02.24.11; https://www.youtube.com/watch?v=SdwEMknYr7s

The Art of War

442 Stephen Spykerman, *Britam.org,* The Oldest Title Deed in the World; *http://www.britam.org/PROMISEDLAND.html*

443 James Arlandson, The Truth about Islamic Crusades and Imperialism, *American Thinker,* 11.27.05; http://www.americanthinker.com/articles/2005/11/the_truth_about_islamic_crusad.html

444 FoxNews, Afghanistan Officials Promise Investigation After Video Surfaces of Stoning Deaths, *Fox News* stoning-death.html

445 Laura Smith-Spark and Michael Martinez, Who was Jordanian pilot Moath al-Kasasbeh, killed by ISIS?, CNN, 02.03.15; http://www.cnn.com/2015/01/29/middleeast/who-is-jordan-pilot-isis-hostage/index.html

446 Ted, Muslims Behead Man in Cold Blood, *Shoebat.com,* 10.21.13; http://shoebat.com/2013/10/21/Muslims-behead-man-cold-blood/

447 Bare Naked Islam, Muslim children being trained in the art of beheading, 10.01.14; http://www.barenakedislam.com/2014/10/01/Muslim-children-being-trained-in-the-art-of-beheading-warning-graphic/

448 Daniel Greenfield, Muslim Rape Culture, *Frontpage mag, 02.02.14;* http://www.frontpagemag.com/fpm/217818/Muslim-rape-culture-daniel-greenfield

449 Rebecca Perring, Shocking moment Muslim woman is publicly executed by al-Qaeda supporters for 'adultery,' 01.17.15; http://www.express.co.uk/news/world/552423/al-Qaeda-Muslim-woman-executed-shot-head-Syria

450 Wikipedia, Samir Kuntar; https://en.wikipedia.org/wiki/Samir_Kuntar

451 *The New England Journal of Medicine,* 03/18/10

452 WaterSheer, *Start-up Nation Central;* http://finder.startupnationcentral.org/c/watersheer

453 ReWalk, http://rewalk.com/

454 Company Overview of TAHAL Group International BV, *Bloomberg*, *http://www. bloomberg.com/research/stocks/private/snapshot.asp?privcapid=99723216*

455 Lifestraw; lifestraw.com

Morality at Missouri U

456 Michael B. Thomas, Report gives new details on U. of Missouri swastika story, *CBSnews*, 11.12.15; http://www.cbsnews.com/news/university-of-missouri-swastika-campus-police-report/

Changing Minds

457 Jew Hatred on Campus Awareness Week, *The 10 Campuses With The Worst Anti-Semitic Activity*, 02.21.15; http://archive.jewhatredoncampus.org/news/10-campuses-worst-anti-semitic-activity

458 Joy Resmovits, Bill Gates Comes to the Defense of the Common Core, 03.14.14; http://www.huffingtonpost.com/2014/03/14/bill-gates-common-core_n_4964026.html

459 Think common Core Standards were a State Initiative?, Utah's Republic, 03.01.12; http://www.utahsrepublic.org/common-core/

460 Beckwith, Bill Ayers and Bernadine Dohrn, *The Obama File*; http://www.theobamafile.com/_associates/BillAyers.htm

461 Pat Gray, The Blaze, Arne Duncan: *You're a Liar, Common Core Will Destroy American Education*, 02.26.14; http://www.theblaze.com/contributions/arne-duncan-youre-a-liar-common-core-will-destroy-american-education/

462 Pamela Engel, *This May be The Biggest Problem with America's 'Common Core' Education Standards, Business Insider*, 07-04-14; http://www.businessinsider.com/heres-the-biggest-problem-with-common-core-2014-7

463 *YouTube*, Suffolk Forum – Mary Calamia, LCSW, 20.28.13; https://www.youtube.com/watch?v=oCaXTNcNJRI

464 Melissas Dykes, 4th Grade Common Core Math Problem Takes 108 Steps to Complete, *Truth Stream Media.com*, 12.18.13; http://truthstreammedia.com/2013/12/18/4th-grade-common-core-math-problem-takes-108-steps-to-complete/

465 *Wikipedia*, A People's History of the United States; https://en.wikipedia.org/wiki/A_People%27s_History_of_the_United_States#Overview

466 Ibid.

467 History Alive! The Ancient World, Middle School Social Studies; https://www.teachtci.com/social-studies/middle-school-social-studies/

468 Ibid.

469 Lt. Col. James G. Zumwalt, USMC (Ret), US Colleges: Middle East Money Speaks to Silence Socrates, *Family Security Matters*, 02.14.16; http://www.familysecuritymatters.org/publications/detail/us-colleges-middle-east-money-speaks-to-silence-socrates?f=must_reads

470 What Does Islam Teach About ... Homosexuality, What makes Islam so Different?; http://www.thereligionofpeace.com/pages/quran/homosexuality.aspx

471 Simon Cottee, Boys of Pleasure: Sexual abuse of children betrays Isis hypocrisy, 01.14.2015; http://www.ibtimes.co.uk/boys-pleasure-sexual-abuse-children-betrays-isis-hypocrisy-1483322

472 Onan Coca, Mufti of Gaza Hassan Al-Laham, Eagle Rising; http://eaglerising.com/30664/Muslim-religious-leader-hit-your-wife-just-dont-make-her-ugly/

473 Hibo Wardere, Cut: One Woman's Fight Against FGM in Britain Today, Amazon; https://www.amazon.com/Cut-Womans-Fight-Against-Britain-ebook/dp/B010MH19UU/ref=sr_1_5?s=books&ie=UTF8&qid=1456326823&sr=1-5&keywords=FGM

474 Fox News, Muslim Students in Britain Reportedly Taught to Chop off Hands of Thieves, Hate Jews, 02.09.11; http://www.foxnews.com/world/2011/02/09/Muslim-students-taught-chop-hands-thieves.html

475 Rachel Stephens, Video: ISIS beheads 15-year-old boy for listening to pop music, 02.20.16; http://www.africanseer.com/news/468455-video-isis-beheads-15-year-old-boy-for-listening-to-pop-music.html

476 Ann Corcoran, Refugee Resettlement, *YouTube,* 04.20.15; https://www.youtube.com/watch?v=6PzT8vEvYPg

477 *Kent State University,* Safe Spaces, http://www.kent.edu/cas/safespaces

478 Beth Davies-Stofka, Sacred Space, *Religion Library: Islam;* http://www.patheos.com/Library/Islam/Ritual-Worship-Devotion-Symbolism/Sacred-Space

479 Chedoh, Berkeley: white students to purchase free-speech insurance, *The People's Cube,* 01.30.16; http://thepeoplescube.com/peoples-blog/uc-berkeley-white-students-must-purchas-free-speech-insurance-t17497.html#!

Mobocracy in Academia

480 Marshall Frank, *Militant Islam in America (Brutally Frank),* Amazon, 06.25.06; https://www.amazon.com/Militant-Islam-America-Brutally-Frank/dp/097187090X

481 *Missions & Values,* Connecticut College; http://www.conncoll.edu/at-a-glance/mission--values/

482 Wikipedia, *Code of Silence,* https://en.wikipedia.org/wiki/Code_of_silence

483 Institutional Equity and Inclusion, Connecticut College; http://www.conncoll.edu/equity-inclusion/

484 Sam Sewell, How to Create a Crisis and Steal a Nation, *Investigating Obama,* 02.24.09; http://investigatingobama.blogspot.com/2009/02/how-to-create-crisis-and-steal-nation.html

485 Lama Dakker, Why Hate Speech is Not Free Speech in an "Inclusive Excellence" Community, College Voice, 03.03.15; http://thecollegevoice.org/2015/03/03/why-hate-speech-is-not-free-speech-in-an-inclusive-excellence-community/comment-page-1/#comment-301764

486 Noah Beck, More Anti-Israel Hate at Connecticut College, *Frontpage Mag, 03.10.16;* http://thecollegevoice.org/2015/03/03/why-hate-speech-is-not-free-speech-in-an-inclusive-excellence-community/comment-page-1/#comment-301764

487 Taglit-Birthright Israel, Summer 2017; http://taglitww.birthrightisrael.com/letsgo/Documents/global.html

488 Brief information on Organization of Islamic Cooperation (OIC) and the OIC Ministerial Conference on the Role of Women in Development; http://kemlu.go.id/Documents/OIC%20Meneg%20PP/Informasi%20Singkat%20OKI%20dan%20KTM%20Perempuan%20ENGLISH.pdf

489 Justus Reid Weiner, The Threat to Freedom of Speech about Israel: Campus Shout-downs and the Spirit of the First Amendment, *Jerusalem Center for public Affairs,* 12.30.13; http://jcpa.org/article/the-threat-to-freedom-of-speech-about-israel/

490 Remi Kanazi, Wikipedia; https://en.wikipedia.org/wiki/Remi_Kanazi

491 Jasbir Puar, Wikipedia; https://en.wikipedia.org/wiki/Jasbir_Puar

492 John Bacon and Aamer Madhani, University of Missouri names black interim president, *USA Today,* 11.12.15; http://www.usatoday.com/story/news/nation/2015/11/12/controversial-u-missouri-professor-may-keep-job/75642556/

Joy of Witlessness

493 Dennis Prager, Ethical Monotheism, *Jewish Virtual Library,* 04.25.85; http://www.jewishvirtuallibrary.org/ethical-monotheism

494 See related videos/original was removed from site, Arab Muslims Slave Trade of Africans, YouTube; http://www.bing.com/videosearch?q=Muslims+began+black+slave+trade&&view=detail&mid=36DF27AIDB9E8A9AA3D36DF27A1DB9E8DA9AA3D&rvsmid = 4EEF6CC DFA48E604DD2D4EEF6CCDFA48E604DD2D&fsscr =0&FORM=VDFSRV

495 Operation Moses – Aliyah of Ethiopian Jewry (1984); *Ministry of Aliyah and Immigrant Absorption*

496 Palestinian Incitement Exposed, *YouTube Ad Blitz,* 03.21.16; https://www.youtube.com/watch?v=j1leD-D2Dpc&sns=em

497 IsraAid *Wikipedia;* https://en.wikipedia.org/wiki/IsraAid

498 YouTube: https://player.vimeo.com/video/154464174

499 Chapter Two, Offensive War to Spread Islam; http://www.answering-islam.org/BehindVeil/btv2.html

500 AZ Quotes, Hassan al-Banna; http://www.azquotes.com/quote/772017

501 Robert Spencer, Quote of the day: Khomeini spits on those who say Islam is peaceful, *Jihad Watch,* 07.14.10; https://www.jihadwatch.org/2010/07/quote-of-the-day-khomeini-spits-on-those-who-say-islam-is-peaceful

502 Viva Sarah Press, Israel in 'Top 5 Happiest Countries in the World,' *Israel 21c,* 06.09.15; http://www.israel21c.org/israel-in-top-5-happiest-countries-in-the-world/

Of Villainy in Vassar

503 Jewish Voice for Peace, *Wikipedia*; https://en.wikipedia.org/wiki/Jewish_Voice_for_Peace

504 David Israel, Report: Syrian Heart-Eating Rebel Killed, *The Jewish Press;* 04.06.16; http://www.jewishpress.com/news/breaking-news/report-syrian-heart-eating-rebel-killed/2016/04/06/

505 UA 235/10 – Man Sentenced for Homosexuality; http://www2.amnesty.se/uaonnet.nsf/df ab8d7f58eec102c1257011006466e1/617d3970afac5d40c12577d900 3a1369/$FILE/52301310.pdf

506 Islam and Pedophilia, *WikiIslam*; http://wikiislam.net/wiki/Islam_and_Pedophilia

507 Noorhan Abbas & Dr. Eric Atwell, Chapter Name: Al-Ahzab Verse No:50, *The University of Leeds: Qurany Tool*; http://www.comp.leeds.ac.uk/nora/html/33-50.html

508 Islam and Pedophilia, *WikiIslam;* http://wikiislam.net/wiki/Islam_and_Pedophilia

509 Topic Thighing, *CEMB Forum;* http://www.councilofexMuslims.com/index. php?topic=9668.0

510 Hal Herzog PhD., The Problem with Incest, *Psychology Today, 10.11.12; https://www. psychologytoday.com/blog/animals-and-us/201210/the-problem-incest*

511 Mission & Vision, *Open Hillel;* http://www.openhillel.org/about

512 Isabel Kershner, 19 Yemini Jews Arrive in Israel, Ending Secret Rescue Operation, *The New York Times,* 03.21.16; https://www.nytimes.com/2016/03/22/world/middleeast/yemen-jews-israel.html?_r=0

513 Richard Spencer, Saudi Arabia is Building a 600-Mile 'Great Wall' to Shield Itself from ISIS, *Business Insider,* 01.14.15; http://www.businessinsider.com/saudi-arabia-is-building-a-600-mile-great-wall-to-shield-from-isis-2015-1

514 Bill Warner, The Annihilation of Civilizations, *Political Islam,* 08.08.11; https://www. politicalislam.com/the-annihilation-of-civilizations/

515 The Jerusalem Center, Jerusalem: 4000 Years in 5 Minutes, *YouTube,* 05.30.11; https://www.youtube.com/watch?v=2mR2W43t6tI

516 Archaeological Evidence for the Kingdom of David and Solomon, *Mosaic Magazine,* 04.05.16; https://mosaicmagazine.com/picks/2016/04/archaeological-evidence-for-the-kingdom-of-david-and-solomon/

517 Infidels, Islam has massacred over 669+ million non-Muslims since 611AD, *Iranaware,* 03.10.16; http://iranaware.com/2016/03/10/islam-has-massacred-over-669-million-non-Muslims-since-622ad/

518 Adi Schwartz, Head of UNRWA admits it should not exist, *Portfolio,* 11.26.10; http:// www.adi-schwartz.com/israeli-arab-conflict/unrwa-should-not-exist/

519 Yoel Meltzer, The Arab-Israeli conflict: Time to move on, Op-ed, y-net Opinion, 04.06.16; https://www.ynetnews.com/articles/0,7340,L-4786722,00.html

520 Alex Safian, PhD, Why Palestinians Still Live in Refugee Camps, *CAMERA;* http://www. camera.org/index.asp?x_context=18&x_article=960

521 Barbara J Stock, Israel: then and now, *Renewamerica,* 09/.19.12; http://www.renewamerica. com/columns/stock/120919

Offense by Design

522 Origins of the Tignon, *frenchcreoles.com*; http://www.frenchcreoles.com/ArtTheater/ tignon/origins%20of%20tignon.htm

523 *Etsy;* https://www.etsy.com/search?q=tichel+scarf

524 Women 'Veiling' What is the Hijab and Why do Women Wear it?, Arabs in America; http://arabsinamerica.unc.edu/identity/veiling/hijab/

525 James M Arlandson, Top ten reasons by sharia (Islamic law) is bad for all societies; http:// answering-islam.org/Authors/Arlandson/top_ten_sharia.htm

526 Aaron Homer, Wearing a Hijab is 'Passive Terrorism,' says U.S. Military Publication, *Inquisitr,* 02.25.16; http://www.inquisitr.com/2826731/wearing-a-hijab-is-passive-terrorism-says-u-s-military-publication/

527 Muslim Brotherhood Fact Sheet, *StandWithUs;* http://www.standwithus.com/news/ article.asp?id=1757

528 Sheila Musaji, Muslim Brotherhood Document of the Muslim or Islamophobic Lunatic Fringe?, *The American Muslim,* 05.13.15; http://theamericanMuslim.org/tam.php/features/ articles/Muslim_brotherhood_document1

529 FBI: Americans hate Jews more than Muslims, *Rehmat's World,* 11.27.13; https://rehmat1. com/2013/11/27/fbi-americans-hate-jews-more-than-Muslims/

530 Myths of Mohammed, *The Religion of Peace;* http://thereligionofpeace.com/pages/ Mohammed/persecution-medina.aspx

531 Bernie, Muslims Slaughtered 100 million Hindus, *Planck's constant blog,* 04-08-14; http:// plancksconstant.org/blog1/2014/04/Muslims_slaughtered_100_million_hindus.html

532 What makes Islam so different?, *The Religion of Peace;* http://www.thereligionofpeace.com/

Offense by Design, pt. 2

533 Tabitha Korol, Offense by design, *Renewamerica,* 06.20.16; http://www.renewamerica. com/columns/korol/160620

534 The Holocaust, *Wikipedia;* https://en.wikipedia.org/wiki/The_Holocaust

535 David Eaglehawk, How many concentration camps are there?, *Answers;* http://www. answers.com/Q/How_many_concentration_camps_are_there

536 Rauschning, Hitler speaks, pg. 87, Hitler Quotes; http://www.simpletoremember.com/ articles/a/hitler-quotes/

537 Dinesh d'Souza, Hillary's America, About the Film; http://hillarysamericathemovie. com/#synopsis

538   Nicholas Tampio, David Coleman's plan to ruin education, *Aljazeera America,* 12.05.14; http://america.aljazeera.com/opinions/2014/12/common-core-collegeboardeducation.html

539   Creeping Sharia, Why did Hundreds Common Core Implementers Meet in Dubai?, *The Counter Jihad Report,* November 2, 2014; https://counterjihadreport.com/tag/dubai-common-core-conference/

540   The Muslim Brotherhood's Strategic Plan, part 12, *Sharia, the threat to America;* http://shariahthethreat.org/a-short-course-1-what-is-shariah/a-short-course-14-the-Muslim-brotherhood%E2%80%99s-strategic-plan/

541   What makes Islam so different?, *The Religion of Peace;* http://www.thereligionofpeace.com/

542   Jacob Gershman, Obama Administration Sues Pennsylvania Town for Rejecting Mosque Plan, *The Wall Street Journal,* 07.22.16; for-rejecting-mosque-plan/

543   Josh Clark, What was America's first terrorist threat?, *How stuff work; Culture;* http://history.howstuffworks.com/history-vs-myth/first-terrorist-threat2

544   External Source, *Israel, Islam and EndTimes,* 03/08/16; https://www.israelislamandendtimes.com/muslims-massacred-669-million-non-muslims-since-622ad/

545   Muslim Brotherhood Hitler; http://www.billionbibles.org/sharia/hitler-Muslim-brotherhood.html

546   The Mufti and the Fuhrer (November 1941), *Jewish Virtual Library,* http://www.jewishvirtuallibrary.org/the-mufti-and-the-fuhrer

547   What makes Islam so different? Violence, *The Religion of Peace;* http://www.thereligionofpeace.com/pages/quran/violence.aspx

548   *Honor Based Violence Awareness Network;* http://hbv-awareness.com/

549   Brown Shirt, *The Free Dictionary;* http://www.thefreedictionary.com/Brown+Shirt

550   Tammi Rossman Benjamin, The Jewish Exception to Free Speech on Campus, *jns.org, Jewish News Service,* 07.29.16; http://www.jns.org/latest-articles/2016/7/29/the-jewish-exception-to-free-speech-on-campus#.V5vS1mWd7AB=

An Education in Corruption

551   Mark Alexander, The Clinton Crime Syndicate, *The Patriot Post,* 08.24.16; https://patriotpost.us/alexander/44454

552   Patrick Frye, Hillary Clinton is 'Nasty' to Secret Service, Agents Hate Protecting Bill Clinton's Wife, *Inquisitr,* 08.08.14; http://www.inquisitr.com/1400560/hillary-clinton-is-nasty-to-secret-service-agents-hate-protecting-bill-clintons-wife/

553   Lending Tree, Gallup: Barack Obama the Most Divisive President in History, *Conservative Tribune;* http://conservativetribune.com/obama-divisive-president/

554   Peter Suderman, Watch Obamacare Architect Jonathan Gruber Explain Why "Lack of Transparency" was key to Passing the Health Care Law, *reason.com,* 11.10.14; http://reason.com/blog/2014/11/10/watch-obamacare-architect-jonathan-grube

555   Dean Kalahar, The Birth of Common Core, *Education News,* 09/16/14; http://www. educationviews.org/birth-common-core/

A Choice of One

556   CBN.com, What is the Muslim Understanding of "Ummah"?, *CBN-The Christian Broadcasting Network;*   http://www1.cbn.com/onlinediscipleship/what-is-the-muslim-understanding-of-%22ummah%22%3F

557   Agence France-Press, Violence creating 'lost generation' of Middle East men – study, *Inquirer. net,* 08.08.17; http://newsinfo.inquirer.net/921134/violence-creating-lost-generation-of-middle-east-men-study

558   Springer, Mental Illness, suicide and violence creating lost generation in the Middle East, *EurekAlert! The Global Source for Science News,* 08.07.17; https://www.eurekalert.org/pub_releases/2017-08/s-mis080717.php

559   What Makes Islam so different, *The Religion of Peace;* https://www.thereligionofpeace.com/

560   Muslims Establishing No-Go Zones in America, Youtube, *FoxNews* 01/14/15; MEDIA https://www.youtube.com/watch?v=iqAJGXI5I88

Good Morning, Little Comrades

561   Heath Fogg Davis, How we're redefining gender in the 21st century, *CNN,* 08.01.17; *http://www.cnn.com/2017/08/01/opinions/gender-neutral-drivers-license-opinion-davis/index.html*

562   Bob Unruh, California Wants Lesbians as mandatory 'Role' Models, *WND;* 02/11/11; *http://www.wnd.com/2011/02/262485/*

563   Rush Limbaugh, Can We Salvage Public Education?, *Rush Limbaugh Show,* 04.17.09; *https://www.rushlimbaugh.com/daily/2009/04/17/can_we_salvage_public_education/*

564   The Importance of Cursive, CursiveLogic; http://www.cursivelogic.com/why-cursive/

565   Robert Pondiscio, Opinion contributor, Common Core's Surprisingly Deep Roots, *USNews,* 02.26.16;   https://www.usnews.com/opinion/knowledge-bank/articles/2016-02-26/common-core-has-made-higher-standards-and-tougher-tests-the-new-normal

566   Allie Bidwell, The History of Common Core State Standards, *USNews,* 02.27.14; *https://www.usnews.com/news/special-reports/articles/2014/02/27/the-history-of-common-core-state-standards*

567   The Consequences of Fatherlessness, *National Center for Fathering;* http://www.fathers.com/statistics-and-research/the-consequences-of-fatherlessness/

568   Nancy Flory, Schools are Teaching Islam but Banning Christianity: These Jersey Moms Want to find Out Why, *the Stream,* 02/23/17; *https://stream.org/schools-are-teaching-islam-but-banning-christianity-these-moms-want-to-find-out-why/*

569   Bianca Padro Ocasio, Police Group Director: Obama caused a war on cops, *Politico.com,* 07.08.16;https://www.politico.com/story/2016/07/obama-war-on-cops-police-advocacy-group-225291

570   Judith Shulevitz, In College and Hiding from Scary Ideas, *NYT Sunday Review,* 03.21.15; https://www.nytimes.com/2015/03/22/opinion/sunday/judith-shulevitz-hiding-from-scary-ideas.html

571   Robert Heller, Are our Universities creating Socialists, Communists and Fascists?, *Dr. Rich Swier,* 09.19.17; http://drrichswier.com/2017/09/19/are-our-universities-creating-socialists-communists-and-fascists/

572   Best Friends Are Now Banned, News, *MSN* video, 09.20.17; https://www.msn.com/en-us/video/newsvideos/best-friends-are-now-banned/vp-AAsePv8

573   Identifying signs of stress in your children and teens, *American Psychological Association;* http://www.apa.org/helpcenter/stress-children.aspx

PART THREE: THE MEDIA

The Value of One

574   Simon Plosker, The Guardian's Anti-Semitic Explanation for Shalit Deal, HonestReporting, 10.24.11; http://honestreporting.com/the-guardians-anti-semitic-explanation-for-shalit-deal/

575   Al-Hayat Al-Jadida, Mother of 4 terrorists serving 19 life sentences for murder honored by PA, Palestinian Media Watch, 08.26.10; http://palwatch.org/pages/news_archive.aspx?doc_id=3029526; Leonard Doyle, Muslims 'slaughter their own people': Bosnia bread queue massacre was propaganda ploy, UN told, Independent, 08.21.92; http://www.independent.co.uk/news/Muslims-slaughter-their-own-people-bosnia-bread-queue-massacre-was-propaganda-ploy-un-told-1541801.html

576   Osama bin Laden, Why Islamic Terrorists Commit Attacks – in their own words, The Religion of peace, May 98; https://www.thereligionofpeace.com/attacks/in-the-name-of-allah.aspx

Foul Play

577   Israel Size Comparison Maps, http://www.iris.org.il/sizemaps.php

578   How did the Zionists acquire land in Palestine? http://www.palestinefacts.org/pf_early_palestine_zionists_land.php

579   Shira Schoenberg, United Kingdom Virtual Jewish History Tour; http://www.jewishvirtuallibrary.org/united-kingdom-virtual-jewish-history-tour

580   Daily Mail Reporter, The Mecca of the city: In a London street, the faithful find a way to pray as their mosque overflows, DailyMail.com, 02.03.12; http://www.dailymail.co.uk/news/article-2096263/The-Mecca-city-In-London-street-faithful-way-pray-mosque-overflows.html

581   Admin., Muslims March Through London: "USA go to Hell, UK to to Hell," Call for War!...Video!; Logan's Warning, 04.04.11; http://loganswarning.com/2011/04/04/Muslims-march-through-london-usa-go-to-hell-uk-go-to-hell-call-for-war-video/

582   Terrence McCoy, How Hamas uses its tunnels to kill and capture Israeli soldiers, The Washington Post, 05.21.14; https://www.washingtonpost.com/news/morning-mix/wp/2014/07/21/how-hamas-uses-its-tunnels-to-kill-and-capture-israeli-soldiers/?utm_term=.2d3d810c5b53

583 Gil Ronen, Arabs Harass Female 'Peace' Activists; Left Silences Victims. Arutz Sheva, 09.21.10; http://www.israelnationalnews.com/News/News.aspx/139738#.TkASaIKwVgQ

584 Comfort Women, Wikipedia; https://en.wikipedia.org/wiki/Comfort_women

585 Daled Amos, "Humanitarian Activists" Trying to Bury Palestinian Rape of One of Their Own, Haaretz, 07.14.10; http://daledamos.blogspot.com/2010/07/humanitarian-activists-trying-to-bury.html

586 CPTnet, Jerusalem: The case of Rachel Corrie, Christian peacemaker teams, 06.06.14; http://cpt.org/cptnet/2014/06/09/jerusalem-case-rachel-corrie

587 Lee Kaplan, The Divestment Conference at Georgetown, Frontpagemag.com, 03.17.06; http://archive.frontpagemag.com/readArticle.aspx?ARTID=5159

NPR, Notorious for Palestinian Revisionism

588 Sheera Frankel, Attacks Target Palestinians in Israeli Towns, npr, 11.18.11; http://www.npr.org/2011/11/18/142186667/attacks-target-palestinians-in-israeli-towns?textSize=small\

589 Ilan Lior, Tel Aviv to Build Affordable Housing for Jaffa's Arab Residents, Haaretz, 02.28.11; http://www.haaretz.com/tel-aviv-to-build-affordable-housing-for-jaffa-s-arab-residents-1.346102

590 Chris Mitchell and Julie Stahl, Palestinians Trying to 'Wipe Out Jewish History,' CBN News, 11.20.11; http://www.cbn.com/cbnnews/insideisrael/2011/november/palestinians-trying-to-wipe-out-jewish-history/?mobile=false

591 The Hasmonean Dynasty, Jewish Virtual Library; http://www.jewishvirtuallibrary.org/the-hasmonean-dynasty

592 David M Weinberg, Who's Destroying Antiquities in Jerusalem, The Jerusalem Post, 11/17/11; http://www.jpost.com/Opinion/Op-Ed-Contributors/Whos-destroying-antiquities-in-Jerusalem

Restricted Vision

593 Rachel Corrie, Wikipedia, https://en.wikipedia.org/wiki/Rachel_Corrie

594 International Solidarity Movement, Wikipedia, https://en.wikipedia.org/wiki/International_Solidarity_Movement

595 Human shield, Wikipedia; https://en.wikipedia.org/wiki/Human_shield

596 Guerilla warfare, Wikipedia; https://en.wikipedia.org/wiki/Guerrilla_warfare

597 Palestinian political violence, Wikipedia; https://en.wikipedia.org/wiki/Palestinian_political_violence

598 Armored bulldozer, Wikipedia; https://en.wikipedia.org/wiki/Armored_bulldozer

599 Tom Gross, Wikipedia; https://en.wikipedia.org/wiki/Tom_Gross

600 Arabs Harass Female 'Peace' Activists; Left Silences Victims, Gil Ronen, Arutz Sheva, 09.21.10; http://www.israelnationalnews.com/News/News.aspx/139738#.TkASaIKwVgQ

601 Daled Amos, "Humanitarian Activists" Trying to Bury Palestinian Rape of One of their Own, Haaretz; http://daledamos.blogspot.com/2010/07/humanitarian-activists-trying-to-bury.html

A Twist of Hate

602 Title VI of the 1974 Civil Rights Act, The US Department of Justice; https://www.justice.gov/crt/title-vi-1964-civil-rights-act

603 jalisco555, San Francisco Dispatch: West Bank (Bay Area anti-Semitism), NewRepublic, 06.17.02; http://www.freerepublic.com/focus/f-news/701515/posts

604 Michelle Merlin and Michael Tabb, Swastikas etched onto car, tires slashed outside ZBT house, Student Life, 03.19.12; http://www.studlife.com/news/police-beat/2012/03/19/swastikas-etched-onto-car-tires-slashed-outside-zbt-house/

605 Anti-Semiticv/Anti-Israel Events on Campus, Anti-Defamation League, 05.14.02; http://archive.adl.org/campus/campus_incidents.html

606 American Association of University Professors' Anti-Semitism, Mitchell Langbert's Blog, 08.11.11; http://mitchell-langbert.blogspot.com/2011/08/american-association-of-university.html

607 Dhimmi, Wikipedia; https://en.wikipedia.org/wiki/Dhimmi

Hardtalk, Hard to Swallow

608 Sarah Montague, BC Radio 4's: 'Today' joins 'Newsnight' in breach of editorial guidelines, 01/09/14; https://bbcwatch.org/tag/sarah-montague/page/2/

609 US Leaders From Both parties Agree: America Should have Bombed Auschwitz, The Wyman Institute; http://www.wymaninstitute.org/bombedauschwitz.php

610 The Tragedy of S.S. St. Louis (May 13 – June 20, 1939), Jewish Virtual Library; http://www.jewishvirtuallibrary.org/the-tragedy-of-s-s-st-louis

611 President Harry S. Truman and US Support for Israeli Statehood, MidEastWeb for Coexistence, 2001; http://www.mideastweb.org/us_supportforstate.htm

612 Background & Overview (October – November 1956); Jewish Virtual Library; http://www.jewishvirtuallibrary.org/background-and-overview-sinai-suez-campaign

613 Adam Nagourney, In Tapes, Nixon Rails about Jews and Blacks, The New York Times, 12..10.10; http://www.nytimes.com/2010/12/11/us/politics/11nixon.html

614 Clinton Uses Waiver to Avoid Moving US Embassy to Jerusalem, Jewish Virtual Library, http://www.jewishvirtuallibrary.org/Clinton-uses-waiver-to-avoid-moving-u-s-embassy-to-Jerusalem

615 Michael Goodwin, Israel: Beware of Obama, NYPost, 3.22.15; http://nypost.com/2015/03/22/israel-beware-of-obama/

616 Staff Writer, Innovations from Israel, Breaking Israel News, 06.19.13; https://www.breakingisraelnews.com/868/innovations-from-israel/

617   Raymond ibrahim, The Historical Reality of the Muslim Conquests, Catholic Lane, 03.04.12; http://www.freerepublic.com/focus/f-religion/2854410/posts

618   Anjem Choudary calls for the UK to be a caliphate, Search Forums; http://www.sciforums. com/threads/anjem-choudary-calls-for-the-uk-to-be-a-caliphate.101421/

619   Palestinians rocket Sderot, Gush Katif, ICEF/International Christian Embassy Jerusalem; https://int.icej.org/news/headlines/palestinians-rocket-sderot-gush-katif

620   Armistice Lines (1949-`1967), Israel Ministry of Foreign Affairs; http://www.mfa.gov.il/ mfa/aboutisrael/maps/pages/1949-1967%20armistice%20lines.aspx

621   Obama overrides Congress, signs waiver to send $192 million to Palestinian Authority, the right scoop, 04/27/12; http://therightscoop.com/obama-overrides-congress-signs-waiver-to-send-192-million-to-palestinian-authority/

622   Editorial Guidelines, BBC; http://www.bbc.co.uk/editorialguidelines/guidelines/

623   Jordan's Desecration of Jerusalem (a948-1967), Jewish Virtual Library; http://www. jewishvirtuallibrary.org/jordan-s-desecration-of-jerualem-1948-196775

624   Inventing the Palestinian People, YouTube, Memri TV, 09.22.14; https://www.youtube. com/watch?v=aYMviMHH0nc

625   James M. Arlandson, The Ultimate Goal of Islam, http://www.answering-islam.org/ Authors/Arlandson/ultimate_goal.htm

626   Historyguy.com, The Arab-Israeli Wars & Conflicts; http://www.historyguy.com/arab_ israeli_wars.html

627   Jamie Glazov, The Oslo Syndrome, Frontpagemag.com, 11.25.05; http://archive. frontpagemag.com/readArticle.aspx?ARTID=6565

628   Isi Liebler, Candidly speaking: Concerning 'self-hating Jews', jpost.com, 06.13.12; http:// www.jpost.com/Opinion/Columnists/Candidly-Speaking-Concerning-self-hating-Jews

629   Spanish Reconquist, Spanish Fiestas; http://www.spanish-fiestas.com/history/reconquest/

Lourdes of the Lies

630   Daniel Greenfield, Economics and Peace in the Palestinian Authority, Frontpage mag, 12/27/13; http://www.frontpagemag.com/point/214041/economics-and-peace-palestinian-authority-daniel-greenfield

631   Prof. Efraim Karsh, What Occupied Territories? Commentary Magazine, 07.2002; http:// emperors-clothes.com/israel/karsh-occ.htm

632   Mudar Zahran, UNRWA: The Palestinians' Worst Enemy, Gatestone Institute, 03.21.12; https://www.gatestoneinstitute.org/2962/unrwa-the-palestinians-enemy

633   Khaled Abu Toameh, How Much is Mahmoud AbbasWorth?, Gatestone Institute, 05.18.12; https://www.gatestoneinstitute.org/3066/how-much-is-mahmoud-abbas-worth

634   Market News, Israel sought $1 bln IMF loan for Palestinians, Reuters, 07.02.12; http://in.reuters.com/article/palestinians-israel-imf-idINL6E8I24JH20120702

60 Minutes of Mendacity

635   Christianity Near Extinction in the Ancient Lands of its origin, Daily Alert Archives, 12.24.10; http://www.dailyalert.org/rss/tagpage.php?id=20294

636   David Lev, Christians in Israel Well-Off, Statistics Show, Arutz Sheva, 12.24.12; http://www.israelnationalnews.com/News/News.aspx/163468

637   Michael B. Sauter, The Happiest Countries in the World, Yahoo Finance, 05.22.12; http://finance.yahoo.com/news/the-happiest-countries-in-the-world.html?page=all94

The Palestine Khouri Doesn't Know

638   Zahi Khouri, The Palestine Romney doesn't now, The Washington Post, 08-09-12; https://www.washingtonpost.com/opinions/the-palestine-romney-doesnt-know/2012/08/09/5de0bcdc-e235-11e1-98e7-89d659f9c106_story.html?utm_term=.fcc352f48197

639   WikiAnswers Community, What defines a civilization?, Answers.com; http://www.answers.com/Q/What_defines_a_civilization#ixzz28XZpBc00

640   What makes Islam so different?, The Religion of Peace; http://www.thereligionofpeace.com/

641   Chapter Two, Offensive War to Spread Islam, answering-islam.org; http://www.answering-islam.org/BehindVeil/btv2.html\

642   Raymond Ibrahim, The Historical Reality of the Muslim Conquests, Middle East Forum, 03.01.12; http://www.meforum.org/3182/history-Muslim-conquests

643   Meaning and Origin of: Khouri, family education; https://www.familyeducation.com/baby-names/name-meaning/Khouri?role=family

644   Jewish exodus from Arab and Muslim countries, Wikipedia; https://en.wikipedia.org/wiki/Jewish_exodus_from_Arab_and_Muslim_countries

645   Israel is a monster that stabs and eats children, Palestinian Media Watch, 12-22-13; http://palwatch.org/site/modules/videos/pal/videos.aspx?fld_id=latest&doc_id=7163

Oren on Honesty

646   Michael Oren, Falling for Hamas's media manipulation, The Washington Post, 11.28.12; https://www.washingtonpost.com/opinions/falling-for-hamass-mediamanipulation/2012/11/28/4d7b9498-39a1-11e2-8a97-363b0f9a0ab3_story.html?utm_term=.0d409e41ea15

647   Israel Today Staff, Jewish baby nearly killed by Palestinian stone thrower, Israel today, 12.30.12; http://www.israeltoday.co.il/Default.aspx?tabid=178&nid=23594

648   Palestinian rocket attacks on Israel, Wikipedia; https://en.wikipedia.org/wiki/Palestinian_rocket_attacks_on_Israel

649 Al Fadi, Women under Sharia Law: Family Security Matters, 07.13.11; http://www. familysecuritymatters.org/publications/id.9930/pub_detail.asp

650 Yaakov Lappin, Dealing with Hamas's Human Shield Tactics, The Jerusalem Post, 11/30/12; http://www.jpost.com/Defense/Dealing-with-Hamass-human-shield-tactics

651 David De Piciotto, Beating a tsunami, thanks to an Israeli early warning system, Start-up Israel, 02.02.12; http://www.timesofisrael.com/beating-a-tsunami-thanks-to-an-israeli-early-warning-system/

652 Update from the Israeli Consulate in Los Angeles, StandWithUs, 11.20.12; https://www. standwithus.com/news/article.asp?id=2499

653 TheFogelfamily+slaughter,Google;https://www.google.com/search?num=10&hl=en&site=img hp&tbm=isch&source=hp&biw=1007&bih=536&q=the+Fogel+family+%2B+slaughter&oq= the+Fogel+family+%2B+slaughter&gs_l=img.12...1140.6734.0.8484.28.16.0.2.0.1.281.531.2-2.2.0...0.0...1ac.1.kY3MRTuIwBM&gws_rd=ssl

654 France2; "Reuters apologizes for having provided us with old images of demonstrations in Lebanon as being in Syria," Uprooted Palestinian, 05.11.11; http://uprootedpalestinians. blogspot.com/2011/05/france2-reuters-apologizes-for-having.html

655 Hassan A El-Najjar, The Gulf War: Overreaction & Excessiveness, Chapter X, Amazone Press 2001; http://www.gulfwar1991.com/Gulf%20War%20Complete/Chapter%2010,%20 Palestinians%20in%20Kuwait,%20Terror%20and%20Ethnic%20Cleansing,%20By%20 Hassan%20A%20El-Najjar.htm

656 What makes Islam so different?, The Religion of Peace; http://www.thereligionofpeace.com/

657 Stoyan Zaimov, Muslim Mobs Burn Down Churches, The Christian Post, 01/19/15; http://www.christianpost.com/news/Muslim-mobs-burn-down-churches-pastors-homes-in-niger-for-charlie-hebdos-prophet-Mohammed-cartoons-10-people-dead-in-protests-132757/

658 Shira Sorko-Ram, Why Syria's Assad Can't Stop Killing His Own People, Maoz Israel Report, 03.2012; http://www.maozisrael.org/site/News2?page=NewsArticle&id=9174

Times Un-Square

659 Dylan Byers, Elliot Abrams slams NYT's Judi Rudoren, Politico, 12.19.12; http://www. politico.com/blogs/media/2012/12/elliott-abrams-slams-nyts-jodi-rudoren-152407

660 Daniel Tauber, New York Times' Jerusalem Chief Admits Anti-Israel Bias, JewishPress. com, 12/20/12; http://www.jewishpress.com/blogs/hadar/new-york-times-jerusalem-chief-admits-anti-israel-bias/2012/12/20/0/?print

661 Balfour Declaration, Wikipedia; https://en.wikipedia.org/wiki/Balfour_Declaration 119 Jay, "3000 Year Old Biblical Castle Found in Israel – Disproves Muslim Claims to Land," Israel Today, 04/2013; http://www.fivedoves.com/letters/apr2013/jay426-2.htm

662 Tiffany Gabbay, NY Times Magazine Cover: 'If there is a Third Intifada, We Want to Be The Ones Who Start it,' The New York Times Magazine, 03.19.03; http://www.theblaze. com/stories/2013/03/19/ny-times-magazine-cover-if-there-is-a-third-intifada-we-want-to-be-the-ones-who-started-it/

663   Defend Israel Forever, Palestinian Arabs Attack Motorists in Samaria, YouTube, 01.16.12; https://www.youtube.com/watch?v=8L7VuMenYdo

664   Billy Hollowell, 'Terror': Israeli Baby in Critical Condition After Palestinians Reportedly Throw Rocks at Jewish Vehicles, theblaze, 03/15/13; http://www.theblaze.com/stories/2013/03/15/terror-israeli-baby-in-critical-condition-after-palestinians-reportedly-throw-rocks-at-jewish-vehicles/

665   Gaza: Palestinian Rockets Unlawfully Targeted Israeli Civilians, hrw.org, 12.24.12; https://www.hrw.org/news/2012/12/24/gaza-palestinian-rockets-unlawfully-targeted-israeli-civilians

666   Itamar Marcus, Barbara Crook, Nan Jacques Zilberdik, Eye-witnesses; Hamas used human shields in Gaza war, Palestinian Media Watch, 09.16.09; http://www.palwatch.org/main.aspx?fi=157&doc_id=1304

667   Ziv Hellman, Why the Oslo Accords Failed, My Jewish Learning; http://www.myjewishlearning.com/article/why-the-oslo-accords-failed/

Two-Time Oscar Winner Two-Times

668   Haifa bus 37 suicide bombing, Wikipedia, https://en.wikipedia.org/wiki/Haifa_bus_37_suicide_bombing

669   Photos of Fogel Family Murder, Arutz Sheva, 03/13/11; http://www.israelnationalnews.com/News/News.aspx/142846

670   International aid to Palestinians, Wikipedia; https://en.wikipedia.org/wiki/International_aid_to_Palestinians

671   Gaza Disengagement Plan: Israel Transfers Gush Katif Hothouses to Palestinians, Jewish Virtual Library, 09.07.05; http://www.jewishvirtuallibrary.org/israel-transfers-gush-katif-hothouses-to-palestinians-september-2005

672   Archbishop of Canterbury welcomes Grand Imam of Al-Azhar to Lambeth Palace, ACNS Anglican Communion News Service, 06.11.15; http://www.anglicannews.org/news/2015/06/archbishop-of-canterbury-welcomes-grand-imam-of-al-azhar-to-lambeth-palace.aspx

673   Thomas More Law Center, Islamic Society with Questionable Background joins forces with Justice Department to Intimidate Citizens Opposing Mosque, The Counter Jihad Report, 04.19.17; https://counterjihadreport.com/tag/islamic-lawfare/

674   Philip Johnston, Why are we still threatening to arrest Israeli politicians?, The Telegraph, 02-15-10; http://www.telegraph.co.uk/comment/columnists/philipjohnston/7240581/Why-are-we-still-threatening-to-arrest-Israeli-politicians.html

Polluted Waters

675   England: Sharia law in UK is unavoidable – Rowan Williams, BBC News, VirtueonLine, 02-07-08; http://www.virtueonline.org/england-sharia-law-uk-unavoidable-rowan-williams-3-stories

676   Itamar Attack, Wikipedia; https://en.wikipedia.org/wiki/Itamar_attack

677   Peace Walls, In Your Pocket; https://www.inyourpocket.com/belfast/Peace-Walls_28463v

678 Declaration of the Establishment of the State of Israel, Wikipedia; https://simple.
wikipedia.org/wiki/Declaration_of_the_Establishment_of_the_State_of_Israel

679 Philistia-Philistines-Sea People, Philistia, Wikipedia; http://www.crystalinks.com/
philistia.html

680 Politically motivated mythology of "Palestine," Eretz Yisroel.Org; http://www.
eretzyisroel.org/~peters/mythology.html

681 Soeren Kern, Britain's "Islamic Emirates Project," Gatestone Institute, 02.21.11; https://
www.gatestoneinstitute.org/2278/britain-islamic-emirates-project

682 IPT News, Muted Response to Hamas Jihad Program for School Kids, Investigative Project
on Terrorism, 04.29.13; http://www.investigativeproject.org/4001/muted-response-to-
hamas-jihad-program-for-school

683 Giulio Meotti, Why Does Scandinavia Hate Jews?, Arutz Sheva, 03.30.11; http://www.
israelnationalnews.com/Articles/Article.aspx/10114

684 Jacob Bojesson, 40,000 Jews have fled France in 10 years amid rising Anti-Semitism,
Daily Caller, 01.10.17; http://dailycaller.com/2017/01/10/40000-jews-have-fled-france-
in-10-years-amid-rising-anti-semitism/

685 Paul Alster, Hamas leader's kin gets Israeli medical aid even as terror group blasts
Jewish state, Fox News World, 08-12-12; http://www.foxnews.com/world/2012/08/12/
hamas-leader-kin-gets-israeli-medical-aid-even-as-terror-group-blasts-jewish.
html#ixzz2RcLwsLbs

686 Francis M Deng, Sudan – Civil War and Genocide, The Middle East Quarterly, Winter
2001; http://www.meforum.org/22/sudan-civil-war-and-genocide

687 Steve Kramer, Col Kemp defends Israel, The Times of Israel, 10,01.14; http://blogs.
timesofisrael.com/col-kemp-defends-israel/

688 What Makes Islam do different? TheReligionofPeace; http://thereligionofpeace.com/

Honor for Dishonor

689 Ron Radlauer, An Engineered tragedy, Statistical analysis of Casualties in the Palestinian-
Israeli Conflict, Eretz Yisroel,Org; September,2000; http://www.eretzyisroel.org/~jkatz/
mostly.html

L'Americaine

690 The New World Order, Jeremiah Project; http://www.jeremiahproject.com/the-new-
world-order/

Probing the Propaganda

691 Wilhelm Marr, The Victory of Judaism over Germanism, KevinMacDonald, 2009; http://
www.kevinmacdonald.net/Marr-Text-English.pdf

692 Greg Bradsher, The Nurenberg Laws, National Archives, Prologue Magazine, Winter 2010,
Vol.42, No.4; https://www.archives.gov/publications/prologue/2010/winter/nuremberg.html

693 Saint Martin Luther's Birthday is November 10, http://www.reformation.org/saint-martin-
luther-birthday.html

694   Beer Hall Putsch, Wikipedia; https://en.wikipedia.org/wiki/Beer_Hall_Putsch

695   Joseph Goebbels, bio; http://www.biography.com/people/joseph-goebbels-9313998

696   Schutzstaffel, Wikipedia; https://en.wikipedia.org/wiki/Schutzstaffel

697   The Holocaust: A Learning Site for Students, United States Holocaust Memorial Museum; https://www.ushmm.org/outreach/en/article.php?ModuleId=10007697

698   Holocaust Encyclopedia; https://www.ushmm.org/learn/holocaust-encyclopedia/

699   Nazi Propaganda, Holocaust Encyclopedia; https://www.ushmm.org/wlc/en/article.php?ModuleId=10005202

700   Jonathan Kirsch, The Short, Strange Life of Herschel Grynzpan: A Boy Avenger, a Nazi Diplomat, and a Murder in Paris, Amazon, 05.06.13; https://www.amazon.com/Short-Strange-Life-Herschel-Grynszpan/dp/0871404524

Nuremberg Revisited

701   World War II in Europe, The History Place; http://www.historyplace.com/worldwar2/timeline/boycott.htm

702   Five Takeaways form the ASA Debacle, Louis d. Brandeis Center, 12.27.13; http://brandeiscenter.com/blog/five-takeaways-from-the-asa-debacle/

703   JTA, Shurat HaDin Files Racism Lawsuit against Sydney U BDS Supporter, Jewish Press, 11.02.13; http://www.jewishpress.com/news/breaking-news/shurat-hadin-files-racism-lawsuit-against-sydney-u-bds-supporter/2013/11/02/

704   In the News, Parti de Gauche endorses BDS campaign, 11.19.13; https://bdsmovement.net/news/parti-de-gauche-endorses-bds-campaign

705   Katrina Bishop, UK government set to issue Islamic bonds, CNBC, 10-29-13; http://www.cnbc.com/2013/10/29/uk-government-set-to-issue-islamic-bonds.html

706   Itamar Eichner, Ireland: Israeli products marked with yellow sticker, ynet, 05.11.13; http://www.ynetnews.com/articles/0,7340,L-4449775,00.html

707   Malcolm Lowe, British Methodists: Palestine First, Germany Next?, Gatestone Institute, 06.13.11; https://www.gatestoneinstitute.org/2190/british-methodists-palestine-germany

708   Teachers Union of Ireland calls for Academic Boycott of Israel in unanimous vote; first academic union in Europe to do so, Ireland Palestine Solidarity Campaign; http://www.ipsc.ie/press-releases/teachers-union-of-ireland-calls-for-academic-boycott-of-israel-in-unanimous-vote-first-academic-union-in-europe-to-do-so

709   Scottish council boycotts 'apartheid Israel,' The Commentator, 03.22.13; http://www.thecommentator.com/article/3007/scottish_council_boycotts_apartheid_israel

710   David Greene, The Long Death of Creative Teaching, UN News, 03-17-14; https://www.usnews.com/opinion/articles/2014/03/17/how-common-core-standards-kill-creative-teaching

711   Nuremberg Laws, Wikipedia; https://en.wikipedia.org/wiki/Nuremberg_Laws

712 Law for the Prevention of Hereditarily Diseased Offspring, Wikipedia; https://en.wikipedia.org/wiki/Law_for_the_Prevention_of_Hereditarily_Diseased_Offspring

713 Tiffany Gabbay, Indoctrination and Data Mining in Common Core: Here's Why America's Schools May Be in More Trouble Than You Think, the blaze; 03-27-13; http://www.theblaze.com/news/2013/03/27/indoctrination-and-data-mining-in-common-core-heres-why-americas-schools-may-be-in-more-trouble-than-you-think/

714 Corinne Lestch, Student data-compiling system outrages, Daily News, 03-13-13; http://www.nydailynews.com/new-york/student-data-compiling-system-outrages-article-1.1287990

715 Valerie Strauss, $1.1 million-plus Gates grants: 'Galvanic' bracelets that measure student engagement, The Washington Post, 06-11-12; https://www.washingtonpost.com/blogs/answer-sheet/post/11-million-plus-gates-grants-galvanic-bracelets-that-measure-student-engagement/2012/06/10/gJQAgAUbTV_blog.html?utm_term=.8d7aadfe16f2

716 Editorial, Obama's Military Coup Purges 1197 Officers in Five Years, Investors Business Daily, 10-29-13; http://www.investors.com/politics/editorials/197-military-officers-purged-by-obama/

717 100,000 Americans to Obama: Homeschooling a Right, WND, 04-09-13; http://www.wnd.com/2013/04/100000-americans-to-obama-homeschooling-is-a-right/

718 Sarah Fruchnicht, 50 College Students Killed by Islamic Extremists as They Slept in their Dorms, OpposingViews, 09-29-13; http://www.opposingviews.com/i/religion/islam/50-college-students-killed-islamic-extremists-they-slept-their-dorms

719 Mike Adams, If Obama is opposed to guns, why did his administration just purchase 1.6 billion rounds of ammunition and sniper rounds?, Natural News, 12-20-12; http://www.naturalnews.com/038407_ammunition_homeland_security_civil_war.html

720 Ashley Alman, Dianne Feinstein Gun Control, The Huffington Post, 11.04.13; http://www.huffingtonpost.com/news/dianne-feinstein-gun-control/

721 Dean Garrison, Louie Gohmert Exposes Obamacare Secret Security Force, Freedom Outpost, 11-16-13; http://freedomoutpost.com/louie-gohmert-warns-americans-obamacare-secret-security-force/

722 Janna Brocvk – Sharia Swim: Muslim Girls Only Swim Started by St. Paul YMCA and Police Dept., Freedom Outpost, 11-23-13; http://freedomoutpost.com/st-paul-ymca-and-police-department-start-Muslim-girls-only-swim-practice/#uQAejFZOXvP2MYma.99

We Have MET the Enemy

723 About Berkshire Fine Arts, BFA, http://www.berkshirefinearts.com/about-us_page.htm

724 Rampell, "The Death of Klinghoffer": controversial history in opera, People's World, 04-04-14; http://www.peoplesworld.org/article/the-death-of-klinghoffer-controversial-history-in-opera/

The Metropalistan Opera

725 https://static1.squarespace.com/static/56325ab7e4b00a5559bd6090/t/58a70ea85016e19b b70ad9e4/1487343275121/ISIS_FeatureMessage.pdf

726 Bill Warner, Tears of Jihad, Political Islam, 03.03.08; https://www.politicalislam.com/tears-of-jihad/

727 John Hall, Inside the sickening school for mini-jihadis: Pictures show children as young as five getting combat and weapons training at ISIS military camp, Daily Mail, 10.29.14; http://www.dailymail.co.uk/news/article-2812406/Sickening-school-mini-jihadists-Pictures-children-young-five-getting-combat-weapons-training-ISIS-military-camp.html

The Board Gets Nailed

728 DI Editorial board, Editorial: GOP's anti-Sharia plank offensive, unnecessary, The Daily Iowan, 06.16.14; http://www.dailyiowan.com/2014/06/16/Opinions/38015.html

729 CBSstaffnews, No Pray, No Play, CBSnews, 09-02-00; http://www.cbsnews.com/news/no-pray-no-play/

730 Tara Dodrill, Ohio Teacher fired for having a Bible in the Classroom fighting termination in the State's Highest Court, Inquisitr; http://www.inquisitr.com/547015/ohio-teacher-fired-for-having-a-bible-in-the-classroom/

731 Sue Epstein, US Supreme Court rejects NJ football coach's appeal of team prayer ruling, NJ Advance Media for NJ com, 03.02.09; http://www.nj.com/news/index.ssf/2009/03/supreme_court_rejects_east_bru.html

732 Ken Amaro, Clay County Debate over Prayer around Flagpole, FCN, 10.21.11; http://middleburg.firstcoastnews.com/news/news/62838-clay-county-debate-over-prayer-around-flagpole

733 Hunter Stuart, Ten Commandments Plaques Pulled from School Walls in Muldrow, OK, The Huffington Post, 05.15.13; http://www.huffingtonpost.com/2013/05/15/ten-commandments-oklahoma-muldrow_n_3279658.html

734 Texas Woman Told to Remove 'Offensive' American Flag from Office, Fox News, 05.29.09; http://www.foxnews.com/story/2009/05/29/texas-woman-told-to-remove-offensive-american-flag-from-office.html

735 Katherine Kersten, April 9: Teacher questions Muslim practices at charter school, Star Tribune, 05.19.08; http://www.startribune.com/april-9-teacher-questions-Muslim-practices-at-charter-school/17406054/

736 Janna Brock, Common Core Islamic Indoctrination Textbook has Floridians Outrages, Freedom Outpost, 11-05-13; http://freedomoutpost.com/common-core-islamic-indoctrination-textbook-world-history-has-floridians-outraged/

737 Paparock, Jihad being taught in taxpaper-funded California public schools, Israel Military, Aug.2006; http://www.israelmilitary.net/showthread.php?p=43811

738 John Griffing, Students made to wear burqas — in Texas, WND, 02.24.13; http://www.wnd.com/2013/02/students-made-to-wear-burqas-in-u-s-state/

739 Joseph Klein, Islamizing the Public Schools, FrontPage mag, 06.12.13; http://www.frontpagemag.com/fpm/193058/islamizing-public-schools-joseph-klein

740 Todd Starnes, Students take Field Trip to Mosque, Receive Koran, Foxnews.com; http://radio.
     foxnews.com/toddstarnes/top-stories/students-take-field-trip-to-mosque-receive-koran.html

741 Muslim Logic: Moses was a great Muslim who liberated Palestine from Egypt . . .,
     Bare Naked Islam, 08.27.12; http://www.barenakedislam.com/2012/08/27/so-if-moses-
     and-jesus-were-both-Muslims-why-are-Muslims-trying-to-to-so-hard-to-wipe-their-
     descendants-off-the-face-of-the-earth/

742 AFP, Erdogan says Muslims, not Columbus, discovered Americas, Yahoo News, 11.15.14;
     https://www.yahoo.com/news/erdogan-says-Muslims-not-columbus-discovered-
     americas-162759161.html?ref=gs

743 What Muslim Leaders say about Islam Dispels the Myth that Jihadists are a "Fringe"
     Element, Citizen Warrior; http://www.citizenwarrior.com/2010/10/what-Muslim-leaders-
     say-about-islam.html

744 Pamela Engel, The terrorist threat is worse now than it was before 9/11, Business Insider,
     09/11/16; http://www.businessinsider.com/are-we-safer-now-than-on-911-2016-9

745 David Morgan, Poll: 26% of Young U.S. Muslims OK Bombs, CBS News, 05.22.07;
     http://www.cbsnews.com/news/poll-26-of-young-us-Muslims-ok-bombs/

Guardian with Guile

746 Serunas Milne, Gaza: this shameful injustice will only end if the cost of it rises, the
     Guardian,   07-16-14;   https://www.theguardian.com/commentisfree/2014/jul/16/gaza-
     shameful-injustice-israel-attacks-occupied-people

747 Hamas Covenant, Wikipedia; https://en.wikipedia.org/wiki/Hamas_Covenant

748 Iran's Islamic regime, women, living in Hell, wn.com, 05-23-11; https://wn.com/islamic_regime

749 Simon Plosker, Foreign Journalists Acknowledge Hamas' Human Shields Tactics,
     HonestReporting, 07-23-14; http://honestreporting.com/foreign-journalists-acknowledge-
     hamas-human-shields-tactics/

750 Ben Cosgrove, Nilanjana Bhowmick, Terror at the Olympics: Munich, 1972, TIME,
     08.05.13; http://time.com/24489/munich-massacre-1972-olympics-photos/

751 Daniel Pearl, Wikipedia; https://en.wikipedia.org/wiki/Daniel_Pearl

752 2014 kidnapping and murder of Israeli teenagers, Wikipedia; https://en.wikipedia.org/
     wiki/2014_kidnapping_and_murder_of_Israeli_teenagers

753 Alan Dershowitz, Hamas' Phony Statistics on Civilian Deaths, the Algemeiner, 08.07.14;
     http://www.algemeiner.com/2014/08/07/hamas%E2%80%99-phony-statistics-on-
     civilian-deaths/

754 Joel Leyden, Hamas Murders Children in Palestine, Blames Israel, Israel News Agency;
     http://www.israelnewsagency.com/hamasterrorgazaisrael48770611.html

755 Joshua Levitt, BBC Wakes Up to Hamas's Exaggerations, Warning 'Caution Needed With Gaza Casualty Figures', the Algemeiner, 08.08.14; http://www.algemeiner. com/2014/08/08/bbc-wakes-up-to-hamass-exaggerations-warning-caution-needed-with-gaza-casualty-figures/

756 Taqiyya, Holy Deception, Qur'an 5:32, Winds of Jihad; http://sheikyermami.com/taqiyya-holy-deception-quran-532/

757 Islam and Pedophilia, WikiIslam; http://wikiislam.net/wiki/Islam_and_Pedophilia

758 Nonie Darwish, Cruel and Usual Punishment, Amazon; https://www.amazon.com/Cruel-Usual-Punishment-Nonie-Darwish/dp/159555209X

759 Child suicide bombers in the Israeli-Palestinian conflict; Wikipedia; https://en.wikipedia.org/wiki/Child_suicide_bombers_in_the_Israeli%E2%80%93Palestinian_conflict

760 Admin, Muslims worldwide, the Muslim issue, 08.01.14; https://theMuslimissue.wordpress.com/2014/08/01/hamas-terrorist-hangs-position-kids-on-a-fence-in-front-of-a-house-to-ensure-the-idf-will-not-strike-the-building/

Men of Ideals

761 Terrorism: Hijacking of the Achille Lauro, Jewish Virtual Library; http://www.jewishvirtuallibrary.org/hijacking-of-the-achille-lauro

762 Robert Spencer, Islamic State recaptures Palmyra, displays severed heads of Assad forces, Jihad Watch, 12.15.16; https://www.jihadwatch.org/2016/12/islamic-state-recaptures-palmyra-displays-severed-heads-of-assad-forces

763 Tzedakah: Charity, Judaism 101; http://www.jewfaq.org/tzedakah.htm

764 Five Pillars of Islam, Wikipedia; https://en.wikipedia.org/wiki/Five_Pillars_of_Islam

765 Yoni Kempinski, Ari Yashar, Special Needs Soldiers are 'Great in Uniform,' 08.05.14; http://www.israelnationalnews.com/News/News.aspx/180413

766 Fact sheet, Female genital mutilation, World Health Organization, February 2017; http://www.who.int/mediacentre/factsheets/fs241/en/

767 Doug Giles, Religion of Peace: ISIS teaches their kids to decapitate the infidels, Clash Daily, 08.24.14; http://clashdaily.com/2014/08/religion-peace-isis-teaches-kids-decapitate-infidels/

768 Suicide Attacks (and Islamic Paradise), Religion of Peace; http://www.thereligionofpeace.com/pages/quran/suicide-bombing.aspx

No, No, Norah

769 Simon Plosker, CBS Anchorwoman: Synagogue Attack Took Place at "Contested Religious Site", HonestReporting, 11.19.14; http://honestreporting.com/cbs-anchorwoman-synagogue-attack-took-place-at-contested-religious-site-1/

770 Muslims Play Soccer with the Heads of their Victims, Stop Islamization of the World; http://www.siotw.org/news_english.item.1415/Muslims-play-soccer-with-the-heads-of-their-victims.html

771 Reprint from Arutz Sheva, Exclusive: Dumped Temple Mount Rubble Yields Jewish Artifacts, Temple Institute, 04.14.05; https://www.templeinstitute.org/archive/14-04-05.htm

En Garde!

772 The Guardian, Wikipedia; https://en.wikipedia.org/wiki/The_Guardian

773 Ministry of Women's Affairs, http://www.unwomen.org/~/media/headquarters/media/stories/en/palestinianauthoritynationalstrategytocombatpdf.pdf

774 Women in Arab societies, Wikipedia; https://en.wikipedia.org/wiki/Women_in_Arab_societies

775 JPost.com Staff, Israel ranked 11th happiest country in the world, The Jerusalem Post, 04.24.15; http://www.jpost.com/Israel-News/Israel-ranked-as-11th-happiest-country-in-the-world-399075

Bias at the BBC

776 Ben Cohen, BBC Reporter's Apology for Anti-Semitic Question at Paris Unity Rally Fails to Convince, the Algemeiner, 03.26.15; http://www.algemeiner.com/2015/01/12/bbc-reporters-apology-for-anti-semitic-question-at-paris-unity-rally-fails-to-convince-video/

777 More BBC promotion of the 'Jewish lobby' trope, BBC Watch, 11.10.14; https://bbcwatch.org/2014/11/10/more-bbc-promotion-of-the-jewish-lobby-trope/

778 Vladimir Duthiers, Faith Karimi, Greg Botelho, Boko Haram: Why terror group kidnaps schoolgirls, and what happens next, CNN, 05.02.14; http://www.cnn.com/2014/04/24/world/africa/nigeria-kidnapping-answers/index.html

779 Abbas admits PA sent terrorists to kill Israelis, Official Palestinian Authority TV, PalWatch, 02.14.05; http://www.palwatch.org/site/modules/videos/popup/video.aspx?doc_id=459

780 Michael Omer-Man, This Week in History: Israel's Deadliest Terror Attack, The Jerusalem Post, 03/01/11; http://www.jpost.com/Features/In-Thespotlight/This-Week-in-History-Israels-deadliest-terror-attack

BBC, A Mission Astray

781 Rafael Israeli, Israel Studies an Anthology: The Impact of Palestinian Nationalism on Israel, Jewish Virtual Library, May 2013; http://www.jewishvirtuallibrary.org/israel-studies-an-anthology-palestinian-nationalism

782 Israel Bus Attack, Aug.18, Breaking News, http://www.breakingnews.com/topic/israel-bus-attack/

783 Ethiopian Jews, Israel's History and People, Blogspot, 11.10.10; http://skushnir13.blogspot.com/2010/11/on-may-23-1991-aircraft-supplied-by-iaf.html

784 What makes Islam so different?, The Religion of Peace, May; http://www.thereligionofpeace.com/index.aspx

785 Simon Schama, The Story of the Jews, WVIZ Passport, 04.01.; http://www.pbs.org/wnet/story-jews/video/episode-five-return/

786 Fact Sheet: Jewish Refugees from Arab Countries, Jewish Virtual Library, December 2015; http://www.jewishvirtuallibrary.org/jewish-refugees-from-arab-countries

787 Mitchell Bard, The Palestinian Refugees: History & Overview, Jewish Virtual Library; http://www.jewishvirtuallibrary.org/history-and-overview-of-the-palestinian-refugees

788 Mitchell Bard, The Arab Lobby, Amazon, 12.06.11; https://www.amazon.com/The-Arab-Lobby-Invisible-Undermines/dp/0061725978

Disassociated Press

789 Sidney Smith, Israel not flooding Gaza? Al Jazeera Retracts, Daily Mail corrects, iMediaEthics, 02.26.15; http://www.imediaethics.org/israel-not-flooding-gaza-al-jazeera-retracts-daily-mail-corrects/?new

790 Gaza flotilla raid, Wikipedia; https://en.wikipedia.org/wiki/Gaza_flotilla_raid

791 Steven Erlanger and Far4es Akram, Middle East, The New York Times, 07.08.14; https://www.nytimes.com/2014/07/09/world/middleeast/by-phone-and-leaflet-israeli-attackers-warn-gazans.html?_r=2

792 White phosphorus, Wikipedia; https://en.wikipedia.org/wiki/Allotropes_of_phosphorus#White_phosphorus

793 Ryan Jones, UN Report: Israel doing utmost to prevent civilian casualties in Gaza, Israelandstuff.com, 07.14.14; https://www.israelandstuff.com/un-report-israel-doing-utmost-to-prevent-civilian-casualties-in-gaza

794 WashingtonsBlog, 90% of All Deaths in War are CIVILIANS, 05.16.14; http://www.washingtonsblog.com/2014/05/90-deaths-war-civilians.html

795 Algemeiner Staff, Analysis: I Don't Trust the AP's Report on Civilian Deaths in Gaza and Neither Should You, the algemeiner, 02.14.15; http://www.algemeiner.com/2015/02/14/analysis-i-dont-trust-the-aps-report-on-civilian-deaths-in-gaza-and-neither-should-you/

Muslims Are Not Jews

796 Nicholas Kristof, Would You Hide a Jew From the Nazis?, The New York Times Sunday Review, 09/17/16; https://www.nytimes.com/2016/09/18/opinion/sunday/would-you-hide-a-jew-from-the-nazis.html?_r=0

797 German Jewish Refugees, 1933-1939, Holocaust Encyclopedia; https://www.ushmm.org/wlc/en/article.php?ModuleId=10005468

798 Phyllis Chesler, Lies on the Front Page, the Truth Buried on the Back Page, Pajamas Media, Phyllis Chesler Organization, 03.02.08; https://phyllis-chesler.com/articles/lies-on-the-front-page-the-truth-buried-on-the-back-page

799 Benjamin P. Sisney, ACLJ Demands Answers on Why Homeland Security Secretary Doesn't Know if Terrorists Were Wrongly Granted Citizenship, ACLJ; https://aclj.org/executive-power/aclj-demands-answers-on-why-homeland-security-secretary-doesnt-know-if-terrorists-were-wrongly-granted-citizenship

800 Daniel Greenfield, Obama June Surge of Syrian Muslim Migrants Excludes Christians, Frontpage Magazine, 07.01.16; http://www.frontpagemag.com/point/263373/obama-june-surge-syrian-Muslim-migrants-excludes-daniel-greenfield

801 Ann Corcoran, Refugee Resettlement and the Hijra to America, Center for Security Policy; http://www.centerforsecuritypolicy.org/wp-content/uploads/2015/04/Refugee_ Resettlement_Hijra.pdf

802 Information about Israel: Government, Israel Science and Technology Homepage, 1999-2017; http://www.science.co.il/gov/Government.php

803 A list of Quran hate quotes, World Media Monitoring, 09.14.13; http://worldmedia monitoring.com/list-quran-hate-quotes/

804 Islamic Relief and the Myth of the Non-Discriminating Muslim Charity, What makes Islam so different? The Religion of Peace; https://www.thereligionofpeace.com/pages/ articles/islamic-relief.aspx

805 Oli Smith, Dhaka flooded with Blood as Eid animal sacrifices stain Bangladesh roads red, Sunday Express, 09.15.16; http://www.express.co.uk/news/world/710852/Dhaka-flooded-BLOOD-Muslims-slaughter-animals-Eid

806 Sharia Law; http://www.billionbibles.org/sharia/sharia-law.html

807 Chase Stephens, Video Accurately Diagnosis Hillary as an Ameriphobe, Dailywire. com, 09.23.16; http://www.dailywire.com/news/9436/video-accurately-diagnoses-hillary-ameriphobe-chase-stephens

808 Dr. Judhi Jasser, Obama using Refugees to Unravel our National Identity, Live Leak, 09.15.16; https://www.liveleak.com/view?i=cb6_1473988037

809 Edwin Mora, Breitbart, The Counter Jihad Report, 09.29.16; https://counterjihadreport. com/2016/09/29/fbi-director-terrorist-diaspora-like-never-before-may-follow-islamic-state-defeat/

The Times That Try Men's Souls

810 Khaled Abu Toameh, Palestinians: The Message Remains No and No, Gatestone Institute, 11.16.16; https://www.gatestoneinstitute.org/9334/palestinians-rejectionism

811 114th Congress 2d Session H.R.; https://roskam.house.gov/sites/roskam.house.gov/files/ Protecting%20Israel%20Against%20Economic%20Discrimination%20Act_Final.pdf

812 UNESCO's Denial of Jewish History and the Western Servility That Enables It, Mosaic, 10.20.16; https://mosaicmagazine.com/picks/2016/10/unescos-denial-of-jewish-history-and-the-western-servility-that-enables-it/

813 Conversion of non-Islamic places of worship into mosques, Wikipedia; https:// en.wikipedia.org/wiki/Conversion_of_non-Islamic_places_of_worship_into_mosques

814 Ira Stoll, The New York Times' Obsession with Settlements Means it Misses Other News, the Algemeiner, 10.6.16; https://www.algemeiner.com/2016/10/06/the-new-york-times-obsession-with-settlements-means-it-misses-other-news/

815 Muslim Crowds Shout 'Allahu Akar'and Declare To Italians – 'Build us Mosques or we will take over the Vatican!", TradCatKnight, 11.12.16; http://tradcatknight.blogspot. com/2016/11/Muslim-crowds-shout-allahu-akbar-and.html

816 Pamela Geller, Hamas-CAIR Leader Calls for Overthrow of U.S. Government, Freedom Outpost, 11.13.16; http://freedomoutpost.com/hamas-cair-leader-calls-for-overthrow-of-u-s-government/

Israel in Dispute

817 Gilead Ini, At the New York Times, Special Words Reserved for Certain Territories, The New York Times, January, 2017; http://www.thetower.org/article/at-the-new-york-times-special-words-reserved-for-certain-territories-israel-west-bank/

818 Alan Baker, A current digest of media, polls and significant interviews and events, Independent Media Review Analysis IMRA, 08.16.16; http://www.imra.org.il/story. php3?id=71257

819 Publie par Jean-Patrick Grumberg, Israel is the legal occupant of the West Bank, says the Court of Appeal of Versailles, France, dreuz.info, 01/13/17; http://www.dreuz. info/2017/01/13/israel-s-the-legal-occupant-of-the-west-bank-says-the-court-of-appeal-of-versailles-france/

Asylum!

820 Cecil123, Muslim Leaders Declare Aim of World Domination. Rome, London, Spain, Paris, America, ISIS.; **YouTube**, 06/18/14; https://www.youtube.com/ watch?v=ZmGRshS0PAw

821 Nonie Darwish, NonieDarwish on the Barak Lurie Podcast, **NonieDarwish.org**, 01/22/16; http://www.noniedarwish.org/

822 WND, Airport protests just the start of 'chaos' planned by Muslim Brotherhood, **TeaParty,** 01/29/17; https://www.teaparty.org/3-triggers-islamic-uprising-trump-presidency-215581/

Made in the USA
Middletown, DE
24 July 2019